BHARTṚHARI
PHILOSOPHER AND GRAMMARIAN

BHARTṚHARI
PHILOSOPHER AND GRAMMARIAN

Proceedings of the First International Conference on Bhartṛhari

(University of Poona, January 6-8, 1992)

Edited by
SAROJA BHATE
JOHANNES BRONKHORST

MOTILAL BANARSIDASS PUBLISHERS
PRIVATE LIMITED • DELHI

First Indian Edition: Delhi, 1994
Reprint: Delhi, 1997

First published: Bern, 1993

ISBN: 81-208-1198-4

MOTILAL BANARSIDASS
41 U.A. Bungalow Road, Jawahar Nagar, Delhi 110 007
8, Mahalaxmi Chamber, Warden Road, Mumbai 400 026
120 Royapettah High Road, Mylapore, Chennai 600 004
Sanas Plaza, Subhash Nagar, Pune 411 002
16 St. Mark's Road, Bangalore 560 001
8 Camac Street, Calcutta 700 017
Ashok Rajpath, Patna 800 004
Chowk, Varanasi 221 001

PRINTED IN INDIA

BY JAINENDRA PRAKASH JAIN AT SHRI JAINENDRA PRESS,
A-45 NARAINA, PHASE I, NEW DELHI 110 028
AND PUBLISHED BY NARENDRA PRAKASH JAIN FOR
MOTILAL BANARSIDASS PUBLISHERS PRIVATE LIMITED,
BUNGALOW ROAD, DELHI 110 007

TABLE OF CONTENTS

ACKNOWLEDGEMENTS

The Bhartṛhari conference was held at the University of Poona, January 6-8, 1992, under the joint auspices of the University of Poona (India) and the University of Lausanne (Switzerland). The University of Poona put its facilities at the disposal of the conference organisators.

Financial help was received from the University of Poona, the Faculty of Letters of the University of Lausanne, the Fondation du 450e anniversaire of the University of Lausanne, the Swiss Academy of Humanities and Social Sciences. The present publication has been made possible with the help of the Faculty of Letters of the University of Lausanne, and the Swiss Asia Society. Thanks are further due to all those students and researchers from the Universities of Poona and Lausanne who spared no efforts to make the conference successful.

J.B.

AN INTRODUCTION TO THE STUDY OF BHARTṚ-HARI*

Ashok Aklujkar, University of British Columbia

kāle varṣatu parjanyaḥ, pṛthvī stācchasya-śālinī/
deśo 'stu kṣobha-rahitaḥ, sajjanāḥ santu nirbhayāḥ //[1]

1.1 Professor S.D. Joshi, Pandit Bhagavat, my other respected teachers in the audience, Dr. Gaurinath Sastri, other fellow members of the Bhartṛhari scholarly community, students present in the audience whose work in the future I hope will soon overtake what we achieve in the conference, ladies and gentlemen: I am grateful to the main organizers of this conference, Professors Saroja Bhate and Johannes Bronkhorst, for the opportunity they have given me of making the first and relatively more extensive presentation of the conference. I hope it leads to well-informed and well-defined, and hence mutually rewarding, discussions in the sessions to follow, as was my intention in suggesting that such an introductory presentation be arranged.

1.2 I would like to dedicate the presentation to the memory of Professor Bimal Krishna Matilal. Professor Matilal's untimely death has removed from among us one of those rare scholars who could combine excellent philological skills with comparative work on the broadest scale possible at present, who had a remarkable talent for discovering the essence behind overwhelming detail, and who, above all, would have very much enjoyed

* I was able to study many of the sources used in the preparation of this lecture because of financial assistance provided at various times since 1969 by the University of British Columbia Humanities and Social Sciences Research Committee, the Social Sciences and Humanities Research Council of Canada, the Shastri Indo-Canadian Institute, the American Council of Learned Societies, and the Alexander von Humboldt Stiftung of the Federal Republic of Germany.
The oral style of the lecture given on 6 January 1992 has deliberately been retained to a significant extent. The references given in the appendix were then made available to the audience in the form of a handout.

1 I have changed the quarters 'b' and 'c' of this purāṇic *maṅgala* from *pṛthivī śasya-śālinī* and *deśo 'yaṁ kṣobha-rahitaḥ*. My reason for accommodating the verbs *stāt* and *astu* is that without them the quarters fall out of step with 'a' and 'd,' which contain *varṣatu* and *santu,* and thus lack the force that benedictive utterances should have.
In a period of ecological concerns, regional disturbances, and fundamentalist pressures being exerted on historians, the vision of the *maṅgala* is something that we should cherish.

participating in a conference like this, dedicated as he was throughout his scholarly life to establishing that India did have a rich and rewarding tradition of philosophy, even if philosophy were to be sharply distinguished from religion and theology and taken in the relatively recent narrow sense of analytical or linguistic philosophy. I shall miss Bimal as a friend and a thinker.

1.3 My lecture has been described as introductory and to some extent it *will* be introductory. However, please note that it will not be introductory in the sense of a presentation proceeding on the assumption that the audience knows nothing or little about Bhartṛ-hari (hereafter abbreviated to "B") and the works associated with him and hence the principle goal should be to give to the audience some very basic or preliminary information in that regard. Rather, I am principally going to talk about what research has achieved so far, what parameters are emerging, and what we could expect in the future. From the observations made along these lines and the information given in the appendix, it should be possible for you to infer, if you do not already know, what basic factual information and surmises made by scholars there are regarding B, his works, and his commentators.

1.4 Secondly, while trying to reach the goal I have set for myself, I am going to inject, wherever appropriate, observations regarding Sanskritic or Indological research in general. The more these observations, strictly speaking 'asides' or 'side-glances', provoke you, like the asides of the jester in Sanskrit plays or like the side-glances of the heroine in classical Sanskrit poetry - which imagery to use I shall leave for you to decide - the happier I shall be. However, I shall not deliberately try to provoke you. My intention will still be to give an honest expression to the situation as I see it, and I shall be as careful as I can be to ensure that one-sided treatment and distortion are avoided. Nevertheless, I acknowledge that there is an unavoidable element of subjectivity in a presentation like this. One scholar's nectar of facts can sometimes indeed make another scholar a victim of food-poisoning. But, while noting this, I must also point out that B research is a part of many larger circles of research activity and that unless its relationship with at least the immediately next larger circle, the one of Indological research in general, is explored, we will not know how it is faring and how it is likely to fare.

2.1 I hope you will excuse me if there appears a personal dimension in a part of my presentation. Even if I exclude the year 1962-63, when Professor Bhate and I read the Vākyapadīya with Professor Arjunwadkar as a part of our Junior M.A. curriculum, my serious engagement with B is now about twenty-five years old. It was in 1967 that I, rather suddenly, decided to work on B for my Ph.D. dissertation. My decision was principally due to the realization that the time available to me for completing the Ph.D. degree program would not have been sufficient to prepare myself in Vedic or Indo-European studies, and that I always internally suffered much if I had to write on something about which I could not either think clearly or think with a sense of having something new to say. But, in retrospect, it seems that my decision to revisit B was due also to the discussions in philosophy of language, philosophy of grammar, and philosophy approached linguistically that were taking place around me through the writings of Willard van Orman Quine, Roman Jacobson, Noam Chomsky, etc. The relevance of ancient Indian *śāstra* statements to these discussions could not be missed even by my mind which seems to have a special knack for unsystematic and erratic reading of Indological literature.

2.2 Having embarked upon a study of B - this time largely voluntary and not occasioned by textbooks - and having read whatever I could find to read upon him, it somehow occurred to me that what I needed to do first was to determine the parameters of his thought - to come up with a set of theoretical positions with which any interpretation of a piece of his philosophy must agree in order to be acceptable as *his* view. Thus, I set aside a comparative approach with respect to modern Western theoreticians as well as with respect to ancient and medieval Indian thinkers such as Maṇḍana, Śaṅkara, Kauṇḍa-bhaṭṭa, or Nāgeśa. I also decided not to concentrate on placing B historically - to *pretend* ignorance of wider issues of history, particularly of the history of ideas. Furthermore, I resolved to separate at each step the evidence available in ancient commentators from the evidence available in B's own words to the extent I could reasonably be sure about what his own words were. And, although I was being confronted by textual problems practically on every page of printed B works, I decided temporarily to push all such problems under the rug. This is not to say that I denied the usefulness of the comparative approach, played down the importance of historical or philological research, distrusted the traditional commentators, and glossed over textual difficulties. In fact, I used everything that I found relevant, justifiable, and reliable in all activites of the indicated kind. However, I used those things the way Pāṇini uses meaning in his grammar: implicit as background but not applied as a major criterion of presentation.

2.3 In writing a dissertation that focused on determining the basic or fundamental ideas attributable to B, it was possible to follow two paths. One was to let an overarching structure of presentation emerge out of the specific individual observations collected as a result of a careful and comprehensive consultation of primary sources, that is, to figure out what the broad categories were into which the particular determinations of B's views fell and to turn those categories into major sections or chapters of the dissertation. The second possible path was to follow the major concepts the ancient and medieval Indian tradition and the preceding generations of modern scholars seemed to associate with B and to investigate each of them or the more important among them from the point of view of determining, accurately and thoroughly, their nature and scope, as understood by B. Among such concepts, the ones that rather readily come to mind are: *brahman (śabda-tattva-brahman, śabda-brahman), vākya, pada, āgama, jāti (ākṛti, sāmānya), dravya, saṁbandha, guṅa, diś, sādhana* or *kāraka, kriyā, kāla, puruṣa* or grammatical person, *saṁkhyā, upagraha* or the *'parasmai-pada:ātmane-pada'* kind of verbal aspect, *vṛtti* or the grammatical phenomenon of composition or compounding, Veda, *śābda-pūrva yoga,* forms or levels or phases of *vāc* such as *vaikharī, sphoṭa, dhvani* and *nāda* with their *prākṛta* and *vaikṛta* divisions, *pratibhā, śābda-bodha, śabda (anvākhyeya* and *pratipādaka), artha* with its divisions such as *apoddhāra-padārtha* and *sthita-lakṣaṇārtha* or as *bāhyārtha (vastvartha)* and *śabdārtha, avidyā, vivarta, pariṇāma, vikāra, prakṛti*, etc.[2]

2.4 In the end, I decided to follow the first path, that of letting a new structure emerge, in the main body of my dissertation. However, in the introduction to the dissertation, I briefly clarified my understanding of those concepts *(sphoṭa, prākṛta dhvani, vaikṛta dhvani, āgama, pratibhā, śabda-tattva, śabda,* Veda, *avidyā, vivarta, vikāra, prakṛti, jāti, ākṛti*, and

2 As can be seen from this listing, the concepts indicated by the division of B's *magnum opus*, the Trikāṇḍī or the Vākyapadīya, and by those technical expressions in his Mahābhāṣya-ṭīkā or Mahābhāṣya-dīpikā which are not found in the earlier grammatical or philosophical works, such as Patañjali's Mahābhāṣya, form a subset of the set of concepts I have in mind.

sāmānya) which were intimately connected with the content of my main chapters and which I could ignore only at the risk of giving the reader the impression that I was unaware of what other scholars had perceived as major topics in interpreting B.

2.5 My reasons for following the first path were mainly two at that time: (a) In scores of research writings, Indologists, particularly the late Professor K.A. Subramania Iyer - who must occupy a place of high honor among those who have worked on B - had already followed the line of inquiry based on Sanskrit concepts,[3] and, although I had some contribution to make to the elucidation of the concepts, there was not that much benefit for me in retaining the old overall framework of approaching B. (b) If I allowed what were traditionally felt to be prominent concepts associated with B to dictate the selection and sequence of my items of investigation, I would not be able to present the investigation as a logically integrated whole. I would be suppressing what arose internally with what someone else saw as his or her agenda. In particular, I would be presupposing that B wrote his magnum opus, the Trikāṇḍī (abbreviated hereafter to "TK") or the Vākyapadīya, primarily as a work of general linguistics, philosophy, or philosophy approached linguistically, so that its division of content could be my division of content. However, clearly the TK is not written primarily as a work in general linguistics, philosophy, or philosophy with a linguistic turn. Its immediate context and concern are Pāṇinian grammar and that grammar's immediate (Mahā-bhāṣya, etc.) and larger (especially Vedic) tradition (as expressed, for example, in the notions of Veda, *praṇava*, and *vāc*). Because B achieves so much in so few words and because there is an amazing wealth of linguistic and philosophical observations in his work, it does not follow that general explorations in linguistics and philosophy constitute the major purpose of his work. And if I had to isolate precisely that general linguistics and philosophy from his work, there could be a serious spill between what flowed from his lip and what the cup of my dissertation sought to catch. B's clothes may be fine and attractive, but I must wear the coarse ones that fit me.

3 Recall his numerous papers beginning with "Who are the *anitya-spota-vādinah*" in 1935/37 and his massive 1969 monograph: Bhartr-hari[:] a study of the Vākyapadīya in the light of the ancient commentaries.

2.6 With these considerations, I organized my findings on B's fundamental thought in six chapters: "The epistemological point of view," "The nature of cognition," "The cognizor," "Language," "Meaning," and "What there is." Only after this organization emerged did I realise that it corresponded to what B had himself indicated as the very basic modes of his theoretical reflections: *jñāna, śabda,* and *artha.*[4] The most ancient accessible commentator of the TK, Vṛṣabha or Vṛṣabha-deva (p. 181; cf. p. 182 line 8), provided further support: *etaddhi tat sarvaṁ yad uta jñānaṁ vāg arthaś ceti* 'This is all that there is: cognition, language, entities.' A little later, I realised that the organization corresponded to the distinctions (a) epistemic or epistemological, (b) linguistic, and (c) ontic or ontological that were explicit or implicit in most of modern Western philosophy understood in the narrow sense of analytical philosophy or linguistic philosophy. However, it was not until I began to think about the histories of the rise of linguistically oriented philosophies in India and in the West, particularly in the context of Nāgārjuna and B, that it occurred to me that the organization which had emerged had a larger significance. Not only were the antecedents of language-based philosophies generally similar in the two regions,[5] the modes, angles, or approaches that assumed prominence once the language-based philosophies came into existence were also surprisingly similar. Thus, the Sanskrit tradition may not have words corresponding to epistemology and ontology and it may not have branches of knowledge explicitly recognized with those words and having precisely the same scope, but it came pretty close to having them *de facto* in *jñāna* and *artha* as understood by B.

2.7 My completed dissertation could have been published in Professor Matilal's then newly established Journal of Indian Philosophy. However, Professor Matilal did not think he could publish the whole dissertation together in one issue, and, in my view, on the other hand, the chapters of the dissertation were too interdependent to withstand segmented publication. Thus, it remained unpublished. I did not make any effort to have it published elsewhere either, for by that time almost every

4 (a) *śabdādi-bhedaḥ* ... TK 1.123, *jñāna-śabdārtha-viṣayāḥ* ... TK 3.1.103, *evam arthasya śabdasya jñānasya ca* ... TK 3.3.59.
(b) A variant reading *ṣaḍjādi-bhedaḥ* is found for the first citation given in (a), but it is clear from Vṛṣabha's explanation that the original reading must have been *śabdādi*°.

5 This is expanded upon in an old lecture of mine on Nāgārjuna and B, which I am now readying for publication.

established scholar who was known to be interested in B had either read it or had acquired a photocopy of it and I had moved on to (or returned to) an activity I had deliberately suspended to complete the dissertation, namely the activity of settling the TK text . Recently, I have once again been advised by kind colleagues in the field that I should do the minimally necessary revision and have the dissertation published. But now it seems wasteful to publish it without coordinating the textual references with the better or more convenient editions I think I will be able to finish in the next few years.

2.8 A word of explanation about these editions, I believe, is in order, not in order to blow my own trumpet, but in order to submit a kind of progress report to co-workers in the field and to avoid the possibility of work being needlessly duplicated. Since about 1973 I have accomplished much work toward preparing a critical edition of the entire TK. Such an edition has been considerably facilitated but has not been made unnecessary either by Professor Rau's edition of the TK kārikās executed with informed and perceptive hard work and amazing care or by Professor Iyer's editions of all *kāṇḍas* with all known ancient commentaries completed with great dedication to learning in defiance of indifferent health and practical difficulties. For one thing, it can be proven that the kārikā manuscript (abbreviated to 'ms.' hereafter) tradition (from this point on, please refer to the appendix at all appropriate points) to which Rau devoted his highly disciplined scholarship originated out of the kārikāvṛtti ms. tradition. The need to integrate the results achieved by him with the results one could achieve by a truly critical edition of the kārikā-vṛtti mss., therefore, remains. Without taking that step, we cannot claim to have made all possible effort to rèach the most ancient determinable form of the TK, a text of unparalleled importance in its area.[6] Secondly, although Iyer's editions and translations contain much valuable information and have contributed greatly to the progress of B studies, they cannot be said to have been prepared with full application of the principles of textual criticism. Not only was Iyer hampered by the fact that

6 In the present state of our sources, the principal physical feature of the most ancient determinable form would be this division: (a) *kārikās* of the two *kāṇḍas* accompanied by the Vṛtti to the extent it is available and (b) *kārikās* of the third *kāṇḍa*. It is interesting to note that in the more than one hundred years of TK printing (the first edition appeared in 1884/1887) not a single complete edition with this kind of text division has appeared.

in most cases he had to rely on transcripts instead of original mss. or photocopies, he did not in most instances try to establish genealogies of mss. or to follow them consistently - a very important part of the procedure of textual criticism, for it is not the number of mss. having a particular reading that counts but the number of versions or recensions to which the mss. supporting a particular reading belong. Furthermore, rarely did Iyer try to check if the reading he selected for a kārikā was the reading presupposed by the ancient commentator of that kārikā. As individuals closer to B by several centuries than our earliest available mss., the commentators frequently provide clues as to older and, therefore, probably genuine readings. Moreover, either because he began the text-critical and translational work late in his life or because he simply wanted to take the first step of giving a general sense of the contents of the TK, Iyer did not spend much time on problematic passages or try very hard to think of emendations - emendations that would be supported by testimonia or by transcriptional probability, so that such passages would make contextually acceptable sense. He was also unfortunate in not having conscientious printing presses for his early editions. The actual number of printing errors far exceeds the ones for which there are corrections in his errata. If this is the case with his constituted main texts, one cannot have much confidence that the variant readings given in footnotes are printed exactly according to his press copy. Since such variants are frequently meaningless, the errors committed in their printing, one feels, could have often gone undetected and uncorrected.

2.9 Having briefly established the need for a new edition, let me state what the main physical features of this edition will be. Its first volume will contain a critically constituted TK text divided into two main sections: (a) the kārikās and Vṛtti (abbreviated to "V" hereafter) of the first two *kāṇḍas* and (b) the kārikās of the third *kāṇḍa* divided into fourteen *samuddeśas* or chapters. Regardless of what view one holds of the authorship of the V, it makes sense to replicate in an edition the text associations as they are evidenced in the most ancient line of mss. and in the writings of all *śāstra* authors, beginning with Maṇḍana and probably as early as Dignāga. The numbers assigned to kārikās in this volume will correspond to those in Rau's edition, not because all the verses included in Rau's edition belong to the original kārikā text but (a) because Rau's is the only flawless enumeration based on actual ms. evidence that we have, (b) because there is no realistic hope at present of our being able to recover the entire kārikā text, and (c) because readers wishing to compare both the editions would find it convenient to have the kārikās identically numbered in them.

2.10 The second volume of the edition will contain text-critical notes, getting into (a) a discussion of why a reading is to be preferred or rejected, wherever the established objective criteria are insufficient to decide the issue, and (b) a discussion of what the problems presented by available readings are when no definite decision can be made. This volume will also have a register of references to TK passages made in other Sanskrit works. The ground for such a register was prepared by Charudeva Shastri in the footnotes to his painstakingly produced editions of the first two *kāṇḍas*[7] and by Professor K.V. Abhyankar and Ācārya V.P. Limaye in the highly informative appendices to their edition of the TK kārikās. However, these notices of later references to B by Charudeva Shastri and Abhyankar and Limaye are scattered and hence cannot be very efficiently used. Also, they do not consistently concentrate on highlighting the differences of readings found between their constituted TK text and the work in which a TK segment is quoted. Furthermore, there are numerous other references to TK passages which have understandably escaped even the formidable memories of Charudeva Shastri and Abhyankar-Limaye or which can be noticed only now because new texts have been published or because we have better indices available now. A fresh attempt, therefore, will be made in the second volume of my edition to collect conveniently and systematically as much of these testimonia as may be possible.

2.11 The third and final volume of the edition will contain a *pāda* index and word indices to both the kārikās and the V. Rau has published a *pāda* index and also a word index for the kārikās. Mine, like the text in the first volume of the edition and the record of variants in the second volume, will be in the Nāgarī script and will be based on the text as constituted by Rau as well as the text as constituted by me.

2.12 As some of you know, this major textual project of mine has been hybernating for some years due to my other professional responsibilities. However, not all has been quiet on my B front. I have published several articles on textual issues concerning the TK and on concepts such as Veda and *prāmāṇya* which I had only briefly touched upon or deliberately side-

7 The second *kāṇḍa* edition remained incomplete and only a few printed formes of it were somehow circulated, probably as a book.

tracked in writing my Ph.D. dissertation. I have also used the intervening years to achieve computer input of the TK commentaries of Vṛṣabha, Puṇya-rāja (this name should be followed by a question mark, as in the appendix), and Helā-rāja and of the Mahābhāṣya-ṭīkā of B. The accuracy of these texts typed by student assistants is yet to be checked, and, except for the Vākya-kāṇḍa-ṭīkā ascribed to Puṇya-rāja and Helā-rāja's commentary on the Saṁbandha-samuddeśa, none of the computerized commentary texts yet incorporates my critical observations. But having them available on the computer would facilitate future work considerably. At present my plan is to publish critical editions of Vṛṣabha's commentary and of the Vākya-kāṇḍa-ṭīkā and a semi-critical edition[8] of Helārāja's commentary, after or while I complete the work on the three-volume critical edition of the TK outlined earlier.

3.1 I realise that I have taken you on a rather long trip of personal narration. I hope it would not be seen as a display of self-centrism. In addition to capturing a part of the history of B research and stating what you can expect from me in the future, I have incidentally given in this *ātmopākhyāna* an indication of the major directions that B research can take. These directions are happily well reflected in the first international conference on B which was inaugurated a short time ago. We have here papers comparing B with modern linguists and philosophers, relating B's views to predecessors and successors in Indian *darśanas*, elucidating concepts such as *pratibhā* and *vivakṣā*, and exploring relationships between texts. I look forward to learning more about B from the paper presenters in all of these areas. However, it may not be inappropriate if I first touched upon some general issues that concern the areas and summarised what I consider to be definite achievements of B research so far.

3.2 Several Indologists are quite uneasy about comparing an ancient Indian philosopher with a non-Indian philosopher or with a modern philosopher. They feel that such attempts invariably result in distortions or inattention to specific contexts of an individual philosopher's thinking or amount to expressions of nationalistic pride ('see, our philosopher said so many centuries ago what your philosopher could say only recently' or 'see, our philosopher had a solution for that which baffled your

8 What is mainly meant by a semi-critical edition is that mss. will be selectively consulted and the edition will not be held up for a comprehensive consultation of all mss. The evidence collected by Iyer will be put to better use.

philosopher'). Now, nationalistic pride is clearly inappropriate in pure research, and distortion is obviously to be avoided by any researcher worth his salt. I would even concede that Indians may be showing a particularly agressive interest in pointing out the achievements of their medieval and ancient philosophers because their present offers them few springboards for self-elevation at the international level. But it is worth asking: Who planted 'being first in something' as a wide-spread value on the Indian soil? And, is it fair to deny Indians the opportunity of asserting themselves on the basis of being first in something when they are being put down in other spheres precisely by pointing out in one way or the other that they are not first there - that they are underdeveloped, that they are lagging behind? Secondly, the validity of comparativist conclusions is frequently a matter of temperamental difference. It depends on whether one is a person concentrating on the trees or on the forest. Thirdly, while it is true that many comparativists work through secondary literature and display a very shaky grasp of the literature in one or both the sides of comparison, it does not follow that sound philological interpretation and comparative study are necessarily mutually exclusive. There is no logical reason why they should be. Most important of all, it is important to bear in mind that one can never tell which thought, insight, or approach seen in a particular tradition will be useful in making sense of, or in making a better sense of, something baffling in another tradition. Frequently, one needs to compare in order to be able to understand - to complete the philological endeavour. The opposition or incompatibility seen between a philological approach and a comparative approach is thus a phoney issue. The two approaches can clash only in individual instances of practice, not as principles in methodology.

3.3 If this is acceptable, the comparative dimension seen in the study of B should be welcomed. It should also be all right if those of us who value Sanskrit as a treasure of knowledge and human experience pointed out to the rest of the world that B, a writer in our Sanskrit, distinguished between meaning and reference (*śabdārtha* and *vastvartha)* a long time before Gottlieb Frege did, argued for sentence as the primary unit of language at least fifteen centuries ahead of Willard van Orman Quine, anticipated Bertrand Russell's and A.N. Whitehead's Principia Mathematica in noting that a number is a class of classes *(saṁkhyeya-saṁgha-saṁkhyāna-saṁghaḥ saṁkhyeti kathyate* 3.11.19), came close to realising the possibility of propositional calculus when he declared *so 'yam ity abhisaṁbandho buddhyā prakramyate yadā / vākyārthasya tadaiko 'pi varṇaḥ pratyāyakaḥ kvacit //* 2.40), gave a linguistic turn to philosophy, and so on.

3.4 You will have noticed that under the pretext of discussing a methodological issue I have already stated one reason for B's importance. Only because we do not know how much was original to him - the traditional *śāstra* style would not let him preface his original observations with "I propose" or "I think" - we cannot determine if in the number of insights of fundamental importance he, as an individual philosopher, surpassed the Russells and Quines of the modern world, but it cannot be doubted that even the relatively little that survives of his work contains many more fundamental insights than the works of several modern language philosophers put together (cf. Sadhu Ram 1956:51-52).

3.5 B's position in the Sanskrit tradition itself gives him high importance of another sort. Not only does he combine in his philosophy the insights we tend to associate with Sāṁkhya, Mīmāṁsā, Vedānta, Yoga, Kashmir Śaivism, and Mādhyamika-Yogācāra Buddhism, he preserves for us precious pieces of information from the otherwise inaccessible periods of these as well as other systems like the Vaiśeṣika. It is perhaps only the Yukti-dīpikā that can rightly be compared with his works in this respect. Furthermore, B is our oldest available and so far clearest link to the tradition of *vāc* mysticism that has obviously survived in India right down from the Vedic period, albeit without receiving recognition in literature as a *darśana* in itself.

3.6 Within Vyākaraṇa itself, with which the relationship of B's surviving *śāstra* works is most explicit, B's standing seems to be next only to that of the *muni-traya*. I have not yet come across a statement in the work of any old grammarian to the effect that, although such and such form is sanctioned, employed, or cited by B, it is *asādhu* or incorrect. In the present state of our sources, B's works are chronologically the first that combine in them clearly and systematically the elements of what later became the traditions of *śabda-* or *prakriyā-granthas* and *artha-* or *darśana-granthas* written by Vaiyākaraṇas.[9]

9 Patañjali's Mahābhāṣya is of course the first available work that goes beyond formal grammar. But the place occupied by *artha* or *darśana* discussions in it is clearly secondary and incidental. The same applies to the Vārttika text which, at present, is accessible to us only through the Mahābhāṣya.

4.1 There is much that can be said about interpreting B, both in terms of the general direction of interpretation one should take (e.g., whether he does really take a linguistic approach to typically philosophical problems and thus try to dissolve rather than solve epistemological and ontological issues) as well as in terms of the interpretation of individual passages and words. The available time makes it clearly impossible for me to say all that I would like to say. However, it seems that I must make time for the following few observations.

4.2 Considerable progress has recently been registered in interpreting B. Particularly the achievement of the team of scholars organized by the Bhandarkar Oriental Research Institute for the purpose of re-editing and translating the Mahābhāṣya-ṭīkā is a cause for celebration. The concentrated attention that this text received at the hands of several capable and widely informed scholars has served to clarify many passages. It has also resulted in most specific and minute problems being flushed out into the open. Our explicit awareness of them and their possible solutions was the first thing needed for further progress. Congratulations, I am sure, are in order for Pandit Bhagavat and Drs. Palsule, Saroja Bhate, and Johannes Bronkhorst. A grateful tribute also to the departed scholars Professors Abhyankar and Devasthali and Ācārya Limaye. The pioneering work of V. Swaminathan should also be acknowledged in this context. One wishes that the unpublished part of his edition would still be published, but with greater accuracy of printing. The printing of the first part, he told me in a 1977 meeting, did injustice to his effort and press copy.

4.3 As for the TK, Iyer was the first to render the whole of it into English - an outstanding example of dedication. It is, on the whole, a very useful translation, but its intention was to make the original Sanskrit generally accessible (cf. Iyer 1965:xi, 1971:ix, 1974:11), not to push for making sense of knotty passages. As a result, Iyer rarely comes to the rescue of an informed Sanskritist. Where such a Sanskritist has problems with the text, Iyer usually has nothing to offer by way of solution. Being neither consistently literal nor completely geared to the needs of a non-Indologist or non-Sanskritist, the translation is unfortunately like most other translations of Sanskrit *śāstra* works.[10] If the perception that India has

10 One can easily see from Karl H. Potter's massive bibliography that there is no dearth of translations of Sanskrit philosophical texts. But can we name ten translations that we would give in the hands of an intelligent non-specialist with the confidence that he would

only religion and no philosophy is still widespread, as I think it is, our translations of Sanskrit philosophical texts must be to some extent responsible for it. The important lesson to draw is that Sanskritists must better define the readerships for their philosophical translations. We need both literal translations attentive to and explicit with regard to philological detail as well as explanatory essays ultimately based on such translations but pretending that the translations do not exist and the reader knows no Sanskrit. Any translation that is not consistent in either activity, literal translation and straight-forward exposition, will satisfy neither the Sanskritists nor the non-Sanskritists.

4.4 Dr. Madeleine Biardeau's (French) translation of the first *kāṇḍa* kārikās and V, in contrast to Iyer's, is on the whole more helpful to Sanskritists wishing to approach B. It tries to account for all words in the original and thus a Sanskritist can easily ascertain how she construes and interprets the sentences of the original. It displays a sharper sense of who its reader is supposed to be.

4.5 In recent years, a trend to take up parts of the more extensive third kāṇḍa for close study is developing. Dr. Peri Sarveswara Sharma's work on Kāla-samuddeśa and Giovanni Bandini's work on the Kriyā- and Puruṣa-samuddeśas paved the way. Dr. Roland R. Bergdahl, Jr., has worked on a part of the Sādhana-samuddeśa and intends to continue working on it and the Kriyā-samuddeśa. Messers Jan Houben and Yves Ramseier have selected the Saṁbandha-samuddeśa and the Jāti-and-Dravya-samuddeśas, respectively, for their dissertations. Dr. Peter Scharf also intends to work on the Jāti-samuddeśa. Helā-rāja's commentary on the third *kāṇḍa*, which matches in maturity the classics like Śaṁkara's commentary on the Śārīraka-mīmāṁsā (popularly known as Brahma-sūtras), finally seems to be receiving the attention it deserves.

4.6 Telugu and Gujarati translations of the TK kārikās have appeared. Substantial Hindi elucidations, if not translations, seem to have been undertaken by Dr. Shiv Shankar Awasthi. I understand that a Japanese translation is being planned or is already in progress.

understand them without knowing the original Sanskrit? I teach a course on Indian analytical philosophy for undergraduates who are not expected to have any knowledge of Sanskrit. It is my experience that I am hard-pressed to find adequate translations for the students in that course.

4.7 Thus, the prognosis for understanding B and making his works accessible is good. It is obviously not possible to mention or review here all interpretational activity. Its extent can be gathered from the bibliographies on B. However, while thus feeling on the whole optimistic, we have to protect the field from the publications of those who pay little or no attention to the research, particularly the textual research, accomplished and who cannot judge the accuracy of translations on which they depend. Although we cannot do much to stop such publications, we should do everything possible to discourage them. Otherwise, the field of B studies will soon resemble that of Śaṁkarite Advaita Vedānta - hundreds of books and articles to read but very few which really add to knowledge.

5.1 There is much that could be said on the content of B's works and on the larger issues such as his date (definitely not later than 425-450 A.D.), his religious affiliation, his identity with or difference from B the poet, from B the follower of Gorakhnath, from B the author of the Bhāga-vṛtti, and from Bhaṭṭi the author of the Rāvaṇa-vadha, the sequence of his works, his relationship with other philosophers and grammarians like Vasurāta, Dignāga, and Candra, his intellectual antecedents, and the impact of his work on the later tradition. However, the time available would not allow me to do justice to any of these exciting and challenging themes. Nor am I qualified or prepared to speak on them. Therefore, instead of touching on them in a half-hearted or rushed manner, I would, in the remaining time, like to quickly run through some conclusions on the external or textual aspects of B's studies and their implications.

5.2 It is probably an indirect consequence of the loss of importance that Sanskrit studies suffered under the British Raj that the texts of many or most important Sanskrit works first appear in poorly published editions based solely on locally available mss. Another contributing factor to this sorry state could be that a Sanskrit pandit has as little interest in preparing critical editions as a devout Christian has in historical studies of the Bible. Both are primarily interested in content or message, and not in wording or problems of ascription, etc. Anyway, whatever the causes may be, scholars are frequently forced to depend on such editions, and research is misled for several generations to come. B studies have had more than their fair share of wrong leads.

5.3 The first edition that began to appear in 1884 and was published in a separate volume in 1887 or 1888 contained the kārikās of the first two *kāṇḍas* and a commentary on each of those *kāṇḍas*. The title page simply announced *vākyapadīyaṁ ... puṇya-rāja-kṛta-prakāśākhya-ṭīkā-yutam*. That in the very same edition the colophon at the end of the first *kāṇḍa* read *iti śrī-mahāvaiyākaraṇa-hari-vṛṣabha-viracita-vākyapadīya-prakāśe* and the colophon of the second *kāṇḍa* read *iti śrī-puṇya-rāja-kṛtā vākyapadīya-dvitīya-kāṇḍa-ṭīkā samāptā* was not at all reflected in the editor's title page. Nor did he feel compelled to explain the discrepancy in his brief Sanskrit introduction. It was not realised until the 1930s, that is, for nearly fifty years after the publication of the edition, that the first *kāṇḍa* commentary had nothing to do with Puṇya-rāja, that its name was not Prakāśa, and that it was in fact an abridgement of a larger commentary which should be called V and which could be ascribed to B himself. Because the abridgement was not intelligible at places and it was the first to receive circulation, progress in B research was held up. Some traditional scholars like Dravyeśa Jhā, Nārāyaṇa-datta Tripāṭhī, and Sūrya-nārāyaṇa Śukla wrote new commentaries on the kārikās without taking the position that their interpretations must conform to the wording of the kārikās as well as of the commentary published in 1888, for they had no way of suspecting that there could be a common author for both the compositions. At present the commentaries of Jhā, Tripāṭhī, and Śukla are useful only to a scholar who does not accept B's authorship of the V commentary or to a scholar who wishes to go through the 'academic' exercise of checking how someone would interpret the kārikās if not given the benefit of the V. Even if it were held that the V is not authored by B, it is abundantly clear that the V is so close to B in time and thought that there is very little, if any, gain in trying to interpret the kārikās by ignoring what it has to say. In my view, much precious scholarly energy has been wasted because of the wrong lead supplied by the first edition.[11]

5.4 Nor was the first edition right in calling the second *kāṇḍa ṭīkā* Prakāśa or, as I have argued elsewhere (Aklujkar 1974), in ascribing it to Puṇya-rāja. One should here, in fairness to the editor, hasten to add that the ascription to Puṇya-rāja did not originate with him. The ms.(s) accessible to him could have given the name of the author as Puṇya-rāja, for there

11 Even after 1934, several scholars like Gaurinath Sastri (1959) wrote on B as if the V and Charu Deva Shastri's edition of it did not exist.

are many mss. which so ascribe the work. But all these mss. are later than the mss. which either do not contain the line of ascription or ascribe the commentary to Helā-rāja.[12] The second *kāṇḍa ṭīkā* available at present should be held to be a shortened version of Helā-rāja's as yet unrecovered commentary on that *kāṇḍa*.[13] I have recently come to the further conclusion that Puṇya-rāja is identical with Phulla-rāja, who filled two gaps in Helā-rāja's commentary on the third *kāṇḍa*, since the variation 'Puṇya:Phulla' is attested elsewhere also and is probably due to a misreading of the Śāradā script.

5.5 Despite a suggestion to the contrary in its brief Sanskrit introduction, the 1888 edition, continued in 1905, was partly instrumental also in giving rise to the wrong view that the comprehensive title for B's three *kāṇḍas* was Vākyapadīya. I have pointed out at length elsewhere that at least until the time of Helā-rāja and Vardhamāna, the author of the Gaṇa-ratna-

12 I am aware that Dr. Peri Sarveswara Sharma (1983) has argued against my position. Some of his observations are indeed good and valid. However, I am sure I can answer his really relevant objections and will do so at the time of a revised publication of my article. The only change needed in my position, as I have indicated in my contribution to The Philosophy of the Grammarians (volume 5 of the Encyclopedia of Indian Philosophies), is that the extant *ṭīkā* of the second *kāṇḍa* is not in its original form but is a short recast of what Helā-rāja must have composed.

13 It should be noted that I am not proposing that Puṇya-rāja/Phulla-rāja did not write the summary verses found toward the end of the Vākya-kāṇḍa-ṭīkā mss. or that Puṇya-rāja/Phulla-rāja could not have made the abridgement himself. All I am saying is that the work is not his original composition and is essentially taken over from Helā-rāja. As the summary verses conclude with *śaśāṅka-śiṣyāc chrutvaitad vākya-kāṇḍaṁ samāsataḥ / puṇya-rājena tasyoktā saṁgatiḥ kārikāśritā* //, it is possible (if *samāsataḥ* 'briefly' is intended to go with *śrutvā* and not with *uktā*) that the shorter version was available to Śaśāṅka-śiṣya, Puṇya-rāja's guru for the Vākya-kāṇḍa, who has been on very probable grounds identified with Sahadeva, the author of the earliest known commentary on Vāmana's Kāvyālaṁkāra-sūtra-vṛtti (Aklujkar 1974:182-83), about whose time the only definite thing is that he lived after Mukula-bhaṭṭa (900-925 A.D.). Such an early existence of the shorter version would agree with the guess that Helā-rāja's original commentary could probably have not made it to the north Indian heartland and that even Helā-rāja's Prakīrṇa-prakāśa seems to have left his residence or family only after the damage its ms. had suffered in two places was repaired by Phulla-rāja/Puṇya-rāja (see below 5.4, 12-15). It should be added, however, that a Śūra-varman could also be held to be the author of the summary verses. There are difficulties in taking *śūra-varma-nāmnā* as simply an adjective of *puṇya-rājena* (Aklujkar 1974:169). As a change of metre usually indicates conclusion of a composition, Śūra-varman mentioned in the preceding *āryā* metre verse would be the author of the summary verses and Puṇya-rāja the fashioner of the abridgement. Puṇya-rāja's very probable identification with Phulla-rāja, based on independent transcriptional grounds, indicates that he was capable of such work.

mahodadhi, and most probably in the time of Vṛṣabha, Vākyapadīya was understood to cover only the first two of the three *kāṇḍas* and that we should use the title Trikāṇḍī when we wish to refer to the entirety of the three *kāṇḍas*. A significant modification I have recently made in my view is that Yudhiṣṭhira Mīmāṁsaka (saṁvat 2019:349-50, revised edn. samvat 2030:400) was right when he suggested that Vākyapadīya was originally the title of only the second *kāṇḍa*.[14] Thus, it needs to be added by way of clarification that the range of Vākyapadīya understood by Vṛṣabha, Helā-rāja and Vardhamāna does not represent the first but the second stage in the use of the title.

5.6 How the first edition, without meaning to have that effect, got TK studies started on a wrong foot is, I suppose, amply illustrated by what I have said so far. The second volume of that edition, begun in 1905 and finished in 1937, proved to be a further impediment in the development of TK studies. It printed the text of the only extensive and generally undamaged commentary on the TK, namely the Prakīrṇa-prakāśa or the Prakīrṇaka-prakāśa of Helā-rāja, in such a perfunctory and incorrect (not to mention unattractive) manner[15] that it is not surprising that the first international conference on B could not take place until the year 1992. Between 1935 and 1942, the deficiencies of this second volume of the *editio princeps* were partly made up for by the carefully printed editions of Sāmba-śiva Śāstrī and Ravi Varma. But it was not until 1963 that the real rescue of the invaluable Prakīrṇa-prakāśa began at the hands of Iyer.

5.7 It is obvious that, however important B may be, his study cannot progress unless we have reliable and easy access to the contents of what he wrote.[16] As I have indicated so far, after making a bad start, which was perhaps inevitable, we have recently seen considerable progress in providing good access to his works. However, we are still nowhere near that level of tools which are available for the study of important authors of European Classical heritage. In addition to Iyer's work, which I think will be useful in years to come primarily for the third *kāṇḍa*, we have

14 However, Yudhiṣṭhira Mīmāṁsaka's reasoning in arriving at this conclusion is not correct.

15 Cf. Sadhu Ram 1956:52-53, Satyavrat Śāstrī 1963/1966:42-45, Iyer 1963:vii, xiii-xiv.

16 Thus, in the preceding paragraphs lies a partial explanation of the paradox that, on the one hand, B is a remarkable linguist-philosopher, perhaps the most interesting of all Indian philosophers to modern linguists and philosophers, and yet, on the other hand, he has not been extensively studied. The paragraphs also provide a partial explanation of why some have found B to be a difficult philosopher to follow.

Charudeva Shastri's edition of the first *kāṇḍa* and partly of the second *kāṇḍa* as an important landmark in B studies.

Rau's accounts of mss., critical edition of the kārikās, edition of the Vākyapadīya-prameya-saṁgraha, kārikā *pāda* index, kārikā word index, and painstaking tracing of Vedic quotations exemplify a down-to-earth, largely non-speculative scholarship of a high order. The work on the Mahābhāṣya-ṭīkā recently completed in Pune has been a substantial addition to scholarship. Better editions of the V (particularly of the second *kāṇḍa*), of the Ṭīkā on the second *kāṇḍa*, and of Vṛṣabha's commentary on the kārikās and V of the first *kāṇḍa* are what we need somewhat urgently. Iyer's work in these areas is not adequate.[17]

5.8 I mentioned our author's major work getting currency under a wrong name. The same is happening to his Mahābhāṣya-ṭīkā. The first incomplete edition by Brahma-datta Jijñāsu (= Jigyāsu) carried the objectively indefensible (cf. Aklujkar 1971) component °*dīpikā* in its title. Swaminathan correctly opted for °*ṭīkā*. Abhyankar and Limaye reverted to °*dīpikā*. I would have been happier if at the time of revising the Abhyankar-Limaye edition the scholars associated with the otherwise very valuable recent Pune edition had revised the title also. By way of reaction to my remark, the well-known Shakespearean adage "What's in a name" may be thrown at me and it may be protested that I am making too much of names. Let me, therefore, clarify that I too am aware of the tolerent attitude implict in *nāma-mātre vivādaḥ*. But that tolerence is all right when it has some practical purpose to serve, such as reducing the level of social friction, or when the available evidence does not allow a choice between two or more names. Scholarship concerned with reconstructing history must aim at being precise, as far as possible. More importantly, in the present case, inattention to the histories of the titles Vākyapadīya and Mahābhāsya-dīpikā results in some valuable historical insights being obscured. These are: (a) The three books of what we call Vākyapadīya or TK seem to have been originally conceived as relatively independent treatises. (b) When the thought to combine them in a unified work occurred, it could not be carried to completion. The author probably did not live to complete the V of the third *kāṇḍa*. (c) Hence the first two *kāṇḍas* which had the V gained currency together. (d) The third *kāṇḍa*

17 As stated earlier, these are my priorities, plus an index to the V, although while meeting theses priorities I shall be reworking the other sections of the TK as well, for I believe that there is still scope to bring about much improvement of detail.

had to be supplemented with a V by Dharmapāla. (e) The extending of the Mahābhāṣya commentary to only three *pādas*[18] of the Mahābhāṣya[19] was also probably a consequence of the uncertainties of life.[20] It is not likely that the work was planned to be complete with a treatment of three *pādas*, but that the author could not for some reason take it beyond three *pādas*.[21] Thus, the rather colourless names Trikāṇḍī and Tripādī,[22] conveyed in the oldest available unambiguous statements of two specialists of the Pāṇinian system, namely Helāraja and Vardhamāna, do not arise out of the author's choice. To name one's work as TK or Tripādī, without at least one content-indicating word preceding, would be like naming one's child "Two-eyed" or "Two-nostrilled." Nor are TK and Tripādī to be preferred because they were coined by some ancient specialist of the field as titles capable of reflecting the contents of the works. We should prefer them only because their very mechanicalness, their being based on nothing but enumeration pure and simple, distorts historical reality the least.

5.9 My remark that the three *kāṇḍas* or books of the TK could have originally been conceived as practically independent may have come to some of you as a surprise. Please note that I am not saying that their earliest circulation was necessarily as separate works. What I am saying minimally amounts to asserting that the three books were not intended to develop one argument progressively. They obviously have many links of detail with each other and they do present one thinker's philosophy consistently as far as I can judge. But it is not the case that the first book establishes a central thesis on which the central thesis of the second book logically depends, and the second book, in turn, provides logical underpinnings for the third book, or that the principal statement of the first book is explained, elaborated upon, and defended in the second book, and the main contention of the second book is similarly served in the third book. The content-based titles, Āgama-samuccaya, Vākyapadīya, and

18 Probably the first three *pādas*.

19 And, indirectly, those of the Aṣṭādhyāyī too.

20 At present the commentary is available only for a part of the first *pāda*. In the time of Helā-rāja and Vardhamāna it was known as a work covering three *pādas*. See Aklujkar 1969:555 and 1971.

21 This too must not necessarily be taken as a precise statement on the extent. The commentary could have covered only a part of the third *pāda*.

22 Helā-rāja's brilliant pun (see Aklujkar 1969:555) *trailokyagāminī yena trikāṇḍī tripadī-kṛtā* at the conclusion of his Prakīrṇa-prakāśa notwithstanding, there is nothing particularly suggestive about the names Trikāṇḍī and Tripādī/Tripadī.

Prakīrṇa/Prakīrṇaka, of the three books indicate this fact. Of these, Āgama-samuccaya 'Collection of traditionally received knowledge' and Prakīrṇa 'Miscellany' are transparent enough. For the middle one, the oldest known references that also go beyond mere recording of the title and throw some light on the nature of the work are those by Prabhākara[23] and Jayāditya-Vāmana.[24] Both indicate very strongly that Vākyapadīya is not simply a text that deals with *vākya* and *pada* but is particularly a text that tries to determine whether *vākya* is the primary unit of language or whether it is *pada* that should be accorded linguistic primacy.[25] This connotation fits only the second book of the TK.[26]

5.10 There is a tendency among TK specialists to view the alternative nomenclature of the three books, Brahma-kāṇḍa, Vākya-kāṇḍa, and Pada-kāṇḍa, as based on content.[27] A little reflection, however, will reveal that *brahma*, *vākya*, and *pada* do not capture the contents of the three books fully or precisely. The first book is largely devoted to matters other than

23 Bṛhatī, part I, p. 389: *te ete 'nvitāḥ padārthāḥ. eṣāṁ abhidhānāni padāni. tad idaṁ vākyapadīyam.*

24 (a) Kāśikā 4.3.88: *śabdārtha-saṁbandhīyaṁ prakaraṇaṁ vākyapadīyam.*
(b) A third reference revealing the nature of Vākyapadīya is in Helā-rāja's introduction to *kārikā* 3.1.1: *iha padārthāṣṭaka-vicāra-paratvād vākyapadīyasya.* The eight *padārthas* to which this remark refers are listed in TK 1.24-26. Being divisible under *śabda* 'expression,' *artha* 'meaning,' and *saṁbandha* 'relation (between *śabda* and *artha*),' the eight can be subsumed under the Kāśikā's *śabdārtha-saṁbandha.* Of them, only the relation conducive to *dharma (dharmāṅga saṁbandha)* and perhaps the rather obvious communicating relation *(pratyayāṅga saṁbandha)* can be said not to have found place or explicit discussion in the second book. They are, however, definitely discussed in the first book. Thus, Helā-rāja's remark on the nature of the Vākyapadīya would seem to imply inclusion of the first book as well in the Vākyapadīya. This, however, should not be viewed as invalidating what I assert here. It is quite consistent with the way Helā-rāja uses the word Vākyapadīya elsewhere. There can be no doubt that in his understanding, or by his time, Vākyapadīya meant the first two books. What I am concerned with here is not this second stage in the reference of the title but a stage preceding it.

25 Prabhākara's statement, as Śālika-nātha's explanation suggest, should be viewed as sarcastic. He is in effect saying to the Vaiyākaraṇas (with probably principally B in mind): 'I have shown you what the real vākyapadīya is. You fellows got it wrong.'

26 In the light of the foregoing discussion, the first part of my 1969 article needs to be revised.

27 Thus, relying on this understanding, some scholars have argued that restricting the name Vākyapadīya to the first two books (as Helā-rāja does and as I initially did) would be inappropriate; the Pada-kāṇḍa must be a part of the Vākyapadīya if the *pada* in the *dvandva* basis *vākya-pada* were to be fully significant (see Aklujkar 1969:550 for names of the scholars). Presumably, these scholars would argue similarly against the view that Vākyapadīya originally stood for only the second *kāṇḍa.*

brahman. The third is said to have once contained a Bādhā-samuddeśa and a Lakṣaṇa-samuddeśa,[28] which can only arbitrarily be held as discussions confined to *pada*. The second, as I have been stating, is not merely a discussion of *vākya*, but of *vākya* vis-à-vis *pada* with the intention of determining which of the two is more fundamental to language. On the other hand, a disarmingly simple explanation of the origin of the nomenclature Brahma-, Vākya-, and Pada- can be given once it is understood as not intended for expressing the entire contents of the books: *brahman* is the most important or central notion of the first statement of the first book, *vākya* of the first statement of the second book, and *pada* of the first statement of the third book.[29] The titles Brahma-kāṇḍa, Vākya-kāṇḍa, and Pada-kāṇḍa are as mechanically coined as the title TK and must have either given rise to it or must have been occasioned by it. Just like it, they seem not to originate from the author.

5.11 I believe I have done justice to my point about the importance of being careful about names, an otherwise innocuous matter regarding which one should normally not be insistent.

The question of the authorship of the V has had and will probably continue to have a considerable bearing on how we interpret B and what historical conclusions we accept regarding him and his works. I have something to say on it specifically in my second presentation. Therefore, I shall at present leave it aside, and come to some interesting facts that a careful textual study can reveal about the commentaries in general.

5.12 One unusual feature of the TK textual tradition is the existence of abbreviated versions of commentaries. Scholars of course know that having

28 (a) Sadhu Ram (1956:71-79) puts forward the view that the *samuddeśas* mentioned here were parts of B's commentary on the Mīmāṁsā-sūtras. Like Iyer (1969:8), I find Sadhu Ram's arguments unconvincing.
(b) Iyer (1969:7-8) speaks also of the loss of an Upamā-samuddeśa. The evidence he adduces from Puṇya-rāja in support of this assertion is not as clear as he assumes it to be. Most probably, it is only that part of the extant Vṛtti-samuddeśa which discusses compounds based on similitude that Puṇya-rāja had in mind in employing the expression *upamā-samuddeśa*.

29 Respectively, (a) *anādi-nidhanaṁ brahma śabda-tattvaṁ yad akṣaram / vivartate 'rtha-bhāvena prakriyā jagato yataḥ //*, (b) *ākhyātaṁ śabda-saṁghāto jātiḥ saṁghāta-vartinī / eko 'navayavaḥ śabdaḥ kramo buddhyanusaṁhṛtiḥ //padam ādyam pṛthak sarvaṁ padaṁ sākāṅkṣam ity api / vākyaṁ prati matir bhinnā bahudhā nyāya-darśinām*, and (c) *dvidhā kaiścit padaṁ bhinnaṁ caturdhā pañcadhāpi vā / apoddhṛtyaiva vākyebhyaḥ prakṛti-pratyayādivat //*

a shorter and a longer version is not uncommon in the case of Sanskrit works. What is remarkable in this case is the relative profusion. I have already noted that the so-called Prakāśa commentary on the first *kāṇḍa* in the first edition turned out to be an abridgement of the V. The commentary on the second *kāṇḍa* in the same edition, usually ascribed to Puṇya-rāja, can, with a great deal of certainty, be viewed as an abridged version of Helā-rāja's as yet undiscovered and hence probably lost Vākya-kāṇḍa commentary. The summary verses of Śūra-varman or Puṇya-rāja and the Vākyapadīya-prameya-saṁgraha (the latter published by Rau) are further abridgements of that commentary.[30]

5.13 Noting the irony that a complex of texts which contains a mild rebuke of *saṁkṣepa-ruci vaiyākaraṇas* (TK 2.481) itself underwent *saṁkṣepa*, we should ask overselves: What is it that could have prompted the abridgements? The original being too extensive or the original being in such a corrupt state that its significant parts became unintelligible and its essence needed to be preserved in a different form (*sarva-nāśe samutpanne ardhaṁ tyajati paṇḍitaḥ*) are the possibilities that come to mind. I am inclined to think that in the case of the first two abridgements I listed, the shorter version of the V of the first book and the shorter version of Helā-rāja's commentary that passes under the name of Puṇya-rāja, corruption is the probable cause. For the latter two, the summary verses and the Vākyapadīya-prameya-saṁgraha, convenience was in all likelihood the motive behind making an abridgement.

5.14 It is quite revealing, I think, that all the abridged versions belong only to north India and there too overwhelmingly to the Varanasi area. North India suffered from heavy disruption of its lines of ms. transmission in the period of Muslim aggression, and Varanasi tried for a long time to save whatever it could of traditional learning in the midst of an ocean of unfavorable conditions. Of the abridged V, two mss. have been noticed in Calcutta and five in Varanasi. One of the Calcutta mss. is dated in Kāśī-saṁvat, and the remaining, upon examination, may also turn out to be a

30 It need not be supposed that these shorter versions were created strictly by dropping parts of the original – that no expression of his own was added by the adapter. Some connecting words, phrases, and remarks could easily be added by anyone reasonably familiar with the system. The presence of such elements, seen when, for example, the Vākya-kāṇḍa-ṭīkā is compared with the Vākyapadīya-prameya-saṃgraha, does not prove that the shorter commentaries are not abridgements or essentially abridgements.

copy made in Kashi-Varanasi or from a ms. in the Kashi-Varanasi area. Of the Vākya-kāṇḍa-ṭīkā, the so-called Puṇyarājīya, no south Indian ms. has come to light.[31] The Vākyapadīya-prameya-saṁgraha does not exist out of the Sarasvatī-bhavana Library at the Sampurnanand Sanskrit University in Varanasi. On the other hand, there is no genuine ms. of the longer version of the V coming from the north Indian heartland.[32] The only available north Indian mss. of the longer V belong to the southeastern and southwestern extremities of north India, Rau's B1-B3 to Calcutta and a ms. that became available to me in Ahmedabad obviously to Gujarat. Also, no ms. of Vṛṣabha's commentary, which explains the longer V, has been located in north India. The message is clear. The longer V and Helā-rāja's original commentary on the second book (if the latter ever went beyond Helā-rāja's family or Kashmir) have disappeared from most of north India for a long time.[33] The intellectual giants such as Bhaṭṭoji-dīkṣita and Nāgeśa must have been forced either to rely on the abridgements or to give second-hand references. The complete absence in their writings of any reference to Vṛṣabha's commentary also reveals their relative impoverishment.[34]

5.15 With proper attention to the objective evidence that mss., etc. provide, one can progress even further in determining the vicissitudes that B's works and the commentaries thereon have gone through. It can be proved that even the Vṛtti-samuddeśa, the last chapter of the third book,

31 E[15] listed as preserved at Trivandrum in Rau's (1971:34) account is a Devanāgarī transcript made as late as 1782-83 A.D. evidently from a north Indian original.

32 Rau's B[9], preserved at Varanasi, is a transcript made in 1936 (at least as far as folios 7A-49 go), that is, two years after Charudeva Shastri's edition was published, but apparently written without a knowledge of that edition. Most of it appears to have been based on an exemplar in a script that the copyist could not properly read.

33 (a) For the unreliability of Nāgeśa's references to Helārājīya on the second *kāṇḍa*, see Aklujkar 1974:176-77.
(b) A ms. containing fragments of Hari-vṛsabha's commentary on the first and the second books is mentioned under no. 116 on p. 437 of the 1878/1889 anonymous Catalogue of Sanskrit Manuscripts in the Sanskrit College Library at Benares (for the details of the catalogue, see Janert 1965:27, no. 14). Normally, a ms. with such a description should be a ms. of the longer version of the V. However, in reality, no. 116 (= no. 38,025 in the new catalogue of mss. belonging to the Sarasvati-bhavana Library) contains a fragment of the Vākya-kāṇḍa-ṭīkā ascribed to Puṇya-rāja.

34 It should be borne in mind that although Vṛṣabha's commentary is simple in wording, it displays much well-digested and well-concealed learning. Some of the details he preserves are so important that it is extremely implausible that a mind like Bhaṭṭoji's or Nāgeśa's would not have invoked them.

is incomplete and that we should not suppose that only the Bādhā and Laksana samuddeśas have been lost. Rāma-bhadra-dīkṣita's Patañjali-carita, probably composed in the seventeenth or eighteenth century, contains a 'prediction' that is borne out by the present state of the Mahābhāṣya-ṭīkā; that is, like the Bhaviṣya-purāna, the Patañjali-carita states a fact as a future event. While preparing my draft critical edition of the first kāṇḍa V, I have come to the conclusion that some relatively short parts of the first kāṇḍa V were missing as early as Vṛṣabha's time, a commentator who could have flourished before the time of Kumārila and Prabhākara. The full text of the second kāṇḍa V was not accessible to the author of the available Vākya-kāṇḍa-ṭīkā.[35] What was missing in the north and south (Gujarat and Kerala) were different sections. The few available mss. indicate a very bad line of transmission for the Vākya-kāṇḍa V, probably from very early days, perhaps going back to B's own time. As for Helā-rāja's commentary, it could have left his family or place of residence[36] and begun to circulate a long time after it was completed - when it had reached a stage in which a few parts were already missing or had become hopelessly damaged and had to be replaced by Phulla-rāja (most probably identical with Puṇya-rāja, as suggested above).

6.1 Finally, I would like to touch very briefly upon the larger implications of B textual research. Perhaps because it was so neatly presented and because it was given the benefit of a very useful word-index by Chitrao and Pathak, we have tended to look upon Kielhorn's edition[37] of the Mahabhāṣya as definitive. We should now recognise that the manuscript base of that edition was not sufficiently wide. We badly need to check, at first selectively, the oldest available non-Devanāgarī mss., particularly from South India, and, if they indicate the desirability of preparing a new edition of the Mahabhāṣya, then plan for such an edition. The work to be done being highly demanding, we will probably need the services of young

35 Hence Helā-rāja's (who, I think, wrote the original of this *ṭīkā*) phrase *kāṇḍa-dvaye yathā-vṛtti* appearing at the beginning of his commentary on the third *kāṇḍa* may not mean only 'in accordance with the V of the two *kāṇḍas*' but probably also 'as far as the V of the two *kāṇḍas* was available.'

36 I mention the second possibility because Helā-rāja could have been a *mahāvratin* living away from his family if he is the same as the Helā-rāja mentioned by Kalhaṇa in the Rāja-taraṅgiṇī.

37 How far Kielhorn was helped by local pandits is a consideration that might become relevant in writing an accurate history of Indology.

scholars who are very much at home in Pāṇinian prakriyā[38] - services of scholars to whom the words *mīmāṁsaka, yuvan*, and *medhāvi-saṁmata* of the *ślokas* quoted in Mahabhāṣya 3.2.123 would apply (in a non-sarcastic sense).

6.2 Secondly, we will need to extend a similar textual treatment to the *bhāṣya*, usually ascribed to Vyāsa, on the Yoga-sūtras. As has already been felt by some scholars, this *bhāṣya* has many links with B's TK (and, I may add, with the Mahabhāṣya-ṭīkā). A critical edition of it will probably throw new light on its authorship as I have suggested in another paper.

6.3 I realise that I may have been too specific and may have tried the patience of some of you. Manuscript work is usually very time-consuming, largely boring, and frequently quite discouraging. But unless the text is presented in a dependable form and is studied well, scholarship progresses no faster than in a three-legged race. I hope I have conveyed to at least some of you a sense of how exciting, like a detective's work, textual criticism can be. There is an Indian folktale in which a king's favorite old minister correctly guesses merely from a camel's footprints and grazing pattern a number of things about the animal, right down to (or, perhaps I should say, right up to) the camel's being blind in the left eye. We should do well if we recalled that story.

Thank you.

38 The preceding detail regarding what is needed is based on a comment of Professor George Cardona.

Appendix

1. The works of Bhartṛ-hari, the linguist-philosopher:

Available (but in an incomplete form):

(a) Trikāṇḍī 'Three Books,' printed under the title Vākyapadīya and nowadays commonly known with that inaccurate title

(b) Mahābhāṣya-ṭīkā or Tripādī, edited, except by V. Swaminathan, under the title Mahābhāṣya-dīpikā and gaining currency under that inaccurate title

Unavailable at present:

(a) Śabda-dhātu-samīkṣā

(b) A commentary on Jaimini's Mīmāṁsāsūtras?

2. Arrangement and titles of the sections of the Trikāṇḍī:

Book1: Āgama-samuccaya or Brahma-kāṇḍa

Book2: Vākyapadīya or Vākya-kāṇḍa

Book3: Prakīrṇa(ka) or Pada-kāṇḍa, divided into chapters called samuddeśas

3. Available ancient commentaries of the Trikāṇḍī (tentatively understood as a text consisting of kārikās only, not as a composite of kārikā and Vṛtti)

Book 1:	Vṛtti	longer or original version	Hari-vṛṣabha → (Bhartṛ-)hari[39]
	Vṛtti	shorter or later version	redactor unknown
	ṭīkā	called Paddhati or Sphuṭākṣarā	
		explanation of kārikā + (longer) Vṛtti	Vṛṣabha or Vṛṣabha-deva
Book 2:	Vṛtti		Hari-vṛṣabha → (Bhartṛ-)hari
	ṭīkā	called Vākya-pradīpa?	
		explanation of kārikās only	Puṇya-rāja (= Phulla-rāja?) or Rājānaka-śūra-varman[40]
		a summary in verses of the ṭīkā	Puṇya-rāja (= Phulla-rāja?) or Rājānaka-śūra-varman
		Vākyapadīya-prameya-saṁgraha, a summary of the ṭīkā	redactor unknown
Book 3:	ṭīkā	called Prakīrṇa(ka)-prakāśa	
		explanation of kārikās only	Helā-rāja (two gaps filled by Phulla-rāja)

39 The 'kārikā + Vṛtti' work is ascribed to Hari-vṛṣabha in those manuscripts from 4 (a) below which contain colophons. The name Hari-vṛṣabha must be due to a conflation of the names (Bhartṛ-)hari and Vṛṣabha. There is overwhelming evidence favouring (Bhartṛ-)hari's authorship of both the kārikās and the vṛtti. No evidence that really serves even to cast a serious doubt on this authorship – evidence that is objective and factually or logically sound – has *so far* been offered, although doubts have been expressed more than once.

40 Most probably only as a summarizer of Helā-rāja's unavailable commentary, not as an original commentator.

4. Available manuscript traditions of the Trikāṇḍi (in the order of their origin):

(a)	'kārīkā + longer Vṛtti' manuscripts	first two books[41]
(b)	manuscripts of Vṛṣabha's ṭīkā of the 'kārikā + Vṛtti' text	first book[42]
(c)	'karīkā' manuscripts	all three books
(d)	'karīkā + Prakīrṇa-prakāśa ṭīkā' manuscripts	third book
(e)	'kārikā' + (shortened) ṭīkā' manuscripts	second book
(f)	Vākyapadīya-prameya-saṁgraha	second book
(g)	'kārikā + shorter Vṛtti' manuscripts	first book

5. The Mahābhāṣya-ṭīkā in its present form covers only (parts of) the first seven āhnikas of the first pāda in Patañjali's Mahābhāṣya. Up to the 11th/12th century A.D., it could have extended to at least three pādas (probably corresponding to the first three pādas of Pāṇini's Aṣṭādhyāyī). It survives in only one late, fragmentary, and corrupt manuscript written in north India.

6. Significant achievements in making the Trikāṇḍi accessible:

1887	Gaṅgādhara-śāstrī Mānavalli's edn. (a) of the kārikās and shorter Vṛtti of the first book and (b) of the kārikās and ṭīkā of the second book
1934	Chāru-deva Śāstrī's edn. (a) of the kārikās and (longer) Vrtti of the first book and (b) of excerpts from Vṛṣabha's ṭīkā
1935	K. Sāmba-śiva-śāstrī's edn. of chapters 8-13 of the third book and Helārāja's ṭīkā thereto
1941?	Chāru-deva Śāstrī's incomplete edn. of the kārikās and Vṛtti of the second book
1942	L.A. Ravi Varma's edn. of chapter 14 of the third book and Helā-rāja's ṭīkā thereto
1963	K.A. Subramania Iyer's edn. of chapters 1-7 of the third book and Helā-rāja's ṭīkā thereto

41 A tradition of third book (or Prakīrṇa) kārīkā manuscripts may have existed between the times of Bhartṛ-hari and Dharmapāla. With Dharmapāla, who wrote a Prakīrṇā-vṛtti, this manuscript line may have been turned into a 'kārikā + vrtti' manuscript line or allowed to continue as it was at least until the time of Helā-rāja. The tradition of Dharmapāla-vṛtti manuscripts or 'third book kārikās + Dharmapāla-vṛtti' manuscripts seems to have become defunct sometime after the days of Durveka-miśra and Helā-rāja (10th-11th century A.D.).

42 (a) If any commentary explaining the 'second book kārikās + vrtti' text was ever written is not known.
(b) Some commentaries explaining the kārikās of the third book and distinct from Dharma-pāla's vṛtti could have been written prior to the ṭīkā in (b), but we cannot determine if they are intended in Helā-rāja's references with *kecit, anye,* etc. to those who preceded him in the explanation of the third book.

1966 K.A. Subramania Iyer's edn. of the complete text of Vṛṣabha's ṭīkā to the first book

1973 K.A. Subramania Iyer's edn. of chapters 8-14 of the third book and Helā-rāja's ṭīkā thereto

1977 Wilhelm Rau's edn. of the kārikās of the three books on the basis of kārikā manuscripts

7. Major attempts at elucidation of Trikāṇḍī thought or Vaiyākaraṇa-darśana *in general*:
Prabhat-chandra Chakravarti 1930, 1933, David Seyfort Ruegg 1958, Gaurinath Shastri 1959, K. Kunjunni Raja 1963, Madeleine Biardeau 1964, K. A. Subramania Iyer 1965, 1969, etc., Aklujkar 1970 (unpublished Ph. D. thesis).

8. Significant achievements in making the Mahābhāṣya-ṭīkā accessible:
V. Swaminathan 1964, K.V. Abhyankar and V.P. Limaye 1967-70, G.B. Palsule 1983, V.P. Limaye, G.B. Palsule, V.B. Bhagavat 1984, V.B. Bhagavat, Saroja Bhate 1986, Johannes Bronkhorst 1987, G.B. Palsule 1988, G.V. Devasthali, G.B. Palsule 1989, V.B. Bhagavat, Saroja Bhate 1990, G.B. Palsule 1991.

A list of monographs and articles specifically referred to in the lecture

Details of other publications referred to indirectly can be gathered with the help of the appendix and the bibliographies on Bhartṛ-hari.

Aklujkar, Ashok. 1969. "Two Textual Studies of Bhartṛhari." Journal of the American Oriental Society 89.547-63.

Aklujkar, Ashok. 1970. The Philosophy of Bhartṛ-hari's Trikāṇḍī. Ph.D. dissertation, Harvard University. Unpublished.

Aklujkar, Ashok. 1971. "Mahābhāṣya-dīpikā or Tripādī?" Adyar Library Bulletin 35: 159-71.

Aklujkar, Ashok. 1974. "The authorship of the Vākya-kāṇḍa-ṭīkā." Pandit Charu Deva Shastri Felicitation Volume, pp. 165-88. New Delhi: Charu Deva Shastri Felicitation Committee.

Aklujkar, Ashok. 1991. "Vākyapadīya" summary in the Grammarian volume of the Encyclopaedia of Indian Philosophies, pp. 121-174; 179. Princeton University Press. Delhi: Motilal Banarsidass. With Karl H. Potter.

Gaurinath Sastri. See Sastri, Gaurinath.

Iyer. See Subramania Iyer.

Janert, Klaus Ludwig. 1965. An annotated bibliography of the catalogues of Indian manuscripts. Part 1. Wiesbaden.

Peri Sarveswara Sharma. See Sharma.

Rau, Wilhelm. 1971. Die handschriftliche Überlieferung des Vākyapadīya und seiner Kommentare. München: Wilhelm Fink Verlag. Abhandlungen der Marburger Gesellschaft no. 1.

Sadhu Ram. 1956. "Authorship of some kārikās and fragments ascribed to Bhartṛhari." Journal of the Ganganath Jha Research Institute. 13.57-79.

Sastri, Gaurinath. 1959. The Philosophy of Word and Meaning. Calcutta: Sanskrit College. Calcutta Sanskrit College Research Series. No. 5. Studies No. 2.

Sastri, Satyavrat. 1963/1966. Essays on Indology. Delhi: Meharchand Lachmandass.

Satyavrat Sastri. See Sastri, Satyavrat.

Sharma, Peri Sarveswara. 1983. "Puṇyarāja's ṭīkā on the Vākya-kāṇḍa of the Vākyapadīya of Bhartṛhari." Bhāratīya Vidyā 42:1-21.

Subramania Iyer, K.A. 1935/1937. "Who Are the Anitya-sphoṭa-vādinaḥ." Proceedings of the VIIIth All India Oriental Conference, pp. 258-263. Poona: Bhandarkar Oriental Research Institute.

Subramania Iyer, K.A. 1963. (Ed.) Vākyapadīya of Bhartṛ-hari with the Commentary of Helārāja. Kāṇḍa III, Part 1 [samuddeśas 1-7]. Poona: Deccan College Postgraduate and Research Institute. Deccan College Monograph Series no. 21.

Subramania Iyer, K.A. 1965. (Tr.) The Vākyapadīya of Bhartṛhari with the Vṛtti. Chapter I. Poona: Deccan College. Deccan College Building Centenary and Silver Jubilee Series. No. 26.

Subramania Iyer, K.A. 1969. Bhartṛ-hari[:] a study of the Vākyapadīya in the light of the ancient commentaries. Poona: Deccan College Postgraduate and Research Institute. [Deccan College] Building Centenary and Silver Jubilee Series no. 68.

Subramania Iyer, K.A. 1971. (Tr.) The Vākyapadīya of Bhartṛ-hari, chapter III, pt. i, English translation. Poona: Deccan College Postgraduate and Research Institute. Deccan College Building Centenary and Silver Jubilee Series no. 71.

Subramania Iyer, K.A. 1974. (Tr.) The Vākyapadīya of Bhartṛ-hari, chapter III, pt. ii, English translation with exegetical notes. Delhi, etc.: Motilal Banarsidass.

Yudhiṣṭhira Mīmāṁsaka. 1961. [saṁvat 2019]. Saṁskṛta Vyākaraṇa-śāstra kā Itihāsa. Dvitīya Bhāga [= vol. II]. Ajmer: Bhāratīya Prācya-vidyā Pratiṣṭhāna. Revised edition 1972 [saṁvat 2030]. Saṁskṛta Vyākaraṇa-śāstra kā Itihāsa. Sonipat: Ram Lal Kapur Trust. Hindi.

PRATIBHĀ AND THE MEANING OF THE SENTENCE IN BHARTṚHARI'S VĀKYAPADĪYA

Akihiko Akamatsu, Fukuoka

1.1 In the second book of the Vākyapadīya (VP), Bhartṛhari sets forth a theory that *pratibhā* 'intuition' or 'flash of understanding' is the meaning of the sentence (*vākyārtha*). He discusses the issue of *pratibhā* in kārikās 2.143-152. The first kārikā of this section is as follows[1]:

> When we understand the meanings [of the individual words in a sentence] by discriminating them from each other, there arises flash of understanding (*pratibhā*) which is totally different [from every knowledge of the meanings of the words]. We call that [*pratibhā*], caused by the meanings of the words, the meaning of the sentence.

As a beginning, by placing this statement in the philosophical and historical context about the linguistic theory in India, I will reconsider the reason Bhartṛhari introduced the concept of *pratibhā* into his linguistic theory.

2.1 In the VP, Bhartṛhari makes a distinction between two types of meaningful unit of language: (1) the word and (2) the sentence. The question whether the word could be the linguistic unit is one of the famous subjects discussed in many grammatical and philosophical works; for example, the views of Vṛttikāra in the Śābarabhāṣya. Central to this issue is the problem of the existence of the word, as a meaningful unit, which is distinguished from the constituent phonemes[2]. Vṛttikāra declares: "[When we hear a word, *gauḥ* for example,] the word [as a meaningful unit], which is different from the constituent phonemes /*g*/-/*au*/-/*ḥ*/, is not perceived immediately by us. We hear only the individual phoneme /*g*/ and so on[3]. Therefore [the collection of] the individual phonemes is truly *pada*[4]."

* The author is happy to acknowledge the financial assistance he received from the Kyushu University Fukuoka, which enabled him to present this paper at the Bhartṛhari Conference at the University of Poona (January 6-8, 1992).

1 VP 2.143: *vicchedagrahaṇe 'rthānāṃ pratibhānyaiva jāyate /*
vākyārtha iti tām āhuḥ padārthair upapāditām //

2 Cf. ŚBh 38.9-10: *ato gakārādivyatirikto 'nyo gośabdo 'sti, yato 'rthapratipattiḥ syāt.*

3 ŚBh 40.7-9: *na ca pratyakṣo gakārādibhyo 'nyo gośabda iti. ... gakārādīni hi pratyakṣāṇi.*

4 ŚBh 40.12: *tasmād akṣarāṇy eva padam.*

Because anything not being grasped by our perception (*pratyakṣa*) does not exist, he denies the existence of the word as a meaningful unit.

Posterity regards this statement as criticism of the *sphoṭa*-theory. If, then, the upholders of the *sphoṭa* insist on the independent existence of the word as a meaningful unit against this criticism, they must show the perceptibility of it.

The later grammarians, for example, state that *pada-sphoṭa* (indivisible linguistic unit of word) can be grasped through perception (*pratyakṣa*). But Bhartṛhari himself states nowhere clearly how or by which means of cognition (*pramāṇa*) one recognizes the word as a single unit, though I find a reference to an 'indivisible word' view in the VP. It is the following[5]:

> The indivisible (*avibhakta*) word expressing (*vācaka*) the meaning arises from [a certain number of] individual [phonemes] (*vibhakta*). Therefore the word [as an indivisible unit] (*śabda*) whose nature is the meaningfulness goes to the state of being mixed together [with the individual phonemes as component parts of an audible word].

"According to Bhartṛhari," says S.D. Joshi, "the listener may perceive each phoneme, but he cannot perceive the word as a whole. Only the perception of the phonemes gives rise to the mental image of a single whole[6]." This drives us to the important question. If the word as a single meaningful unit could be perceived by perception, as the later grammarians contend, it would be possible to regard it as arising in the mind with a concrete image. Does Bhartṛhari too think so? 'The mental image of a single whole' has a concrete form? This question concerns his views on perception as well as on the meaning of the word. I shall return to this point later.

2.2 Another type of meaningful unit of language is the sentence. In the VP, he draws an analogy between the words and the sentences. The words, however, are extracted from the indivisible sentence analytically, and the meanings of the words from the indivisible meaning of the sentence[7]. Therefore between two meaningful units, the word and the sentence,

5 VP 1.45: *avibhakto vibhaktebhyo jāyate 'rthasya vācakaḥ /*
śabdas tatrārtharūpātmā saṃbhedam upagacchati //

6 See Joshi 1967: 39 (Introduction).

7 Cf. VP 2.10: *yathā pade vibhajyante prakṛtipratyayādayaḥ /*
apoddhāras tathā vākye padānām upapadyate //
VP 2.269: *vākyasyārthāt padārthānām apoddhāre prakalpite /*
śabdāntareṇa sambandhaḥ kasyaikasyopapadyate //

Bhartṛhari considers the latter as the primary. If so, Dharmakīrti's following argument, which treats the sentences on a level with the words, is not to the point.

> The sentence [as a meaningful unit] (*vākya*), which is different from the constituent phonemes (*varṇa*), does not exist. It is because we have no means to perceive it[8]. In fact, when we hear a word or a sentence, '*Devadatta*' for example, we perceive there no appearance of the mental image [of a single whole] but of the individual phoneme /*d*/ and so on. ... If [the mental image] that is regarded as an object of the cognition does not appear anywhere in the cognition, we cannot determine it as existent or as different[9]

Clearly this is the same type of criticism as Vṛttikāra's mentioned before. Dharmakīrti refuses the existence of the single whole on the grounds of its non-perceptibility.

3.1 When we place the statement of Bhartṛhari quoted at the beginning between these two criticisms of Vṛttikāra and of Dharmakīrti, we shall understand clearly the motive he regards *pratibhā* as the meaning of the sentence. According to Bhartṛhari, the sentence would be the primary unit of language. He examines language always from the point of view of meaningfulness. The sentence is the primary meaningful unit, and the words as meaningful units, extracted from the sentence analytically, are only fictional parts. We understand the meaning as a single whole immediately after the speaker's utterance of a sentence. The meaning, in this case, is not brought forth by relating with each other the different meanings of individual words articulated one by one according to the arrangement of things in the external world. Understanding of the meaning must be the immediate and intuitive grasp of the world as a whole.

From the structuralist point of view, it would be reasonable to say that there is no word besides the phonemes, nor is there any sentence besides the phonemes and the words, as Vṛttikāra or Dharmakīrti insists[10]. Bhartṛhari, opposing these standpoints, declares: "There are no phonemes

8 PV I. kārikā 247cd: *vākyam na bhinnaṃ varṇebhyo vidyate 'nupalambhanāt //*

9 PV I. 127.2-5.

10 Cf. VP 1.73: *na varṇavyatirekeṇa padam anyac ca vidyate /*
vākyaṃ varṇapadābhyāṃ ca vyatiriktaṃ na kiṃ ca na //

in the word; nor are there any parts in the phoneme. It is entirely impossible to separate the words from the sentence[11]."

Bhartṛhari introduced the concept of *pratibhā* (intuition) with a view to maintaining the idea that the sentence is an indivisible linguistic unit. Against the criticism of the existence of the sentence as a linguistic unit on the grounds of the non-perceptibility, he points out the fact that the meaning of the sentence is understood intuitively and immediately, and he supports the existence of the sentence as a linguistic unit, namely the sentence as a meaningful indivisible unit.

4.1 But why does Bhartṛhari not say that the meaning of the sentence is perceived by perception (*pratyakṣa*)? Does he suggest that *pratibhā* is a different type of cognition from perception? What characteristics distinguish *pratibhā* from perception? These are our next questions. In kārikās 2.144-147, Bhartṛhari gives the following explanation[12]:

> *Pratibhā* cannot be explained [concretely] (*anākhyeya*) to others in the form 'this is that'. Though *pratibhā* is accepted in common as being realized in every person, it is not defined even by its author.
> *Pratibhā*, understood incorrectly, seems to make a combination of the meanings [of individual words].
> *Pratibhā*, which appears to have all shapes [of the things denoted by the individual words], acts as object [of the cognition].
> When we understand what to do, we cannot go beyond [the knowledge of] *pratibhā*, that is either caused immediately by the language or formed according to the impression of regular practice [in the previous lives as well as the present life].
> The whole world accepts *pratibhā* as a reliable means for action [in everyday life]. Even animals begin their activities by its force.

Aklujkar says: "The *pramāṇas* presupposed by Bhartṛhari are *pratyakṣa*, *anumāna*, and *āgama*[13]." Basically I agree with his conclusion. However, considering these two points: (1) It is after Dignāga that the *pramāṇa*-

11 VP 1.74: *pade na varṇā vidyante varṇeṣv avayavā na ca /*
vākyāt padānāṃ atyantaṃ pravibhāgo na kaś cana //

12 144: *idaṃ tad iti sānyeṣāṃ anākhyeyā kathaṃ ca na /*
pratyātmavṛtti siddhā sā kartrāpi na nirūpyate //
145: *upaśleṣam ivārthānāṃ sā karoty avicāritā /*
sārvarūpyam ivāpannā viṣayatvena vartate //
146: *sākṣāc chabdena janitāṃ bhāvanānugamena vā /*
itikartavyatāyāṃ tāṃ na kaś cid ativartate //
147: *pramāṇatvena tāṃ lokaḥ sarvaḥ samanugacchati /*
samārambhāḥ pratāyante tiraścām api tadvaśāt //

13 See Aklujkar 1989: 153.

theory is systematized, (2) Bhartṛhari discusses chiefly the authority of *āgama* and the insufficiency of *anumāna* by contrast in VP 1.30-43, it ought to be admitted that Bhartṛhari's ideas about *pratyakṣa* remain obscure. I only suppose that Bhartṛhari regards *pratyakṣa* as a direct cognition of external objects by perception, especially by seeing (*darśana*), and *anumāna* as an indirect cognition of it through reasoning (*yukti*).

4.2 Here I would like to note the similarity of terminology between two sections; kārikās 1.35-37, in which Bhartṛhari discusses 'extraordinary perception' (cf. Aklujkar 1989:154), and kārikās 2.143-152, the section of *pratibhā*, discussed above[14]. Kārikā 35 is as follows[15]:

> The expert's knowledge of precious stones and metals, that is inexplicable (*asamākhyeya*) to others, is caused only by regular practice (*abhyāsa*); it is not the knowledge derived from an inference.

Bhartṛhari insists that extraordinary perceptions result from regular practice (*abhyāsa*) and/or from lasting invisible force accumulated by regular practice in previous lives (*karman/adṛṣṭa/dharma*), and that this invisible force is ultimately dependent on *āgama*[16] of which the essential characteristic is uninterrupted continuity.

As Subramania Iyer already pointed out and we have seen above, *abhyāsa*, *āgama* and *bhāvanā* are mentioned by Bhartṛhari as causes of *pratibhā*[17]. Clearly Bhartṛhari treats *pratibhā* as the same type of cognition as extraordinary perceptions. Aklujkar is correct when he says: "It is clearly stated in TK (= VP) 2.117 that *pratibhā* arises out of all kinds of linguistic expressions, which implies that it does not depend exclusively on means of any special kind. There are also several other indications in the TK to the effect that, in the philosophy of B (= Bhartṛhari), the domain of *pratibhā* is not concomitant with the domain of the extraordinary[18]." However, I think that *pratibhā* and extraordinary perceptions share the characteristics regarding the process of cognition.

14 Subramania Iyer (1969: 89-90) suggested already this resemblance in Bhartṛhari's terminology. See also Aklujkar 1989: 154, n.12.

15 VP 1.35: *pareṣām asamākhyeyam abhyāsād eva jāyate /*
maṇirūpyādivijñānaṃ tadvidāṃ nānumānikam //

16 Cf. Subramania Iyer 1969: 93. See also Aklujkar 1989: 155.

17 Ibid. 89.

18 Aklujkar 1989: 154, n.12.

5.1 In that case, *pratibhā* and extraordinary perceptions have what characteristics in common? I want to refer to the views of Dignāga as to this point. As Hattori pointed out[19], Dignāga adopted the concept of *pratibhā* from Bhartṛhari to establish his views on the meaning of the sentence[20]. After declaring that 'the meaning of the sentence, which is called *pratibhā* (intuition), first arises by dint of that [meaning of the word]' (PS V. 46cd), Dignāga continues[21]:

> Even when there is no external object, from [only hearing] the sentences, various understandings are produced not only on account of regular practice (*abhyāsa*) but also in conformity with [listener's] own notions (*svapratyaya*).

Dignāga regards *pratibhā* as cognition without reference to the external objects. Concerning this point, Bhartṛhari would take the same view. The important point to note is the fact that Dignāga mentions as causes of *pratibhā* the listener's own notions as well as regular practice. As to the latter, Bhartṛhari regards it as one of the causes of *pratibhā* as we have seen before, but the listener's own notions, according to him, are the cause of various understandings of the meaning of the word[22]. The meaning of the word is extracted analytically from the meaning of the sentence. Therefore the understanding of the meaning of the word is a false cognition caused by the listener's illusion for Bhartṛhari. Dignāga, in this point, confuses the meaning of the sentence and the meaning of the word. To Dignāga, these two are the same linguistic illusional cognition since they are formed by conceptual construction, not taking account of the external objects. Bhartṛhari could not allow this confusion. Certainly the meaning of the sentence, namely *pratibhā*, does not have a counterpart in the external world, but it is a trustworthy cognition based on *āgama*, beyond perception (*pratyakṣa*) and inference (*anumāna*), like extraordinary perception[23].

19 Hattori 1979: 64.

20 PS V. kārikā 46cd: *vākyārthaḥ pratibhākhyo 'yaṃ tenādāv upajāyate//* I have quoted Hattori's translation (1979: 63).

21 PS V. kārikā 47. See Hattori 1979: 65. Jayanta Bhaṭṭa criticizes the view that *pratibhā* is the meaning of the sentence in NM 335.24-336.9. It is not Bhartṛhari's, but this Dignāga's view to which he referred there.

22 Cf. VP 2.135: *vaktrānyathaiva prakrānto bhinneṣu pratipattiṣu / svapratyayānukāreṇa śabdārthaḥ pravibhajyate //*

23 Cf. VP 1.36: *pratyakṣam anumānaṃ ca vyatikramya vyavasthitāḥ / pitṛrakṣaḥpiśācānāṃ karmajā eva siddhayaḥ //*

5.2 In the philosophy of Bhartṛhari, the sentence represents wholeness and reality. *Pratibhā* is the essential cognition of the world as a whole. In this sense, *pratibhā* cannot be *pratyakṣa*. *Pratyaksa* is a direct perception of the parts of the world, various things as meanings of the words (*padārtha*). *Pratibhā*, on the other hand, is the internal cognition of the world as a whole, that is to say the sentence as a meaningful unit.

Abbreviations

NM = Sukla's edition: *Nyāyamañjarī of Jayanta Bhaṭṭa.* Part I, edited with notes by S.N. Sukla. Vanarasi 1971.

PV I = Gnoli's edition: *The Pramāṇavārttikam of Dharmakīrti, the first chapter with the autocommentary.* Roma 1960.

PS V = Hattori's edition: *The Pramāṇasamuccayavṛtti of Dignāga, with Jinendrabuddhi's Commentary, Chapter Five: Anyāpohaparīkṣā, Tibetan Text with Sanskrit Fragments.* Kyoto 1982.

VP = Bhartṛhari's Vākyapadīya; references to the kārikās follow W. Rau's critical edition of the kārikās (Rau 1977).

ŚBh = Frauwallner's edition: *Materialien zur ältesten Erkenntnislehre der Karmamīmāṃsā.* Wien 1968. (Österreichische Akademie der Wissenschaften Philosophisch-Historische Klasse. Sitzungsberichte 259. Band, 2. Abhandlung).

Bibliography

Aklujkar, Ashok, 1989: The Number of Pramāṇas According to Bhartṛhari. *WZKS* 33.151-158.

Biardeau, Madeleine, 1964: *Théorie de la connaissance et philosophie de la parole dans le brahmanisme classique.* Paris - La Haye. (École Pratique des Hautes Études - Sorbonne. Sixième Section: Sciences Économiques et Sociales. Le Monde d'Outre-Mer. Passé et Présent. Première Série: études XXIII).

Hattori, Masaaki, 1979: Apoha and Pratibhā, in: *Sanskrit and Indian Studies. Festschrift in Honor of Daniel H.H. Ingalls.* Dordrecht - Boston. 61-73.

Joshi, S.D., 1967: *The Sphoṭanirṇaya of Kauṇḍa Bhaṭṭa.* Poona.

Rau, Wilhelm, 1977: (ed.) *Die mūlakārikās nach den Handschriften herausgegeben und mit einem pāda-index versehen von Wilhelm Rau.* Wiesbaden. (Abhandlungen für die Kunde des Morgenlandes XLII, 4).

Subramania Iyer, K.A., 1969: *Bhartṛhari. A Study of the Vākyapadīya in the Light of the Ancient Commentaries.* Poona. (Deccan College Building Centenary and Silver Jubilee Series 68).

ONCE AGAIN ON THE AUTHORSHIP OF THE TRIKĀṆḌĪ-VṚTTI*

Ashok Aklujkar, University of British Columbia

1.1 I keep an open mind on the issue of the authorship of the Vṛtti (hereafter "V" in abbreviation) of the first two kāṇḍas of the Trikāṇḍī (abbreviated to "TK" in the following lines) or Vākyapadīya. My interest is not in arguing for a position by implicitly assuming the adversarial system analogous to that of the British or North American judiciary. That is why when I discussed the problem in 1972 I tried to consider in as much detail as possible all the pieces of evidence that had the potential to disturb the traditional authorship of the V. For example, I collected all cases of double or multiple glossing in the V and attempted to determine if each of them indicated alternative possibilities of meaning entertained by an uncertain commentator or whether the different glosses were in fact intended by the kārikā author - whether what we had in front of us were, in effect, cases of sophisticated *śāstra* punning. In the end, the time-consuming investigation I invited upon myself revealed that the latter indeed was the case. Wherever we had more than one explanation given for a kārikā expression, the content of each explanation was acceptable to the kārikā author on some level or in some specific context. The alternative explanations could not be thought of as signs of uncertainty of understanding and thus be an evidence of the V author's difference from the kārikā author.

1.2 I do not at all mind being ultimately proven wrong with regard to the position I took in 1972 (if there is any such thing as the ultimate in Indology or historical writing). After all, one works with the evidence one has to the best of one's ability. However, I do think that neither the 1964 attempt by Dr. Madeleine Biardeau nor the 1988 and 1991 attempts by Professor Johannes Bronkhorst constitute the way one should go about proving a different authorship for the V. These attempts are, largely if not

* In addition to the various institutions and agencies which have so far supported my research, I would like to thank co-workers in the field of Bhartṛ-hari studies for the sources, knowledge, and stimulation they have provided. While I express my disagreement with Professor Johannes Bronkhorst in the present article, I very much value the considerable energy, time, and talent he has devoted to ensure that Bhartṛ-hari is studied widely and critically.

entirely, flawed in a basic methodological respect. They do not at every crucial stage ask the vital question: 'Does the argument made here ultimately have a *necessary* and *specific* bearing on the issue of the authorship of the V? In other words, in there a real and logically tight implication?'

2.1 As I have a separate refutation of Biardeau's remarks awaiting finalization for publication, I shall deal here only with Bronkhorst 1988 and 1991. My main counter-observations, in addition to the very general one stated above, are as follows:

(a) It is not sufficient to treat here and there a few details of the other position's arguments. Such treatment, if valid (see 2.3-8), will at the most weaken those details. Before a broader conclusion to the contrary is reached, a researcher is still obliged to account for the remaining details. A *sthālī-pulāka-nyāya* cannot justifiably be invoked in all cases.

(b) Tip-toeing around the evidence available in ancient commentaries, when it is inconvenient to one's position, should not be done. Frequently, there are answers already in these commentaries for the problems of interpretation or the cases of strained interpretation that a modern researcher senses.[1]

(c) The relative weight and number of the pieces of evidence on either side needs to be noted. Objective evidence, which does not need the intervention of a researcher's interpretation (e.g., clear colophons of manuscripts, some older author's explicit statement, citations, and borrowing or imitation of phrases, etc.), should normally carry more weight than the evidence which becomes relevant only through some kind of explaining or accounting, that is, which involves one additional step in the form of 'logic' supplied by the researcher. Bronkhorst in the aforementioned articles not only ignores evidence of elephantine proportions in favor of some little fly of an evidence found here or there, he does not take into consideration the roundaboutness involved in turning his pieces of information into relevant evidence.[2]

1 (a) This is not to say that the commentaries should be slavishly followed in each instance. But to show no recognition of the possible solution they might contain certainly amounts in most instances, as far as the ancient and medieval Sanskrit *śāstra* tradition is concerned, to an unjustifiable disrespect for scholars who seem to have spent their lifetimes studying particular systems, authors, and text.
(b) See 2.4 below for an instance in which Vrsabha's commentary already indicates an answer to the problem perceived by Bronkhorst. Additional instances in which my observation applies to both Bronkhorst and Biardeau will be found in my detailed treatment (under preparation) of Biardeau's arguments.

2 Moreover, I get the feeling in reading Bronkhorst's reconstructions of the early period

(d) It is not enough to show that there is a close correspondence between the kārikās and the Mahābhāṣya-ṭīkā (in abbreviation "MBT" hereafter). The close correspondence seen of the MBT with those parts of the V which do not replicate the kārikā content and which, for this reason, cannot be attributed to the presence of the kārikās still needs to be accounted for. How did it come to be there - in details, in diction, in preferred theoretical positions? The extent of such correspondence unique to the 'V:MBT' pair is not small.

2.2 Given these relatively general methodological observations against Bronkhorst's way of establishing that the V has been authored by a person other than the kārikākāra, it should not be necessary to deal with his specific arguments. However, because some of them may leave lingering doubts in the minds of researchers, I shall briefly address them in the order in which they have been offered in Bronkhorst's 1988 article. The 1991 article contains but one argument. So I shall take it up at the end of this section in 2.8. To save space, I shall in most instances only give the essence of my response, leaving it to the readers to acquaint themselves in Bronkhorst's own words with the arguments to which I am responding.

2.3 (Pp. 109-111): The fact that a reference is made to tatra-bhavat in the V and a view attributable to tatra-bhavat is expressed in a kārikā does not imply that the author of the kārikā in question must be tatra-bhavat, must further be the author of all the kārikās, and hence different from the V author. Holding a view and writing a kārikā need not be done by one and the same individual. An author V can refer to author T's view and again give expression to that view in a verse. It is not necessary that author T himself must write the verse.[3]

of the *śāstras* that he presses into service conclusions weak on account of the specified reasons to reach some other conclusions. The usual mode of that second-level argumentation is: 'As I have shown 'x' in article A, 'y' in article B follows.' That 'x' itself was not conclusively proved or that the objections raised against 'x' by fellow researchers were not adequately answered is not taken into account.

3 (a) The argument based on the presence of alternative explanations in the V is already taken care of in Aklujkar 1972. It is surprising that Bronkhorst (pp. 111-12) does not refer to that article and to Aklujkar 1977-78 and writes as if the possibility of the concluding verses of the Vākya-kāṇḍa being composed by someone other than Bhartṛhari and the possibility of different authorship based on the occurrence of alternative explanations in the V are being raised for the first time.
(b) What Bronkhorst (pp. 112-13) has to say about the so-called discrepancy of *vāc* levels (*vaikharī*, etc.) between the kārikā and the V will be taken care of by what I have to say in my examination of Biardeau's arguments. I shall, therefore, leave it out here. Iyer

2.4 Bronkhorst's (pp. 113-14) point that *śabdānāṁ yata-śaktitvam* in TK 1.6 is explained in the V in an incongruent way is not correct. Although superficially the V may seem to be pointing out only differences of word forms (or, to be precise, differences of phonetic features in the case of what could be viewed as essentially the same words) in different Vedas or in different branches of the same Veda,[4] the reality is not so if the TK thought regarding *smṛti* is taken into account. Words with only certain phonetic features are held to be capable of conveying meaning and producing *abhyudaya*-causing merit in different contexts and periods.[5] That the V wants us to look at *śabdānāṁ yata-śaktitvam* in this way is evident from its gloss *tathārtha-prayāyane sāmarthyāt, tathābhyudaya-hetutvāt*, where *tathā* means 'in *that* form, in that very shape.' To take *yata-śaktitvam* 'state of having a fixed or specific capacity' as signifying 'identity of meaning despite difference of phonetic form,' as Bronkhorst does, will make the import of TK 1.6c overlap with that of TK 1.6b.[6] Besides, an interpretation like Bronkhorst's will at least not be any less specific (and, to that extent, any less arbitrary)[7] than the interpretation found in the V.[8]

2.5 (P. 114): The change from *māṭhara* of TK 2.349 to *kauṇḍinya* in the V thereto, which change is made without a comment, in fact indicates that the V author takes such liberties with the kārikā as an author would take

(1965:xxxv) points out a possible confusion in Biardeau's statement on the matter but does not demonstrate, as is possible to do, that the kārikās must be understood as recognising four levels of *vāc*.

4 The examples given by the V are: *deva-sumnyor yajuṣi kāṭhake* and *simasyātharvaṇe 'nta udāttaḥ*.

5 (a) Cf. ***tathārtha-pratyāyane*** *iti. yena rūpeṇa svareṇa ca yukto yasyāṁ śākhāyām uktaḥ sa tatraivārtham abhidhatte, na śākhāntare. ato 'rtha-kriyā-niyamena śakti-niyamaḥ* ***abhyudaya-hetutvāt*** *iti. tatraiva tathaivābhyudayaṁ jñānataḥ prayogato vā karoti. kāṭhake eva tathā sādhutvam iti.* Vṛṣabha p. 27.

(b) As for difference of capacities with difference of time, note *pratikālaṁ dṛṣṭa-śabda-sva-rūpa-vyabhicārāṇi* in V 1.43, *viśiṣṭa-kālāvadhi-pravibhāgāṁ yathā-kālaṁ dharmādharma-sādhana-bhāvena samanvitāṁ śabda-śaktim* in V 1.171, and Vṛṣabha's (p. 100, 223) statement regarding *nyāṅkava* and *naiyaṅkava*.

6 There too, it is only through comprehending the meaning, through *pratyaya*, that the instrumentality of all *śākhās* or Veda-branches in a common ritual act is realised.

7 Note the restriction of *yata-śaktitva* 'having a controlled or circumscribed capacity' to 'having an identity of meaning' which is implicit in Bronkhorst's interpretation.

8 Bronkhorst's (p. 114) statement that the interpretation of *artha-vāda-rūpāṇi* in V 1.8 is doubtful is probably nothing but an echo of Biardeau's (1964:5, 37) statement to the same effect. He does not even indicate why he considers the V interpretation to be doubtful. It would, therefore, be appropriate if I addressed the argument in my examination of Biardeau's treatment of the matter of V authorship.

with his own composition. The observation would support unity of authorship, contrary to what Bronkhorst wishes to prove.

2.6 (Pp. 115-16): *ātma-bhedaṁ/ātma-bhedas* of TK 1,46 is not a certain case of V showing awareness of variant readings. Since what would be obvious in the prose order *kecit purāṇagāḥ 'tayoḥ ātma-bhedaḥ asti' iti āhuḥ* has been obscured by metrical restrictions in the verse order *'ātma-bhedas tayoḥ' kecit 'astī'ty āhuḥ purāṇagāḥ* - *kecit* has appeared between a split *iti*-clause, as if it were a part of the *iti*-clause, the author could have thought of advising the reader that *kecit purāṇagāḥ tayoḥ ātma-bhedam āhuḥ* was not the intended construction, for failing to offer which he should be faulted, that is, viewed as having written ungrammatical Sanskrit.

At worst, one could suppose that the remark *ātma-bhedasya bruvi-karmatve dvitīyā, vākya-sva-rūpānukaraṇe tu prathamā* was written by someone in the margin of an ancient kārikā-vṛtti manuscript and then it entered the subsequent manuscripts. The remark has that kind of 'note-to-oneself' ring about it, and there are many instances in Sanskrit works of such marginal remarks having become part of texts.[9]

In either case, the remark does not furnish a definite proof of awareness of variant readings on the part of the V author.

2.7 Bronkhorst (pp. 116-21) makes the argument that even after syntactic completion by the V some kārikās remain incomplete.[10] One feels like asking: "Does this really imply anything that has a definite bearing on the matter we are investigating?" What is logically relevant in the context is that there really be a syntactic bond between the V and the kārikā. Whether that syntactic flowing of the one into the other will satisfy all expectations of a reader in terms of intelligibility is another matter. The flowing could be hampered by such factors as loss or corruption of the

9 Vṛṣabha (p. 103) explains only the grammatical considerations involved in the remark. Neither the possibility that the remark could be seen as existence of variant readings nor the possibility that its presence could have implications for the identity of authorship which he assumes seems to have occurred to him.

10 (a) There are some details of this argument extending over five pages which are inaccurate or too general to be of any use in the particular problem of the authorship of the V. However, I shall leave them aside because at present we need to note only the incapacity of the main point to imply the result it seeks.
(b) If some kārikās remain incomplete despite borrowing words from the V, what about the others that borrow words from the V and become syntactically complete? How does one account for their dependence on the V under the hypothesis of different authorships for the kārikās and the V? Bronkhorst does not raise this question.

preceding or following text matter or by a reader's inability to interpret accurately. As long as it does not happen at the point at which the V and the kārikā meet, it cannot be used to invalidate the argument for common authorship based on syntactic unity.

2.8 In his 1991 article (pp. 17-18), Bronkhorst offers an argument which he characterizes with admirable forthrightness as 'neither the most important nor strongest." He thinks that the interpretation of TK 1.99 (*deśādibhiś ca saṁbandho dṛṣṭaḥ kāyavatām api / deśa-bheda-vikalpe 'pi na bhedo dhvani-śabdayoḥ //*) given in the V is "more forced and artificial" than the one he offers. According to him, the literal sense of TK 1.99d 'there is no difference between sound and word' "makes good sense in the context of *sphoṭa* conceived as a universal, for universals and individuals represent the same thing, be it from its real and from its unreal side." "According to the Vṛtti, on the other hand, there is no denial of difference between sound and *sphoṭa* in this stanza, but denial of difference of location. And pāda c ... which [Bronkhorst translates as] 'even though we distinguish different locations [in the case of sound]' is, of necessity, interpreted in the Vṛtti as 'even though we wrongly distinguish different locations [for sound and *sphoṭa*]. But this makes little sense, for the tendency is to confuse sound and *sphoṭa*, not to assign different locations to them." Continuing with the same assumption regarding the tendency, Bronkhorst finds the V consideration of objections based on two different presuppositions ('the contacts and separations of articulatory organs are the manifestors' and 'the sounds following each other are the manifestors') absurd.[11]

The essence of this argumentation, as of some others we have noted and as Bronkhorst himself has indicated, is that the V interpretation is not natural, relative to the alternative offered, and hence is unlikely to be a statement of the kārikākāra.

11 The assumptions in the foregoing thinking that the kārikā author could not have said anything absurd – that only a commentator removed in time from the author of the text being commented upon can say something absurd – and that an absurd proposition is necessarily non-genuine and therefore indicative of different authorship are interesting. However, as my intention at this point is to deal with textual details of arguments, I shall not expand upon the implications of the assumptions.

First, let me point out that the proposed alternative is not natural.[12]

(a) Given all his pronouncements elsewhere, it is unthinkable, in the first place, that B would *literally* assert the identity of *dhvani* and *śabda/sphoṭa*.[13] Any statement appearing to be an identity statement must be intended in some indirect sense or must owe its apparent identity form to constraints of wording that a metrical composition imposes.

(b) How can Bronkhorst assume the tendency to confuse sound and *sphoṭa* in a context in which there are clear indications that the discussion is about spatial (*deśa*) distinctions? The common tendency or, to be precise, the superficially accepted view, as B has discussed at considerable length, is to impute a temporal sequence and differences of speed to *sphoṭa*. Would people, or even theoreticians not thinking rightly in B's view, think that *sphoṭa*, which is an abstract linguistic unit in the mind or the intellect,[14] is the same as *dhvani*, which they hear outside and normally conceive as something concrete or physical? Theoreticians of other pursuasions may not agree to accepting *sphoṭa* in addition to *dhvani*, but would they commonly think that spatially both are the same?

(c) Would not a statement like "there is no difference between sound and word (i.e. *sphoṭa*), even though we distinguish different locations [in the case of sound]"[15] amount to an arbitrary assertion? Would not a listener of this statement ask why there is no distinction if only one of the two is amenable to different locations?

12 It should be noted that, in order to prevent the discussion from becoming too long, I am here leaving aside Bronkhorst's problematic view of universals in B's thought. I am also leaving aside his suggestion that somehow a particular notion of *sphoṭa* is necessary for interpreting the verse properly. Having discussed the *jāti* and *vyakti* views of *sphoṭa*, as well as the view of one *akrama, antaḥ-saṁniveśin śabda-tattva* that transcends the *jāti-vyakti* distinction, at various points between TK 1.67-97, B is evidently concerned in TK 1.98-103 with objections to the thesis of *śabda/sphoṭa* manifestation itself. Until that point, except *perhaps* in an inevitable reference to the other possibility in TK 1.71, he has proceeded on the assumption that all theoreticians of word accept that the word is manifested or revealed. Whether *sphoṭa* is viewed as *jāti* or *vyakti* or as a permanent sequenceless principle not subject to distinctions does not really matter in TK 1.98-103. Many expressions denoting manifestation – *vyaktiḥ (= abhivyaktiḥ), abhivyaktiḥ, vyaṅgya-vyañjaka-bhāvena, prakāśakam, prakāśakānāṁ,* and *prakāśyaḥ* – occur in close succession in this not too long a statement, which fact establishes that the author's main concern is with making a case for manifestation as the process.

13 Even in TK 1.105, which makes *sphoṭa* a phonetic entity under a certain *anitya-pakṣa* the distinction of *sphoṭa* and *dhvani* is maintained.

14 *sphoṭa* must be so, especially if Bronkhorst's view that it is *jāti-sphoṭa* or *śabdākṛti* that is intended in the present context is assumed.

15 Bronkhorst's translation of TK 1.99cd.

(d) How would the assertion connect with the preceding half of the kārikā? Why say even corporeal objects come into contact with space etc., that is, acquire spatial and other distinctions, if the intention is not to assert the same in the case of *both* word and sound? On the other hand, if an assertion of the indicated kind is to be made only with respect to sound, why make a pronouncement on the identity of word and sound at all?

(e) What justification is there in the context to import the words "in the case of sound" into the translation of the kārikā's second half?

As for the naturalness of what we find in the V, in addition to (a) of the preceding point, note the following:

(a) The double objection or the two-tiered *pūrva-pakṣa* in the V that Bronkhorst finds absurd is related to clear indications in TK 1.105, which expresses *karaṇa-saṁyoga-vibhāga* as the cause of *sphoṭa* production under the *anitya-pakṣa*, and in TK 1.76-97, which assume *saṁyoga-vibhāgaja dhvani*[16] as the cause of *sphoṭa* manifestation under the *nitya-pakṣa*. It cannot, therefore, be maintained that the objections are not based views that go back to the kārikā author's time.

(b) That such objections were quite conceivable in B's time and have not been imagined by a commentator desparately trying to make sense of someone else's composition - that they could be a part of the historical context of B's thought - is revealed by Vātsyāyana's comments under Nyāya-sūtra 2.2.13: *kim ayaṁ [= śabdaḥ] samāna-deśo 'bhivyajyate, rūpādivat, atha saṁyogajācchabdācchabda-saṁtāne sati śrotra-pratyāsanno gṛhyata iti?*

3.1 As the preceding comments, offered with as much brevity as possible, indicate, no truly valid or relevant evidence that would seriously threaten the traditional ascription of the V has as yet been offered. Yet relatively few scholars seem to be ready to speak with confidence of Bhartṛ-hari's authorship of the V. The situation reminds me of a man or woman accused in the newspapers of some unethical or illegal conduct. The poor person may not have in fact assaulted anyone or be guilty of anything like embezzlement. But after the news appears, almost everyone begins to stay away from or behave cautiously with him or her. The authorship of the V,

16 Occasionally, the synonym or near-synonym *nāda* appears in the place of *dhvani*, but that is of no consequence in the present context.

I feel, has at present become a matter not only of what the evidence indicates but also of the psychology of B researchers.[17] We seem to be going too far in our suspicion, substantiating the proverb *pāṇau payasā dagdhe, dadhy api bālo phūtkṛtya bhakṣayati.*

3.2 It needs to be recognised that the objective evidence favoring B's authorship of the V is much more multi-sided than in the case of most Sanskrit works. Internal evidence of both organizational and syntactic nature has been offered (Aklujkar 1972:189-96). It can be demonstrated quite objectively that the kārikā mss. have arisen out of the kārikā-vṛtti mss. We have citations of the V by authors at least as old as Maṇḍana, if not as old as Dignāga and Malla-vādin.[18] There are many cases of sharing of unusual diction even where a V passage is far removed from a kārikā displaying similar diction - even where the situation is not one of explaining a similarly worded kārikā or of citing *pratīkas*. At least a dozen parallels have been pointed out by scholars like Charudeva Shastri, Abhyankar-Limaye, and Palsule in their notes to the V or to the MBT that hold good only in the case of the V without the mediacy of the kārikās.[19] Both works contain references to an author Dhyānakāra or Dhyānagrahakāra hardly attested elsewhere.[20] They have some not-so-common quotations in similar context indicating shared associations. The nature and extent of the author's/authors' knowledge and the general world of ideas are similar in them. On the whole, the same atmosphere seems to be breathing through them. Are these connections really likely to be due to mere imitation or borrowing? Can an imitator work so deep under the skin?

17 No historian worth his salt, I hasten to add, will object to the position that it is always safe to distinguish between the thought found in the kārikās or *sūtras* and the thought found in a commentary. If not a difference of authorship, a sense of an author's progression in thought may emerge from maintaining this kind of distinction.

18 When a prose part of the extant V as preserved in its manuscripts (as distinct from a prose part reconstructed from other sources) is attested in the works of Dignāga and Malla-vādin, we would be able to infer confidently that the V was known to them. As long as only a few verses are noticed as citations in their works as well as the V, the possibility that Dignāga and Malla-vādin could have taken those verses over from the same source as the V and that they may not be indebted to the V itself would remain. The fact that the works of Dignāga and Malla-vādin are only partly available in the original Sanskrit creates further uncertainties in determining if they were aware of the V. Cf. Bronkhorst 1988:131-32.

19 I have noticed several more such parallels and will point them out in future publications.

20 See Limaye 1966. Dhyāna-graha is attested as a work only in Bhāmaha's Kāvyālaṁkāra outside the ones associated with Bhartṛ-hari.

Note also that the available evidence comes from many mutually independent sources. The tradition is solidly consistent. Should the tone of investigation really be one of asking the tradition to prove itself?

3.3 What do we have by way of objective or semi-objective evidence on the side of the thesis of different authorship? The name Hari-vṛṣabha found in a few colophons and a feeling that the styles (sentence lengths, etc.) of the MBT and the V are different, although the thought and diction have much in common.

Of these, as regards Hari-vṛṣabha, how far probable is it that a sequence of authors named Hari, Hari-vṛṣabha, and Vṛṣabha and removed from each other by centuries would emerge in the tradition of an advanced text belonging to an intellectually demanding branch of learning that was, even in the best of cultural periods, cultivated or taken ahead by only a few individuals? How many authors named Vṛṣabha are known in Indology? Is it really likely that a very original and valuable text that the V is was cited by widely informed and highly learned authors like Maṇḍana and Jayanta for more than four centuries but none of them would know its author as Hari-vṛṣabha?

Coming to stylistic difference, the only relatively precise statement I have read on the matter is the following: "... while there may be, ... parallel passages here and there in the Vṛtti and in Bhartṛ-hari's commentary on the Mahābhāṣya, there seems to be a marked difference in the style of the two works. ... In contrast to the highly formal and literary style of the Vṛtti, that of the Mahābhāṣya commentary is more conversational. It consists of short and idiomatic sentences and reminds one of the style of the Mahābhāṣya itself. One does not find those long involved sentences which are a characteristic of the Vṛtti. Both the works are commentaries and it is reasonable to expect a similarity of style in them. But one does not find this similarity of style, though ... there are parallel passages." (Iyer 1969:32)[21] Is this characterization of the difference sufficient? Could the

21 (a) Iyer has in the same place these other non-comparative observations to offer on the style of the V: "The Vṛtti is written in a rather unusual style. There is a certain strangeness or obscurity about it which must be distinguished from the fact of being merely archaic. It gives the impression of having been composed under the influence of a different tradition of writing. Sometimes it reminds me of the style of the Vyāsabhāṣya on the Yogasūtras of Patañjali. The impression of obscurity is not due to the presence of unknown words or the author's use of his own new technical terms. Some of the obscurity is due to the nature of the subject matter itself. Some of it, however, is due to the peculiar construction of sentences and compound words. Sometimes the language is very terse. Too much is taken for granted. There are not those indications, usually found

difference perceived not be due to the same author's development or to the different notions about a *ṭīkā* type of commentary and a *vṛtti* type of commentary?[22] There is no reason why difference of sentence length should imply difference of authorship.

3.4 If at all B's authorship of the V is a misunderstanding, the misunderstanding must have come into existence at a very early period in the life of the TK kārikās - so early as to have been in existence before the kārikās began to circulate beyond their author's immediate surroundings, for the tradition does not seem to know anything other than the so-called misunderstanding.[23]

We must then imagine scenarios like the following:

(a) B wrote the kārikās and a student of his[24] wrote the V. The student could pay extraordinary attention to the diction and thought not only of the kārikās but also of other works of B, such as the MBT, and could include much from them, as well as possibly add logical extrapolations and amplifications of the notions and views found in them[25] at

in other works, which compel one to understand the words and sentences in a particular way. There is a tendency to use long and rather involved sentences. Sometimes the whole commentary on a Kārikā consists of just one sentence. Those on Vāk. I.2, 46, 54, 91, 139 [147]; II, 14, 17 [these numbers, unlike the other numbers in this article, do not refer to Rau's edition but, I suppose, to Iyer's own editions. AA] may be mentioned as examples. Another noteworthy feature of the language of the Vṛtti is the addition of the word '*ātman*' to other words and though there is usually a distinct addition to meaning, sometimes it is not clear what extra meaning the compound word thus formed expresses." Iyer 1969:32.

(b) I do not understand what the nature of the indications referred to by Iyer in the sentence "There are not ... particular way' is.

(c) The compounds with *ātman* can be shown to add the sense of 'unit, a reified entity.' They are found, among other texts, in the Yoga-sūtra-bhāṣya, Śabara's Mīmāṁsā-sūtra-bhāṣya, the MBT, and the TK kārikās themselves. While it may be worthwhile to ask why they are so common in the V, they do not seem to be unique or original to it as a stylistic feature.

22 Iyer comes close to realising this possibility when he remarks in the passage quoted in note 21 that the V "gives the impression of having been composed under the influence of a different tradition of writing."

23 Even in Bronkhorst's (1988:132) view, the ascription of the V to B could precede Dignāga's time.

24 I specify 'a student' because that kind of assumption will go well with *praṇīto guruṇāsmākam ayam āgama-saṁgrahaḥ* (= TK kārikās under one natural interpretation) occurring in the verses at the end of the V. But it is not necessary that the V author be a student of B.

25 A *preliminary* comparison of the theoretical thought contents of the MBT and the V indicates that when there are common ideas in the two works (e.g. in the reference to *sphoṭa, prākṛta dhvani, vaikṛta dhvani*) the V usually contains more details even when the

all appropriate points,[26] without ever giving a sense of disjunction. In other words, he was a master imitator. He was also probably very self-effacing, for he did not record his authorship of the V and, by the time the TK began to circulate with the V, he was already forgotten as a contributor.

(b) Vasurāta, said to have been B's *upādhyāya, guru*, or teacher,[27] composed the kārikās that form the TK and B, the well-attested author of the MBT, wrote the V, imitating his teacher's diction to a considerable extent. Somehow Vasurāta's involvement was forgotten, and none of the kārikās was cited as his composition. B displayed different styles as far as sentence length etc. are concerned in the MBT and the V.

How far these scenarios are likely to be true is a matter of personal taste at this point in B's studies, not of history writing based on known evidence, and, in that sense, inconsequential.

The scenarios are inconsequential in another sense too. Under either of them, the period intervening between the composition of the TK kārikās and the composition of the V would be so short as to be insignificant from the point of view of our being able to delineate a historical development of ideas. We would have something comparable to the case of the Tattva-saṁgraha and its Pañcikā. We would have a difference of authorship, but we would not be able to say confidently that important notions such as *vivarta* or *avidyā* are different in the two works. Almost all of the considerable difference of philosophical atmosphere that someone like Biardeau (1964: introduction) sees in the kārikās and the V will have no hard temporal basis.

3.5 What have we learned from the discussion of V authorship that can be considered a gain for Indology?

content it shares with the kārikās is excluded. Therefore, if someone wrote the V on the basis of the MBT, he must, it seems, extrapolate and amplify the MBT statements to bring them to the level of the statements at present found in the V.

26 That the sequence for the introduction of ideas in the MBT and the V would be different is only to be expected. The former, being a commentary on the Mahābhāṣya must follow the Mahābhāṣya author's order of discussion, whereas the latter must abide by the order of the TK kārikās. A person using a work like the MBT to comment on the TK will have to engage in much transposing of observations.

27 The Vākya-kāṇḍa-ṭīkā, the summary verses at the end of the Vākya-kāṇḍa-ṭīkā, and the Dvādaśāra-naya-cakra of Malla-vādin either state or suggest that Vasurāta was B's teacher.

(a) We should not conclude that a commentary has a different author only because it gives alternative explanations of certain expressions. We should remember that the Sanskrit tradition was fashioned by authors who had a very sharp eye for punning possibilities.

(b) Merely because a sub-commentator like Vṛṣabha refers to the author of a *sūtra* or kārikā text and the author of a commentary thereto with different designations such as *granthakāra* and *vṛttikāra* it does not follow that he is thinking of two historical persons. He may be thinking simply of two different roles of the same person - of two different litterary persona.[28]

Bibliography of publications specifically referred to

Aklujkar, Ashok. 1972. "The authorship of the Vākyapadīya-vṛtti." Wiener Zeitschrift für die Kunde Südasiens 16:181-98.

Aklujkar, Ashok. 1977-78. "The concluding verses of Bhartṛ-hari's Vākya-kāṇḍa." Annals of the Bhandarkar Oriental Research Institute, 58-9 (Diamond Jubilee Volume), pp. 9-26.

Biardeau, Madeleine. 1964. (Ed., tr.) Vākyapadīya Brahmakāṇḍa avec la Vṛtti de Harivṛṣabha. Paris: Editions E. de Boccard. Publications de l'Institut de Civilisation Indienne. Série IN-8°. Fascicule 24.

Bronkhorst, Johannes, 1988. "Etudes sur Bhartṛ-hari, 1: L'auteur et la date de la Vṛtti." Bulletin d'Etudes Indiennes 6: 105-143.

Bronkhorst, Johannes. 1991. "Studies on Bhartṛhari, 3: Bhartṛhari on sphoṭa and universals." Asiatische Studien/Études Asiatiques XLV.1: 5-18.

Iyer: see Subramania Iyer.

Limaye, Vishnu Prabhakar. 1966. "Dhyānagrahakāra or Dhyānakāra: a Pre-Bhartṛhari Grammarian." Vishveshvarananda Indological Journal 4.228-9.

Subramania Iyer, K.A. (1965. (Tr.) The Vākyapadīya of Bhartṛhari with the Vṛtti. Chapter I. Poona: Deccan College. Deccan College Building Centenary and Silver Jubilee Series. No. 26.

Subramania Iyer, K.A. 1969. Bhartr-hari[:] a study of the Vākyapadāya in the light of the ancient commentaries. Poona: Deccan College Postgraduate and Research Institute. [Deccan College] Building Centenary and Silver Jubilee Series no. 68.

28 This has been independently pointed out in the context of the authorship of the Dhvanyāloka-vṛtti by Rewa Prasad Dwivedi in his excellent Hindi monograph on Ānanda-vardhana (Bhopal: Madhyapradeśa Hindi Grantha Akādamī, 1972). Thus, a confirmation has been provided from an unrelated corner.

वा. बा. भागवत, पुणे

श्रीमद्भर्तृहरिः नागेशश्च

तत्रभवान् भर्तृहरिः यथा महावैयाकरणः, एवं महान्तत्त्वज्ञो ऽपि । तेन विरचिते वाक्यपदीये यद्यपि आपाततो व्याकरणशास्त्रविषयाणां विवरणं प्रतिभासते, तथापि चिरायाभ्यासकस्य संदिग्धे मतिः 'किमिदं व्याकरणग्रन्थरत्नमुताहो तत्त्वज्ञानपरमिति'। प्रथमे द्वितीये विशिष्य च तृतीये काण्डे अनेन महाप्रज्ञेन महाभागेन विचारितान् समर्थितांश्च जातिद्रव्यगुणकालादीन्समीक्ष्य कोऽपि प्रेक्षावान्विपश्चित् सर्वथा तत्त्वज्ञानग्रन्थो ऽयमित्येव निश्चिनुयात् । एवंस्थितेऽपि शब्दस्यात्मभूतमर्थतत्त्वं विस्तरेण लक्षणप्रमाणपूर्वकं विमर्शयितुम् इदंप्रथमतया प्रवृत्तमिदं वाक्यपदीयं भाषास्वरूपाभ्यासकानां नितराम् उपकारकं व्याकरणस्य कात्स्न्यर्मित्यत्र न कोऽपि संशयीत । व्याकरणनिकाये सांप्रतं श्रीमद्भर्तृहरियुगं प्रचकास्ति । सांप्रतिकानां विश्वस्मिन्विश्वे भाषाविशेषाभ्यासकानां विद्वद्वराणां तत्रभवति भर्तृहरौ श्रद्धाविशेषं प्रतीत्य प्राचीना शास्त्रपरंपरा संतोषातिशयं समनुभवति ॥

यद्यप्ययं विद्वान्वाक्यपदीयस्य द्वितीयकाण्डस्यान्ते खण्डितां व्याकरणशास्त्रपरंपरां स्मारं स्मारमनुशोचति, तां च पुनः संजीवयितुमयमागमसंग्रहः कृत इति प्रतिजानीते, तथापि तममुमागमसंग्रहं स्वाध्यायपरंपरायां द्रढयितुं प्राय उदासांचक्रिरे भर्तृहरेरुत्तराः

पाणिनीयाः । तत्र च उदासनायां निदानं जिज्ञासमानेन मया पाणिनीयव्याकरणपरंपरायां शेखरायमाणः तत्रभवान् पातञ्जले महाभाष्ये कृतभूरिपरिश्रामः नागेशभट्टः पृष्टः, यतः पाणिनीयपरंपरायां यानि मतानि, ये वा सिद्धान्ताः, तेषां समेषामग्र्यया बुद्ध्या परीक्षणे स एव सर्वथालंभविष्णुः इति मन्वेऽहम् ॥

अयं नागेशः स्वग्रन्थेषु बहुत्र श्रीमद्भर्तृहरिसंदर्भान् नामग्राहमन्यथा वा प्रमाणरूपेण समर्थनार्थम्, दूष्यत्वेन निराकर्तुं वा निर्दिशति । बहुत्र वाक्यपदीयकारिकाः महाभाष्यदीपिकावाक्यानि निर्दिशन् अयं वाक्यपदीयमिव दीपिकामपि साक्षाच्चक्रे इत्यनुमीयते ।

नागेशभट्टः साक्षात्परंपरया वा भर्तृहरिमतानि निर्दिश्य तानि बहुत्र दूषयति तत्र कानिचनात्र उदाह्रियन्ते ।

I. महाभाष्ये पस्पशायामुपक्रमे शब्दस्वरूपविचारणायां 'सामान्यभूतं' विवरणावसरे दीपिकायां तत्रभवान्भर्तृहरिः विवृणोति 'भूतशब्द उपमानवाची' इति । अत्र विवरणे तत्रभवान्कैयटः प्रदीपे सर्वथा समर्थयते दीपिकाविवरणम्, परं नागेशः उद्द्योते द्रढीयः खण्डयति 'एवं हि वृक्षवदाम्र इत्याद्यापत्तेः सामान्यश्रुतेः सर्वसामान्यविषयत्वेन प्रवृत्तायाः संकोचे कारणाभावाच्च नेदं युक्तम्, किन्तु स्वरूपवाची सः । पितृभूत इत्यत्राप्यन्यत्रान्यशब्दप्रयोगः सादृश्यपर इति सादृश्यप्रतीतिर्न त्वस्य सादृश्यवाचकत्वे मानमस्ति ।'

II. 'लृकारस्य लपरत्वं वक्ष्यामि' इति 'तुल्यास्यप्रयत्नं ...' (१.१.९) सूत्रभाष्ये दीपिका "व्याख्यास्यामीत्यर्थः, कथम् ? प्रत्याहारः 'रट् लण्' इति लकारे योऽकारः असौ अनुनासिकः प्रतिज्ञास्यते ।" अत्र उद्द्योते नागेशः "लण्सूत्रस्थस्याकारस्यानुनासिकत्वे 'अतो

ऌरान्तस्य' (७.२२) इति सूत्रे पाणिनिर्लकारं नोच्चारयेत्। प्रत्याहारेणैव निर्वाहात्, तस्मादपूर्वं वचनं कार्यमित्येव भाष्याशयः।"

III. अनेकार्थशब्दस्य प्रयोगे विवक्षितार्थनिर्णयार्थमुपकारीणि संयोगादीनि चतुर्दश कारणानि भर्तृहरिणा वाक्यपदीये द्वयोः कारिकयोः संगृहीतानि। (वा.२. ३१५, ३१६) तानि निर्दिश्य लघुमञ्जुषायां नागेशः लिखति 'अत्र सामर्थ्यमिवैकं मुख्यं निर्णायकम्, संयोगादयः तद्व्यञ्जकः प्रपञ्चः, तैः सामर्थ्यस्यैवाभिव्यक्तेः'।*

IV. 'निपात एकाजनाङ्'(१.१.१४) इति सूत्रे दीपिकायां 'गुणभूतस्य हलः सनः कित्त्वातिदेशे न भवति संख्याविशेषस्य विवक्षा' अत्र नागेशः 'विधेयविशेषणं विवक्षितमनुवाद्यविशेषणमविवक्षितमिति मीमांसकमर्यादैव ज्यायसी, भाष्यसंमता चेतीदं चिन्त्यम्। वाक्यपदीये तृतीयकाण्डे जातिसमुद्देशे प्रसक्तानुप्रसक्त इति संख्याविवक्षाऽविवक्षाविषयः उपक्षिप्तः, अनयैव सर्वशास्त्रसंमतमीमांसकमर्यादाप्रतीपया सरण्या निर्णयपथं प्रापितः।'

V. सर्वनामसंज्ञासूत्रे (१.१.२७) भाष्ये 'एतेषां चापि शब्दानां यो विषयः ... सर्वनामकार्यं प्राप्नोति' इत्यत्र दीपिकायां भर्तृहरिः 'इदं न्यायविदो भाष्यकारस्याप्ययुक्तमिव दृश्यते' इति महाभाष्यकारं तिरस्करोति। नागेशः महाभाष्यं समर्थयते।

VI. तत्रैव सूत्रभाष्ये अन्ततः 'उदाहरणमात्रम्' इति महाभाष्यप्रतीकं गृहीत्वा भर्तृहरिः 'भाष्यकारस्याप्युदाहरणमात्रमन्यान्यपि संनिवेशाश्रयाणि कार्याणि विद्यन्ते भावत्यमिति मा भूत्' इति महाभाष्य-

---

* [Note of the editor:] See *Vākyapadīya* (ed. K. V. Abhyankar and V. P. Limaye, Poona 1965), Appendix III, p. 233.

कारस्य न्यूनतां दर्शयति । नागेशो ऽत्र 'आदिपदसंग्राह्यमित्यर्थः' इति भाष्यन्यूनतां परिहरति ।

नागेशः एतानि खण्डनानि कैयटेन प्रदीपटीकायां निर्दिष्टानि मतान्यभिलक्ष्य प्रस्तौति । साक्षाद्दीपिकायां भर्तृहरिं वा नामग्राहं नैव गृह्णाति । परं भर्तृहरिकृतां दीपिकां नागेशः निश्चप्रचं जानीते । यतः प्रत्याहाराह्निकान्ते सः स्वभाष्यटीकायामुद्द्योते 'अत एवैतत्प्रतीकमुपादाय हरिणास्याक्षरसमाम्नायस्य ... इति व्याख्यातम्' इति नामग्राहं भर्तृहरिमुल्लिखति । अव्ययीभावश्चेति सूत्र (१.१.४१) टीकान्ते 'इति मतं हरिटीकायां स्पष्टं' इत्युल्लिख्य तन्मतं भाष्यविरुद्धमिति तिरस्करोति । नामग्राहं निर्दिष्टौ एतौ द्वौ विषयौ सांप्रतमुपलब्धायां दीपिकायां मनागिवान्यथानुपूर्व्या उपलभ्येते ।

उपाध्यायः तत्रभवान् कैयटः स्वटीकाया उपक्रमे एव प्रतिजानीते 'तथापि हरबद्धेन सारेण ग्रन्थसेतुना । क्रममाणः शनैः पारं तस्य प्राप्तास्मि पङ्गुवत् ॥' इति । अतः सः सर्वत्र भर्तृहरिमतमाश्रयति, प्रायशः समर्थयते च । यन्मतं तस्यानभिमतं तत्र मौनमवलम्ब्योदास्ते । नागेशस्तु मुनित्रयं तत्रापि महाभाष्यकारं भगवन्तं पतञ्जलिं परमं प्रमाणं मन्वानः कदाचिदपि भाष्यकारस्य खण्डनम्, उपहासं, तिरस्कारं वा न स्वप्नेऽपि सोढुं शक्नुयात् । या श्रद्धा नागेशस्य त्रिषु मुनिषु प्रायशः, स्वल्पया न्यूनाधिकभेदकणिकया सैव प्राचीनपरंपराप्रवाहमग्नानां समेषां विदुषाम् । दीपिकाकृता श्रीमता भर्तृहरिणा बहुत्र महाभाष्यकारमतानि स्वारुचिं प्रदर्श्य निरस्तानि । परम् 'इग्यणः संप्रसारणम्' (१.१.४५) इति सूत्रविवरणे 'आलस्यात्तु सकृदुच्चारितम्' इति शास्त्रविनोदमातन्वन् सूत्रकारमप्युपहसतीव ।

इत्थंकारं सूत्रकृदुपहासः, महाभाष्यविरोधः, सर्वशास्त्रसंमतसिद्धान्तविरोधः वृथाप्रपञ्चः इत्यादयो दोषाः तत्रभवता नागेशेन परंपरायां पण्डितमण्डल्या च नैकत्र भर्तृहरिकृतौ साक्षात्कृताः । अन्येऽपि केचन दोषाः दृढशास्त्रसंस्कारसंस्कृतमतीनां प्राचीनविदुषां चेतांसि दुःखाकुर्वन्ति ।

अनुज्झितार्थसंबन्धः प्रबन्धः शास्त्रमुच्यते । इति हि शास्त्रसामान्यलक्षणम् । पुराणसदृशी शिथिला बहुविस्तारविस्तीर्णा रचना भर्तृहरिकृतावुपलभ्यते । तत्र वाक्यपदीयकारिकासु पञ्चविधाः कारिकाः संकीर्णा उपलभ्यन्ते I प्रस्तुतार्थाः प्रसन्नाः II प्रस्तुतार्थाः अप्रसन्नाः III प्रसक्तानुप्रसक्तार्थाः प्रसन्नाः IV प्रसक्तानुप्रसक्तार्थाः अप्रसन्नाः V अर्थवादपराः ।

अतः भर्तृहरिग्रन्थमधीयानाः धीराः सक्तुमिव तितउना पुनन्तः कारिकाः, सूक्ष्मया बुद्ध्या अन्विष्यान्विष्य कासुचन एव कारिकासु परिष्कृतं शास्त्रत्वं द्रढयितुं प्रकल्पेरन् न सर्वासु । तत्र प्रथमे काण्डे आहत्य एकशतं पञ्चपञ्चाशत् कारिकाः सांप्रतमुपलभ्यन्ते । तत्र प्रायः अशीतिः कारिकाः शास्त्रबुद्धितितउना कृते पवनसंस्कारे शास्त्रत्वं विन्देरन् । अवशिष्टानामप्रस्तुतत्वम् अर्थवादरूपता वा अङ्गीकर्तव्या आपद्येत ।

कासांचन कारिकाणां तदन्तर्निहितपदानां वा समीचीनम् अभिप्रायमाविष्कर्तुं स्वयं स्वोपज्ञटीकापि अनलंभविष्णुः, तत्का कथा अन्येषामभ्यासकवशकानाम् । 'अर्थप्रवृत्तितत्त्वानाम् ...' (१ .१३) इत्यस्य षडर्थविवरणानि स्वोपज्ञटीकायां प्रदत्तानि, तावद्भिरपि न विदुषां सन्तोषः । एवमेव 'उपकारः स यत्रास्ति ...' (३.३.५) इति

कारिकाविवरणे हेलाराजः नागेशश्च कथं प्रयतेते, कारिकाकर्तुः निगूढमभिप्रायमाविष्कर्तुं कीदृशं महान्तं प्रयासमवलम्बेते तदिदम् अपरोक्षं प्रेक्षावताम् । एतादृशीं निगूढां संदेहकारिणीम् अबोधिकामत एवाप्रसन्नां रचनाशैलीमयं ग्रन्थकारः क्रियासमभिहारेण समाश्रयति इति संभवति प्राचीनपरंपराग्रहः ।

ग्रन्थकारोऽयं नितरां सूक्ष्मान् गूढांश्च विमर्शान् यथा वैदिकान् तथैव अवैदिकानपि संगृह्णाति यथायथं समर्थयते चापि । सर्वेषु वैदिकेषु अवैदिकेषु चागमदर्शनेषु समानमादरभावं दधानोऽयं द्वितीय-काण्डान्ते वस्तुतत्त्वं जिज्ञासमानानभ्यासकान् समानादरभावफलं बोधयति, समर्थयते च —

प्रज्ञा विवेकं लभते भिन्नैरागमदर्शनैः ।
कियद्वा शक्यमुन्नेतुं स्वतर्कमनुधावता ॥ २.४८६
तत्तदुत्प्रेक्षमाणानां पुराणैरागमैर्विना ।
अनुपासितवृद्धानां विद्या नातिप्रसीदति ॥ २.४८७

वस्तुतो विचार्यमाणे वाक्यपदीयकर्ता भर्तृहरिरत्यन्तं प्रतीपत्वेन आभासमानयोः द्वयोः वैदिकावैदिकपरम्परयोः गङ्गायमुनयोरिव संगमः, पारावारयोस्तीरयोः सेतुः, समेषां विदुषां वैदुष्यसारः इत्येवानतिरिक्तं वचः, अत एव वाक्यपदीयीयाः बहवः संदर्भाः खण्डनार्थं मण्डनार्थं समर्थनार्थं वा विविधेषु शास्त्रग्रन्थेषु निर्दिष्टा उपलभ्यन्ते । तथापि शब्दविशेषप्रामाण्योपहता चिराय क्षुण्णं वर्त्म अनुसरन्ती वैदिकशास्त्रपरंपरा विविधेषु विचारेषु समानमादरभावं समर्थयमानममुं वाक्यपदीयकर्तारं स्वकीयमित्यनुमन्तुं न जातुचिद्

अधृष्णोत्, प्रत्युत 'अयं बाह्यः' 'प्रच्छन्नबौद्धः' इत्येव समर्थयांचक्रे (प्रा. का. वा. अभ्यंकर – आचार्य वि. प्र. लिमये संपादिते पुणे विद्यापीठ-प्रकाशिते १९६५ प्रस्तावनायां पृष्ठं VI)।

यद्यप्यादौ निर्दिष्टाः केचन दोषा ग्रन्थान्तरेषु बहुषु सन्ति, तथापि परंपरया ते ग्रन्थाः

गुणदोषौ बुधो गृह्णन् इन्दुक्ष्वेडाविवेश्वरः ।
शिरसा श्लाघते पूर्वं परं कण्ठे नियच्छति ॥

इतीमां बुधबुद्धिमवलम्ब्य स्वकीयत्वेनाभ्युपगताः । परमन्ततो निर्दिष्टः दोषः तत्रभवतः भर्तृहरेः सर्वान्दोषान्, महिष्ठान् गुणानप्यतिशेते येन सः प्राचीनशास्त्रपरंपरायां नातीवादरभाजनमित्येव वक्तुं सांप्रतमिति प्रतीमः ।

'बुद्धेः फलमनाग्रहः' एतादृशि बहूनि सुभाषितवचांसि विद्वांसः प्रस्तुवन्ति, क्वचनाभिनन्दन्त्यपि । तेनैव कारणेन श्रीमान् भर्तृहरिः ममापि मतौ महिष्ठमादरभाजनम् । परं परंपरा किमित्युदास्ते इत्यन्विष्यन्नहं प्रतिनिधिरूपेण नागेशं पर्यैक्षिषि, अन्यानपि विदुषः आपाततः पर्यालोचये । तावता मम बुद्धौ ये विचारतरङ्गाः, तान्विदुषां पुरतः स्थापयितुमयमुद्यमः । यतो ममेदं मतं केवलं संभवरूपमनुमानं मन्थरायमाणमेव अतः तत्प्रमाणपूतमन्यथा वा तन्निर्जये विद्वांस एव प्रभवन्ति ॥

BHARTṚHARI ON LANGUAGE AND REALITY

Saroja Bhate, Pune

The present paper is an attempt to sum up Bhartṛhari's views on the relation of language with reality. It is, in fact, a further extention of the problem posed by Dr. J. Kelley in his paper, namely, whether the *Vākyapadīya* (VP) can be looked upon as an argument about the limitations of a formal system of analysis to describe linguistic phenomena[1]. I would like to go a step further and pose the problem whether the VP represents an argument about the limitations of language to describe reality.

Bhartṛhari accepts perception, inference and word as valid means of knowledge. However, he acknowledges highest authority to word. He declares in the *Brahmakāṇḍa* that there is no knowledge which does not assume the form of a word[2]. All knowledge must culminate in verbal knowledge. No object which is not expressed in words exists. Language is the only window to the world. Our knowledge of reality is shaped by the language we use. Thus Bhartṛhari has initially accepted an intimate relationship of language with reality.

However, Bhartṛhari shows the superficial character of this intimacy by pointing out how language falls short of reality. At several places in the VP he describes language not only as an inadequate tool to represent reality but also as a wrong means, which, in fact, never takes us to reality. It is very intriguing that the VP begins with a declaration that there is no world beyond language, whereas it ends up with a note of disharmony between the two and declares that reality transcends language. What follows is a résumé of the views presented in the VP about the nature of language in relation to reality.

(All references to the *Vākyapadīya* (VP) are from the edition of VP by K.V. Abhyankar and V.P. Limaye, Poona, 1965.)

1 John D. Kelly's paper entitled 'Meaning and the limits of analysis: Bhartṛhari and the Buddhists, and post-structuralism' elsewhere in this volume.

2 VP. I.123:
na so 'sti pratyayo loke yaḥ śabdānugamād ṛte /
anuviddham iva jñānaṃ sarvaṃ śabdena bhāsate //

In the begining of the *Sādhanasamuddeśa* Bhartṛhari describes the world as an aggregate of multiple powers[3]. He also describes the meaning as all-powerful in contrast with the word which has limited powers[4]. Thus as far as their respective powers are concerned, both language and reality are not on the same footing. However, the word with its restricted powers excercises its control over reality[5] and checks its powers through *vivakṣā* 'speaker's intention'[6]. Bhartṛhari's exposition of gender illustrates this point. According to him every object possesses all the three powers, namely, *āvirbhāva* 'manifestation', *tirobhāva* 'disappearance' and *sthiti* 'maintaining status' which are respectively manifested in the masculine, feminine and neuter genders. A word expressing an object is, however, used not in all genders but in a specific gender whose selection is based on *vivakṣā* as well as the association of the object with the external world[7]. The infinite reality being thus checked by the finite powers of the word, we naturally get a suppressed view of reality through words.

At another place Bhartṛhari refers to the skindeep relationship between language and reality. A word is, according to him, a mere indicator of an object[8]. Like a lamp it merely reveals an object. It does not provide any information about the object. When the word *ghata* is, for instance, uttered, nobody understands its shape, size or colour[9]. These are understood from our repeated observation and usage rather than from words[10].

3 VP. III.7.2:
śaktimātrāsamūhasya viśvasyānekadharmanaḥ /
sarvadā sarvathā bhāvāt kvacit kiñcid vivakṣyate //

4 VP. II.431: ... *arthasya sarvaśaktitvāt* ... / VP. III.12.14 ...
... *niyatāḥ śabdaśaktayaḥ /*

5 VP. II.434:
sarvātmakatvād arthasya nairātmyād vā vyavasthitam /
atyantayataśaktitvāc chabdā eva nibandhanam //

6 See note 3 above.

7 VP. III.13.19-20:
sthiteṣu triṣu liṅgeṣu vivakṣāniyamāśrayaḥ /
kasyacic chabdasaṃskāre vyāpāraḥ kaścid iṣyate //
sannidhāne nimittānāṃ kiñcid eva pravartakam /
yathā takṣādiśabdānāṃ liṅgeṣu niyamas tathā //

8 VP. II.435:
vastūpalakṣaṇam śabdo nopakārasya vācakaḥ /
na svaśaktiḥ padārthānāṃ saṃsprastuṃ tena śakyate //

9 VP. II.123:
ghaṭādīnāṃ na cākārān pratyāyayati vācakaḥ /

10 VP. II.120:
prayogadarśanābhyāsād ākārāvagrahas tu yaḥ /
na sa śabdasya viṣayaḥ sa hi yatnāntarāśrayaḥ //

Similarly, although the word *go* is used by a speaker to refer to a certain cow with specific colour, shape and certain ornaments etc. the listener never understands these features when the word is utterred[11]. The remark in the VP, namely, *na hi sarveṣām satāṃ śabdo 'bhidhāyakaḥ* (VP II.38) 'a word is not expressive of all existing (features of an object)' implies that an object in its totality is never understood from the word which is used to denote it. As far as this inherent incompetence of verbal knowledge is concerned it is compared to *pratyakṣa* 'perception' which always fails to present a complete view of reality[12]. There are many examples in the VP which illustrate this inadequate nature of language. The word *salila* conveys, for instance, water. However, it fails to convey whether that water is in the form of a drop or a river[13]. All such illustrations and arguments given above lead to the conclusion that language is a mismatch for reality.

It is further argued in the VP that language is not only a mismatch for reality; it also misrepresents reality. Here again verbal knowledge is compared to perception. Bhartṛhari offers a number of illustrations to show how our perception is often deceptive. For example, one sees water in both, a river and a mirage; but the water in the mirage is not a reality[14]. A miniature of a giant mountain seen through a mirror is similarly not a reality[15]. According to our perception of a fire-circle produced by the circular movement of a fire-brand, we use the word *alātacakra* 'fire-circle'. However, there is no such object as a fire-circle although there is the

11 VP. II.153-154:
yathā saṃyogibhir dravyair lakṣite 'rthe prayujyate /
gośabdo na tv asau teṣām viśeṣāṇām prakāśakaḥ //
ākāravarṇāvayavaiḥ saṃsṛṣṭeṣu gavādiṣu /
śabdaḥ pravartamāno 'pi na tān aṅgīkaroty asau //

12 VP. II.156:
durlabhaṃ kasyacil loke sarvāvayavadarśanam /
kaiścit tv avayavair dṛṣṭair arthaḥ kṛtsno 'numīyate //

13 VP. II.158:
saṃkhyāpramāṇasaṃsthānanirapekṣaḥ pravartate /
bindau ca samudāye ca vācakaḥ salilādiṣu //

14 VP. II.287:
darśanaṃ salile tulyaṃ mṛgatṛṣṇādidarśanaiḥ /
tulyatve darśanādīnāṃ na jalaṃ mṛgatṛṣṇikā //

15 VP. II.294:
mahān āvriyate deśaḥ prasiddhaiḥ parvatādibhiḥ /
alpadeśāntarāvasthaṃ pratibimbaṃ tu dṛśyate //

word[16]. Words like *śaśaśṛṅga* 'hare's horn', *khapuṣpa* 'skyflower' refer to non-reality. Thus the word not only presents an incomplecte picture of reality; it also conveys non-reality.

Further, even when the word expresses reality, it is not expressed in its own form. Often an object is expressed by a word in terms of its properties rather than its own form[17]. In the *Vṛtisamuddeśa* Bhartṛhari describes how our analytical mind sees diverse properties in a single object and accordingly manifests them in the language[18]. Here again, *vivakṣā* plays an important role in making selection of properties[19].

Thus an object is partially understood from a word, and that too, in terms of its properties rather than its real form. While referring to this invariable appearance of a property in an expression Bhartṛhari observes, just as pure knowledge without an object is impossible so also knowledge of an object without a property connected with it is impossible[20]. He further remarks, just as knowledge becomes impure due to being coloured by an object, an object understood from a word is similarly coloured with some property and thus deviates from its own form[21]. Both knowledge and the object of that knowledge thus render each other impure.

The properties expressed by a word do not always accord with reality. Often there are properties which are not existent. For instance, in expressions like *paṭasya śuklaḥ* "white colour of the cloth" and *dārāḥ* 'wife' non-existing features like singularity or plurality and masculinity (in case of *śukla* and *dārā*) are expressed. Bhartṛhari concludes, when a feature of

16 VP. I.130:
atyantam atathābhūte nimitte śrutyupāśrayāt /
dṛśyate 'lātacakrādau vastvākāranirūpaṇā //

17 This is indicated by the following verse:
VP. III.11.6:
svabuddhyā tam apoddhṛtya loko 'py āgamam āśritaḥ /
svadharmād anyadharmeṇa vyācaṣṭe pratipattaye //

18 VP. III.14.571:
aṅgadī kuṇḍalī ceti darśayan bhedahetubhiḥ /
caitram īdṛśam ity āha buddhyavasthāparigrahāt //

19 VP. III.14.573:
buddhyavasthāvibhāgena bhedakāryam pratīyate /
janyanta iva śabdānām arthāḥ sarve vivakṣayā //

20 VP. III.11.8:
yathaivāviṣayam jñānam na kiñcid avabhāsate /
tathā bhāvo 'py asaṃsṛṣṭo na kaścid upalabhyate //

21 VP. III.3.58:
yathā ca jñānam ālekhād aśuddhau vyvatiṣṭhate /
tathopāśrayavān arthaḥ svarūpād viprakṛṣyate //

an object is being expressed by a word it hardly matters whether the feature actually exists or not[22].

Bhartṛhari's observations recorded above may be summed up as follows:

Although language is the only window to the world, it is too small to give us a complete picture of reality. Further, whatever view it offers is not necessarily faithful to reality. Words often misrepresent and distort the facts of the external world. The linguistic world and the external world thus do not match with each other.

Bhartṛhari finally declares that although language claims to have a control over reality by virtue of its being the only tool to represent it, it never does, in fact, represent reality. Reality transcends language.

Do we then ever know reality? If yes, how?

Bhartṛhari's answers to these questions are: No! Reality is never understood by an ordinary person, only *ṛṣis* 'sages' are capable of knowing it. Further, whatever reality is understood by the *ṛṣis* can never be expressed in words[23]. Language has thus no power enough to hold reality.

What is it then that we understand from language? What about the close intimacy between language and reality proclaimed in the Brahmakāṇḍa? How to reconcile these opposite statements?

Bhartṛhari offers a very simple solution. He distinguishes between *sampratisattā* 'present reality' and *aupacārikī sattā* 'secondary reality'[24]. It is the latter which is intimately connected with language. We may name the former, 'Reality', and the latter, 'reality'. While language is in perfect harmony with reality (in fact, the whole VP aims at establishing this harmony), it is far away from Reality. It is even detrimental to Reality as pointed out above.

The *aupacārikī sattā* with which language is directly connected exists in the mind. Bhartṛhari shows how the conception of this reality is a solution to logical fallacies involving our usage. The expression, *aṅkuro jāyate* 'a sprout is born' is, for example, fallacious, because it involves contradiction. Since the very utterance of the word *aṅkura* implies its

22 VP. III.11.10:
paradharmasya na hy atra sadasattvaṃ prayojakam //

23 VP. II.139:
ṛṣīṇāṃ darśanaṃ yac ca tattve kiñ cid avasthitam /
na tena vyavahāro 'sti na tac chabdanibandhanam //

24 VP. III.3.39:
vyapadeśe padārthānām anyā sattaupacārikī /
sarvāvasthāsu sarveṣām ātmarūpasya darśikā //

existence it would be redundant to say *jāyate* 'is born'. If it is argued that *aṅkura* is non-existent and that *jāyate* implies that it comes into existence, how can a non-existent object become existent[25]? The VP points out fallacies also in other expressions like *nāsti* 'does not exist' where both existence and its negation are simultaneously conveyed[26]. The only solution to problems of this kind is to accept that objects like *aṅkura* and even the existence conveyed by *asti* in the expression *nāsti* exist in the mental world. Thus whatever is expressable in words 'exists' in the *aupacārikī sattā*, may it be a flower or a skyflower. Even *abhāva* 'non-existence' exists in this world. The mental world is thus extended far beyond the boundaries of Reality. It does not maintain temporal and spatial distinctions[27]. It is because of this world that an object possesses some properties which may contradict each other[28]. All objects are infused with life in this *sattā*[29]. Bhartṛhari further says that it is this reality rather than the Reality which is the basis of worldly transactions.

According to Bhartṛhari *buddhi* 'intellect' plays a vital role in creating and shaping this reality. It is the *buddhi* which has power to do and undo. On a number of occassions Bhartṛhari acknowledges this extraordinary power of *buddhi*[30].

However, in spite of the wonderful *buddhi*, it is the cognition which narrows down the view of reality. Bhartṛhari remarks, since cognition of a complete reality is not possible, words based on such cognition present

25 VP. III.3.43:
yadi saj jāyate kasmād athāsaj jāyate katham /

26 VP. III.3.48:
prāk ca sattābhisambandhāt mukhyā sattā katham bhavet /
asaṃś ca nāsteh kartā syād upacāras tu pūrvavat //

27 VP. III.3.50-51:
abhinnakālām arthesu bhinnakālesv avasthitām /
pravṛttihetum sarveṣām śabdānām aupacārikīm //
etām sattām padārtho hi na kaś cid ativartate /
sā ca sampratisattāyāḥ pṛthag bhāṣye nidarśitā //

28 VP. III.3.41:
tadvac chabdo 'pi sattāyām asyām pūrvam vyavasthitaḥ /
dharmair upaiti sambandham avirodhivirodhibhiḥ //

29 VP. III.14.327:
acetanesu saṃkrāntam caitanyam iva dṛśyate /
pratibimbakadharmeṇa yat tac chabdanibandhanam //

30 VP. III.14.15:
budhhyaikam bhidyate bhinnam ekatvam copagacchati /
buddhyāvasthā vibhajyante sā hy arthasya vidhāyikā //

objects different from their own form[31]. And as far as cognition and expression are concerned there is no difference, according to Bhartṛhari, between a learned scholar and an ignorant child[32].

To sum up the foregoing observations: According to Bhartṛhari language is not at all connected with the external world. It is connected with the mental reality of which it presents a restricted view due to the restricted nature of cognition. The mental reality is a creation of *buddhi* which has a boundless capacity to create objects. Due to the inherent incompetence of language as well as due to the limited nature of cognition language fails to reflect reality in its own form. Often it misrepresents and obscures reality. Further, language and reality are so opposed to each other that reality starts where language ends. Language can never reach reality (Reality). Bhartṛhari has, finally, extended the notion of *apoddhāra* 'abstraction' which is peculiar to grammar, also to language which implies that for him language is as fictitious as grammar[33].

31 VP. III.3.54:
akṛtsnaviṣayābhāsaṃ śabdaḥ pratyayam āśritaḥ /
artham āhānyarūpeṇa svarūpeṇānirūpitam //

32 VP. III.3.55:
rūpaṇavyapadeśābhyāṃ laukike vartmani sthitau /
jñānaṃ praty abhilāpaṃ ca sadṛśau bālapaṇḍitau //

33 VP. III.11.6:
svabuddhyā tam apoddhṛtya loko 'py āgamam āśritaḥ /
svadharmād anyadharmeṇa vyācaṣṭe pratipattaye //

VP. III.11.9:
bhedena tu samākhyānaṃ yal loko 'py anuvartate /
āgamāc chāstrasadṛśo vyavahāraḥ sa varṇyate //

STUDIES ON BHARTṚHARI, 5: BHARTṚHARI AND VAIŚEṢIKA[1]

Johannes Bronkhorst, Lausanne

There are reasons to think that Bhartṛhari's writings may shed light on the early history of Vaiśeṣika. One of these is that he obviously knew the Vaiśeṣika system. Almost all of its categories play a role in his work. Separate sections (*samuddeśa*) of the *Vākyapadīya* are dedicated to the categories *jāti*, *dravya*, *guṇa* and *kriyā*. The relationship called *samavāya* - a special feature of Vaiśeṣika - is mentioned and used repeatedly. Vaiśeṣika substances appear as 'powers' (*śakti*), most notably *kāla* (time) and *diś* (space).

A second reason is Bhartṛhari's chonological position. I have argued in another publication that Praśastapāda's *Padārthadharmasaṁgraha*, as well as Dignāga's *Pramāṇasamuccayavṛtti* before it, were heavily indebted to the *Kaṭandī*, a work written not long before Dignāga. This *Kaṭandī*, I further argued, exerted a dominating influence on all Vaiśeṣika literature that came after it, including perhaps the versions of the *Vaiśeṣika Sūtra* itself, not to speak of the surviving commentaries on this Sūtra work.[2] Bhartṛhari, on the other hand, lived long enough before Dignāga that someone different from Bhartṛhari could write a commentary on the first two kāṇḍas of his *Vākyapadīya* still before Dignāga. Bhartṛhari, therefore, lived and worked most probably before the *Kaṭandī*! If his work provides information on Vaiśeṣika, it would then be one of the very few sources of information dating form the pre-*Kaṭandī* period of this system.

In what follows we shall consider some possible links between Bhartṛhari's *Vākyapadīya* and the Vaiśeṣika of his days.

1 I thank A. Wezler and J. Houben for critical comments. The earlier articles in this series have appeared in the following periodicals: no. 1, *Bulletin d'Etudes Indiennes* 6 (1988), 105-143; no. 2, *Studien zur Indologie und Iranistik* 15 (1989), 101-117; no. 3, *Asiatische Studien / Etudes Asiatiques* 45 (1991), 5-18; no. 4, *Asiatische Studien / Etudes Asiatiques* 46, 1 (1992), 56-80.

2 See Bronkhorst, forthcoming.

1. The variegated colour (citrarūpa)

Karl H. Potter explains the variegated colour in his *Encyclopedia of Indian Philosophies* vol. II, which deals with the tradition of Nyāya-Vaiśeṣika up to Gaṅgeśa, in the following terms (1977: 118): "Consider a substance with a mottled surface of more than one shade. Nyāya-Vaiśeṣika insists on treating this substance as a single entity with one color of its own, but surely it is evident that it has several colors. Does this mean that one thing can be both, say, red and green all over at once? Uddyotakara seems to have originated one sort of answer to this, which is that in the list of shades one has to count as one kind of color that called 'variegated color' (*citrarūpa*)."

The problem which the variegated colour is meant to solve is clear. An object is, in Vaiśeṣika ontology, different from its parts; it is a completely different entity, which has, necessarily, a colour of its own, different from the colours of its parts. What is the colour of a whole whose parts do not all have the same colour?

The problem is inherent in the most fundamental assumptions of Vaiśeṣika, and is likely to be as old as the system itself. Why then do we not find this particular answer until Uddyotakara, a Nyāya author who may have been a contemporary of Praśastapāda?

The reason why we don't find the variegated colour mentioned in our earliest Vaiśeṣika texts appears to be that we have so few of them. There is reason to believe that the variegated colour played a role in the system already before Praśastapāda.

Otto Grohma (1975: 151f.) has drawn attention to the passage in Vasubandhu's *Abhidharmakośa Bhāṣya* which polemicizes against the existence of a whole cloth as different from its parts. Vasubandhu mentions here the variegated colour in the following lines (p. 189 l. 24-26): "In case the threads have different colours ... the cloth could not have a colour .... If [you accept] 'variegated' as its colour ... there would be production of [a colour] belonging to a different universal (from the colours in the threads)." (*bhinnarūpajātikriyeṣu tantuṣu paṭasya rūpādyasaṁbhavāt/ citrarūpāditve vijātīyārambho 'pi syāt*).

It must be admitted that the variegated colour in this passage from the *Abhidharmakośa Bhāṣya* is rather hypothetical, and does not prove beyond doubt that anyone known to Vasubandhu believed in it.

Vyomaśiva's commentary on the *Padārthadharmasaṁgraha*, called *Vyomavatī*, cites a sūtra in its discussion of the variegated colour. The sūtra reads:[3] "Because there cannot be, in one non-omnipresent substance, [several] specific qualities (*viśeṣaguṇa*) that are perceived by the same sense-organ." It is not impossible that this sūtra was indeed meant to justify variegated colour as a quality. Unfortunately it is only known through this passage of the *Vyomavatī*; it does not occur in the different versions of the *Vaiśeṣika Sūtra* that have been preserved, nor does it appear to be cited by any other commentator.

For the most certain attestation of the variegated colour in early Vaiśeṣika we have to turn to the following verses of Bhartṛhari's *Vākyapadīya*:[4]

> Just as the single variegated colour is described by way of different [colours] such as blue etc., which point to divisions [in the one and indivisible variegated colour]; in the same way the single sentence, which is completely self-sufficient, is described by way of other linguistic units (viz. words) which require one another.

It is not necessary to recall here that for Bhartṛhari the sentence is the real unit of language, the individual words being the result of an artificial analysis. The comparison with the variegated colour is therefore particularly appropriate, for that colour too cannot be looked upon as a collection of constituent colours. The comparison further reminds us of the fact that Bhartṛhari's observations on the sentence as an indivisible unit are of an ontological rather than linguistic or psychological nature.

2. *Sound (1)*[5]

Sound (*śabda*), in classical Vaiśeṣika, is a quality of ether (*ākāśa*). It is already described as such in the *Padārthadharmasaṁgraha* of Praśastapāda, in Candramati's **Daśapadārthī*, and in some of the Vaiśeṣika sūtras. The *Padārthadharmasaṅgraha* gives the following description:[6]

> *śabdo 'mbaraguṇaḥ śrotragrāhyaḥ kṣaṇikaḥ .../ sa dvividho varṇalakṣaṇo dhvani-* (v.l. *'varṇa-) lakṣaṇaś ca/ tatra akārādir varṇalakṣaṇaḥ śaṅkhādinimitto dhvanilakṣaṇaś*

3 Vy vol. 1, p. 63 l. 20: *avibhuni dravye samānendriyagrāhyāṇāṁ viśeṣaguṇānām asambhavāt.*

4 VP 2.8-9: *citrasyaikasya rūpasya yathā bhedanidarśanaiḥ/ nīlādibhiḥ samākhyānaṁ kriyate bhinnalakṣaṇaiḥ// tathaivaikasya vākyasya nirākāṅkṣasya sarvataḥ/ śabdāntaraiḥ samākhyānaṁ sākāṅkṣair anugamyate//*

5 I thank W. Halbfass for some useful observations.

6 N p. 287-88, Ki p. 262, Vy vol. 2 p. 237.

> *ca* (v.l. *'varṇalakṣaṇaḥ)/ tatra varṇalakṣaṇasyotpattir ātmamanasoḥ saṁyogāt smṛtyapekṣād varṇoccāraṇecchā/ tadanantaraṁ prayatnaḥ/ tam apekṣamāṇād ātmavāyusaṁyogād vāyau karma jāyate/ sa cordhvaṁ gacchan kaṇṭhādīn* (v.l. *uraḥkaṇṭhādīn) abhihanti/ tataḥ sthānavāyusaṁyogāpekṣamāṇāt* (v.l. *-āpekṣāt) sthānākāśasaṁyogād varṇotpattiḥ/*
>
> Sound is a property of ether. It is perceptible by the ear. It is momentary. ... It is of two kinds – (1) in the form of speech sounds and (2) in the form of noise in general. [Sound] in the form of speech sounds is [the sounds] *a* etc. [Sound] in the form of noise in general is produced by the blowing of a conch and such things. Sound of the former kind proceeds from the contact of the mind and soul as influenced by remembrance: – First of all there is desire for pronouncing the sound; this is followed by an effort on the part of the speaker; and when this effort brings about the conjunction of the soul with wind, there is produced in this wind a certain motion; this wind moving upwards strikes such places as the throat and the like; this contact of the places of articulation and the wind brings about contact of the places of articulation with *ākāśa*; and this contact produces the speech sounds. (tr. Gaṅgānātha Jhā, modified)

This passage is quite clear that speech sounds are the sounds of the alphabet (*a* etc.) and are momentary. Words and phrases, on the other hand, are combinations, or rather sequences, of speech sounds. They present, therefore, a problem which resembles to some extent that of the variegated colour, discussed above. There are, however, important differences. Words and phrases are sequences of speech sounds, and cannot in any way be looked upon as collections of simultaneously existing sounds. Moreover, words and phrases do not, unlike the variegated colour, have a different substrate from their constituent sounds. It is further of some interest to note that the sūtra cited in the *Vyomavatī* and discussed above, which was supposedly meant to justify the existence of the variegated colour, confines itself explicitly to non-omnipresent substances. It may here be recalled that ether, the substrate of sound, is omnipresent.

How, then, did the Vaiśeṣikas look upon words and phrases?

No statements from early Vaiśeṣika texts are known to me that attribute or deny ontological status to words and phrases. But some passages discuss the link between words and the things they denote. VS 7.2.19/19/19 *śabdārthāv asambaddhau* claims that "words and designated objects have no connection", and VS 7.2.24/20/20 *sāmayikaḥ śabdād arthapratyayaḥ* adds that "the understanding of an object from a word is based on convention". It seems clear that the presence of an 'existent' link between words and things is here rejected. This, however, would seem to imply that the 'existence' of words is not in doubt.

A similar position appears to be taken in Vyomaśiva's *Vyomavatī*. This commentary raises the problem that the definition of *samavāya* risks to cover the relation between a word and its designated object as well, as happens in the case of the word 'ether' and its designated object.[7] The solution to the problem presented by Vyomaśiva has no relevance to our question. The fact that he does not point out that the word *ākāśa* ('ether') does not 'exist' creates however the impression that Vyomaśiva, too, accepts the existence of whole words. Yet in another passage he points out that we understand the meaning 'cow' when we hear the sequence *g-au-ḥ*.[8]

Candrānanda's commentary on *Vaiśeṣika Sūtra* 7.2.23 (which has no parallel in the other versions of this text) discusses the link that exists between sound and ether, and the one between ether and objects. The combined link which thus exists between a word and the object it denotes is not accepted, because it leaves a doubt as to which object is denoted by which word. But Candrānanda, too, fails to point out that the designating words do not exist in the first place. He seems to have no difficulty accepting the existence of whole words.

Turning now to the *Vākyapadīya*, we notice that Bhartṛhari knows the conception of sound as a quality of ether. This we must conclude from a number of stanzas in the *Sambandhasamuddeśa*, which discuss the relation, in Vaiśeṣika terms, between words and objects. We find here, for example, the following statement (VP 3.3.16ab):

> *svāśrayena tu saṁyuktaiḥ saṁyuktaṁ vibhu gamyate*
> What is 'omnipresent' is known, being in contact with [objects] that are in contact with its own substrate.

We know from the *Padārthadharmasaṅgraha* (Ki p. 148 l. 16; N p. 141 l. 5; Vy vol. 2 p. 72 l. 19) that omnipresent objects have no mutual contact. We may therefore conclude that 'its own substrate' is omnipresent. But it seems certain that 'it' is sound (more precisely, the word *vibhu* 'omnipresent [object]'); it would be difficult to make sense of the surrounding stanzas without this assumption. This in its turn means that sound has as substrate an omnipresent substance, which can only be ether. From stanza 3.3.13 we learn, moreover, that the relation with the own substrate is

7 Vy vol. 1 p. 26 l. 13-17: *tathā hy ākāśaśabdenākāśam abhidhīyata ity anayor ādhāryādhārabhāve sati vācyavācakabhāvaḥ .../ tadvyavacchedārtham avadhāraṇam ādhāryādhārabhūtānām eva yaḥ saṁbandhaḥ sa samavāya iti.*

8 Vy vol. 2 p. 241 l. 23-25: *yatra yatra gakāraukāravisarjanīyānām itthambhūtānupūrvīm upalabhase, tatra tatra gotvaviśiṣṭo 'rthaḥ pratipattavyaḥ pratipādayitavyaś ceti saṅketagrahe sati tathāvidhaṁ śabdam upalabhamānas tam arthaṁ pratipadyate pratipādayati ceti.* See also the discussion on p. 184f.

samavāya (*samavāyāt sva ādhāraḥ ... pratīyate*); that is to say, the relation between the word 'ether' and ether is *samavāya*. Sound is therefore clearly looked upon, in this passage of the *Vākyapadīya*, as a quality of ether.

But this passage does more than this. Like the passages from Vyomaśiva and Candrānda discussed above, and like the *Vaiśeṣika Sūtra* itself, it does not appear to find fault with the idea that whole words (such as *vibhu* 'omnipresent [object]' and *ākāśa* 'ether') are treated as 'existing' entities, about the 'existence' of whose links with the denoted objects one can reasonably discuss.[9]

It may be worthwhile to recall at this point that there were thinkers in the age concerned who did not look upon words as entities in their own right. An example is found in the *Śābara Bhāṣya*, the classical commentary on the *Mīmāṁsā Sūtra* which is probably earlier than the *Padārthadharmasaṅgraha.*[10] According to this text words are nothing but collections of speech sounds, which alone 'exist'. This point of view is introduced in the so-called *Vṛttikāragrantha* on sūtra 1.1.5, and attributed to someone called Upavarṣa.[11]

3. Sound (2)

There is a further problem with sound in early Vaiśeṣika. The Vaiśeṣika sūtra that enumerates all the qualities, no. 1.1.5, does not mention sound, nor several of the other qualities that figure in the classical list. Instead of the classical number of 24 qualities, it lists 17 of them. This smaller number is confirmed by the Jaina author Jinabhadra, in his *Viśeṣāvaśyakabhāṣya.*[12] We are entitled to assume that the Vaiśeṣika sūtras that do mention or treat sound as a quality are later additions to the text. Their removal offers valuable insights into the earlier construction of the *Vaiśeṣika Sūtra.*

9 Bhartṛhari does not even hesitate to speak about the universals residing in (whole) words; see Bronkhorst, 1991: 9f.

10 There are reasons to think that Bhartṛhari did not yet know the *Śābara Bhāṣya*; see Bronkhorst, 1986, 1989.

11 Frauwallner, 1968: 38: *atha 'gaur' ity atra kaḥ śabdaḥ? gakāraukāravisarjanīyā iti bhagavān upavarṣaḥ/* Compare this passage with the one from the *Vyomavatī* cited above.

12 See Halbfass, 1980: 285 n. 55; Wezler, 1983: 36 n. 5.

These sūtras occur in two groups, in Āhnikas 2.1 and 2.2 respectively. The first group follows sūtra 2.1.20/19/20 which presents leaving and entering a place as the inferential mark of ether (*niṣkramaṇaṁ praveśanam ity ākāśasya liṅgam*).[13] This inferential mark is rejected in the then following group of sūtras, and replaced by another inferential mark, sound, which is proved to be a quality of ether. This whole discussion - which covers sūtras 21-26 in Jambuvijaya's edition, 20-30 in Thakur's, and 21-27 and 30-31 in Sinha's - is therefore added onto another, older inferential mark meant to prove the existence of ether. Since ether is enumerated as one of the substances in sūtra 1.1.4, we may safely assume that in earliest - or at any rate, earlier - Vaiśeṣika the motions of leaving and entering a place were deemed to prove the existence of the substance ether. This conclusion also teaches us to regard with suspicion any discussions that may occur within the body of the *Vaiśeṣika Sūtra*.

Sound is again discussed in Āhnika 2.2. The context is, again, peculiar. Sūtra 2.2.19/17/17 introduces the topic, which is doubt (*saṁśaya*); this topic continues until 2.2.23/21/20. Then the topic sound is introduced, in 2.2.24/22/21, and the following sūtra 25 (it occurs only in Candrānanda's version) makes clear that this topic is meant to illustrate a particular case of doubt: is sound a substance, an action, or a quality (*tasmin dravyaṁ karma guṇa iti saṁśayaḥ*)? This illustration now steals the show completely, and is the sole topic of discussion - according to the commentators - until the end of the Āhnika. It seems clear that this long excursus on sound is an intrusion into the text, and that Adhyāya 2 originally ended with a discussion of 'doubt'.

Vaiśeṣika, then, underwent a change in its conception of sound. The new conception, according to which sound is a quality of ether, is already known to *Nyāya Sūtra* 1.1.12-14. *Caraka Saṁhitā*, *Sūtrasthāna* I.49, moreover, enumerates the Vaiśeṣika qualities in such a manner that it is clear that its author knew the expanded list: mention is made of *guru* etc., and we may conclude that sound, too, was considered a quality.[14] All this suggests that the change took place at a rather early date.

However, Jinabhadra's *Viśesāvaśyakabhāṣya* states in so many words that the number of Vaiśeṣika qualities is 17, as we have seen. This text

13 Compare this with "giving room" (*avakāśadāna*), mentioned as mark of ether in the (according to Ruben, spurious) Nyāya sūtra *gandhakledapākavyūhāvakāśadānebhyaḥ pāñcabhautikam*, see Ruben, 1928: 64.

14 Cf. Adachi, 1990: 909 (35); Narain, 1976: 108f.

may have been composed in the year 609 C.E.,[15] i.e., much later than Bhartṛhari. It appears, therefore, that the earlier conception of sound existed for a long time side by side with the one that came to replace it. It is, for this reason, not impossible that it was still known to Bhartṛhari.

Before we deal with this question, we must address another one: what conception did early Vaiśeṣika have of sound?

Note first that it is not possible to assume that the author of sūtra 1.1.5, which enumerates the qualities, simply overlooked sound. Such an argument may be possible in the case of 'heaviness' (*gurutva*), 'fluidity' (*dravatva*), 'viscidity' (*sneha*), and the other qualities (*saṁskāra, dharma, adharma*) that do not figure in the original list. Sound is too obviously a 'thing' - besides colour, taste, smell, and touch, all of them accepted as qualities in early Vaiśesika - not to be given a place in the Vaiśeṣika scheme of what there is.

What then was sound? Given the Vaiśeṣika ontological scheme, it must have been a substance, a quality, an action, a universal, a particular, or the special type of relationship which is called *samavāya*. It seems clear that, out of this list, sound can only belong to the categories substance or quality. Since quality is excluded, sound must then have been looked upon as a kind of substance. Which substance? Vaiśeṣika enumerates nine substances, among them the five elements earth, water, fire, wind and ether. If we are forced to make a choice, wind (*vāyu*) seems most appropriate. It seems therefore a priori not unlikely that for the early Vaiśeṣikas sound was a form of wind.

The link between sound and wind is obvious where speech sounds are concerned. The *Padārthadharmasaṁgraha* explains how the movement of wind plays a crucial role in the production of speech sounds in the passage which we studied in the preceding section. A verse cited in the *Vṛtti* on Bhartṛhari's *Vākyapadīya* describes the same process in almost the same terms, with this difference that here wind itself is stated to become sound:[16]

15 Chatterjee, 1978: 109. Unfortunately I have had no access to the *Viśeṣāvaśyakabhāṣya*.

16 Ed. Iyer, Kāṇḍa 1, p. 173; included in Rau's edition as 1.111. Śabara's Bhāṣya on Mīmāṁsā sūtra 1.1.22 ascribes to the Śikṣākāras the words: *vāyur āpadyate śabdatām*. (D'Sa, 1980: 79 n. 8, surprisingly, ascribes this position to the Vaiśeṣikas; see however further below.) Śabara makes a further remark which may explain how sound could be conceived of as wind: *vāyavīyaś cec chabdo bhaved vāyoḥ saṁniveśaviśeṣaḥ syāt* "If sound were made of wind, it would be a special configuration of wind". The idea that sound is wind occurs elsewhere, too; cp. Somānanda's *Śivadṛṣṭi* 2.36: *vāco vāyvātmatā na kim?*

> *labdhakriyaḥ prayatnena vaktur icchānuvartinā/*
> *sthāneṣv abhihato vāyuḥ śabdatvaṁ pratipadyate//*
> The wind set in motion by the effort corresponding to the desire of the speaker, strikes at the different places of articulation and is transformed into sounds. (tr. Iyer, modified)

The parallelism between these two passages, combined with the fact that *icchā* (desire) and *prayatna* (effort) are qualities of the soul in the Vaiśeṣika scheme of things, suggests that the quoted stanza in the *Vṛtti* draws upon Vaiśeṣika ontology, and may even express a Vaiśeṣika point of view. This point of view, however, is that wind becomes sound, in other words, that sound is wind.

Consider now the following passage of the *Padārthadharmasaṁgraha*. It reads, in the translation of Gaṅgānātha Jhā (p. 129):[17]

> Sound cannot be the property of those substances that can be touched - (1) because, being perceptible, its production is not preceded by any quality in the material cause of the substance (to which it belongs); (2) because it does not pervade over, and is not coeval with, the substance to which it belongs; (3) because it is perceived elsewhere than in the substratum wherein it is produced. It cannot be regarded as belonging to the soul, (1) because it is perceptible by an external sense-organ; (2) because it is perceived by other souls; (3) because it is not found to inhere in the soul; and (4) because it is perceived as apart from all idea of 'I'. It cannot be the quality of space (*diś*), time and mind, (1) because it is perceptible by the ear, and (2) because it is a *viśeṣaguṇa* (a specific quality). And thus the only substance to which it could belong as a quality, and be a distinguishing feature of, is *ākāśa*. As the distinguishing feature of sound is common to all *ākāśa*, this is regarded as one only. From this unity follows its individual separateness or isolation. *ākāśa* being spoken of as *vibhu* (omnipresent or all-pervading), it points to its dimension being the largest or highest. In as much as *ākāśa* is spoken of as the cause of sound, it follows that it has conjunction and disjunction.

Every sentence in this passage reflects a Vaiśeṣika sūtra;[18] this is not

17 Pdhs Ki p. 71-74, N p. 58, Vy vol. 1 p. 108: *śabdaḥ pratyakṣatve saty akāraṇaguṇapūrvakatvād ayāvaddravyabhāvitvād āśrayād anyatropalabdheś ca na sparśavadviśeṣaguṇaḥ/ bāhyendriyapratyakṣatvād ātmāntaragrāhyatvād ātmany asamavāyād ahaṅkāreṇa vibhaktagrahaṇāc ca nātmaguṇaḥ/ [śrotragrāhyatvād vaiśeṣikaguṇabhāvāc ca na dikkālamanasām/ pariśeṣād guṇo bhūtvā ākāśasyādhigame liṅgam/] śabdaliṅgāviśeṣād ekatvaṁ siddham/ tadanuvidhānād ekapṛthaktvam/ vibhavavacanāt paramamahat parimāṇam/ śabdakāraṇatvavacanāt saṁyogavibhāgāv iti/*. The part in brackets has been omitted in Ki, no doubt by mistake.

18 Compare with the preceding note the following sūtras (2.1.24-26) found in Jambuvijaya's edition: *kāraṇaguṇapūrvaḥ kārye guṇo dṛṣṭaḥ, kāryāntarāprādurbhāvāc ca śabdaḥ sparśavatām aguṇaḥ/ paratra samavāyāt pratyakṣatvāc ca nātmaguṇo na manoguṇaḥ/ liṅgam ākāśasya/*. Corresponding sūtras are found in the other two versions of the text.

however indicated. Yet it is Praśastapāda's habit to give an indication to that effect when he refers to a sūtra. The final portion of our passage illustrates this. Consider the sentence "*ākāśa* being spoken of as *vibhu*, it points to its dimension being the largest or highest". This refers to sūtra 7.1.28/24/22: *vibhavān mahān ākāśaḥ* "because of its omnipresence ether (*ākāśa*) is large". The sūtra contains an argument (if perhaps a bad one), which Praśastapāda could have simply repeated. Instead he invokes the authority of the sūtra. This only makes sense on the assumption that Praśastapāda prefers referring to a sūtra to repeating its contents on his own authority.

This assumption, if correct, has far-reaching consequences. It implies that all the other sūtras whose contents are repeated in this passage, were not yet recognized as such by Praśastapāda. In other words, some of the Vaiśeṣika sūtras which describe sound as a quality were not yet considered sūtras by Praśastapāda. Others, to be sure, were. The *Padārthadharmasaṅgraha* (Ki p. 235 l. 1-3; N p. 239 l. 14-16; Vy vol. 2 p. 200 l. 14-15) cites VS 2.2.26/x/22 from a 'śāstra', most probably from the *Vaiśeṣika Sūtra*. Moreover, Praśastapāda expresses in no uncertain terms that he looks upon sound as a quality.

Our passage refers explicitly to two sūtras. The first one has already been discussed. The second one cannot but be 2.2.36/30/31: *saṁyogād vibhāgāc chabdāc ca śabdaniṣpatteḥ / -niṣpattiḥ* "sound originates from conjunction, from disjunction, and from (other) sound". We may assume that this second sūtra was accepted as such by Praśastapāda, and may therefore be older than at least some of the sūtras which describe sound as a quality. With this in mind we turn to Bhartṛhari's *Vākyapadīya*.

Consider *Vākyapadīya* 1.105:

> *yaḥ saṁyogavibhāgābhyāṁ karaṇair upajanyate/*
> *sa sphoṭaḥ śabdajāḥ śabdā dhvanayo 'nyair udāhṛtāḥ//*
> Others declare that the *sphoṭa* is what is produced by the organs [of speech] by means of contact and separation; the sounds born from [this initial] sound are the *dhvanis*.

Note the similarity of this verse, at least of certain parts of it, with the Vaiśeṣika sūtra (2.2.36/30/31) which appears to be old. It seems likely that

The version edited by Sinha contains some additional elements in the sūtras 2.1.27, 30-31: *pariśeṣāl liṅgam ākāśasya/ śabdaliṅgāviśeṣād viśeṣaliṅgābhāvāc ca/ tadanuvidhānād ekapṛthaktvaṁ ceti/.* Sūtra 28 *tattvaṁ bhāvena* refers back to 1.2.18 *salliṅgāviśeṣād viśeṣaliṅgābhāvāc caiko bhāva iti.*

Bhartṛhari had this sūtra in mind when he wrote the verse. Our next question must be: how is this verse to be understood?[19]

To begin with, note that this verse describes the opinion of 'others'. It offers, by doing so, an alternative to the opinion of 'some', which is presented in the preceding verses. The first of these preceding verses is nr. 1.96, which reads:[20]

> Some consider that the *sphoṭa* is the universal revealed by the various individual instances, and they consider that the individuals belonging to this [universal] are the *dhvanis*.

We see that two alternatives are placed side by side. According to the first alternative, the *sphoṭa* - that is the real, eternal word - is a universal; according to the second one the *sphoṭa* is produced by the speech organs. But what is produced by the speech organs? Several factors combine to show that the *sphoṭa*, on the second alternative, is some form of substance (*dravya*).

Recall, to begin with, that for Bhartṛhari the world has two sides: the one real and eternal, the other unreal and non-eternal. Regarding the real, eternal side, Bhartṛhari does not care much what we call it. Some consider the eternal aspect of an object to be its universal, others its substance. We are free to choose, as long as we agree that every object has an eternal aspect. The second verse of the *Jātisamuddeśa* (3.2) states therefore:[21]

> In the analysis of objects denoted by words, the eternal objects denoted by all words have been described as 'universal' or as 'substance'.

The remainder of the *Jātisamuddeśa* occupies itself with the alternative that the eternal part of all objects is its universal; the then following *Dravyasamuddeśa* takes up the alternative view that *substance* constitutes their eternal part.

What is true for all 'things', is true for words, too. The real, eternal part of words is either a universal or a substance; both views are acceptable. The conclusion cannot but be that the verse (1.105), which appears

19 See in this connection also Bronkhorst, 1991: 14f.

20 VP 1.96: *anekavyaktyabhivyaṅgyā jātiḥ sphoṭa iti smṛtā/ kaiścid vyaktaya evāsyā dhvanitvena prakalpitāḥ//*

21 VP 3.1.2: *padārthānām apoddhāre jātir vā dravyam eva vā/ padārthau sarvaśabdānāṁ nityāv evopavarṇitau//*

to draw its inspiration from the Vaiśeṣika sūtra, concerns the *sphoṭa* as substance.

This conclusion is confirmed by verse 1.110, which is one of the verses that elaborate the notions introduced in 1.105. This verse states how different schools of thought conceive of sound:[22]

> Some accept that sound is wind, [others] that it is atoms, [others again] that it is knowledge; for in the presentations the different points of view are endless.

The identification sound = knowledge looks puzzling at first. But obviously any idealistic school of thought will maintain that substance derives its reality from, is nothing but, thought or knowledge. In fact, Bhartṛhari himself says so in a passage of his commentary on the *Mahābhāṣya*.[23] We may conclude that the three points of view according to which sound is wind, atoms, and knowledge respectively, share in common that sound is substance.

We have seen that the view in which sound is knowledge must belong to an idealistic school of thought. The view that sound is atoms is part of the world-view of the Sarvāstivādins and the Jainas.[24] Remains the view according to which sound is wind. The fact that Bhartṛhari appears to refer to a Vaiśeṣika sūtra in this very passage, suggests that this view belonged to the early Vaiśeṣikas.

It would seem, then, that Bhartṛhari knew indeed both the positions of Vaiśeṣika with regard to sound: the more recent one according to which it is a quality of ether, and the older one according to which it is wind.

One final observation. Bhartṛhari may not yet have known Śabara's Bhāṣya on the *Mīmāṁsā Sūtra*.[25] He may therefore be earlier than Śabara, or roughly contemporaneous with him. For Śabara, sound is eternal and resides in the omnipresent ether. The fleeting sounds we hear are *manifested*, and not *produced* by the speaker who utters them. In this context Śabara adds the following intriguing remark:[26] "But for him who

22 VP 1.110: *vāyor aṇūnāṁ jñānasya śabdatvāpattir iṣyate/ kaiścid darśanabhedo hi pravādeṣv anavasthitaḥ//*

23 CE I p. 22. l. 19-20, AL p. 27 l. 4-5, Sw p. 32 l. 11-13: *'dravyaṁ hi nityam'/ nityaḥ pṛthivīdhātuḥ/ pṛthivīdhātau kiṁ satyam/ vikalpaḥ/ vikalpe kiṁ satyam/ jñānam/ ...*

24 For a description of the way in which, according to the Sarvāstivādins, sound joins other atoms in order to form a molecule, see La Vallée Poussin, 1980: I: 144-145. For the position of the Jainas, see Jaini, 1920: 118 (*Tattvārtha Sūtra* 5.24).

25 See note 10, above.

26 Śabara on sūtra 1.1.13 (p. 93 l. 5-6): *yasya punaḥ kurvanti tasya vāyavīyāḥ saṁyogavibhāgā vāyvāśritatvād vāyuṣv eva kariṣyanti, yathā tantavas tantuṣv eva paṭam.*

believes that [contacts and separations] produce [sounds rather than manifest them], contacts and separations, which occur in wind, will produce [sounds] nowhere else than in wind, because they subsist in wind; just as yarns produce a cloth in the yarns themselves." Śabara's ideas are frequently close to those of the Vaiśeṣikas, so that it is possible to believe that he had the Vaiśeṣikas in mind while writing this passage. For the Vaiśeṣikas do indeed believe that sounds are produced, not manifested. It is therefore possible that Śabara, too, still knew of Vaiśeṣikas who believed that sound is wind.

4. The omnipresent soul[27]

VS 5.2.18-20 read, in Candrānanda's version:

5.2.18: *kāyakarmaṇātmakarma vyākhyātam*
5.2.19: *apasarpaṇam upasarpaṇam aśitapītasaṁyogaḥ kāryāntarasaṁyogāś cety adṛṣṭakāritāni*
5.2.20: *tadabhāve saṁyogābhāvo 'prādurbhāvaḥ sa mokṣaḥ*

The first of these sūtras has a different form in the *Vyākhyā* edited by Thakur: *kāyakarmaṇātmakarmadharmayor anupapattiḥ* (5.2.16); as observed by A. Wezler (1982: 659), it is difficult to make satisfactory sense of this reading. Nothing corresponding to this sūtra is found in the version known to Śaṅkara Miśra. The remaining two sūtras, on the other hand, occur in the other versions with only insignificant variations.[28]

Candrānanda's explanation of these sūtras contains some suspect features, most notably the following: 1) Candrānanda interprets *ātman* in 5.2.18 to mean wind (*vāyu*). 2) In his interpretation 5.2.19 is about the *manas.* A straightforward interpretation of the sūtras would rather suggest that 5.2.18 talks about the acitivity of the soul (*ātmakarman*), and that 5.2.19 continues this topic and therefore talks about the soul too.[29] Regarding 5.2.19 we know that already Praśastapāda interpreted it like Candrānanda: his *Padārthadharmasaṅgraha* refers to this sūtra in the

27 Some of the questions here discussed have also been dealt with in a paper called "Mysticisme et rationalité en Inde: le cas du Vaiśeṣika", to be published in the Proceedings of the Colloque 'Mystique et rationalité: Inde, Chine, Japon' (Genève, November 29-30, 1990), Asiatische Studien/Etudes Asiatiques 47 (4), 1993.

28 ..*pītasaṁyogāḥ* instead of ..*pītasaṁyogaḥ*; *'prādurbhāvaś ca* instead of *'prādurbhāvaḥ*.

29 See Wezler, 1982: 654f.

context of the description of the *manas*, in order to show that the *manas* can have *saṁyoga* and *vibhāga.*[30] Note in passing that Praśastapāda's remark shows that he looked upon VS 5.2.19 as a sūtra. Elsewhere in the *Padārthadharmasaṅgraha* it is pointed out that the two activities of the *manas* called *apasarpaṇa* and *upasarpaṇa* are the result of contact between the soul and the *manas*, which depends on *adṛṣṭa*;[31] again the sūtra is interpreted as referring to the *manas*.

There is evidence to show that the above sūtras at one time concerned the *ātman* and its activities. Consider first VS 6.2.19/18/16: *ātmakarmasu mokṣo vyākhyātaḥ*. Wezler (1982: 654) observed already that this sūtra "obviously refers back to VS 5.2.20". It does, however, more than just this: it suggests strongly that 5.2.20, and therefore 5.2.19 as well, concern *ātmakarman* 'the activity of the soul'.

With this in mind we turn to Bhartṛhari's *Vākyapadīya*. The *Sambandhasamuddeśa* of this work explores the question what connection exists – to be described in Vaiśeṣika terms, i.e., combinations of *saṁyoga* and *samavāya* – between a word and the object it designates. This leads to no satisfactory results. Indeed, VP 3.3.17 points out that this approach would not limit the designation of a word to its appropriate object. Here VP 3.3.18 counters:

> *adṛṣṭavṛttilābhena yathā saṁyoga ātmanaḥ/*
> *kvacit svasvāmiyogākhyo 'bhede 'nyatrāpi sa kramaḥ//*
>
> Just as the *saṁyoga* of the soul is [only] called 'connection of owner and owned' with regard to certain objects, because *adṛṣṭa* operates [in these cases], even though there is no difference [between this special kind of *saṁyoga* and *saṁyoga* in general], just so is the situation in the case of other [relations], too.

This verse cannot but mean that a virtually limitless number of *saṁyogas* of the soul is limited by the operation of *adṛṣṭa* to those few which link the soul to 'its' body, etc. This in its turn implies that, in Bhartṛhari's opinion, the soul of the Vaiśeṣikas is in contact with far more objects than just its 'own' body etc., and therefore most probably infinitely large, as it is in classical Vaiśeṣika.

30 Ki p. 101 l. 16-17; N p. 89 l. 15-16; Vy vol. 1 p. 156 l. 14-15: *apasarpaṇopasarpaṇavacanāt saṁyogavibhāgau.*

31 Ki p. 270 l. 12; N p. 308 l. 22-23; Vy vol. 2 p. 266 l. 6: *apasarpaṇakarmopasarpaṇakarma cātmamanaḥsaṁyogād adṛṣṭāpekṣāt.*

The explicit mention of *adṛṣṭa* in this verse leaves little doubt that Bhartṛhari paraphrases here VS 5.2.19, which he apparently considered to concern the soul. If we now try to translate VS 5.2.18-20 in agreement with the interpretation which Bhartṛhari to all appearances accorded them, we get:

5.2.18: The activity of the soul is explained by the activity of the body.
5.2.19: Retreating, approaching, contact with what is eaten and drunk, contacts with other effects, [these functions of the soul] are caused by *adṛṣṭa*.
5.2.20: When there is no [activity of the soul], there is no contact [with objects that belong to it], no manifestation [of the soul in a body]; that is *mokṣa*.

In view of VP 3.3.18, the contacts of the soul referred to in VS 5.2.19-20 pertain to the subgroup of *saṁyoga*s called 'contact between owner and owned'. Contacts in general exist between each soul and every finite object, the soul being omnipresent; but these general contacts are not relevant in the context of 'activity of the soul'. This 'activity of the soul', too, must be interpreted to bring about the special contacts called 'contact between owner and owned'. These special contacts are confined to the body, and so is therefore this 'activity of the soul'.

It goes without saying that this limitation of the contacts of an infinitely large soul to a restricted number of objects is hard to explain in terms of the Vaiśeṣika categories. *Adṛṣṭa* is meant to explain, or cover up, this mystery, and would not seem to have much to do with *dharma* and *adharma*, which constitute *adṛṣṭa* in the classical system. Indeed, if *adṛṣṭa* in VP 3.3.18 meant *dharma* and *adharma*, also the connection between words and their meanings should be determined by *dharma* and *adharma*, a point of view which Helārāja rects as impossible.

At this point we must pay attention to a passage of the *Nyāya Sūtra*, along with Pakṣilasvāmin's Bhāṣya (3.2.61-73 (Ānanda Āśrama ed.)/ 60-72 (tr. Jhā)/ 59-71 (ed. Ruben)).[32] This passage deals with the formation of the body and with the factors that play a role in it. Sūtra 61/60/59 gives the opinion of the author: "Its formation is due to the persistence of previous acts" (*pūrvakṛtaphalānubandhāt tadutpattiḥ*). Sūtra 67/66/65 explains further: "Just as *karman* is the cause of the formation of the body, so is it also of the connection [of the body with a particular soul]" (*śarīrotpattinimittavat saṁyogotpattinimittaṁ karma*; tr. Jhā). Sūtras 69-73/68-72/67-71 now reject an alternative opinion regarding the formation

32 My attention was drawn to this passage by J.E.M. Houben.

of the body and its connection with its soul (?). The first two of these sūtras are of most interest to us:

69/68/67: *tad adṛṣṭakāritam iti cet punas tatprasaṅgo 'pavarge*
If [it be asserted] that the [formation of the body] is due to *adṛṣṭa*, then [our answer is that in that case] even after final release there would be likelihood of [a body being produced]. (tr. Jhā)

70/71/72: *manaḥ* (v.l. *manasaḥ*) *karmanimittatvāc ca saṁyogānucchedaḥ*
There would be no severance of connection – this being due to the action of mind. (tr. Jhā)

The then following sūtras go on to show absurd consequences of the rejected opinion, but the above two are most important, for they allow us to identify the rejected opinion as that of VS 5.2.19-20, studied above. The link with VS 5.2.19 is again emphasized by the *Nyāya Bhāṣya* on NS 3.2.70/69/68, which raises questions regarding the *apasarpaṇa* and *upasarpaṇa* of the *manas*, using exactly the terms also found in VS 5.2.19.

Two observations must be made here. The first concerns the interpretation of VS 5.2.19 offered in these Nyāya sūtras. NS 3.2.70/69/68 speaks of the activity of the mind (*manaḥkarman*), and this is apparently how it interpreted the Vaiśeṣika sūtra – just like Praśastapāda and Candrānanda, as we have seen. The second observation pertains to the meaning of *adṛṣṭa* in NS 3.2.69/68/67. *Adṛṣṭa* cannot here be identical with *karman*, nor even be the fruit of previous acts (*pūrvakṛtaphala*), because these are presented as the true causes of the formation of the body in sūtras 61/60/59 and 67/66/65 (see above). The author of the *Nyāya Bhāṣya* understood this very well: he offers two interpretations of *adṛṣṭa*, neither of which appears to have much to do with *karman* and its effects.

It appears, then, that NS 3.2.69-70/68-69/67-68 directly criticise VS 5.2.18-20, which they interpret in a way that deviates from the original interpretation. The meaning assigned to *adṛṣṭa*, on the other hand, is still pre-classical. The criticism centres in a way on VS 5.2.20, which describes *mokṣa*, liberation. According to these Nyāya sūtras, liberation would not be possible if VS 5.2.19 were correct.

It is difficult to avoid the conclusion that the Nyāya sūtras just considered must be later than VS 5.2.18-20, so much later that the original interpretation of VS 5.2.19 was no longer known, or used. This is all the more surprising since Bhartṛhari, as we have seen, still knew the original interpretation of VS 5.2.19. Is it possible that the section NS 3.2.61-73/ 60-72/59-71 was added later?

This is indeed likely, for this group of sūtras constitutes an excursion which interrupts the regular order of topics, as was already noted by Ruben (1928: 209 n. 237). It may here further be observed that *tad-* in *tadutpattiḥ* (NS 3.2.61/60/59) supposedly refers to the body; but the body is not mentioned in the preceding sūtras! We may safely conclude that the whole group of sūtras constitutes a later addition to the text.

The results of the above investigation can be presented as follows. A verse of Bhartṛhari's *Vākyapadīya* allows us to catch a glimpse of the earliest interpretation of VS 5.2.18-20. It shows us that then already the Vaiśeṣikas looked upon the soul as infinitely large. This did not prevent them from speaking about the activity or movement of the soul (*ātmakarman*). The soul can be active because besides the general contact (*saṁyoga*) which it has with every finite object, it can have a specific contact - described as 'contact of owner and owned' - with a restricted number of objects, primarily the 'own' body and all that is contained in it. The 'activity' of the soul that brings about, or maintains, these special contacts, coincides therefore normally with the movement of the body. In terms of the Vaiśeṣika system there is something very mysterious about these special contacts; this is why they are stated to be occasioned by *adṛṣṭa*, the unseen. These special contacts, as well as the 'activity' ascribed in this way to the soul, can come to an end; the soul does then no longer manifest itself in a body. This state of the soul is called 'liberation' (*mokṣa*).

The implausibility of this way of speaking about the 'activity' of a none-the-less omnipresent soul is obvious. It does not surprise that the idea was discarded. But discarding an idea proved easier than discarding the sūtras which expressed it. This led to a reinterpretation of the sūtras concerned. We find the first evidence of this in a set of sūtras inserted at an unknown date into the *Nyāya Sūtra*. This set criticizes VS 5.2.18-20, but while doing so it shows that the idea of an activity of the self had been given up. Contact between the soul and 'its' body are now ascribed to the activity of the mind (*manas*), which corresponds to the later, classical doctrine. But the interpretation of the term *adṛṣṭa* had not yet reached its classical form. *Adṛṣṭa* is not yet short-hand for *dharma* and *adharma*, which are the effects of *karman*; *adṛṣṭa* is, on the contrary, contrasted with *karman* and its effects. It will be clear that with the interposition of a *manas* between a soul and its body, the mystery of the special relationship between the soul and its body disappears, and that, consequently, pre-classical *adṛṣṭa* has no more role to play in it. No wonder that our set of Nyāya sūtras attacks this notion.

With Praśastapāda we arrive at the classical exposition of the Vaiśesika system, and apparently also at the classical interpretation of VS 5.2.18-20. It is clear that Praśastapāda knows at least VS 5.2.19 and considers it a sūtra. He believes, furthermore, that it concerns the *manas*. But also *adṛṣṭa* has with Praśastapāda reached its classical meaning; it has become more or less identical with the effect of *karman* (*pūrvakṛtaphala*). Praśastapāda does no longer have to attack the notion of *adṛṣṭa*; the new interpretation of this term allows him to agree with the author of the above set of Nyāya sūtras, while yet accepting the *Vaiśesika Sūtra* as authoritative.

Abbreviations

AL	*Mahābhāṣyadīpikā* of Bhartṛhari, ed. Abhyankar-Limaye
CE	'Critical edition' of Bhartṛhari's *Mahābhāṣyadīpikā*
Ki	*Padārthadharmasaṅgraha* of Praśastapāda, ed. Jetly
N	*Padārthadharmasaṅgraha* of Praśastapāda, ed. Dvivedin
Sw	*Mahābhāṣyadīpikā* of Bhartṛhari, ed. Swaminathan
VP	*Vākyapadīya* of Bhartṛhari, ed. Rau
Vy	*Padārthadharmasaṅgraha* of Praśastapāda, ed. Gaurinath Sastri

References

Adachi Toshihide (1990): "The acceptance of the Vaiśesika padārtha theory in the Carakasaṁhitā." *Journal of Indian and Buddhist Studies* 38 (2), 911-907.

Bhartṛhari: *Mahābhāṣyadīpikā*. 1) Edited by K.V. Abhyankar and V.P. Limaye. Poona: Bhandarkar Oriental Research Institute. 1970. (Post-Graduate and Research Department Series No. 8.) 2) Partly edited by V. Swaminathan under the title *Mahābhāṣya Ṭīkā*. Varanasi: Banaras Hindu University. 1965. (Hindu Vishvavidyalaya Nepal Rajya Sanskrit Series Vol. 11.) 3) Manuscript reproduced. Poona: Bhandarkar Oriental Research Institute. 1980. 4) 'Critical edition', Āhnika 1. Edited and translated by Johannes Bronkhorst. Poona: Bhandarkar Oriental Research Institute. 1987.

Bhartṛhari: *Vākyapadīya*. (i) Critical edition by Wilhelm Rau. Wiesbaden: Franz Steiner. 1977. (Abhandlungen für die Kunde des Morgenlandes XLII,4.) (ii) Kāṇḍa I, edited, with the *Vṛtti* and Vṛṣabhadeva's *Paddhati*, by K.A. Subramania Iyer. Poona: Deccan College. 1966. (Deccan College Monograph Series, 32.)

Bronkhorst, Johannes (1986): "Tantra and prasaṅga." *Aligarh Journal of Oriental Studies* 3 (2), 77-80.

Bronkhorst, Johannes (1989): "Studies on Bhartṛhari, 2: Bhartṛhari and Mīmāṁsā." *Studien zur Indologie und Iranistik* 15, 101-117.

Bronkhorst, Johannes (1991): "Studies on Bhartṛhari, 3: Bhartṛhari on sphoṭa and universals." *Asiatische Studien / Etudes Asiatiques* 45, 5-18.

Bronkhorst, Johannes (forthcoming): "The Vaiśeṣika vākya and bhāṣya." *Annals of the Bhandarkar Oriental Research Institute.*

Chatterjee, Asim Kumar (1978): *A Comprehensive History of Jainism [up to 1000 A.D.].* Calcutta: Firma KLM.

D'Sa, Francis X. (1980): *Śabdaprāmāṇyam in Śabara and Kumārila.* Towards a study of the Mīmāṁsā expercience of language. Vienna. (Publications of the De Nobili Research Library, 7.)

Frauwallner, Erich (1968): *Materialien zur ältesten Erkenntnislehre der Karmamīmāṁsā.* Wien: Hermann Böhlaus. (Österreichische Akademie der Wissenschaften, philosophisch-historische Klasse, Sitzungsberichte, 259. Band, 2. Abhandlung. Veröffentlichungen der Kommission für Sprachen und Kulturen Süd- und Ostasiens, Heft 6.)

Grohma, Otto (1975): "Theorie zur bunten Farbe im älteren Nyāya und Vaiśeṣika bis Udayana." *Wiener Zeitschrift für die Kunde Südasiens* 19, 147-182.

Halbfass, Wilhelm (1980): "Karma, apūrva, and 'natural' causes: observations on the growth and limits of the theory of saṁsāra." *Karma and Rebirth in Classical Indian Traditions.* Edited by Wendy Doniger O'Flaherty. Berkeley - Los Angeles - London: University of California Press. Pp. 268-302.

Hattori, Masaaki (1968): *Dignāga, On Perception*, being the Pratyakṣapariccheda of Dignāga's Pramāṇasamuccaya, from the Sanskrit fragments and the Tibetan versions translated and annotated. Cambridge, Mass.: Harvard University Press. (Harvard Oriental Series, 47.)

Hattori, Masaaki (1968a): "Two types of non-qualicative perception." *Wiener Zeitschrift für die Kunde Südasiens* 12-13 (1968/1969; Festschrift für Erich Frauwallner), 161-169.

Jaini, J.L. (1920): *Tattvarthadhigama Sutra*, edited with introduction, translation, notes and commentary. Reprint: AMS Press, New York. 1974.

Jhā, Gaṅgānātha (tr.)(1915): *Padārthadharmasaṅgraha of Praśastapāda*, with the Nyāyakandalī of Śrīdhara. Varanasi: Chaukhambha Orientalia. 1982. (Chaukhambha Oriental Studies, 4.)

Jhā, Gaṅgānātha (tr.)(1939): *Gautama's Nyāyasūtras*, with Vātsyāyana-Bhāṣya. Poona: Oriental Book Agency. (Poona Oriental Series, 59.)

La Vallée Poussin, Louis de (tr.)(1980): *L'Abhidharmakośa de Vasubandhu.* 5 tomes. Nouvelle édition anastatique présentée par Étienne Lamotte. Bruxelles: Institut Belge des Hautes Études Chinoises. (Mélanges Chinois et Bouddhisques, XVI.)

Narain, Harsh (1976): *Evolution of the Nyāya-Vaiśeṣika Categoriology.* Vol I. Varanasi: Bharati Prakashan.

Pakṣilasvāmin: *Nyāya Bhāṣya.* Edited, with the Nyāya sūtras and Viśvanātha Bhāttācārya's Vṛtti, by Nāgeśa Digambara Śāstrī Jośī. Poona: Ānanda Āśrama. 1922. (Ānandāśrama-saṁskṛtagranthāvali, 91.)

Potter, Karl H. (1977): *Encyclopedia of Indian Philosophies.* II. Indian Metaphysics and Epistemology: The Tradition of Nyāya-Vaiśeṣika up to Gaṅgeśa. Delhi: Motilal Banarsidass.

Praśastapāda: *Padārthadharmasaṅgraha* (Praśastapādabhāṣya). 1) Edited, with the commentary *Nyāyakandalī* of Śrīdhara, by Vindhyesvari Prasad Dvivedin. Second edition. Delhi: Sri Satguru Publications. 1984. 2) Edited, with the commentary *Kiraṇāvalī* of Udayanācārya, by Jitendra S. Jetly. Baroda: Oriental Institute. 1971. 3) Edited, with the commentary *Vyomavatī* of Vyomaśivācārya, by Gaurinath Sastri. Varanasi: Sampurnanand Sanskrit Vishvavidyalaya. 2 vols. 1983-84.

Ruben, Walter (ed., tr.)(1928): *Die Nyāyasūtra's*. Text, Übersetzung, Erläuterung und Glossar. Leipzig. Genehmigter Nachdruck: Kraus Reprint, Nendeln, Liechtenstein. 1966. (Abhandlungen für die Kunde des Morgenlandes, XVIII, 2.)

Śabara: *Mīmāṁsābhāṣya*. 1) Edition in: Mīmāṁsādarśanam: Tarkapāda. Poona: Ānandāśrama. 1976. (Ānandāśramasaṁskṛtāvali, 97.) 2) Translation: Śābara-Bhāṣya, translated by Ganganatha Jha. Vol. I. Baroda: Oriental Institute. 1973. (Gaekwad's Oriental Series, 66.)

Schmithausen, Lambert (1970): "Zur Lehre von der vorstellungsfreien Wahrnehmung bei Praśastapāda." *Wiener Zeitschrift für die Kunde Südasiens* 14, 125-129.

Somānanda: *Śivadṛṣṭi*. Edited, with the Vṛtti by Utpaladeva, by Madhusudan Kaul Shāstri. Srinagar. 1934. (Kashmir Series of Texts and Studies, LIV.)

Tillemans, Tom J.F. (1990): *Materials for the Study of Āryadeva, Dharmapāla and Candrakīrti*. The Catuḥśataka of Āryadeva, chapters XII and XIII, with the commentaries of Dharmapāla and Candrakīrti: introduction, translation, Sanskrit, Tibetan and Chinese texts, notes. 2 vols. Wien: Arbeitskreis für Tibetische und Buddhistische Studien, Universität Wien. (Wiener Studien zur Tibetologie und Buddhismuskunde, 24,1 & 2.)

Vaiśeṣika Sūtra. 1) Edited, with the commentary of Candrānanda, by Muni Jambuvijaya. Baroda: Oriental Institute. 1961. (Gaekwad's Oriental Series, 136.) 2) Edited, with an anonymous commentary, by Anantalal Thakur. Darbhanga: Mithila Institute. 1957. 3) Edited, with a translation of the sūtras, of the commentary of Śaṅkara Miśra and of extracts from the gloss of Jayanārāyaṇa, by Nandalal Sinha. Delhi: S.N. Publications. 1986. The three numbers that specify a sūtra refer to these three editions respectively. Where only one number is given, the reference is to the first of these three.

Vasubandhu: *Abhidharmakośa Bhāṣya*. Edited by P. Pradhan. Second edition. Patna: K.P. Jayaswal Research Institute. 1975.

Vṛṣabhadeva: *Paddhati*. See under 'Bhartṛhari'.

Vyomaśiva: *Vyomavatī*. Edited by Gaurinath Sastri. Varanasi: Sampurnanand Sanskrit University. 2 vols. 1983-84.

Wezler, A. (1982): "Remarks on the definition of 'yoga' in the Vaiśeṣikasūtra." *Indological and Buddhist Studies*, Festschrift J.W. de Jong. Edited by L.A. Hercus et al. Canberra: Faculty of Asian Studies. Pp. 643-686.

Wezler, A. (1983): "A note on concept adṛṣṭa as used in the Vaiśeṣikasūtra." *Aruṇa-Bhāratī*. Professor A.N. Jani Felicitation Volume. Edited by B. Datta et al. Baroda: Oriental Institute. Pp. 35-58.

Yogabhāṣya = Pātañjalayogadarśanam, edited by Nārāyaṇa Miśra. Varanasi: Bhāratīya Vidyā Prakāśana. 1971.

THE CHANGING NOTION OF ŚIṢṬA FROM PATAÑJALI TO BHARTṚHARI

Madhav M. Deshpande, University of Michigan

The word *śiṣṭa* is used by the traditions of Dharmaśāstra as well as Sanskrit Grammar to refer to a community of social and linguistic élites whose socio-cultural and linguistic behavior was considered to set the norm to be described by the respective texts of Dharmaśāstra and Sanskrit Grammar, and to be emulated by others. This notion is by no means static, though the changing nature of this notion has not been sufficiently investigated in previous studies. In this paper, an attempt is made to trace the major changes in the notion of *śiṣṭa* from Patañjali to Bhartṛhari. I have dealt with the notion of *śiṣṭa* in the earlier phase of Sanskrit Grammar, i.e. from Pāṇini to Patañjali, in my previous research (Deshpande 1985, 1979). Here, I will briefly refer to this earlier phase, and will discuss Bhartṛhari's contribution in greater detail.

In the *Aṣṭādhyāyī* of Pāṇini, there is no explicit reference to *śiṣṭas*, though one can build a fairly clear picture of the community whose linguistic behavior Pāṇini was describing. In my forthcoming article "Sociolinguistic Parameters of Pāṇini's Sanskrit" (appearing in Professor A.M. Ghatage Felicitation Volume), I have discussed several issues relating to the earliest phase of Sanskrit Grammar and the nature of the language described by these early grammarians. To summarize the more extensive discussion in that paper, we can state the following things. Pāṇini's grammar dealt with a mass of language data which included within its scope language material from the bygone age of Vedic texts, as well as contemporary regional and scholastic dialects. To the extent his grammar dealt with contemporary usage, it seems to cover the dialects spreading from the Northwestern region of the subcontinent to the eastern region of the subcontinent. Essentially, its linguistic geography is restricted to North India. However, within that region, it does not describe the linguistic usage of everyone. Pāṇini is primarily describing the linguistic usage of the Brāhmaṇa males. The grammar is addressed to an audience of Brāhmaṇa males. Here too, the grammar does not describe all possible usage of this community, but describes how this community should speak correctly. This means that Pāṇini drew a dividing line between what he perceived to be the élite linguistic usage and the non-acceptable lower-class usage. This dividing line was not a totally hard and fast lin It changed from region to region, time to time, and grammarian to grammarian. Thus, to make a cautious statement, Pāṇini's grammar tells us more about what he considered to be proper usage of Sanskrit, and less about what the people actually spoke. In this respect, Pāṇini's grammar is similar to texts like *Manusmṛti*, which tell us more about how the people should behave, and less about how they actually behaved. In general, this is what we can infer from Pāṇini's grammar, but there is no explicit theoretical discussion about this matter in the rules of the *Aṣṭādhyāyī*.

As we move to Kātyāyana and Patañjali, we find more explicit discussion of the question of who sets the standard of usage for Sanskrit. Kātyāyana brings in some important notions. The first notion brought in explicitly by Kātyāyana is that the science of grammar does not create any new facts of language, but it only describes what is already found in the world of linguistic usage. The usage of language is given to the science of grammar. It does not invent this usage. If this is the case, what is the role of grammar? According to Kātyāyana, the role of grammar is to make a religious restriction (*dharmaniyama*), i.e. to specify explicitly which usages found in the world are proper, and therefore lead to the user gaining religious merit, and which usages found in the world are not proper, and therefore do not lead to the user gaining religious merit. Thus, while all linguistic usage described by a grammar is based on the actual linguistic performance observed in the world, grammar does not aim at describing this totality. It describes only a subsection of the total usage found in the world. It describes the proper, correct, and the meritorious linguistic usage, and by exclusion indicates that the rest of the linguistic usage is improper, incorrect, and does not lead to religious merit. However, Kātyāyana himself does not explicitly get into the discussion of how a grammarian decides which linguistic usage is proper.

For the first time, Patañjali goes into an explicit discussion of most of these issues. Yes, the grammar describes only what already exists in the linguistic performance of the world. Yes, the grammar does not describe the entire linguistic usage of the world. Yes, it describes only the merit-conducive usage, and leaves out the rest as being not conducive to religious merit. But, then how do we know which usage is conducive to religious merit? For the first time, Patañjali goes into details of this question. In his *Mahābhāṣya* on P.6.3.109, Patañjali says:[1]

1 *ke punaḥ śiṣṭāḥ / vaiyākaraṇāḥ / kuta etat / śāstrapūrvikā hi śiṣṭir vaiyākaraṇāś ca śāstrajñāḥ / yadi tarhi śāstrapūrvikā śiṣṭiḥ śiṣṭipūrvakaṃ ca śāstraṃ tad itaretarāśrayaṃ bhavati / itaretarāśrayāṇi ca na prakalpante / evaṃ tarhi nivāsataś cācārataś ca / sa*

> Who are the *śiṣṭas*?
>
> They are the grammarians.
>
> How is it?
>
> The linguistic behavior of the élites presupposes the science of grammar, and the grammarians know the science of grammar. [Therefore, the grammarians must be the élites.]
>
> But, if the behavior of the élites presupposes the science of grammar, and if grammar presupposes the behavior of the élites, then this argument becomes circular. Circular arguments are not acceptable.
>
> Then we define *śiṣṭas* by their place of residence and their way of life. That way of life is found only in the region of Āryāvarta.
>
> What is this Āryāvarta?
>
> It lies to the east of [where the river Sarasvatī] disappears [in modern Rajasthan], to the west of Kālaka forest [near modern Allahabad], to the south of the Himālayas, and to the north of the Vindhyas. Those Brāhmanas who live in this Āryāvarta, the land of the Āryas, who store just a basketful of grain, who are not greedy, and who without any motive have attained the highest wisdom in some branch of learning, they are the *śiṣṭas*.
>
> If these *śiṣṭas* are the decisive standard for correctness of language, then what is the function of Pāṇini's *Aṣṭādhyāyī*.
>
> Pāṇini's grammar aims at helping one recognize these linguistic élites.
>
> How can the linguistic élites be recognized by means of Pāṇini's grammar?
>
> A student of Pāṇini's grammar observes another person who has never studied that grammar but who uses constructions taught in that grammar. He [i.e. the student of Pāṇini's grammar] thinks that it must be either divine grace or some innate nature that this person who does not study Pāṇini's grammar still uses constructions taught in it. Perhaps he may know even other usages [which are deemed to be correct but are not taught by Pāṇini]. This way Pāṇini's grammar aims at helping one recognize the élite speakers of Sanskrit [= *śiṣṭas*]. (MB 3:174)

In this major passage discussing the notion of *śiṣṭa*, several clarifications emerge. Patañjali's *śiṣṭas* are restricted to the region of Āryāvarta, which interestingly does not extend to cover even Pāṇini's birthplace of Śalātura, or even his Udīcya region. Secondly, there is evidence in the *Mahābhāṣya* to show that Patañjali's linguistic élites did not use Sanskrit at all times, but only in the context of ritual, while they seem to prefer the use of

cācāra āryāvarta eva / kaḥ punar āryāvartaḥ / prāg ādarśāt pratyak kālakavanāt dakṣiṇena himavantam uttareṇa pāriyātram / etasminn āryanivāse ye brāhmaṇāḥ kumbhīdhānyā alolupā agṛhyamāṇakāraṇāḥ kiñcid antareṇa kasyāścid vidyāyāḥ pāragās tatrabhavantaḥ śiṣṭāḥ / yadi tarhi śiṣṭāḥ śabdeṣu pramāṇam kim aṣṭādhyāyyā kriyate / śiṣṭajñānārthāṣṭādhyāyī / katham punar aṣṭādhyāyyā śiṣṭāḥ śakyā vijñātum / aṣṭādhyāyīm adhīyāno 'nyam paśyaty anadhīyānam yetra vihitāḥ śabdās tān prayuñjānam / sa paśyati / nūnamasya daivānugrahaḥ svabhāvo vā yo 'yaṃ na cāṣṭādhyāyīm adhīte ye cātra vihitāḥ śabdās tāṃś ca prayuṅkte / ayaṃ nūnam anyān api jānāti / evam eṣā śiṣṭaparijñānārthāṣṭādhyāyī /, Mahābhāṣya III, p. 174.

Prakrits on other occasions. Here, I would like to emphasize two points in Patañjali's discussion.

a. The linguistic usage of Sanskrit is already established in the world, and the users of Sanskrit do not necessarily learn this language from studying grammar books. To put it in another way, there is grammar-independent usage of standard Sanskrit, and it is this grammar-independent usage of standard Sanskrit which the grammarians are expected to observe and follow in their description of standard Sanskrit.

b. The grammarian realizes that there is circularity in claiming the grammarians themselves to be the normative speakers of Sanskrit and then claiming that the science of grammar follows the usage of the normative speakers. Patañjali explicitly recognizes this dilemma and tries to find a way by pointing to a speaker of standard Sanskrit who is not a grammarian or a student of grammar.[2] This way he is able to break the inherent circularity discussed above. However, he is able to break out of this circularity only because there supposedly existed grammar-independent usage of Sanskrit. This seems to confirm the belief in the tradition of Sanskrit grammar that the grammarians from Pāṇini to Patañjali were *lakṣyaikacakṣuṣka* "those whose eyes are solely fixed on the usage to be described." This is the period when grammar is believed to have followed the usage of language which existed independent of that grammar. The tradition says that the grammarians who came after Patañjali were *lakṣaṇaikacakṣuṣka* "those whose eyes were solely fixed on the rules of grammar."[3] This is the period when the language is believed to have followed the grammar, implying that the usage of language followed exclusively from the prior study of the grammatical description, and that there was no grammar-independent usage of Sanskrit to be observed any longer.

Around 400 A.D., about 500 years after Patañjali, came Bhartṛhari. According to the later traditional division mentioned above, he indeed

2 This point seems to have escaped the attention of Abhyankar and Limaye (1965: 404) when they explain a Śiṣṭa as: "People of recognized learning and culture. People who have studied and understood the Vyākaraṇa and other śāstras and can speak with authority." To support this interpretation, they approvingly quote the passage *śiṣṭāḥ vaiyākaraṇāḥ / śāstrapūrvikā hi śiṣṭiḥ, vaiyākaraṇāś ca śāstrajñāḥ* (*MB* on P.6.3.109). However, they fail to point out that this is only a prima facie view finally rejected by Patañjali, who explicitly rejects it by pointing out its circularity.

3 The terms *lakṣyaikacakṣuṣka* and *lakṣaṇaikacakṣuṣka* are attested in the works of Nāgeśabhaṭṭa (Cf. *Paribhāṣenduśekhara*,, p. 78 and 145; *Uddyota* on *Pradīpa* on *Mahābhāṣya* on P.8.3.15). Renou's *Terminologie Grammaticale du Sanskrit*, p. 261 also refers to attestations from Nāgeśabhaṭṭa's works.

belongs to that period of Sanskrit grammar when grammarians had their eyes solely fixed on the rules of grammar, since there was no grammar-independent usage of Sanskrit to be found. The particular description of these two phases, using the terms *lakṣyaikacakṣuṣka* and *lakṣaṇaika-cakṣuṣka*, is not found in any work of Bhartṛhari, but belongs to much later works. Hence, we cannot attribute this division directly to Bhartṛhari himself. Then, what do we find in Bhartṛhari? Did he at least implicitly support such a division? While he claims to be an interpreter of Patañjali, is there any indication in his work that he is in fact offering us a new view of Sanskrit grammar and Sanskrit language, a view which is significantly different from the one found in Patañjali, and a view which is a more accurate reflection of the changed situation? I would like to attempt to provide some answers to these questions in this paper. Consider the following passages from Bhartṛhari's works.

> **Passage 1:** *nyaṅkor neti smṛtyanatare pratiṣedha ārabhyate, nyāṅkavam iti / ihāpy av-yutpattipakṣe nyāṅkavam iti śiṣṭaparṣadā uktatvād ayaṃ vyākhyānaṃ saṃsādhnoti /* [Bhartṛhari's *Mahābhāṣyadīpikā* in Palsule 1983: 12]. Translation: "In another Smṛti a prohibitory rule *nyaṅkor na* is framed (to account for the form) *nyāṅkava.* Here (in Pāṇini's grammar) also *nyāṅkava* has been accepted by the whole body of the Śiṣṭas, on the view that the *Uṇādi* words are unanalysable. So, he (the Bhāṣyakāra) gives an explanation." [Palsule 1983: 35]

Comments: A grammatical description is termed *smṛti* "recollection, memory." This implies that, at least in this view of grammar, a grammar is a statement by some authority of his recollection of how the ideal usage is supposed to be. Taken literally, it is simply a descriptive statement. Bhartṛhari then says that the word *nyāṅkava* was used by a body of Śiṣṭas (*śiṣṭa-parṣad*), and this was why Patañjali came up with an explanation for this word. Here, Patañjali is depicted as being responsive to what the Śiṣṭas say, and this fits the description of the role of a grammarian as found in the *Mahābhāṣya* itself. A grammarian is expected to be responsive to the usage of the Śiṣṭas.

> **Passage 2:** *śabdāḥ smaryante abhyudayāya / anye tu doṣāya /* [*Mahābhāṣyadīpikā* in Palsule 1983: 13].
> Translation: "(Correct) words are taught for worldly prosperity in the Smṛtis; the others lead to sin." [Palsule 1983: 35]

Comments: This explains the function of the Smṛtis, which include grammar. This function is very much in agreement with the discussion which goes back to Kātyāyana and Patañjali. I would suggest that we not render the word *abhyudaya* by "worldly prosperity." Such a rendering brings in the contrast between the notions of *abhyudaya* "worldly prosperity" versus *nihśreyasa* "spiritual prosperity" as seen in the works of Śaṅkara, such as the introduction to his *Gītābhāṣya.* This is a very late contrast and is intended neither in Bhartṛhari's work, nor in the works of Kātyāyana and Patañjali.

> **Passage 3:** *'[mṛjer] vṛddhir acaḥ' ity etāvad evāstu / [tataḥ] 'aci kṅiti vā bhavatī'ti / asya ca smartā bhāṣyakāraḥ / ayaṃ cādiśiṣṭa iti /* [*Mahābhāṣyadīpikā* in Palsule 1983: 13].
>
> Translation: "To that end let (the sūtra) be as [*mṛjer*] *vṛddhir acaḥ.* Then *aci kṅiti* (and finally) *vā.* The author of this is the Bhāṣyakāra who is the foremost of the Śiṣṭas." [Palsule 1983: 35]

Comments: This is a very significant passage. Here Patañjali offers a new grammatical formulation [or rather reformulation] which accounts for words not previously accounted for by Pāṇini's grammar. Who is the author of this new grammatical rule? Bhartṛhari says that Patañjali is the Smartā "recounter, rememberer" of this rule. This is the role Bhartṛhari ascribes to grammarians. They do not produce new usage, but recollect the standard usage. So far this is fine. But then Bhartṛhari says that Patañjali is the foremost of the Śiṣṭas. While in Passage 1 above, Bhartṛhari says that Patañjali as a grammarian is responsive to the usage of the body of Śiṣṭas, here he calls him the foremost of the Śiṣṭas. Clearly, there is a conflation of the two functions here which Patañjali himself tried his best to keep separate. Patañjali's logic was that if the grammarians are themselves to be called Śiṣṭas, and if grammar is to follow the usage of the Śiṣṭas, then this argument becomes circular. Therefore, Patañjali tried to find a non-circular definition of the Śiṣṭa. Bhartṛhari has conflated the two roles by saying that the best Śiṣṭa is the best grammarian, and that Patañjali has the honor of being both. This peculiar conflation of the roles is not just casual or occasional in Bhartṛhari, but, as we shall see, it is the hallmark of his thought. Bhartṛhari's recognition of Patañjali as the foremost of the Śiṣṭas has several possible implications. The first implication is that the roles of being a grammarian and a Śiṣṭa need not or cannot be kept separate, and that these roles can be, or perhaps must be, combined. Secondly, by calling Patañjali a Śiṣṭa Bhartṛhari seems to affirm that a Śiṣṭa need not be a contemporary person, but that a person of one era could be considered to be a Śiṣṭa for another era. It seems that for Patañjali himself, the notion of Śiṣṭa seems to carry with it an associated notion of contemporariness. By considering Patañjali to be not only a Śiṣṭa, but the foremost Śiṣṭa, Bhartṛhari seems to be implicitly subscribing to the notion expressed later by Kaiyaṭa in the maxim: *yathottaram munīnām prāmāṇyam* "the later the sage, the greater his authority." Of course, this doctrine applies only to the first three sages of the Pāṇinian tradition, i.e. Pāṇini, Kātyāyana, and Patañjali. This makes Patañjali the most authoritative among these three ancient sages, and the doctrince does not apply to the period after Patañjali, which makes Patañjali the foremost authority for all periods of Sanskrit grammar. By considering Patañjali to be the foremost Śiṣṭa, Bhartṛhari is also subordinating his contemporary Śiṣṭas to the authority of Patañjali. In effect, Bhartṛhari seems to be subscribing to a new notion of Śiṣṭa, a notion not shared by Patañjali himself.

There is also another role-conflation manifest in Bhartṛhari. He calls Patañjali a Smartā, as well as the foremost among the Śiṣṭas. This seems to combine the two views of grammar, one as a *smṛti* "recollection, description of [ideal, but actual] behavior," and the other as a *śāsana* "teaching, ruling, decree, regulation." Taken literally, the first notion seems to view grammar as a purely descriptive enterprise, while the second notion seems to add a prescriptive and a coercive dimension. The coercive nature of the meaning of the verb *śās* can be demonstrated from many examples.[4]

> **Passage 4**: *upadeśam cāntarena samskāravati nirapabhramśe śabdabrahmaṇi labdha-pratiṣṭhānām śiṣṭānām anumānam* / Bhartṛhari's *Vṛtti* on *VP* 1.12 (Iyer 1966: 43). Translation: "It is the means of inferring that those, who, without being taught, are well acquainted with the true word endowed with correctness and free from corruption, are the cultured people." (Iyer 1965: 18).

Comments: This is merely a restatement of Patañjali's discussion in the *Mahābhāṣya* on P.6.3.109.

4 This dichotomy of views goes back to the old contrast between the notions of grammar expressed by the terms *vyākaraṇa* and *anuśāsana.* The coercive value of the verb *anu+śās* is manifest in many passages from the late Vedic literature, e.g. *vedam anūcyācāryo 'ntevāsinam anuśāsti – satyam vada / dharmam cara / svādhyāyān mā pramadaḥ ...*, *Taittirīya-Upaniṣad* 1.11. The content of the message of an *anuśāsana* is full of the usage of imperatives etc. Similarly, while the views of Āpiśali have been quoted in Passage 1 above under the name *Smṛtyantara*, elsewhere in Sanskrit grammatical literature, the same view has been referred to by using the verb *śās.* For instance, in his *Uṇādivṛtti* (p. 11), Ujjvaladatta cites Āpiśali's view as: *Āpiśalis tu nyaṅkor naicbhāvam śāsti.* This particular conflation of *smarati* and *śāsti* is not new for Bhartṛhari. It is simply an instance of continuation of an old conflation.

Passage 5: *sādhuprayogānumitāṃś ca śiṣṭān na veda yo vyākaraṇaṃ na veda /*, Bhartṛhari's *Vṛtti* on *VP* 1.12 (Iyer 1966: 43).
Translation: "He who does not know (among other things) the cultured users (of Sanskrit) recognized from their use of correct language, does not know grammar."

Comment: This is also a continuation of the old notion of how to recognize a Śiṣṭa. Cf. *Mahābhāṣya* on P.6.3.109.

Passage 6: *tatrāmnātā maharṣibhiḥ / sūtrādīnām praṇetṛbhiḥ / vyākaraṇa eva ye sūtrādīnām praṇetāras te vyapadiśyante / tatra sūtrāṇām ārambhād eva śabdānāṃ nityatvam abhimatam / na hy anityatve śabdādīnāṃ śāstrārambhe kiñcid api prayojanam asti / vyavahāramātraṃ hy etad anarthakaṃ na mahāntaḥ śiṣṭāḥ samanugantum arhantīti /* Bhartṛhari's *Vṛtti* on *VP* 1.23 (Iyer 1966: 61-62).
Translation: "What is meant by 'taught there by the great sages', is: by the authors of the sūtras etc. Those who have composed the sūtras etc. of the science of Grammar are referred to. The very fact that the sūtras have been composed shows that they considered the words to be eternal. There would be no purpose in composing the science of Grammar if the words were not eternal. Because they would be a matter of mere usage and great cultured persons would not take the trouble of expounding them." (Iyer 1965: 27).

Comment: This passage identifies the Śiṣṭas as the authors of grammatical texts.

Passage 7: *athavā yaiḥ pratyakṣadharmabhis tatra pravacane sūtrānutantrabhāṣyāṇi praṇītāni tair eva śiṣṭair vyākaraṇe 'pi nityāḥ śabdārthasambandhāḥ ity āmnātam / teṣām ca vyavasthitaṃ loke prāmāṇyam iti /* Bhartṛhari's *Vṛtti* on *VP* 1.23 (Iyer 1966: 63).
Translation: "Or (it might be said) those very sages who have realised the truth and have, in the course of their different teachings, composed Sūtras, Anutantra (vārttikas) and Bhāṣya, have, in the science of Grammar also, declared that the word, the meaning and their mutual relation are eternal. And their authority in the world is established." (Iyer 1965: 28).

Comment: Iyer's translation does not do justice to the expression *tair eva śiṣṭair* in the text. It says: "by the same Śiṣṭas, [it has been declared in the science of grammar.]" This passage also clearly identifies the Śiṣṭas as the authors of grammatical texts. The commentator Vṛṣabhadeva glosses the words *tair eva śiṣṭair* with *pāṇinyādibhiḥ* (Iyer 1966: 63).

Passage 8: *śiṣṭebhya āgamāt siddhāḥ sādhavo dharmasādhanam / arthapratyāyanābhede viparītās tv asādhavaḥ //* *VP* 1.27 (Iyer 1966: 81).
Translation: "The correct words, acquired from the cultured through tradition, are the means of obtaining merit. The incorrect words, while not differing from them as far as conveying of the meaning is concerned, are of an opposite character." (Iyer 1965: 40)

Comment: The words *śiṣṭebhya āgamāt siddhāḥ* are syntactically unclear. Do they refer to two separate sources for the knowledge of correct words, or are they dependent on each other in some way? The next passage from the *Vṛtti* deals with this issue in its own way.

Passage 9: *yathaivānyāni dharmasādhanāni [vi]śiṣṭopadeśapāramparyāgamāvicchedenāgatāni anabhiśaṅkanīyāni vyavasthitāni / ... tathā sādhvasādhuvyavasthānam apy anavacchinnapāramparyam anabhiśaṅkanīyaṃ yathāgamād eva siddham iti / Vṛtti* on *VP* 1.27 (Iyer 1966: 82).

Translation: "Just as other means of attaining merit, received through uninterrupted tradition consisting of successive teaching of the cultured are well established and are not to be doubted, in the same way, the distinction between what is correct and what is not is based on unbroken tradition and is not to be doubted, but is to be accepted according to tradition." (Iyer 1965: 40).

Comments: This passage makes it clear that for Bhartṛhari the conception of Śiṣṭa is not a synchronic conception including only the contemporary Śiṣṭas. For him, this conception represents an *āgama* 'tradition, continuous transmission.' The Śiṣṭas of one generation transmit their knowledge to the next generation of Śiṣṭas in an unbroken way, and presumably the latter-day Śiṣṭas derive their authority from their being in line of transmission from the Śiṣṭas of the older generation.

Passage 10: *nānarthikām imām kaścid vyavasthām kartum arhati / tasmān nibadhyate śiṣṭaiḥ sādhutvaviṣayā smṛtiḥ // VP* 1.29. *ko hi śiṣṭaḥ sambhinnabuddhir api lokam praty abhiniviṣṭo durjñānaṃ duradhyeyam ca svarasaṃskārādiniyamaṃ laukikavaidikānām śabdānām prayojanaṃ vyavasthāpayitum utsaheta / na cānarthako niyamaḥ / kṛto 'pi śiṣṭair aparair na parigṛhyate / pramāṇaṃ vā viduṣāṃ loke na syād iti / tasmād anādir gurupūrvakramāgatā śiṣṭānumānahetur avyabhicārā lakṣaṇaprapañcābhyām paryāyaiḥ śabdavatī cāśabdā ca smṛtir nibadhyate / Vṛtti* on *VP* 1.29 (Iyer 1966: 84-85).

Translation: "Nobody would establish this system of rules without a purpose. Therefore, this tradition relating to correctness is being composed by the cultured. (Comm.:) Which cultured person, even if he has a confused mind and no sympathy towards the world, would undertake the regulation of the accent and other signs of correctness of the words of the Veda and of the world which are so difficult to know and to learn and which are the very purpose of Grammar? And such a regulation would not be useless. (If it were) such a regulation made by the cultured would be unacceptable to the others. And it would not be authority in the world for scholars. Therefore, this tradition (relating to words) beginningless, handed down from teacher to pupil, the means of inferring who the cultured persons are, infallible, consisting of general rules and their elaborations, is being composed in different ways, through direct statements and by implication." (Iyer 1965: 42).

Comments: Here, the verse from the *Vākyapadīya* and the *Vṛtti* seem to be espousing slightly different ideas. To focus on this difference, we can note that the verse says that the grammatical Smṛti is composed by the Śiṣṭas (*śiṣṭaiḥ nibadhyate smṛtiḥ*). On the other hand, the *Vṛtti* says that the grammatical Smṛti is a tool to detect who the Śiṣṭas are (*śiṣṭānumāna-hetuḥ*). Of these two conceptions, the first one is the new conception developed by Bhartṛhari, while the second conception is the old conception found in the *Mahābhāṣya* on P.6.3.109.

Passage 11: *āvirbhūtaprakāśānām anupaplutacetasām / atītānāgatajñānam pratyakṣān na viśiṣyate // VP* 1.37 // *atīndriyān asaṃvedyān paśyanty ārṣeṇa cakṣuṣā / ye bhāvān vacanaṃ teṣāṃ nānumānena bādhyate // VP* 1.38. *Vṛtti: atha ca tapasā nirdagdhadoṣā nirāvaraṇakhyātayaḥ śiṣṭāḥ pratibimbakalpena pratyakṣam iva svāsu khyātiṣu saṃkrāntākāraparigraham avyabhicaritaṃ sarvaṃ paśyanti / ... antaryāmiṇam anugrāmam abhijātinimittanibandhanam anabhivyaktaṃ śabdabrahma śaktyadhiṣṭhānaṃ devatāḥ karmaṇām anubandhapariṇāmaśaktivaikalyāni sūkṣmam ātivāhikaṃ śarīraṃ pṛthag anyāṃś ca tīrthapravādeṣu prasiddhān arthān rūpādivad indriyair agrāhyān sukhādivat pratyātmasaṃvedyān ye śiṣṭā vyāvahārikād anyenaiva cakṣuṣā muktasaṃśayam upālabhante / teṣām anumānaviṣayātītaṃ vacanaṃ vyabhicāribhir anumānair apākartum aśakyam /* (Iyer 1966: 94-96).

Translation: "The knowledge of the past and the future of those whose insight has manifested itself and whose mind is in no way tainted differs in now way from perception (*VP* 1.37). The words of those who, with their divine vision, see things which are beyond the senses and unknowable, cannot be set aside by reasoning (*VP* 1.38). (*Vṛtti*:) But cultured persons, whose impurities have been burnt away by austerities, whose cognitions are free from all limitations, see everything vividly reflected in their cognitions. The supreme inner Controller, the atoms which are the abode of the initial cause of creation, the unmanifested Word-Absolute which is the substratum of its powers, the gods, the residual forces generated by action, leading to particular results and not to others, in their maturity, the divine otherworldly body, and other such things known in all scholarly circles, imperceptible to the senses like colour and beyond the range of inner experience like happiness are undoubtedly perceived by the sages with their extraordinary eye. The words of these sages, dealing with matters beyond the range of inference, cannot be upset by reasoning which is so liable to err." (Iyer 1965: 47-48)

Comments: Here the verses of the *VP* do not mention the Śiṣṭas explicitly. However, the *Vṛtti* takes this to be a description of the Śiṣṭas. A comparison of this description of the Śiṣṭas with the description given by Patañjali on P.6.3.109 shows that while Patañjali is speaking about a real community of ideal speakers residing in the region of Āryāvarta, a community of learned Brāhmaṇas, Bhartṛhari has almost mythologized the conception of Śiṣṭa. It has no specific regionality or temporality, but it has a very high degree of spirituality. This high degree of spirituality seems to indicate that he is not speaking about any contemporary persons, but mythologized great sages of the golden age of Sanskrit grammar. His reference to *ārṣa cakṣus* "vision appropriate to a Ṛṣi", which Iyer wrongly translates as "divine eye," makes it clear that Bhartṛhari's Śiṣṭas are the ancient Ṛṣis, and not any contemporary persons. With this attitude, it makes eminent sense that Bhartṛhari views Patañjali to be the foremost of the Śiṣṭas. By the time of Bhartṛhari, Patañjali has been mythologized into a Ṛṣi, and his *Mahābhāṣya* is referred to as an *ārṣa* text (*VP* 2.481). As Abhyankar and Limaye (1965: 203) point out, these two verses of the *Vākyapadīya* have been quoted by Kaiyaṭa in his *Pradīpa* on *Mahābhāṣya* on P.6.3.109, where he elucidates Patañjali's conception of Śiṣṭa. However, Kaiyaṭa sees no difference between Bhartṛhari's conception and Patañjali's conception. Kaiyaṭa cites these verses to explain the import of the expression *kiñcid antareṇa kasyāścid vidyāyāḥ pāraṃ gatāḥ*. Kaiyaṭa takes this to mean that the Śiṣṭás acquire mastery of knowledge without even being taught by a teacher (*vinaiva abhiyogādinā, Uddyota: abhiyogo gurūpadeśaḥ, ādinā abhyāsādiḥ*). The implication is that they have direct access to all knowledge through their yogic and ascetic practices, and they need neither instruction nor practice. It is almost certain that Patañjali does not have any such thing in his mind. We need to be aware that Kaiyaṭa's understanding of the *Mahābhāṣya* has been significantly colored by his reliance on Bhartṛhari, and that several crucial distinctions escaped his attention.

Passage 12: *astaṃ yāteṣu vādeṣu kartṛṣv anyeṣu asatsv api / śrutismṛtyuditaṃ karma loko na vyativartate // VP* 1.125. *Vṛtti: iha praṇetṛvad āgamānām api pravādeṣu vicchedo 'bhyupagamyate / teṣu pratyastamiteṣu yāvad anye praṇetāro notpadyante, āgamāntarāṇi ca na pratāyante tatrāpy antarāle śrutivihitāni karmāṇi smṛtinibandhanāṃś ca bhakṣyābhakṣyādīn niyamān nātikrāmanti śiṣṭāḥ /* (Iyer 1966: 204). Translation: "Even if the doctrines perish and there are no more authors to compose others, cultured people follow the right path mentioned in the *śrutis* (Scripture) and the *Smṛtis* (written tradition). [Iyer translates this verse under number *VP* 1.133.] [Commentary:] In all discussions, it is admitted that, like the authors, the written traditions themselves can disappear. When they come to an end and before other authors arise and other written traditions are elaborated, there may be an interval during which cultured people do not violate the rites taught in the Scripture nor the regulations relating to what to eat and what not to eat embodied in the written traditions." (Iyer 1965: 120)

Comments: Iyer's translation needs some comment. The verse of the *VP* uses the expression *loko na vyativartate*, which literally means: "the world (or people) do not violate." Under the influence of the *Vṛtti*, Iyer translates the word *loka* as being equivalent to Śiṣṭa. In this particular case, there seems to be some contextual justification to support a restricted meaning for the word *loka*. Since the verse speaks about the "world" not violating the rules laid down in the Vedas and Smṛtis, we can assume that the verse does not refer to the world or people at large, but only to those people who follow the rules laid down in the Vedas and Smṛtis. Therefore, a more restrictive view of the notion of *loka* is justified.[5] There is also no need to bring in any notion of "written" traditions. There is no reference to writing. The verse of the *VP* seems to refer to a decadent age where the ancient traditions have been lost, and yet some people seem to continue to follow the regulations from the ancient traditions, perhaps by instinct. These people could not be the same as the great ancient Ṛṣis, referred to as Śiṣṭas elsewhere. Thus, the Śiṣṭas referred to in the *Vṛtti* of this verse must be good people in a decadent age. Thus, the word Śiṣṭa seems to have been used with some latitude, though mostly to refer to the ancient glorious Ṛṣis.

> **Passage 13:** *sādhutvajñānaviṣayā saiṣā vyākaraṇasmṛtiḥ / avicchedena śiṣṭānām idaṃ smṛtinibandhanam // VP* 1.133. *Vṛtti: yathaiva bhakṣyābhakṣyagamyāgamya-vācyāvācyādiviṣayā vyavasthitāḥ smṛtayaḥ yāsu nibaddhaṃ samācāraṃ śiṣṭā na vyatikrāmanti tatheyam api vācyāvācyaviśeṣaviṣayā vyākaraṇākhyā smṛtiḥ / smṛto hy arthaḥ pāramparyād avicchedena punaḥ punar nibadhyate / prasiddhasamayācārāyāṃ ca smṛtāv anibandhanaśabdāyāṃ śiṣṭasamācārāvicchedenaiva smaryate /* (Iyer 1966: 212-213).
>
> Translation: (Iyer 1965 translates this verse under *VP* 1.141): "Knowledge of the correctness of words is the subject of this tradition called Grammar. It is here that the uninterrupted tradition of cultured people is recorded. (Commentary:) Just as traditions relating to what can be eaten and what cannot be eaten, which woman one can marry and which woman one cannot marry, what can be said and what cannot be said are well established and cultured people do not go against the code of conduct based on them, in the same way, this tradition called Grammar relates

5 Here, we should distinguish the use of the word *loka* in this verse of the *VP* from the use in the first *Vārttika* of Kātyāyana on Pāṇini's grammar: *siddhe śabdārthasambandhe lokato 'rthaprayukte śāstreṇa dharmaniyamaḥ* "With the words, their meanings, and the relationship between them being already established by (the usage of) the world and (with the words) being used to express meanings, the science of grammar makes a restriction as to (which words are conducive) to religious merit." Here, the word *loka* refers to the world at large, i.e. to speakers of correct as well as incorrect words. All this usage of language, correct as well as incorrect, is given to grammarians, and all that the grammarians can do is to say which kind of usage is meritorious. They do not invent linguistic usage, either correct or incorrect. Of this totality of linguistic usage, Patañjali would say that the usage of the Śiṣṭas represents the correct and the meritorious usage. Thus, the Śiṣṭa usage represents a subset of the linguistic usage in the world.

to what particular words can be used and what not. What is remembered from generation to generation, in an uninterrupted manner is again and again embodied in words. A tradition which has no written basis but the observance of which is well-known is preserved by the continuity of the practice of the cultured." (Iyer 1965: 124-125).

Comments: Again, Iyer is not justified in bringing in any notion of writing. In the syntax of the original verb, the genitive form *śiṣṭānām* is somewhat ambiguous. It could be possibly connected as an agentive genitive with the word *nibandhanam*, which makes the Śiṣṭas the authors of these grammatical compositions. Such a view of the role of the Śiṣṭas is justified on the basis of several other passages. The *Vṛtti*, and Iyer who follows it, seem to connect this genitive with *samācāra* "practice." This word is found in the *Vṛtti*, but does not occur in the text of the verse. The verse as interpreted by Iyer does not make any reference to who the authors of the grammatical Smṛti are. However, as shown above, another interpretation is possible.

Passage 14: *tasyāś cāsamkīrṇam vāco rūpaṃ kārtsnyena sāmānyaviśeṣavaty asmin lakṣaṇe vyākaraṇākhye nibaddham / arvāgdarśanānāṃ tu puruṣāṇām prāyeṇa sātiśayāḥ pratighātinyaḥ sāparādhāḥ śaktayaḥ / niraparādhas tu lakṣaṇaprapañcavān anekamārgo 'yaṃ śabdānām pratipattyupāyo darśitaḥ / Vṛtti* on *VP* 1.134. (Iyer 1966: 221) Translation: (Iyer 1965 translates this passage as *Vṛtti* on *VP* 1.142) "The pure form of that word is embodied in this descriptive Science called Grammar, consisting of general and special rules. The powers of those of lower visions, generally admit of degree, are liable to meet obstruction and to commit mistakes. Hence this method of acquiring the words, free from error and consisting of definitions and elaborations and containing many paths, has been developed." (Iyer 1965: 127).

Comments: The commentary *Paddhati* of Harivṛṣabha (Iyer 1966: 221) on the word *niraparādhaḥ* "free from error" says that the grammatical Smṛti texts are free from error because they are composed by the Śiṣṭas (*śiṣṭaiḥ praṇītatvāt*). This comment from Harivṛṣabha shows that the idea of the Śiṣṭas being the authors of grammatical texts was positively endorsed by the commentators of Bhartṛhari's works.

Passage 15: *svabhāvajñaiś ca bhāvānāṃ dṛśyante śabdaśaktayaḥ* // *VP* 1.135cd // *Vṛtti: santi tu sādhuprayogānumeyā eva śiṣṭāḥ sarvajñeyeṣv apratibaddhāntaḥprakāśāḥ / te viśiṣṭakālāvadhipravibhāgāṃ yathākālaṃ dharmādharmasādhanabhāvena samanvitāṃ śabdaśaktim avyabhicāreṇa paśyanti* // (Iyer 1966: 221-223). Translation: (Iyer 1965: 128-129 translates this verse as *VP* 1.143:) "[As] the powers of words are seen by those who know the true nature of things. (Commentary:) There are cultured people and that they are so can be inferred only from their use of correct words. They, whose inner vision is unobstructed in regard to all things to be known, see, without error, the power of words, differing at different periods of time and consisting in their being the means of merit or demerit, according to the times."

Comments: This passage also gives a view of the Śiṣṭas which is far more mythologized and utopian as compared to the conception of Patañjali. The commentary *Paddhati* of Harivṛṣabha offers an interesting explanation of the word *svabhāvajña* in the verse: *ye tu śiṣṭāḥ padārthaśaktim pratyakṣena [paśyanti?] te pṛṣodarādivat sarvān sādhūn vidantīti tān praty anarthakaṃ vyākaraṇam / tacchiṣṭaparijñānārthan tu vyākaraṇam iti /* (Iyer 1966: 222). This argues that the Śiṣṭas, with their mystical powers, directly perceive which words are correct and which are incorrect, and they use them appropriately. They do not need to use a grammar themselves to make this determination. Patañjali's notion of Śiṣṭa assumes that there are people who speak correct Sanskrit without learning it from grammar books. However, Patañjali says that this could be either through divine grace or their own inherent nature. He does not enhance the mystical powers of these Śiṣṭas. He merely seems to refer to "natural" speakers of Sanskrit. By the time of Bhartṛhari and his commentators, this "natural" speaker of Sanskrit has been endowed with supernatural mystical Ṛṣi-like powers. In this sense, the Śiṣṭas have been mythologized.

Passage 16: *anādim avyavacchinnām śrutim āhur akartṛkām / śiṣṭair nibadhyamānā tu na vyavacchidyate smṛtiḥ // VP* 1.136 // *Vṛtti: smṛtis tu nityam avicchidyamānārthā gadyaślokavākyādibhedena pratikālam anyathā śiṣṭair eva nibadhyate //* (Iyer 1966: 223-224).

Translation: (Iyer 1965: 129-130 translates this verse as *VP* 1.144:) "Scripture (*Śruti*) has been declared to be beginningless, continuous and without an author. Written tradition (*Smṛti*) is composed by cultured Ancients and has continuity. (Commentary:) Written Tradition, on the other hand, has continuity of meaning, but is composed by the cultured differently at different times in prose, verses, sentences etc."

Comments: As pointed out before, Iyer's reference to writing is out of place. This passage most clearly connects the Śiṣṭas with the authorship of grammatical texts. Interestingly, the verse has just the word *śiṣṭa*, but Iyer renders it with "cultured Ancients." Iyer's translation obviously reads something into the text which is not there from a very literal point of view, and yet I feel he captures the contextually recoverable intention of the author of the verse. As I have argued before. Bhartṛhari has mythologized the notion of Śiṣṭa and it does not refer to any contemporary speakers of standard Sanskrit. It refers to mythologized and partially deified ancient authors of Sanskrit grammatical texts. Bhartṛhari's conception of Śiṣṭa, therefore, has a utopian quality to it, rather than being something which can be understood purely in sociolinguistic terms.

Passage 17: *atha kasmād ete gośabdasya gāvyādayaḥ paryāyā na vijñāyante /na hi śiṣṭasamācāraprasiddher anyad evamprakāreṣu smṛtinibandhaneṣv artheṣu nimittam abhidhīyate / gāvyādayaś cet paryāyāḥ syur ete 'pi śiṣṭair lakṣaṇair anugamyeran prayujyeraṃś ca // Vṛtti* on *VP* 1.141. (Iyer 1966: 231).
Translation: (Iyer 1965: 134 translates this passage as *Vṛtti* on *VP* 1.149:) "Why is it that *goṇī* etc. are not considered to be synonyms of *gauḥ*? In regard to such matters which are embodied in the written Tradition, no other cause other than being well-known in the practice of the cultured can be adduced. If *gāvī* etc. were synonyms, they would also have been included in their rules and actually used."

Comments: This passage clearly attributes two functions to the Śiṣṭas. The usage of the Śiṣṭas is viewed to be standard usage. However, the Śiṣṭas are also authors of the rules of grammar codifying that standard usage.

Passage 18: *na śiṣṭair anugamyante paryāyā iva sādhavaḥ / te yataḥ smṛtiśāstreṇa tasmāt sākṣād avācakāḥ // VP* 1.142 // (Iyer 1966: 231).
Translation: (Iyer 1965: 134 translates this verse as *VP* 1.150:) "Since they (= incorrect words, *apabhraṃśas*) are not explained like correct synonyms by cultured people in the written Tradition (*smṛtiśāstra*), therefore, they are not directly expressive."

Comments: This verse again clearly confirms the notion that the Śiṣṭas are authors of grammatical texts.

Passage 19: *jñānaṃ tv asmadviśiṣṭānāṃ tāsu sarvendriyaṃ viduḥ / abhyāsān maṇirūpyādiviśeṣeṣv iva tadvidām // VP Kāṇḍa III, Jātisamuddeśa*, verse 46 (Iyer 1963: 51).
Translation: "The knowledge regarding the universal of those who are different from us proceeds from all the senses, just as that relating to the characteristics of precious stones and coins comes through practice in the case of those who know them." (Iyer 1971: 33)

Comments: Iyers rendering of the expression *asmadviśiṣṭānām* as "those who are different from us" does not do justice to the intention of the verse. As Helārāja appropriately points out, this expression seems to mean "those who are superior to us." It refers to the Śiṣṭas with their supernormal cognitive abilities: *tad evam āgamaprāmāṇyād bhāvatattvadṛśaḥ śiṣṭās santy atīndriyārthadarśina iti te yathāyathaṃ gotvabrāhmaṇatvādijātīr āśrayavivekenādhyakṣayanti / tac ca teṣāṃ śiṣṭānāṃ jñānaṃ sarvendriyaṃ pratiniyamānapekṣatvāt / sarvajñā hīndriyāntareṇāpīndriyāntaravyāpāraṃ kurvanti /... brāhmaṇatvādiṣv asti kiñcit sāsnādisthānīyam upavyañjanam asmākaṃ param atīndriyam / śiṣṭais tad avadhārya saṃjñāḥ* *praṇītāḥ / ... tatrabhavatām upadeśād vayam api sampradāyapāramparyād yathāyogaṃ gotvādijātīr adhyavasyāmaḥ // Prakīrṇakaprakāśa* of Helārāja (Iyer 1963: 51-55). Translation: "Thus, on account of the authority of the tradition [we assert] that the Śiṣṭas do exist who see the truth of things and see things which are beyond the reach of senses. They appropriately determine the existence of different universals such as cowness and Brahminness depending upon the difference of the loci of these universals. That knowledge of those Śiṣṭas comes from all senses, since (for such accomplished persons) there is no restriction on which objects are cognized through which sense. Omniscient persons can accomplish the function of one sense with another sense. Just as [for recognizing cowness, there is] the dewlap [in the individual object], similarly there must be some indicator for the universals like Brahminness. However, those indications are beyond our senses. The Śiṣṭas, after comprehending such indications, make the appropriate designations. Because of the teaching of those honored [Śiṣṭas], we also determine the appropriate universals like cowness through continuity of our tradition." Helārāja seems to be true to the spirit of Bhartṛhari, though perhaps even more ebullient. According to him, we the current grammarians do not have the supernatural cognitive abilities which the ancient Śiṣṭas had, and therefore we can do no better than follow the teachings of those ancient Śiṣṭas. This virtually denies the existence of contemporary Śiṣṭas, and does seem to fall in the general line of the doctrine of declining abilities of humans in the course of time. Helārāja, in fact, discusses this notion of decline of abilities with time, and hence the resulting authority of the past sages, in great detail (Iyer 1963: 53). Again, to emphasize our historical perspective, Patañjali himself does not share in this notion of the non-existence of the contemporary Śiṣṭas.

> **Passage 20:** *bhāvatattvadṛśaḥ śiṣṭāḥ śabdārthesu vyavasthitāḥ / yad yad dharme 'ṅgatāṃ eti liṅgaṃ tat tat pracakṣate // Vākyapadīya, Third Kāṇḍa, Liṅgasamuddeśa*, Verse 21. (Iyer 1973: 141).
>
> Translation: "Cultured people who can see the truth and who know the words and meanings adopt whatever gender leads to merit." (Iyer 1974: 114).

Comments: As Helārāja clarifies on this verse, Bhartṛhari is redefining the notion of *loka* "world" in terms of Śiṣṭas. As the older dictum goes: *liṅgam aśiṣyaṃ lokāśrayatvāl liṅgasya* (*Mahābhāṣya*, II, p. 198) "Gender need not be explicitly taught in grammar, since it depends upon the usage of words in the world." While the original statement does not have any reference to Śiṣṭas with mystical supernatural cognitive powers, Bhartṛhari's interpretation elevates the world of usage to the world of Śiṣṭas with supernatural cognitive abilities, who know the absolutely true nature of things and whose cognitive abilities are totally unobstructed: *iha lokaśabdena śiṣṭā vivakṣitāḥ / teṣāṃ ca vastuparamārtha-sākṣātkāritā lakṣaṇam / te hi nirāvaraṇakhyātayo 'bhidheyeṣu samavetaṃ strītvādi liṅgam abhyudaye yad yad yasya śabdasya sādhanatām eti tat tad eva tasyācakṣate /*, *Prakīrṇakaprakāśa* of Helārāja, (Iyer 1973: 141).

Conclusion:

A close study of all the passages cited above indicates that Bhartṛhari has a distinctive conception of Śiṣṭa, a conception which is substantially different from the conception found in Patañjali's *Mahābhāṣya.* Patañjali's Śiṣṭas are a real flesh-and-blood community of Brahmins living in the region of Āryāvarta. While they are selfless and learned, they are still contemporary human beings. Patañjali argues that these Śiṣṭas speak Sanskrit naturally, and their natural usage does not ensue from a study of Sanskrit grammar. Just as they do not study Sanskrit grammar in order to learn Sanskrit, Patañjali does not depict them as being authors of grammatical works either. In fact Patañjali points to the circularity of argument, if grammar were to follow the usage of the Śiṣṭas who were grammarians themselves. He insists on finding a source of grammar-independent usage of standard Sanskrit. Such usage is found in the community of Śiṣṭas. Patañjali's Śiṣṭas thus represent a sociolinguistic unit of élite speakers of Sanskrit. They most likely spoke Sanskrit as a second language, but they could, so it is claimed, acquire Sanskrit without learning it from grammar books. Patañjali exclaims that such persons must be divinely gifted or must have a special nature that they do not learn Sanskrit from grammar books and yet speak it correctly. However, Patañjali does not depict them as being highly mythologized mystical sages of some ancient times whose cognitive abilities were far superior to the contemporaries of Patañjali. Thus, there is no mystique about them. Besides these contemporary Śiṣṭas, Patañjali also refers to mythical sages and their behavior in particular contexts. This is, for instance, the case with the story of the sages called Yarvāṇastarvāṇa narrated in the *Mahābhāṣya* (Vol. I, p. 11):

> *yad apy ucyate ācāre niyama iti yājñe karmaṇi sa niyamaḥ / evaṃ hi śrūyate / yarvāṇastarvāṇo nāmarṣayo babhūvuḥ pratyakṣadharmāṇaḥ parāparajñā viditaveditavyā adhigatayāthātathyāḥ / te tatrabhavanto yad vā nas tad vā na iti prayoktavye yarvāṇastarvāṇa iti prayuñjate yājñe punaḥ karmaṇi nāpabhāṣante /*

> The statement that there is a restriction on the usage [of correct Sanskrit] applies to the context of sacrificial performance. Thus it is heard. There were in ancient times great sages called Yarvāṇastarvāṇa. They had direct insight into the nature of things, knew this and the yonder worlds, had realized what there is to be realized, and had attained the true knowledge of the world as it is. Those highly honored sages used the [incorrect = Prakrit] expressions *yarvāṇa* and *tarvāṇa* when they should have used [the proper Sanskrit] expressions *yad vā naḥ* and *tad vā naḥ*. However, they did not use these incorrect [= Prakrit] expressions during a sacrificial performance.

Thus, in Patañjali's *Mahābhāṣya*, there are two distinct kinds of references, one kind refers to contemporary élite speakers of Sanskrit, i.e. the selfless learned Brahmins of the region of Āryāvarta, and the second kind refers to mythical sages like Yarvāṇastarvāṇa. Only the mythical sages are glorified by a supernormal mystical description, though Patañjali does not invoke their supernormal cognitive powers as an argument. It is simply a rhetorical device. The contemporary Śiṣṭas are described more in terms of their social and scholastic élitism, rather than any supernatural cognitive abilities. There is no doubt that Patañjali argues for grammar being responsive to contemporary Śiṣṭa-usage of Sanskrit. The clear argument is that a grammarian who merely knows what the form would be in terms of the inherited rules of grammar (*prāpti*) is inferior to the one who responds to the desired current standard usage (*iṣṭi*).[6] It says that an inherited system of grammatical rules is inherently an outdated system, and that it needs to be updated and revised by taking into account the contemporary Śiṣṭa usage. While Patañjali is not saying that the current age is as good as the older ages, he does not reach a point of denying the authority of the contemporary Śiṣṭas. While the ancient mythical Yarvāṇastarvāṇa are called Ṛṣis, the contemporary Śiṣṭas are not called Ṛṣis. They are exalted, and yet real human beings.

We should also refer to another distinction which we find in Patañjali's work. This is the distinction between the notions of *ācārya* versus *ṛṣi*. While the word *ācārya* is an expression of respect, it refers to real historical teachers, contemporary or otherwise. Thus, for Patañjali, Pāṇini is an *ācārya*, but the mythical Yarvāṇastarvāṇas are *ṛṣis*. This distinction between contemporary or ancestral teacher and mythical Ṛsi is found in several Dharmasūtras. For instance, the *Āpastambīyadharmasūtra* (1.2.5.4:

6 *evam hi kaścid vaiyākaraṇa āha / ko 'sya rathasya praveteti / sūta āha / āyuṣmann aham prājiteti / vaiyākaraṇa āha / apaśabda iti / sūta āha / prāptijño devānāmpriyo na tv iṣṭijña iṣyata etad rūpam iti / Mahābhāṣya* on P.2.4.56, Vol. I, p. 488.

tasmād ṛṣayo 'vareṣu na jāyante niyamātikramāt) claims that, because of the transgression of restraints, no Ṛṣis are born among the younger generations. However, it routinely refers to contemporary Ācāryas. Similarly, Pāṇini seems to consider other grammatical authorities to be Ācāryas, rather than Ṛṣis. The term *ṛṣi* in Pāṇini's rules seems to refer to Vedic seers (Cf. P.3.2.186: *kartari carṣidevatayoḥ*) or to a Vedic mantra (Cf. P.4.4.96: *bandhane carṣau*). The term *ācārya* refers to teachers whose opinions are cited (Cf. P.7.3.49: *ād ācāryāṇām*).

In Bhartṛhari, an entirely new tone has set in. There is a strong undertone that the current times are decadent, and that there are no truly authoritative persons around. Grammarians in this decadent period must look back to the golden age of the great sages and seek authority in their statements. Thus, the ancient grammarians become the Śiṣṭas with supernormal cognitive and mystical abilities, something the contemporaries of Bhartṛhari could not hope to achieve. Thus, the Śiṣṭas are no longer a contemporary community of standard speakers of Sanskrit, but the ancient sages of a golden age of Sanskrit grammar. This indicates that for Bhartṛhari the ancient grammarians are already mythologized and deified to a great extent. While Patañjali has great respect for Pāṇini, he does not call him a Ṛṣi. On the other hand, Patañjali is already a Ṛṣi for Bhartṛhari, who calls his *Mahābhāṣya* an *ārṣa* text (*VP* 2. 481c: *ārṣe ... granthe*). The later tradition clearly considers all the three sages, i.e. Pāṇini, Kātyāyana, and Patañjali to be Ṛṣis or Munis, and the beginning of this process must have already set in by the time of Bhartṛhari.

This in general confirms the set of beliefs which become more explicit in later centuries when Patañjali is more conclusively regarded as an incarnation of the divinity Śeṣa. The iconographic representation of Patañjali as a serpent divinity appears for the first time in the southern Śiva temple at Chidambaram, and the literary references to Patañjali being an incarnation of Śeṣa also probably originate in the southern tradition.[7]

7 The oldest iconographic representations of Patañjali as a form of the serpent divinity Śeṣa are found in the 13th century A.D. Natarāja temple at Chidambaram in Tamilnadu. Some of this Chidambaram iconography of Patañjali is illustrated in J.F. Staal 1972. The poem *Haracaritacintāmaṇi* by the Kashmirian poet Rājānaka Jayaratha refers to Patañjali as an incarnation of Śesa (Chapter 27, verse 167, p. 236). This poem also belongs to the 13th century. Jayaratha's narrative is in part based on the long lost *Bṛhatkathā* of Guṇāḍhya. However, no other recension of this lost work refers to Patañjali being an incarnation of Śesa. Then there is the 17th century poem *Patañjalicaritam* by the southern poet Rāmabhadra Dīkṣita which elaborates upon this theme. K.V. Abhyankar (1954: 352) suggests that the southern grammarians knew the account of the transmission of the *Mahābhāṣya* and its recovery by Candrācārya from the south, and then they

As we are informed in the concluding verses of the second *Kāṇḍa* of the *Vākyapadīya*, Bhartṛhari's grandteacher Candrācārya recovered the text of the *Mahābhāṣya* from a southern source. It is therefore likely that Bhartṛhari may have been aware of and influenced by these southern traditions regarding Patañjali as a divinity. In a decadent age when one thought that there was no grammar-independent usage of Sanskrit to be found, an identification of ancient grammarians with Śiṣṭas seems to be a way of combining the two previously independent sources of authority. While Patañjali could point to a contemporary community of Śiṣṭas who spoke standard Sanskrit without learning it from grammar books, Bhartṛhari was unable to do that. Thus, this whole argument lost its value. Under such changed conditions, Bhartṛhari created a whole new edifice of authority for Sanskrit grammar by pointing to the golden age of Sanskrit grammar where the great grammarian Ṛṣis were also the great Śiṣṭas. Bhartṛhari seems to argue that these great grammarians had a direct mystical insight into the true nature of Sanskrit and they did not need a grammar book themselves to learn Sanskrit. However, as great compassionate sages, these Munis prepared the grammatical Smṛtiśāstra for generations of lesser abilities to come. Bhartṛhari, who claims to belong to such later generations, accepts this grammatical inheritance with gratitude and reverence. Here is the beginning of the *lakṣaṇaikacakṣuṣka* phase of the Sanskrit grammatical theory.

created the elaborate myths about Patañjali appearing in Chidambaram. However, this does not explain why Patañjali should have been regarded as an incarnation of Śeṣa, rather than of some other divinity.

Bibliography

Āpastambīyadharmasūtra. Edited by Georg Bühler. 3rd edition. 1932. *Bombay Sanskrit Series*, Nos. XLIV and L. Pune: Bhandarkar Oriental Research Institute.

Abhyankar, K.V. 1954. *Prastāvanā Khaṇḍa* (Introductory Volume). Introduction to the 6 volume Marathi translation of Patañjali's *Mahābhāṣya*. Vol. 7. Pune: Deccan Education Society.

Abhyankar, K.V., and Limaye, V.P. 1965. *Vākyapadīya of Bhartṛhari*. Edited. *University of Poona Sanskrit and Prakrit Series, Vol. II*. Pune: University of Poona.

Deshpande, Madhav M. 1985. "Historical Change and the Theology of Eternal Sanskrit." In *Zeitschrift für vergleichende Sprachforschung*, Vol. 98, No. 1, pp. 122-149.

–. 1979. *Sociolinguistic Attitudes in India, An Historical Reconstruction*. Ann Arbor: Karoma Publishers, Inc.

–. (Forthcoming). *Sanskrit and Prakrit: Sociolinguistic Issues*. Delhi: Motilal Banarsidass.

–. (Forthcoming). "Sociolinguistic Parameters of Pāṇini's Sanskrit." In *Professor A.M. Ghatage Felicitation Volume*.

Haracaritacintāmaṇi, by Rājānaka Jayaratha. *Kāvyamālā Series*, No. 61. Edited by Pandit Shivadatta and Kashinath Pandurang Parab. Originally published by Nirnaya Sagara Press, Bombay. Reprinted in 1983 by Bharatiya Vidya Prakashan, Delhi.

Iyer, K.A. Subramania. 1974. *The Vākyapadīya of Bhartṛhari*, Chapter III, pt. ii, English Translation with Exegetical Notes. Delhi: Motilal Banarsidass.

–. 1973. *Vākyapadīya of Bhartṛhari, with the Prakīrṇakaprakāśa of Helārāja, Kāṇḍa III, Pt. ii.* Critically edited. Pune: Deccan College.

–. 1971. *The Vākyapadīya of Bhartṛhari*, Chapter III, pt. i, English Translation. Pune: Deccan College.

–. 1969. *Bhartṛhari: A study of the Vākyapadīya in the light of the Ancient Commentaries*. Pune: Deccan College.

–. 1966. *Vākyapadīya of Bhartṛhari, with the Vṛtti, and the Paddhati of Vṛṣabhadeva, Kāṇḍa I.* Critically edited. *Deccan College Monograph Series, No. 32.* Pune: Deccan College.

–. 1965. *The Vākyapadīya of Bhartṛhari with the Vṛtti, Chapter I, English Translation.* Pune: Deccan College.

–. 1963. *Vākyapadīya of Bhartṛhari with the commentary of Helārāja, Kāṇḍa III, Pt. 1.* Edited. Pune: Deccan College.

Mahābhāṣya of Patañjali. Edited by Franz Kielhorn in 3 volumes, 1880-1885. 3rd revised edition by K.V. Abhyankar, 1962-1972. Pune: Bhandarkar Oriental Research Institute.

Palsule, G.B. 1983. *Mahābhāṣyadīpikā of Bhartṛhari.* Fascicule I, Āhnika III. Critically edited and translated with notes. *Post-Graduate and Research Department Series, No. 22.* Pune: Bhandarkar Oriental Research Institute.

Paribhāṣenduśekhara of Nāgeśabhaṭṭa. Critically edited with the commentary *Tattvādarśa* of Vāsudev Shastri Abhyankar, by K.V. Abhyankar. Part 1. Pune: Bhandarkar Oriental Research Institute.

Patañjalicarita, by Rāmabhadra Dīkṣita. *Kāvyamālā Series*, No. 51 1895. Edited by Pandit Shivadatta and Kashinath Pandurang Parab.. Bombay: Nirnaya Sagara Press.

Staal, J.F. 1972. *A Reader on the Sanskrit Grammarians.* Cambridge: MIT Press.

BHARTṚHARI'S SOLUTION TO THE PROBLEM OF *ASAMARTHA* COMPOUNDS

Brendan S. Gillon, McGill University

As is well known, the first systematic treatment of compound formation for any language is that of Pāṇini's in his *Aṣṭādhyāyī.* The basic idea is that each compound should, in the unmarked case, be paired with a canonical phrasal paraphrase. A compound and its canonical phrasal paraphrase are grammatically linked by sharing a common derivational ancestor. The canonical phrasal paraphrase retains its stems and its abstract inflectional affixes; while the compound loses all abstract inflectional affixes but those affixed to the head stem, and a fixed linear order is imposed on all the remaining elements. Moreover, it is clear that the derivation presupposes that a common derivational ancestor has constituent structure (A 2.1.1) and the deletion involved in compound formation applies cyclically (*Mahābhāṣya* to A 2.1.1).

It is agreed that the second and fourth expressions are grammatical and synonymous while the first is ungrammatical (*Mahābhāṣya* to A 2.1.1).

(1.1) *[NP1 [AP6 ṛddhasya] (rāja < puruṣaḥ)]
(1.2) [NP1 ((ṛddha < rāja) < puruṣaḥ)]
(1.3) [NP1 [NP6 [AP6 ṛddhasya] rājñaḥ] puruṣaḥ]
(1.4) [NP1 [NP6 [AP6 ṛddhasya] rājñaḥ] puruṣaḥ]
rich king man
servant of a rich king

And this is precisely the distribution of facts which is captured by the *Aṣṭādhyāyī*. Indeed, the treatment has the universal result of preventing elements outside of a compound from being construed with subordinate elements within it.

Interestingly, a distribution, similar to that found in (1) above, holds for English.

(2.1) *(bombing < report) of cities
(2.2) [NP report [PP of the bombing [PP of cities]]]
(2.3) [NP report [PP of (city < bombing)]]
(2.4) ((city < bombing) < report)

Here, "city" is construed with "bombing" in all cases but the first, where, as an element external to a compound, it cannot be construed with subordinate elements within it. This fact of English compound formation has prompted DiSciullo and Williams (1987: p. 30) to treat such a prohibition as a constraint on compound formation within Universal Grammar.

In Sanskrit, however, there are expressions comprising a compound and another inflected word, where the inflected word is construed with an element, an uninflected word, subordinate within the compound. Compounds found in such a configuration are known as *asamartha*, or non-constitutive, compounds. An example, due to Patañjali (*Mahābhāṣya* to A 2.1.1; MBh 1.360.20), is the first of the four expressions given below.

(3.1) [NP1 [NP6 Devadattasya] (guru<kulam)]
(3.2) [NP1 (Devadatta<guru)<kulam]
(3.3) [NP1 [NP6 (Devadatta<guroḥ)] kulam]
(3.4) [NP1 [NP6 [NP6 Devadattasya] guroḥ] kulam]
Devadatta's teacher's family

In the first expression, the inflected word "Devadattasya", external to the compound "guru-kulam", is construed with the compoound's subordinate element "guru".

Asamartha compounds would be of little linguistic interest if they were simply isolated occurrences. But, the evidence is that they are not; for, *asamartha* compounds occur with the frequency of such routine phrasal constructions as indirect questions and relative clauses, not with the frequency of such marked formations as *aluk* compounds (i.e., compounds whose subordinate elements retain their inflectional morphology).

This conclusion is based on two investigations. A study of approximately three-hundred sentences, chosen essentially at random from the best representatives of the Classical Sanskrit corpus, reveals thirteen unequivocal cases of *asamartha* compounds. (See Appendix I below.) And a study of the first approximately five-hundred sentences of a single text reveals forty-three clear cases. (See Appendix II below.) On the one hand, the first sample has more occurrences of *asamartha* compounds than of indirect questions; while the second sample has more occurrences of *asamartha* compounds than of relative clauses. On the other hand, neither sample has a single *aluk* compound.

The productivity of this formation presents a serious challenge not only to Pāṇini's treatment of Sanskrit compound formation but also to DiSciullo and Williams' treatment of compound formation, which aims to provide a framework for the analysis of compound formation, whatever language it may occur in.

A successful treatment of these compounds begins with an empirically adequate characterization of the circumstances under which elements external to a compound can be construed with an element subordinate within it. The only attempt I know of to provide such a characterization is Bhartṛhari's in his *Vākyapadīya.*

(4) VP 3.14.47
sambandhi-śabdaḥ sāpekṣaḥ nityaṃ sarvaḥ prayujyate
sva-artha-vat sā vyapekṣā asya vṛttau api na hīyate.

It is always the case that relational words are all used as expressions in need <of something else>. Their need, like their denotation, is not given up, even in <word> formation.

Bhartṛhari is suggesting that at least some cases of *asamartha* compounds are cases where the subordinate element in the compound expresses a relation. It is tempting, in light of Bhartṛhari's description, to conjecture that only relational words license *asamartha* compounds and to view such cases as configurations in which the subordinate lexical element in the compound has a *kāraka* (roughly, in terms of contemporary linguistic jargon, a thematic role), which is assigned to the inflected lexical item external to the compound.

A survey of the cases found in the samples mentioned above shows that, for the most part, such is the case: the subordinate lexical element is a deverbal noun or adjective, either subcategorizing for an noun phrasal complement or having associated with its verbal root a *kāraka*, which the denotation of the external lexical item can serve as. Here is an excerpt from a sentence in *Śakuntalā* which contains two cases of *asamartha* compounding.

(5) Ś 3.9.16 <SGSC 3.1.6>
[NP1 [NP3 [NP7 tasyām] (snigdha<dṛṣṭyā)] (sūcita<abhilāṣaḥ)-B]
... whose affection was indicated by his gaze being fixed on her

In this sentence, "tasyām" is construed with "snigdha", which is known to take a 7th case noun phrasal complement (i.e.,, an NP7); and "sūcita", being a perfect passive participle, may take optionally a third case noun phrasal complement (i.e., NP3).

As attractive as this characterization might appear, it is wrong, as shown by the very examples furnished by Patañjali and repeated by Bhartṛhari. In the expression "Devadattasya gurukulam", the word "guru" is not a deverbal noun. However, it is a relational noun, but not one with which a *kāraka* is associated. It is clear, then, that relational nouns must be taken to include not only words with which *kārakas* are associated, but nouns whose meanings presuppose some kind of relation, that is, nouns such as "bhrātā" (i.e., "brother"), "rājā" (i.e., "king"), etc.

This revised characterization brings within its purview another interesting case, which, despite its commonness, has not attracted any attention, as far as I can tell, either from the traditional or the contemporary literature on Classical Sanskrit: inflected elements external to a compound can be construed with a *bahuvrīhi* compound subordinate within it. (See Appendix II, Section 3.)

(6) PVS 1.8
[S [NP5 [NP5 [NP6 (artha+(an-artha))<vivecanasya] (anumāna$_1$<āśraya)-B-tvāt] (tat$_1$<vipratipatteḥ)] [NP4 (tat$_1$<vyavasthāpanāya)] [NP1s e] [VP āha]]
Because the discrimination of the beneficial and the unbeneficial has inference for its basis <and> because of misunderstanding about it, in order to settle it, he <i.e., Dharmakīrti> says:

Here, the inflected element "artha+anartha-vivecanasya", external to the compound "anumāna-āśraya-tva", is construed with the subordinate element in it, "anumāna-āśraya", which is itself a *bahuvrīhi* compound. This construal is borne out by the paraphrase of the commentator Karnakagomin (PVST 5.1).

Unfortunately, *asamartha* compounds are not confined to cases where the subordinate element in the compound expresses a relation, onto which the denotation of the external element can be hooked. Consider the following case.

(7) V 2.134 <SGSC 9.1.3>
[AP1 [ADV dṛḍham] [PRT khalu] [NP7 tvayi] (baddha<bhāvā)-B]] [NP1S Ūrvaśī].
Indeed, Ūrvaśī is one whose affection is firmly fixed on you.

Here, there are two elements external to the compound being construed with a subordinate element within the compound. One of the two external elements is construed with the element subordinate within the compound in precisely the way discussed above. In this case, the element external to the compound is the seventh case noun phrase, "tvayi", which is to be construed with the element subordinate within the compound, the perfect passive participle "baddha", which takes a seventh case noun phrasal complement. The other element external to the compound construed with "baddha" is the adverb "dṛḍham", whose occurrence cannot be predicted either from *kārakas* associated with "baddha" or from its meaning.

An important peculiarity of some cases where an adverbial element external to a compound modifies an element within it is that the adverbial element may function adjectivally, as illustrated below, instead of adverbially, as seen above.

(8.1) PVS 3.17
[NP3 aṃśena] [NP1s (((janya + janaka)-tva) < prasangaḥ)]
the absurdity of partial causation

Here, the adverb "aṁśena" is construed with "janya + janaka-tva", functioning to modify it adjectivally, not adverbially. Below, the adverb "bahulam" is construed to function as an adjectival predicate of "pakva", a construal borne out by the Tibetan translation (personal communication from Richard Hayes).

(8.2) PVS 10.15
[s na hi [ABC [NP7 [ADV bahulam] pakva < darśane) api]]
[NP3 ((sthāli < antargamana) < mātreṇa)] [NP1s pākaḥ] [VP _ sidhyati]
[NP5 (vyabhicāra < darśanāt)]]
For, even if the cooked ones are observed to be many, the cooking <of something> is not established by <its> mere inclusion in a pot, because of the observation of deviation.

Another *asamartha* configuration involves elements external to a compound being construed appositionally with subordinate elements within the compound.

(9) PVST 53.21
[s [NP6 [aham iti] (buddhi < rahitasya)] [ADV katham] [AP1 parārthā api]
[NP1s _ pravṛttiḥ]]
How is it that an undertaking by one who is devoid of an idea of self be also altruistic?

Here, "aham iti" is to be construed with "buddhi", an element subordinate within the compound "buddhi-rahitasya".

It might be thought that that "aham iti" forms part of the compound. But this is unlikely, for the appropriate form of the first person personal pronoun, when occurring in a compound, is "mat", not "aham". I suppose one might conjecture that the need for "mat" is obviated by use of "iti", turning "aham" into a name. But this conjecture does not generalize in any plausible way. First, these constructions are not confined to simple words: entire clauses, fully and appropriately inflected, may occur as external elements; and these clauses are not plausibly names in any usual sense of the word. (See Appendix II, Section 2.2, example (23).)

Second, these appositional elements may occur without any "iti"; and when they do, they are inflected for the case the element with which it is in apposition would have were it not in the compound.

(10) PVS 15.20
[S yena [NP5 [NP6 (vacana-ādeḥ)] (((kim-cit) < mātra) < sādharmyāt)]
[NP1s ((sarva < ākāra) < sāmyam)] [VP anumīyeta]]
so that one might infer from the fact that a mere something, say speaking, is common, that every feature is common.

Here, "vacana-ādeḥ" is in apposition with "kim-cit-mātra"; the sixth case noun (i.e., the NP6) of "vacana-ādeḥ" is the case "kimcit-mātra", with which "vacana-ādeḥ" is in apposition, would have were it not in compound. (See Appendix II, Section 2.2, example (24) for another instance.)

Surprisingly, even locative absolutes can be construed with elements subordinate within a compound.

(11) PVS 2.6
[NP1 [ABC [NP7 [NP5 sāmarthyāt] (artha < gatau)]] (((pratipatti < gaurava) < parihāra)ārtham)-B]
whose purpose is to exclude a burden on <one's> understanding, when one understands the meaning <of the definition> through implication.

In this case, the phrase "sāmarthyāt artha-gatau" is construed, not with the entire compound, but with "pratipatti-gaurava", a subordinate element within the compound. (For other cases, see Appendix II, Section 2.3.)

The foregoing evidence suggests several conclusions. First and foremost, *asamartha* compounds are not to be dismissed as bad style or marginal. The cases adduced in this study are found in the best authors of Classical Sanskrit, including Kālidāsa, Bāṇa, and Dharmakīrti. Indeed, Patañjali himself uses *asamartha* compounds. Here are two instances found in his *Paspaśāhnika*:

(12.1) MBh 1.1.15
[AP1 [NP7 (rakṣa < arthe) [NP6 vedānām]] adhyeyam] [NP1s vyākaraṇam]
Grammar is to be studied for the sake of the preservation of the Vedas.

(12.2) MBh 1.9.20
[AP1 mahān] hi [NP1s [NP6 śabdasya] (prayoga < viṣayaḥ)]
For the domain of the usage of verbal expression is large.

In the former sentence, "veda" is to be construed as the patient, or *karma*, of "raksa"; while in the latter, "śabda" is to be construed as the agent, or *kartā*, of "prayoga".

The second conclusion is that the formation is productive. It occurs with a frequency equal to that of relative clauses and indirect questions, hardly arcane constructions in Classical Sanskrit. This frequency contrasts dramatically with the frequency of known marked compound formations, such as *aluk* compounds, which, as it turns out, do not occur at all in either sample assayed.

The third conclusion is that these compounds present a serious empirical and theoretical challenge to the linguistic study of Classical Sanskrit, whether from the point of view of traditional Sanskrit grammar or from the point of view of current linguistics. To begin with, these compounds cannot be accommodated by Pāṇini's treatment of compounds: elements subordinate to other elements subordinate within a compound must lose their inflection, unless they are *aluk* compounds. Now some hope of a theoretically satisfying account of *asamartha* compounds was held out by a marriage of Bhartṛhari's empirical characterization of them with the mechanism of compound formation found in Di Sciullo and Williams (1987). But, as was shown, configurations where the elements external to the compound are adverbs, appositional clauses and noun phrases, and locative absolutes belie Bhartṛhari's empirical characterization and thereby elude any straightforward treatment by the mechanism of compound formation proposed in Di Sciullo and Williams.

Notation

Anaphoric Co-indexation: index to the immediate right.
B: appended to bahuvrīhi cpds, so-called exocentric cpds
Case Marking: occurs at the end of phrasal label following Pāṇinian numbering; AP adjectival phrase NP noun phrase; PP prepositonal phrase; VP verb phrase; NP1s is subject noun phrase.
Parentheses: lexical constituent structure
Square Brackets: phrasal constituent structure
phrasal labels: [ABC] locative absolute
[PC] participial phrase
Subordination: "x<y" means that x is subordinate to y

Abbreviations

A *Aṣṭādhyāyī* <adhyāya.pāda.sūtra>.
K *Kādambarī*; Peterson (ed) 1885 <page.line>.
M *Mālavikāgnimitra*; Iyar (ed) 1896 <act.verse.line>.
MBh *Mahābhāṣya*; Kielhorn (ed) 1880 <volume.page.line>.
P *Pañcatantra*; Kielhorn (ed) 1896 <tantra.page.line>.
PVS *Pramāṇavārttika-svavṛtti*; Gnoli (ed) 1960 <page.line>.
PVST *Pramāṇavārttika-svavṛtti-ṭīkā*; Sankrityayana (ed) 1943 <page.line>.
SGSC Apte 1885 <chapter.exercise.sentence>.
Ś *Śakuntalā*; Godabole (ed) 1933 <page.verse.line>.
V *Vikramorvaśīyam*; Pandit (ed) 1889 <act.verse.line>.
Ve *Veṇīsaṃhāra*; Parab (ed) 1930 <act.verse.line>.
VP *Vākyapadīya*; Iyer (ed) 1973 <kāṇḍa.samuddeśa.kārikā>.

Acknowledgements

This paper is based on work done in 1986 while I was a senior fellow of the American Institute of Indian Studies, affiliated with the Centre for the Advanced Study of Sanskrit at Poona University. While there I had the opportunity to learn from and work with a number of scholars. I am especially grateful to Dr. Siniruddha Dash. I was also privileged to receive advice and guidance from Paṇḍit Śrī T.S. Śrīnivāsa Śāstrī and Śrī Venugopalan of Deccan College.

I also wish to thank Prof. Kamaleshwar Bhattacharya and Prof. Richard Hayes for their advice pertaining to a number of sentences discussed here.

Bibliography

Aklujkar, Ashok 1991 *Sanskrit: An Easy Introduction to an Enchanting Language*. Richmond, British Columbia (Canada): Svādhyāya Publications.

Apte, Vāman Shivarām 1885 *The Student's Guide to Sanskrit Composition. A Treatise on Sanskrit Syntax for Use of Schools and Colleges*. Poona, India: Lokasamgraha Press, 24th edition (1960).

Apte, Vāman Shivarām 1890 *The Practical Sanskrit-English Dictionary*. Poona, India: Prasad Prakashan, revised and enlarged edition (1957).

Bhaṭṭoji Dīkṣita *Siddhānta-Kaumudī*. Sanskrit Edition and English Translation: Vasu, Śrīśa Chandra (ed) (tr) 1906.

Boose, Emery and Gary Tubb 1981 "Rough Draft of Portions of a Handbook Designed to Aid Students in the Use of Sanskrit Commentaries". Unpublished mss., Harvard University.

Cardona, George 1988 *Pāṇini: His Work and Its Traditions. Background and Introduction.* New Delhi: Motilal Banarsidass.

Coulson, Michael 1976 *Sanskrit: An Introduction to the Classical Language*. London, England: Hodder and Stoughton (Teach Yourself Books).

Dash, Siniruddha 1986 *The Syntax and Semantics of Sanskrit Nominal Compounds*. Poona, India: University of Poona, Centre of Advanced Study in Sanskrit.

Deshpande, Madhav M. 1985 *Ellipsis and Syntactic Overlapping: Current Issues in Pāṇinian Syntactic Theory*. Poona, India: Bhandarkar Oriental Research Institute (Post-graduate and Research Department Series no. 24).

Di Sciullo, Anna Maria and Edwin Williams 1987 *On the Definition of Word*. Cambridge, Massachusetts: The MIT Press.

Gnoli, Raniero (ed) 1960 *The Pramāṇavārttikam of Dharmakīrti: The First Chapter with the Autocommentary. Text and Critical Notes.* Rome, Italy: Istituto Italiano per Il Medio ed Estremo Oriente: (Serie Orientale Roma: 23).

Godabole, N.B. (ed) 1933 *Śakuntalā*. Bombay: Nirṇaya Sāgara Press (revised by W.L. Panśīkar).

Iyer, K.A. Subramania (ed) 1973 *Vākyapadīya of Bhartṛhari with the Prakīrṇakaprakāśa of Helārāja*. Poona: Deccan College.

Iyyar, Seshādri (ed) 1896 *Mālavikāgnimitra*. Poona.

Kale, Moreshwar Ramchandra 1894 *A Higher Sanskrit Grammar*. Reprint: Delhi: Motilal Barnasidass, 1977.

Kielhorn, F. (ed) 1880 *The Vyākarana Mahābhāṣya of Patañjali*. Poona, India: Bhandarkar Oriental Research Institute (4th edition revised by R.N. Dandekar 1985).

Kielhorn, Franz (ed) 1896 *Pañcatantra*. Bombay: Government Central Book Depot (Bombay Sanskrit Series: vv. 1, 3, 4). [Tantra 1 edited by Kielhorn; Tantra 2 through 5 edited by G. Buhler.]

Peterson, P. (ed) 1885 *Kādambarī*. Bombay: Government Central Book Depot (Bombay Sanskrit Series: v. 24).

Pandit, S.P. (ed) 1889 *Vikramorvaśīyam*. Bombay: Government Central Book Depot (Bombay Sanskrit Series: v. 16), 2nd edition.

Parab, K.B. (ed) 1930 *Veṇīsaṃhāra*. Bombay: Nirṇaya Sāgara Press, 7th edition (revised by W.L. Panśīkar).

Renou, Louis 1961 *Grammaire Sanscrite*. 2 vols. Paris: Addrien-Maisonneuve.

Sāṁkṛtyāyana, Rāhula (ed) 1943 *Ācārya-Dharmakīrteḥ Pramāṇavārttikam (svārthānumāna-paricchedaḥ) Svopajñavṛttyā Karṇakagomi-viracitayā taṭṭīkayā ca sahitam*. Allahabad, India: Kitab Mahal.

Vasu, Śrīśa Chandra (ed) (tr) 1906 *The Siddhānta Kaumudī of Bhaṭṭoji Dikṣita*. Allahabad, India: The Pāṇini Office. Reprint: Delhi, India: Motilal Banarsidass, 1962.

Whitney, William Dwight 1881 *Sanskrit Grammar: Including both the Classical language, and the older Dialects, of Veda and Brahmana*. Cambridge, Massachusetts: Harvard University Press, 2nd edition (1889), 11th reprint (1967).

APPENDIX I

Study of a Random Sample of Classical Sanskrit Prose

The sample from which sentences below are taken comprise the three hundred exercise sentences of SGSC, taken by V.S. Apte from a variety of Classical Sanskrit texts.

(1) Ś 3.9.16 < = SGSC 3.1.6>
[NP1 [NP3 [NP7 tasyām] (snigdha<dṛṣṭyā)] (sūcita<abhilāṣaḥ)B]
... whose affection was indicated by his gaze being fixed on her.
Remark: "snigdha" subcategorizes for NP7.
NP3 denotes the agent of "sūcita".

(2) K119.14 < = SGSC 3.1.12>
[NP6 [NP6 ... (nija<balasya)] (viśrāma<hetoḥ)]
... in order to rest his own army.
Remark: NP6 denotes the theme (karma) of "viśrāma".

(3) Ś 6.4.4 < = SGSC 6.1.4> <Prakrt>
[AP1 (a-śruta<pūrvaḥ)) [NP3 āvābhyām]] (NP1S [AP1 eṣaḥ] vṛttāntaḥ]
This news had not been previously heard by the two of us.
Remark: NP3 denotes the agent of "śruta".

(4) K 356.13 < = SGSC 8.2.1>
[NP1 [NP5 (janma<karmataḥ)] ((malina-tara)<janam)-B]
... where people are dirtier than their actions or deeds.
Remark: *-tara* subcategorizes for an NP5.

(5) K 356.13 < = SGSC 8.2.1>
[NP1 [NP5 janataḥ] ((nistriṁśa-tara)<(loka<hṛdayam))-B]
... where worldly hearts are more pitiless than the people.
Remark: *-tara* subcategorizes for an NP5.

(6) K 356.13 < = SGSC 8.2.1>
[NP1 [NP5 (loka<hṛdebhyaḥ)]
(((nirghṛṇa-tara)<(sarva<saṁvyavahāra))<(samasta<puruṣam))-B]
... where every person's behavior is always more cruel than their worldly hearts.
Remark: *-tara* subcategorizes for an NP5.

(7) V 2.134 < = SGSC 9.1.3>
[AP1 [ADV dṛḍham] ... [NP7 tvayi] (baddha<bhāvā)-B]] [NP1S Ūrvaśī].
Ūrvaśī is one whose affection is firmly fixed on you.
Remark: "badh" subcategorizes for an NP7.
ADV modifies "baddha".

(8) V 2.129 < = SGSC 14.1.4>
na asmi [NP1 [NP7 bhavatyoḥ] ((īśvara<niyoga)<pratyarthī)]
I am not hostile to the charge to you two of <your> master.
Remark: Verbs of entrusting, such as "niyuj", subcategorize for an NP7 to denote the recipient of the charge.

(9) Ś 3.15.6 < = SGSC 14.2.1>
[AP3 [NP6 ... janasya] (ārti<hareṇa)] [NP3 rajñā] bhavitavyam.
A king must be one who removes the suffering of ... people ...
Remark: NP6 denotes the agent of "ārti".

(10) Ś 7.14.6 < = SGSC 28.1.4>
[NP1 [NP3 (ṛṣi<janena)] [(sarva<damanaḥ) iti] (kṛta<nāmadheyaḥ)] asi
... You are called the queller of all by the sages.
Remark: NP3 denotes the agent of "kṛta".

(11) K 294.5 < = SGSC 28.2.1>
... [NP1S [AP1 [NP6 anayoḥ api] ((a-darśana)<kṛtāḥ] kleśāḥ]
The pains brought about by not seeing those two as well ...
Remark: NP6 denotes the theme (karma) of *darśana*.

In addition, there are a number of cases where an inflected element external to a compound might be construed with one of its subordinate elements, but need not be. These cases may be divided into two, depending on whether the inflected element external to the compound is an argument or not of the compound's subordinate element. The former cases are: Ve 2.26.4 < = SGSC 1.1.5>, V 3.46.18 < = SGSC 2.2.1>, K 292.6 < = SGSC 5.1.7>, V 3.20 < = SGSC 18.1.1>; the latter cases are: Ś 3.5.2 < = SGSC 3.1.4>, M 1.12.7 < = SGSC 6.1.2>, V 2.129 < = SGSC 14.1.4>, Ś 1.7.2 < = SGSC 22.1.2>, and P 1.88.12 < = SGSC 27.1.6>.

APPENDIX II

Study of a Single Text of Classical Sanskrit Prose

The sample from which sentences below are taken comprise the first four hundred and fifty or so sentences of PVS, the preponderance of which are prose.

1. Arguments

(1) PVS 1.7
[AP1 [NP7 atra] (anubaddha<spṛham)-B]
one who has eagerness for this.
Remark: "anubaddha" subcategorizes for an NP7.

(2) PVS 2.2
[NP5 ... [NP7 dṛṣṭānta-dharmiṇi] (sattva<siddheḥ)]
because of the establishment of <its> presence in the corroborating instance.
Remark: NP7 denotes the locus of "sattva".

(3) PVS 2.11
[NP5 [NP6 vaktuḥ] (abhiprāya<vaśāt)]]
by dint of the intention of the speaker.
Remark: NP6 denotes the agent of "abhiprāya".

(4) PVS 3.11
[NP5 [NP6 ... bhavataḥ] (((tat<utpatti)<niyama)<abhāvāt)]]
because of the absence of necessity of the arising from it of an existent.
Remark: NP6 is the agent of "utpatti".

(5) PVS 7.3
[AP7 [NP6 ((sāmagrī<phala)<śaktīnām)] (pariṇāma<anubandhini)]
which depends on the development of the potentialities for the result of <its> causal totality.
Remark: NP6 is the agent of "pariṇāma".

(6) PVS 7.5
[NP5 [NP6 ... śaktīnām] (pariṇāma<apekṣatvāt) ...]
because of the need for the development of the potentialities.
Remark: NP6 is the agent of "parināma".

(7) PVS 8.1
[NP1 [NP6 (rūpa<(upādāna-hetūnām))] (pravṛtti<kāraṇam)]
the cause of the activation of the material causes of color.
Remark: NP6 is the agent of "pravṛtti".

(8) PVS 8.12
[NP5 [NP6 ((a-pratibaddha)<svabhāvasya)-B] ((avinābhāva<niyama)<abhāvāt)]]
because of the absence of the necessity of the indispensability of that whose nature is unrelated.
Remark: NP6 is the complement of "avinābhāva".

(9) PVS 12.23
[ABC [NB7 ... [NP7 (kva-cit)] (abhāva<siddhau) api]]
even if there is the establishement of an absence in some place.
Remark: NP7 denotes the locus of "abhāva".

(10) PVS 12.23
[NP5 [NP6 (a-pratibaddhasya)] ... (abhāva<(a-siddheḥ))]
because of the non-establishment of the absence of what is unconnected.
Remark: NP6 denotes the agent of "abhāva".

(11) PVS 13.4
[NP5 [NP6 (ghaṭa-ādīnām)] (nairātmya<(a-siddheḥ)]
because of the non-establishment of selflessness of such things as pots.
Remark: NP6 denotes the possessor of "nairātmya".

(12) PVS 15.4
[NP3 [NP6 asya api] [NP7 [AP7 (kva-cit)] viśeṣe] (sambhava<āśaṅkayā)]
through uncertainty about the existence of it too in any species.
Remark: NP6 denotes the agent of "sambhava".

(13) PVS 16.1
[NP5 ... [NP6 ((a-dṛṣṭa)<viśeṣāṇām)-B] (((vijātīyatva<upagama)<virodhāt)]
because of the contradiction of the acceptance of the heterogeneity of those things whose special qualities are unobserved.
Remark: NP6 denotes the possessor of "vijātīyatva".

(14) PVS 16.20
[NP5 [NP7 (a-(para<artheṣu))] saṁghātatva<(a-darśanāt))
because of the non-observation of the compositeness of things not for others.
Remark: NP7 denotes the locus of "saṃghātatva".

(15) PVS 17.23
[NP1s [NP6 sādhanasya] ((sādhya<vyabhicāra)<āśaṅkā)]
uncertainty about the deviation of the establisher from the establishable.
Remark: NP6 denotes the agent of "vyabhicāra".

(16) PVS 19.3
[NP5 [NP6 (artha1<antarasya)] (((tat1<anubandha)<niyama)<abhāvāt)]
because of the absence of the necessity of dependence on it of what is other than it.
Remark: NP6 denotes the agent of "anubandha".

(17) PVS 19.20
[ADV ... [NP6 anyasya] (prasiddhi<artham)]
for the sake of the establishment of another.
Remark: NP6 denotes the agent of "prasiddhi".

(18) PVS 20.16
[NP1s ((avaśyam<bhāva)<niyamaḥ) _] ... [NP6 parasya]
the necessity of the inevitable presence of another.
Remark: NP6 denotes the agent of "avaśyam-bhāva".

2. Non-Arguments

2.1 External Element an Adverb

(19) PVS 3.17
[NP3 aṁśena] (NP1s (((janya+janaka)-tva)<prasaṅgaḥ)]
the absurdity of partial causation.
Remark: NP3 modifies "janya-janaka-tva" adjectivally.

(20) PVS 10.15
[s na hi [ABC [NP7 [ADV bahulam] pakva<darśane) api]] [NP3 ((sthāli<antargamana)<mātreṇa)] [NP1s pākaḥ] [VP _ sidhyati] [NP5 (vyabhicāra<darśanāt)]]
For, even if the cooked ones are observed to be many, the cooking <of something> is not established by <its> mere inclusion in a pot, because of the observation of deviation.
Remark: ADV modifies "pakva" adjectivally, as is borne out by the Tibetan. (personal communication: Richard Hayes)

(21) PVS 21.7
[AP1 [NP3 (sattā<upalambhena)] [ADV sarvadā] (((tathā<bhāva)<śaṅkā)<vipralabdhaḥ)]
deceived by his apprehension of <a thing's> presence into the suspicion of <its> always being so.
Remark: ADV modifies "tathā-bhāva".

2.2 External Element an Appositive

(22) PVS 15.20
[S yena [NP5 [NP6 (vacana-ādeḥ)] (((kim-cit)<mātra)<sādharmyāt)] [NP1s ((sarva<ākāra)<sāmyam)] [VP anumīyeta]]
so that one might infer from the fact that a mere something, say speaking, is common, that every feature is common.
Remark: NP6 is in apposition to "kimcit-mātra".

(23) PVS 17.23
[NP5 [[S [NP5 ((eka<dharma)1<sadbhāvāt)] [VP [NP3 (tat1<anyena) api] bhavitavyam]] iti] (niyama<abhāvāt)]
because of the absence of a determination to the effect that, from the existence of one property one different from it too must exist.
Remark: "iti" clause is in apposition with "niyama".

(24) PVS 20.12
[NP3 [NP3 ... a-gatyā] ... (((iti-ādi)<bheda)<prayogaiḥ)]
through the formulation of such differentia as the non-understanding ...
Remark: NP3 is in apposition with "bheda".

2.3 External Element a Locative Absolute

(25) PVS 2.4
[ABC [NP7 (sādhya<abhāve)]] ((a-sattva)<vacana)-vat
like the statement of <its> non-presence in the absence of what is to be established.
Remark: ABC places a condition on "a-sattva".

(26) PVS 2.6
[NP1 [ABC [NP7 [NP5 sāmarthyāt] (artha<gatau)]]
(((pratipatti<gaurava)<parihāra)<artham)-B]
whose purpose is to exclude a burden on <one's> understanding, when one understands the meaning <of the definition> through implication.
Remark: ABC places a condition on "pratipatti".

(27) PVS 12.23
[NP5 [NP6 (a-pratibaddhasya)] [ABC [NP7 (tat<abhāve) [AP7 sarvatra]]] (abhāva<(a-siddheḥ))]
because of the non-establishment of the absence of what is unconnected in every absence of it.
Remark: ABC places a condition on last "abhāva".

3. Internal Element is a *Bahuvrīhi* Compound

(28) PVS 1.8
[S [NP5 [NP5 [NP6 (artha+(an-artha))<vivecanasya] (anumāna1<āśraya)-B-tvāt]
(tat1<vipratipatteḥ)] [NP4 (tat1<vyavasthāpanāya)] [NP1s e] [VP āha]]
Because the discrimination of the beneficial and the unbeneficial has inference for its basis <and> because of misunderstanding about it, in order to settle it, he <i.e., Dharmakīrti> says:
Remark: Commentator construes NP6 with "anumāna-āśraya", construed as a *bahuvrīhi*.

(29) PVS 3.1
[S na [NP1s E] [NP1 arthaḥ api] [NP5 [NP6 (vikalpa<bhedānām) [AP6 svatantrāṇām]]
(an-(artha<āśraya))-B-tvāt]]

<it> is not a fact as well, since conceptual differentiation, being independent <of fact>, does not have a basis in it.
Remark: NP6 is to be construed with "an-artha-āśraya", treated as a *bahuvrīhi.*

(30) PVS 5.2
[s evam [NP1s [NP6 [AP6 anayoḥ] anupalabdhyoḥ] [NP5 ((svaí + viparyaya) < hetu) < (abhāva + bhāvābhyām))] (((sat < vyavahāra)1 < pratiṣedha) < phala)-B-tvam] [AP1 tulyam] [NP5 [NP7 ekatra] saṁśayād] [NP5 [NP7 anyatra] viparyayāt]]
Thus, the fact that both <types of> non-apprehension result in the inhibition of activities with respect to what is present through the absence of a reason for it and through the presence of a reason for its contrary is the same because of doubt in the one case and because of contariety in the other.
Remark: NP6 is to be construed with "sat-...-phala", treated as a *bahuvrīhi.*

(31) PVS 7.10
[s [NP5 (((pūrva < sajāti) < mātra) < hetu)-B-tvāt [NP6 (śakti < prasūteḥ)]] [NP1s [NP6 sāmagryāḥ] yogyatā] [VP [[AP1 (an-(anya < apekṣiṇī))] iti] ucyate]]
The aptitude of a <causal> totality is said not to require anything else because the generation of potentiality has for its cause merely the previous similar <causal totality>.
Remark: NP6 is to be construed with "pūrva-...-hetu", treated as a *bahuvrīhi.*

(32) PVS 9.17
[s na E [NP5 [NP6 (para < arthasya) eva] [NP3 phalatvena] istatvāt [NP5 ((icchā-lakṣaṇa)-B-tvāt) [NP6 phalasya]]]]
<This> is not <so>, because only the benefit of another is intended as a result, since a result is the object of desire.
Remark: NP6 is to be construed with "icchā-lakṣaṇa", treated as a *bahuvrīhi.*

(33) PVS 16.1
[s na [AP evam] [NP1s vākyāni 1] [NP5 [NP6 e 1] ((dṛśya < viśeṣa2)-B-tvāt)] [NP5 [ABC [NP7 (a-dṛśyatve) api [NP6 e 2]]] [NP6 ((a-dṛṣṭa) < viśeṣāṇām)B 3] (((vijātīyatva < upagama) < virodhāt)] [NP5 [NP6 (tat3 < viśeṣāṇām)] [NP7 anyatra api] (śakya < kriyatvāt)] [NP5 [NP6 [AP6 pratyakṣāṇām] śabdānām] (((a-pratyakṣa) < svabhāva)B < abhāvāt)] [NP5 ((bhrānti < nimitta) < abhāvāt) [NP5 [NP5 (bādhaka < abhāvāt)] (bhrānti < a-siddheḥ))]]]
Sentences are not like that <1> because their special qualities are observable, and <2> because, even if they were unobservable, it is contradictory to accept the heterogeneity of those with unobserved special qualities <from those without>, <2.1> because their differences can be created elsewhere too <i.e., in non-Vedic sentences>, <2.2> because perceptible sounds do not have the nature of what is imperceptible, <3> because there is no basis for error <3.1> because error is not established because there is no contravening cognition.
Remark: The NP6 "pratyakṣāṇām śabdānām" is to be construed with "apratyakṣa-svabhāva", treated as a *bahuvrīhi.*

(34) PVS 21.7
[s [NP1s [AP1 [PC [NP2 [AP2 tām] punar [NP6 asya] (((kṣaṇa<sthiti)1<dharma)-B-tām)] [NP2 svabhāvam 2] [NP6 [NP6 (sva2<hetoḥ) eva] (tathā1<utpatteḥ)] paśyan api]] (manda<buddhiḥ)-B [AP1 [NP3 (sattā<upalambhena)] [ADV sarvadā] (((tathā<bhāva)<śaṅkā)<vipralabdhaḥ)] [VP E na vyavasyati]]
A dull-witted person, deceived by his apprehension of <a thing's> existence into the suspicion of <its> always being so, does not ascertain its having the property of persisting <but> a moment to be <its> nature, even though, because a thing arises from its own causes to be that way, he sees it thus.
Remark: NP6 is to be construed with "kṣaṇa-sthiti-dharma", treated as a *bahuvrīhi*.

KAMALAŚĪLA'S INTERPRETATION OF SOME VERSES IN THE VĀKYAKĀṆḌA OF BHARTṚHARI'S VĀKYAPADĪYA

Masaaki Hattori, Kyoto

In the *Tattvasaṃgraha* (abbrev.: *TS*) of Śāntarakṣita (ca. 725-788 A.D.), various views maintained by scholars of different schools are critically examined and repudiated. For the purpose of examination the author Śāntarakṣita often introduces the view of others by the citation from their works.

The 16th chapter of *TS*, viz., Śabdārthaparīkṣā, is devoted to the problem of meaning. As a follower of Dignāga and Dharmakīrti, Śāntarakṣita maintains the *apoha*-theory, i.e., the theory that the function of a word consists not in the direct reference to a real object but in the differentiation (*apoha*) of an object from other things. He begins this chapter with the discussions that a word does not directly denote a specific feature (*svalakṣaṇa*), nor an individual (*vyakti*), nor a universal (*jāti*), nor the relation (*saṃbandha*) between an individual and a universal, and firmly establishes his theory through severe criticism on the views put forward by Bhāmaha, Kumārila and Uddyotakara against the *apoha*-theory. Before introducing their arguments, the author makes reference to some views which recognize something other than *svalakṣaṇa*, etc. as the meaning of a word, and criticizes these views. In that portion he quotes the following six verses (*TS*, 886-891) from the Vākyakāṇḍa of Bhartṛhari's Vākyapadīya (abbrev.: *VP*).[1]

886 asty arthaḥ sarvaśabdānām iti pratyāyyalakṣaṇam /
apūrvadevatāsvargaiḥ samam āhur gavādiṣu // (*VP*, II.119)

1 The editions used are as below.
TS: Bauddha Bharati Ser., 1, vol. 1. Varanasi 1968. (GOS edition gives exactly the same reading. The verse-numbers in it are 887-892.)
VP: (1) R = Rau, W. (ed.), *Bhartṛharis Vākyapadīya*. Wiesbaden 1977 (Abhandlungen für die Kunde des Morgenlandes, XLII, 4).
(2) I = Iyer, K.A. Subramania (ed.), *The Vākyapadīya of Bhartṛhari, Kāṇḍa II, with the Commentary of Puṇyarāja and the Ancient Vṛtti*. Delhi, etc.: Motilal Banarsidass, 1983.
The quotations of *VP*, II.119, 126-128, 132 in *TS* are pointed out in K.V. Abhyankar and V.P. Limaye (ed.), *Vākyapadīya of Bhartṛhari*, Poona 1965 (Univ. of Poona Skt. and Pkt. Ser., 2), Appendix III, pp. 220-223.

887 samudāyo 'bhidheyo vāpy avikalpasamuccayaḥ /
asatyo vāpi saṃsargaḥ śabdārthaḥ kaiś cid iṣyate // (126)

888 asatyopādhi yat satyaṃ tad vā śabdanibandhanam /
śabdo vāpy abhijalpatvam āgato yāti vācyatām // (127)
b: nibandhanām R d: vācyatam R

889 so 'yam ity abhisaṃbandhād rūpam ekīkṛtaṃ yadā /
śabdasyārthena taṃ śabdam abhijalpaṃ pracakṣate // (128)

890 yo vārtho buddhiviṣayo bāhyavastunibandhanaḥ /
sa bāhyaṃ vastv iti jñātaḥ śabdārthaḥ kaiś cid iṣyate // (132)
d: śabdārtha iti gamyate R

891 abhyāsāt pratibhāhetuḥ sarvaḥ śabdaḥ samāsataḥ /
bālānāṃ ca tiraścāṃ ca yathārthapratipādane // (117)
b: sarvaḥ śabdo (śabdaḥ sarvo) 'paraiḥ smṛtaḥ R (I)

Seven views are referred to in these six verses. (1) 886: All words simply mean that 'something exists'. Such words as *apūrva, devatā* and *svarga* do not produce a form of any particular object in the mind of a hearer. They simply make him understand that there exists something which is called '*apūrva*', etc. It is known by extension that the word '*go*' (cow) and the like also mean only that 'something exists'. (2) 887ab: An aggregate free from option (*vikalpa*) and accumulation (*samuccya*) is the denotation of a word. (3) 887cd: The unreal relation of a thing with its universal is the meaning of a word. (4) 888ab: The real with unreal adjuncts is the cause of the application of a word. (5) 888cd, 889: When the form of a word becomes identified with the object, this word is called *abhijalpa*. The meaning of a word is nothing other than the word in the state of *abhijalpa*. (6) 890: When the image of a thing, which is caused by an external object, is externalized, it is recognized as the meaning of a word. (7) 891: All words are the cause of *pratibhā* (intuition) through repeated practice, as in the case of making things understood to infants and animals. This *pratibhā* is the meaning of a word.

These seven views are among those which are enumerated by Bhartṛhari in *VP*, Vākyakāṇḍa, 116ff.[2] It is not known by whom these views were advocated. The seventh view seems to represent Bhartṛhari's own idea, since the concept of *pratibhā* is peculiar to his theory of meaning. However, while Bhartṛhari considers *pratibhā* as the meaning of a sentence

2 In *VP*, II.116, Bhartṛhari states: *avikalpe 'pi vākyārthe vikalpā bhāvanāśrayāḥ / atrādhikaraṇe vādāḥ pūrveṣāṃ bahudhā matāḥ* (*gatāḥ* I) (Although the meaning of a sentence is not diversified, there arises diversification [into the meanings of component words] on the basis of *bhāvanā* [of different persons]. Concerning this subject, the discussions of ancient scholars took place variously.) Then he introduces thirteen views concerning the meaning of a word.

(*vākya*), the idea expressed in *TS*, 891 (*VP*, II.117) is that *pratibhā* is caused by any word, whether it is a single word or a sentence. It may be either that Bhartṛhari admitted that *pratibhā* is caused even by a single word or that *TS*, 891 represents a view maintained by some unknown predecessor of Bhartṛhari.[3]

An elaborate commentary on *TS*, viz., the *TS-Pañjikā* (abbrev.: *TSP*), was written by Kamalaśīla (ca. 740-745 A.D.), a direct disciple of Śāntarakṣita. In this commentary we find a clear and intelligible explanation of each verse quoted above. There is a *ṭīkā* on the Vākyakāṇḍa of *VP* (abbrev.: *VPT*), which is usually ascribed to Puṇyarāja[4], who is supposed to have lived in the first half of the 10th century[5], that is, much later than Kamalaśīla. The explanation of the above-cited verses in *VPT* is not always clear enough to make the meaning of the verse understandable. This deficiency is covered by the appropriate interpretation of the verses presented in *TSP*. I shall cite two examples.

Introducing the verse 127ab which states that *satya* possessing *asatya* as an adjunct (*upādhi*) is the cause of *śabda*, *VPT* states: "*atha satyam evāsatyopādhivicitritaṃ śabdavācyam iti ṣaṣṭhaṃ pakṣam āha*," and gives no further explanation. This *ṭīkā* does not help us understand what is meant by '*satya*' and '*asatya*'. A clear explanation on this verse is furnished in *TSP*: "When the adjuncts, i.e., the particulars such as bracelet, ring, and so on, which are unreal (*asatya*) as the denotation of a word, belong to the real (*satya*), i.e., gold (*suvarṇa*) which is of generic character and permeates all the particulars, then it is called 'real with unreal adjuncts' (*satyam asatyopādhi*)."

Kamalaśīla's interpretation of this verse is based on *VP*, III.2 (Dravyasamuddeśa), kk. 2-4:[6]

3 Dr. J. Houben suggested me in personal communication that Bhartṛhari might have admitted that *pratibhā* is produced even by a single word. He may discuss this point in one of his future articles.

4 At the end of *VPT* there are sixty verses, in which the author mentions his name as Puṇyarāja. However, A. Aklujkar expresses some doubt upon Puṇyarāja's authorship of *VPT*, mentioning that the two older manuscripts ascribe *VPT* to Helārāja, and some other reasons, cf. A. Aklujkar, "The Authorship of the Vākya-kāṇḍa-ṭīkā," *Charudeva Shastri Felicitation Volume*, vol. I, Delhi 1974, pp. 165-188. His view is criticized in Peri Sarveswara Sharma, "Puṇyarāja's Ṭīkā on the Vākya-kāṇḍa of the Vākyapadīya of Bhartṛhari," *Bhāratīya Vidyā*, 42 (1983), pp. 1-21. I should like to express my thanks to Dr. J. Houben for his kindness to make this latter article accessible to me.

5 Cf. P.S. Sharma, *op. cit.*, pp. 6-7.

6 This has been suggested to me by Professor A. Aklujkar on the occasion of the Bhartṛhari Conference in 1992. The idea presented in these verses is close to that refer-

satyaṃ vastu tadākārair asatyair avadhāryate /
asatyopādhibhiḥ śabdaiḥ satyam evābhidhīyate // 2
adhruveṇa nimittena devadattagṛhaṃ yathā /
gṛhītaṃ gṛhaśabdena śuddham evābhidhīyate // 3
suvarṇādi yathā bhinnaṃ svair ākārair apāyibhiḥ /
rucakādyabhidhānānāṃ śuddham evaiti vācyatām // 4

"A real substance is ascertained through its unreal forms. It is in fact what is real that is expressed by the words with unreal adjuncts. Just as Devadatta's house, which is cognized through an impermanent mark, is expressed in its pure form by the word 'house', [or,] just as gold, for instance, which is differentiated by its own impermanent forms, becomes in its pure form the object of such words as '*rucaka*' (golden necklace) and the like." From afar Devadatta's house may be indicated by a crow resting on the roof with the words: "His house is that one with a crow on the roof." However, what is really expressed by the word 'house' is not the house with a crow on the roof, but it is only the house which remains unchanged even after the crow flies away. Similar is the case with such words as '*rucaka*' etc., which are used to indicate gold in the form of necklace, etc. What is expressed by these words is in fact gold as the real substance, which subsists under the change of impermanent, unreal forms.

On the verse 126ab which states that an aggregate (*samudāya*) free from option (*vikalpa*) and accumulation (*samuccaya*) is the denotation of a word, *VPT* states: *"nanu yady ākārasamudāyaṃ samuccitam eva pratyāyayati tarhi bahuvacanam eva tatra syāt. atha vikalpitaṃ pratyāyayati tadā vacanavikalpaṃ syād ity āśaṅkyāha - 'avikalpasamuccayaḥ' iti*. (If [a word] causes to apprehend the aggregate of forms simply as accumulated, then only plural may be used for it. If it causes to apprehend the same as optional, then there may be alternation of number. - Anticipating this [question, the author] says: "free from option and accumulation".) This explanation is not unintelligible, but a far clearer understanding is obtained from the example given in *TSP*: "When the word 'forest' (*vana*) is uttered, the notion arises not through option as: '*dhava* tree or *khadira* tree or *palāśa* tree', nor through accumulation as: '*dhava* tree and *khadira* tree and *palāśa* tree', but *dhava* tree, etc. are apprehended generally. In the same way, when the word '*brāhmaṇa*' is uttered, the apprehension is not in the form: 'austerity (*tapas*) or birth (*jāti*) or learning (*śruta*)', nor is

red to by Patañjali in *Mahābhāṣya* (ed. Kielhorn), Vol. I, p. 7.11-18. Cf. also J. Bronkhorst, *Mahābhāṣyadīpikā of Bhartṛhari*, Fasc. IV: Āhnika I. Poona: Bhandarkar Oriental Research Inst., 1987, pp. 22 (text), 78-79 (translation).

it in the form: 'austerity and birth and learning'; but austerity, etc. distinguished from other correlatives are apprehended in entirety as an assembled whole."[7]

All these seven views are repudiated by Śāntarakṣita. Neither *TSP* nor *VPT* inform us to whom or to which school these views are to be attributed. It draws our attention that the concept of *pratibhā* presented in the verse 891 (*VP*, II.117) is also criticized in *TS*. I have shown elsewhere that Dignāga, who advocated the *apoha*-theory, adopted the concept of *pratibhā* from Bhartṛhari in his discussion on the meaning of a sentence.[8] Śāntaraksita also accepts the view that *pratibhā* is the meaning of a sentence. He is known to have modified Dignāga's *apoha*-theory by laying emphasis on the fact that a word produces a positive mental image (*pratibimba*) in the mind of the hearer. In the process of his counter-attack against Kumārila who criticized Dignāga for the inconsistency of admitting *apoha* as the meaning of a word and *pratibhā* as the meaning of a sentence, Śāntarakṣita considers the term *pratibhā* as synonymous with *apoha* which, according to him, is of the nature of *pratibimba*.[9] When he criticizes the doctrine of *pratibhā* in *VP*, II.117, his discussion is focussed on the problem concerning the relation between *pratibhā* and external object: "*Pratibhā* has also been regarded as the meaning of a word. If it takes an external thing for its object, then, inasmuch as the external thing has only one particular character, how could there be various *pratibhā*-s for different persons who take one and the same thing for their object? If *pratibhā* be held to be objectless, being produced only by dint of the impression of previous experiences (*vāsanā*), then how could there be either apprehension or activity pertaining to external things? It is not appropriate to say that *pratibhā* is baseless, since in that case there would follow an absurd conclusion that it is produced anywhere. If its basis consists in the mutual difference [among things], then that is exactly our view."[10] Thus it is understood that Śāntaraksita does not totally reject the

7 *TSP*, p. 350.9-13.

8 M. Hattori, "Apoha and Pratibhā," *Sanskrit and Indian Studies: Essays in Honour of Daniel H.H. Ingalls*, ed. by M. Nagatomi, et al. Dordrecht, etc.: D. Reidel Publ. Co., 1979, pp. 61-73.

9 Cf. *TS*, 1027: *pratibimbātmako 'pohaḥ padād apy upajāyate / pratibhākhyo jhaṭ ity eva padārtho 'py ayam eva naḥ //*

10 *TS*, 901-904: *pratibhāpi ca śabdārtho bahyārthaviṣayā yadi / ekātmaniyate bāhye vicitrāḥ pratibhāḥ katham // atha nirviṣayā etā vāsanāmātrabhāvataḥ / pratipattiḥ pravṛttir vā bahyārtheṣu katham bhavet // ... nirbījā na ca sā yuktā sarvatraiva prasaṅgataḥ / itaretarabhedo 'syā bījaṃ cet pakṣa eṣa naḥ //*

doctrine of *pratibhā*. To be criticized is the view that *pratibhā* pertains to some real thing in the external world. It is his thought that *pratibhā* does not go beyond the mental realm and has nothing to do with external objects. On this point he is close to Bhartṛhari who maintains that words pertain only to mentally constructed secondary being (*aupacārikī sattā*) and not to the real entity in the external world.[11]

11 Cf. *VP*, III.3 (Sambandha-samuddeśa), k. 39ff.

BHARTṚHARI'S DEFINITION OF *KRIYĀ*

Yoshichika Honda, Kyoto

0. General Introduction

In this paper I will treat Bhartṛhari's and Patañjali's definition of *kriyā* as interpreted by Helārāja in the *Kriyāsamuddeśa* of the *Vākyapadīya*.

In his *Kriyāsamuddeśa*, Bhartṛhari deals with *kriyā* from two different points of view, from that of those who hold that a word denotes the particular (*vyaktivādin*) and that of those who hold that the word denotes the universal (*jātivādin*).[1] It seems that *kriyā* as understood by the *jātivādin* is more interesting than that of the *vyaktivādin*, but here I will limit the discussion to the *vyaktivādin's* understanding of *kriyā*.

1. Bhartṛhari's Definition of kriyā.

1.0. Introduction

It is from the author of the *Nirukta* that Bhartṛhari inherits the idea that an act, which Yāska calls *bhāva*, is continuous (*pūrvāparībhūta*)[2]. And he introduces that idea into the field of grammar (*vyākaraṇa*). And, keeping it in his mind, he gives his definition of *kriyā* 'act' as denoted by *śabda* 'a word' in his *Kriyāsamuddeśa*'s first kārikā. It reads

> *yāvat siddham asiddhaṃ vā sādhyatvenābhidhīyate /*
> *āśritakramarūpatvāt tat kriyety abhidhīyate // (VP.3.8.k.1)*[3]

According to Helārāja, this kārikā gives a scientific definition (*śāstrīyam lakṣaṇam*) of *kriyā* 'act'.[4] We may exemplify the definition briefly as fol-

1 Helārāja on KSk.20 (VPI, page 18, lines 14-15): *evam tāvat padārthānāṃ apoddhāre jātir vā vyaktir eva vā/ iti vyaktivādimatena kriyālakṣaṇo 'poddhārapadārtho nirūtaḥ/ idānīm jātivādimatenāha/*

2 Nirukta 1.1.: *pūrvāparībhūtam bhāvam ākhyātenācaṣte vrajati pacatīti upakramaprabhṛtyapavargaparyantam/* See Helārāja on KS.k.11 (VPI., page 12, line 14).

3 VPR reads *pratīyate* for *abhidhīyate.*

4 Helārāja on KSk.1 (VPI, page 1, lines 2-3): *idānīm sādhyāpekṣatvāt sādhanasya sādhanānantaram uddiṣṭāyāḥ kriyāyāḥ śāstrīyaṃ lakṣaṇaṃ āha/*

lows.[5] In the case of {*apākṣīt* '[he] cooked'}, something is *siddha*. On the other hand, in the case of {*pacati* '[he] is cooking'} and {*pakṣyati* '[he] will cook'}, something is *asiddha*. In both cases, in so far as something is denoted by a word as *sādhya*, that something is called *kriyā*.

1.1 General conception of the act as *sādhya*.

A general account of *kriyā* as *sādhya* can be found in Helārāja's commentary on this kārikā.[6]

Let us observe the process of making a pot of clay, on the level of the actual world. First, there is a lump of clay. Then out of this, a potter makes several parts which will become a body or an ear and so on. Then the parts are united and baked by the potter. After that a pot appears in the actual world.

Now let us leave the actual world and turn to the level of the word. We will examine the expression {*ghaṭaḥ kriyate* 'the pot is being made'}. From this expression we understand the process of a pot being made just in the same way as it happened in the actual world.

Then, what kind of notion does the expression {*ghaṭaḥ*} alone bring about in our mind? The notion which is brought about by {*ghaṭaḥ*} in our mind is not the process of a pot being made, but it is only 'pot'.

Therefore, the process of a pot being made is to be understood from the verb {*kriyate*}. And such a process in temporal sequence is what the word *sādhya* means. In this way, a *kriyā* has many component acts, which have a temporal order and constitute a series.

1.2 The mentally unified whole is the act.

Then, how can a *kriyā* be regarded as a whole such as "the act of cooking"? Bhartṛhari gives an answer to this question in the fourth kārikā of the *Kriyāsamuddeśa*. It reads

5 VSM, page 45, lines 23-24: *'pacati' 'pakṣyati' ityādāv asiddham, 'apākṣīt' ityādau siddhaṃ vā sādhyatvenābhidhīyamānaṃ kriyā/*

6 Helāraja on KSk. 1 (VPI, page 5, lines 11-15): *tathā hi – dravyaśabdāḥ pravartamānāḥ ghaṭaḥ kriyate, paṭaḥ kriyate ityādisādhyamānāvastheṣv api sanmātrākārāvalambanaṃ pratyayaṃ janayanti/ ghaṭasya hi bhāvyamānāvasthā śivakastūpakādīnām avasthānāṃ krameṇa prādurbhāvaḥ/ na cāsau ghaṭaśabdāt pratīyate, kriyata iti kriyāśabdaprayogād eva tadavagateḥ/*

guṇabhūtair avayavaiḥ samūhaḥ kramajanmanām /
buddhyā prakalpitābhedaḥ kriyeti vyapadiśyate // (VP 3.8.k.4)

According to Helārāja, this kārikā can be interpreted as follows. As mentioned above, *kriyā* is a mere continuous series of its component acts. But they aim at a single result (*ekaphaloddeśa*).[7] And on the basis of this singleness of result the component parts can be regarded as a collection (*samudāya*) whose nature is single and total, thanks to the intellectual function of joining.

Therefore, when we pay attention to a collection, we can say that a *kriyā* is single; and on the other hand, when we fix our eyes upon its component parts, we can speak of it as having an order (*krama*) or sequence (*paurvāparya*).

However, this singleness with regard to a collection is nothing but a mental construction (*adhyāropita*), because each component part disappears immediately after it originates and all the parts cannot exist simultaneously to constitute a real collection.

To Bhartṛhari, *kriyā* is a collection conceived as a whole. And it is such a collection that brings about a result.

1.3 Any component part of a composite action is also an act (*kriyā*).

Here there arises a problem. If a process as a whole is *kriyā*, a part of it, for instance, *adhiśrayana* 'putting [a pot] on a fire', could not be called *kriyā*. If so, we could not apply the expression {*pacati*} to a part such as *adhiśrayaṇa*.

Bhartṛhari gives an answer to this question in the fifth kārikā of the *Kriyāsamuddeśa*:

samūhaḥ sa tathābhūtaḥ pratibhedaṃ samūhiṣu/
samāpyate tato bhede kālabhedasya sambhavaḥ // (VP 3.8.k.5.)

According to Helārāja, a man who is beginning to cook aims at eating as the result of cooking from the very beginning. Therefore the whole process

7 Bhartṛhari and Helārāja mention another reason for regarding a *kriyā* as a whole. See Helārāja on *Kālasamuddeśa* k. 90 (VPI, page 78, lines 17-18): *pūrvaṃ kṣaṇasamūhasyaikatvaṃ ekaphaloddeśena samarthitam/ idānīṃ saṅkalanābuddhyupārūḍhasya buddhyākārarūpatvena bhāvikaṃ ekatvaṃ ucyate/*. Here the reason why a *kriyā* is regarded as a whole is singleness of intellect.

is conceptually fixed on each part of cooking such as *adhiśrayaṇa*. In other words, a part (*samūhin*) is regarded as the whole or collection (*samūha*). In this case, we can apply the expression {*pacati*} to a component part, such as *adhiśrayaṇa*, on which the whole process of cooking is superimposed. And when *adhiśrayaṇa*, is finished, we can apply the expression {*apākṣīt*} to it. And with reference to a component part which will happen in the future, we can say {*pakṣyati*}. Helārāja says that this mental construction (*adhyāsa*) occurs, because the notion of cooking continues (*anuvartate*) in each component part.[8]

Then, another problem arises. From the discussion above, it will follow that a component part, such as *adhiśrayaṇa*, is not *sādhya*, though the expression {*pacati*} can be applied to it, because a component part has the concept of the whole fixed on it and therefore it does not have its own parts.

Helārāja gives an answer to this problem in his commentary.[9] He says that a part is constructed conceptually as having the same nature as the whole. In other words, a part is exactly the same as the whole. Accordingly, any component part, having its own component parts in temporal sequence, is *sādhya*.

1.4 The act is not perceptible.

Incidentally it may be remarked that, according to Patañjali, a *kriyā* cannot be perceived, but can only be inferred.[10] However, if the whole is conceived in each part, as I mentioned above, a *kriyā* would be perceptible, because its very last atomic moment is perceptible.[11]

8 Helārāja on KSk.5 (VPI, page 9, lines 22-23): *adhyāsaś ca sarvatra pacatīti pratyayasyānuvṛtter eva jñāyate/*

9 Helārāja on KSk.5 (VPI, page 9, line 25-page 10, line 2): *atrocyate/ na samudāyabuddhyaikatvena, nāpy avayavabuddhyā ayaṃ cāyaṃ ceti samuccayena pratyekaṃ samudāyasyāvayaveṣv āropo 'tra/ kim tarhi? pūrvāparībhūtāvayavatvenaiva/*

10 MBh on P. 1.3.1 (MBh I vol. 1, page 254, lines 15-17): *kriyā nāmeyam atyantāparidṛṣṭā 'śakyā piṇḍībhūtā nidarśayitum/ yathā garbho nirluṭhitaḥ/ sāsāv anumānagamyā/*. See Cardona 1991, page 453-454 (Sec. 5.1.5.).

11 Helārāja holds that the very last atomic moment, which is no longer called *kriyā*, is perceptible. See Helārāja on KSk. 11 (VPI, page 12, lines 18-19): *bhāgaśaḥ pratyakṣatvāc ca na śakyā piṇḍībhūtā pāṃsurāśivat kriyā nidarśayitum ity uktam/*. Cf. Cardona 1991, footnote 54.

Bhartṛhari discusses this problem in the sixth kārikā of the *Kriyāsamuddeśa.*

> *kramāt sadasatām teṣām ātmāno na samūhinām /*
> *sadvastuviṣayair yānti sambandhaṃ cakṣurādibhiḥ// (VP 3.8.k.6).*

The first part of a composite act, for instance, *adhiśrayaṇa* 'putting [a pot] on a fire', has already finished when the second part, namely, *udakāsecana* 'pouring the water [into the pot]', begins. In other words, the first part is non-existent (*asat*) and the second part is existent (*sat*). That is to say, the composite act is both existent and non-existent. And the objects of sense-organs such as the eye are existent things. Accordingly, the composite act, which is both existent and non-existent, cannot be the object of sense-organs. In other words, the composite act is not perceptible. Nor can the component parts of the composite act be perceived. As I mentioned above, the component parts are perfectly equivalent to the composite act and each component part is both existent and non-existent. Therefore they are in the same situation as the composite act, and cannot be perceived either.

Next, *adhiśrayaṇa*, which is a component part of the composite act of cooking, has its own component parts such as *iṣṭakāviniyojana* 'laying out of bricks', *hastaprasāraṇa* 'stretching out the hands', *sthālīvinyāsa* 'putting down the pot' and so on. In this case, the whole is denoted by the verb "*adhiśrayati*".

Now, let us move to the next problem. Each component act is further divided into subdivisions. For example, *hastaprasāraṇa* is further divided. Bhartṛhari speaks of this division in the ninth kārikā of the *Kriyāsamuddeśa*.

> *yathā ca bhāgāḥ pacater udakāsecanādayaḥ /*
> *udakāsecanādīnāṃ jñeyā bhāgās tathāpare // (VP 3.8.k.9)*

The question which we must consider next concerns further subdivisions of the component act. For example, *hastaprasāraṇa* has further subdivisions. And these further subdivisions have their component parts. Finally, the composite act will be divided into atomic moments. Can such minute moments have their own component parts in a temporal sequence? And can the minute moment, too, be *sādhya*? And would it be perceptible?

Bhartṛhari gives the following answer to this question:

> *yaś cāpakarṣaparyantaṃ anuprāptaḥ pratīyate /*
> *tatraikasmin kriyāśabdaḥ kevale na prayujyate // (VP 3.8. k.10)*

That is, a minute moment which has no parts is not called *kriyā*. This means that what is denoted by a word, namely, a verbal act, involves a process.

Here it is important to say that Bhartṛhari approaches the problem of *kriyā* from the viewpoint of a grammarian. He is concerned with what is denoted by the word, not with the actual world, because he is a *śabdapramāṇaka*.[12]

2. *Patañjali's definition of kriyā as interpreted by Helārāja*

2.0 Introduction

Let us now turn to Patañjali's definition of *kriyā*. Patañjali, too, gives a definition of *kriyā* in his *Mahābhāṣya*. It reads "*kārakāṇāṃ pravṛttiviśeṣaḥ kriyā*".[13]

Since it is difficult to give a definitive interpretation of the definition, Helārāja presents six interpretations.

When interpreting this definition, we are confronted with two difficulties.

The first difficulty is how to understand the meaning of the word '*kārakāṇām*'. As is well known, Panini introduces in his *Aṣṭādhyāyī* six *kārakas* 'act-participants': namely, *apādāna* 'starting point', *sampradāna* 'beneficiary', *karaṇa* 'instrument', *adhikaraṇa* 'locus', *karman* 'object' and *kartṛ* 'agent'.[14] The point here is to know what Patañjali means by this plural *kārakāṇām*.

12 Helārāja remarks frequently that *iha vyākaraṇe na vastvartho 'rthaḥ, api tu śabdārtho 'rthaḥ*. For instance, VPI, page 5, lines 6-7.

13 This definition appears twice in MBh. on P.1.3.1. (MBh I., vol. 1, page 258, line 11) and on P.5.3.42. (MBh I., vol. 2, page 410, lines 13-14). This definition is argued originally in a context with reference to *as, bhū* and *vid*, which express mere existence in the *Mahābhāṣya* and Helārāja's commentary on KS. See Helārāja on KSk. 1 (VPI, page 1, lines 7-14): "*astibhavatividyatīnām dhātutvam vaktavyam*" (MBh I., vol. 1, page 255, line 2) *iti coditam/ tathā hi yathā kiṃ karoti? pacati, iti pacādīnāṃ karotinā sāmānādhikaraṇyāt kriyāviśeṣavācakatvādhyavasāyaḥ, na tathā bhavatyādīnām/ na hi bhavati kiṃ karoti? bhavati, ityādīti na te kriyāvacanāḥ syuḥ/ kiṃ ca parispandasvabhāvā loke kriyā prasiddhā/ astibhavatividyatīnām ca na parispandasvabhāvo 'rtha iti sakaladhātuvyāpakaṃ kriyālakṣaṇaṃ bhāṣye praṇītaṃ "kārakāṇāṃ pravṛttiviśeṣaḥ kriyā" iti/*. See 6th view below.

14 The general rules for these act-participants are P.1.4.24. *dhruvam apāye 'pādānam/*, P.1.4.32. *karmaṇā yam abhipraiti sa sampradānam/*, P.1.4.42. *sādhakatamaṃ karaṇam/*, P.1.4.54. *ādhāro 'dhikaraṇam/*, P.1.4.49. *kartur īpsitatamaṃ karma/* and P.1.4.54. *svatantraḥ kartā/*.

The second difficulty is how to understand the compound *pravṛttiviśeṣa*. In this respect, Helārāja presents two alternatives, as follows:[15]

1) *sarveṣāṃ kārakāṇām ekaḥ pravṛttiviśeṣaḥ*

2) *pratikārakam bhinnā pravṛttiḥ*

In the case of the former alternative, the point is how to interpret the compound *pravṛttiviśeṣa*. In the case of the latter, the word *viśeṣa* is explained as *bhinna* 'split or different'. The question here is what the word *pratikārakam* means.[16] Helārāja presents six kinds of interpretation based on these two alternatives. Let us examine them one by one.

2.1 The First View.[17]

The first view is based on the second alternative. In this view, the word "*kārakāṇām*" points to all the act-participants (*kāraka*).

Helārāja quotes Patañjali who says "A root is what denotes an act (*kriyāvacano dhātuḥ*)".[18] If so, a root should denote the different activities (*pravṛtti*) of all the act-participants, because an act is {*pratikārakaṃ bhinnā pravṛttiḥ*} in this view.[19]

Next, the question arises: If *Lakāra*, which is introduced after a root (*dhātu*), denotes a *sādhana* 'means of accomplishing' the act, which is denoted by the root, *Lakāra* will also denote all the act-participants. But Pāṇini limits the function of *Lakāra* to *kartṛ*, *karman* or *bhāva*.[20] Thus, it seems that Helārāja's first interpretation contradicts Pāṇini's prescription.

And this contradiction is due to a difference of approach. I take the word "*svīkāra*" in Helārāja's commentary as a synonym of "*abhyupagama*" "hypothesis", according to the *Nyāyasūtra*.[21] Now, in a sentence such as

15 Helārāja on KSk.1 (VPI, page 1, lines 14-16): *tatra vicāryate sarveṣāṃ vā kārakāṇām ekaḥ pravṛttiviśeṣaḥ, pratikārakaṃ bhinnā vā pravṛttir iti/*

16 For a discussion of the compound *pratikārakam*, see Joshi, S.D. & Roodbergen, J.A.F. [1975], page 27, footnote 93.

17 VPI, page 1, line 16-page 2, line 4.

18 MBh on P.1.3.1. (MBh I., vol. 1, page 254, line 13).

19 Because we can put {*pratikārakaṃ bhinnā pravṛttiḥ*} in the place of the "*kriyā*" in Patañjali's expression {*kriyāvacano dhātuḥ*}. Helārāja on KSk. 1 (VPI, page 1, lines 18-19): *itthaṃ ca kriyāvācī dhātur iti sakalakārakavyāpārābhidhāyī dhātuḥ prāptaḥ/*

20 P.3.4.69. *laḥ karmaṇi ca bhāve cākarmakebhyaḥ*/[P.3.4.68. *kartari*]

21 a) VPŚ. page 402, lines 3-5: .../ *satyam etat/ kin tu 'devadattaḥ kāṣṭhaiḥ sthālyām odanaṃ pacati' ityādau viśeṣeṇa* pacater dhātoḥ sarvakārakavyāpārasvīkāropalabdher akhilakārakavyāpārābhidhāyī dhātur ity upagamāt/* *VPI: *ityādāv aviśeṣeṇa*.

{*devadattaḥ kāṣṭhaiḥ sthālyām odanaṃ pacati*}, we observe that many act-participants are involved in different activities. Therefore, we can hypothesize that different activities are denoted by a verb. However, the activities of an agent (*kartṛ*) and an object (*karman*) gain predominance (*prādhānya*) over those of other act-participants. Therefore, the function of *Lakāra* is to point to an agent and an object, as we can deduce by means of the logical method based on positive concomitance (*anvaya*) and negative concomitance (*vyatireka*), and as Pāṇini teaches in the rule P.3.4.69.

2.2 The Second View.[22]

The second view is also based on the second alternative {*pratikārakaṃ bhinnā pravṛttiḥ*}. This view says that the definition "*kārakāṇāṃ pravṛttiviśeṣaḥ kriyā*" is concerned with the nature of the act (*kriyā*) and not with the meaning of the root (*dhātu*).[23] Here the activities of the *apādāna* and the *sampradāna* are also *kriyā*. But the root does not denote them.[24] This view differs from the first view in that it limits the number of act-participants whose activities are denoted by the root to four, namely, *kartṛ*, *karman*, *adhikaraṇa*, and *karaṇa*, all of which may be considered to have *svātantrya*. But, in that case, in order to express their independence, *karaṇa* and *adhikaraṇa* have to be transformed into a *kartṛ*.[25]

2.3 The Third View.[26]

Unlike the previous two, the third view is based on the first alternative {*sarveṣām kārakāṇām ekaḥ pravṛttiviśeṣaḥ*}. The compound *pravṛttiviśeṣa* is

b) NS 1.1.31. (page 266): *aparīkṣitābhyupagamāt tadviśeṣaparīkṣaṇam abhyupagamasiddhāntaḥ*/. See NKs.v. "*abhyupagama*", 2. *svīkāraḥ/ astu dravyam śabda iti/*

22 VPI, page 2, lines 4-13: *anye manyante.../.../...dhātunābhidhānāt/*

23 Helārāja on KSk.1 (VPI, page 2, lines 8-10): *ataś ca kārakāṇāṃ pravṛttiviśeṣaḥ kriyeti kriyāsvarūpamātraṃ kathitam, na tu dhātuvācyatvam/*

24 Helārāja on KSk.1 (VPI, page 2, lines 4-5): *...sampradānādivyāpāre dhātor na vṛttiḥ/ karaṇādivyāpāra eva tu vṛttiḥ/*

25 Helārāja on KSk.1 (VPI, page 2, lines 11-13): *kācid eva tu dhātunābhidhīyate karmagatā kartṛgatā vā pacyate pacatīti/ ata eva kartṛkarmaṇor evotpadyate lakāraḥ tadvyāpārasyaiva dhātunābhidhānāt/*

26 VPI, page 2, lines 13-15: *anye tu viśeṣapade.../.../...kriyeti vyācakṣate/*

taken as a genitive tatpuruṣa, that is {*pravṛttīnāṃ viśeṣaḥ*},[27] and "*viśeṣa*" means 'distinguishing feature".

In this view, *kriyā* is regarded as a result (*phala*) brought about by the activities of all the act-participants. For example, the activities of all the act-participants in the act of 'cooking' bring about a single specific result, namely, 'softening of rice (*viklitti*)'.

2.4 The Fourth View.[28]

The fourth view is based on the second alternative, {*pratikārakaṃ bhinnā pravṛttiḥ*}. In this view, the predominant act-participant in the form of *kartṛ* is intended by the word '*kāraka*'. And the plural ending in '*kārakāṇām*' does not point to the plurality of the act-participants, but only to that of the *kartṛ*.[29] However, we observe that *Lakāra* can also denote a *karman*. In such cases, the activity of the *karman* is also *kriyā*.

Here an objection is raised. The plural number of *kārakāṇām* could be explained with reference to *karman* only. Because activity is that of which the *karman* constitutes a purpose (*artha*) and the *karman* could also be the predominant *kāraka*. Why should the *kartṛ* be the only predominant *kāraka*?[30]

To this objection, the fourth view answers as follows. The *kriyā* of all roots has a *kartṛ*, but it does not always have a *karman*. In other words, the *kartṛ* pervades all roots. That is the reason why this view considers that the *kartṛ* is the predominant *kāraka*.[31] Here this view quotes a *Mahābhāṣya* passage as a means of proof which says "*anyathā śuṣkaudane kārakāṇi pravartante/anyathā māṃsaudane*".[32] This view interprets this passage as follows. Many act-participants act impetuously towards rice with meat, and slowly towards dried rice. And acting impetuously or slowly is possible only

27 The *ṣaṣṭhī vibhakti* in *pravṛttīnām* denotes *janyajanakabhāva*.

28 VPI, page 2, line 15-page 3, line 18: *apare punaḥ kārakam atra pradhānam.../.../...itīdam darśanam/*

29 Kārakas other than the main agent (*pradhānakartṛ*) also function as agents (*guṇakartṛ*) of their own minor acts (*guṇakriyā*).

30 Helārāja on KSk.1 (VPI, page 2, lines 18-19).

31 Helārāja on KSk.1 (VPI, page 2, lines 19-20): *naitad asti, karmaṇo 'sarvaviṣayatvāt/ kartā punaḥ sarvatra sthita iti vyāpakatvāt sa evātra pradhānaṃ kārakam vivakṣitam/*

32 VPI, page 2, line 21. But the original text reads *anyathā ca kārakāṇi śuṣkaudane pravartante, anyathā ca māṃsaudane* (MBh I, vol. 1, page 258, lines 11-12). This passage is also quoted by the fifth view below.

for a *kartṛ* that is animate (*cetana*). Therefore *kāraka* in the passage of the *Mahābhāṣya* stands only for *kartṛ*.

Now, two questions arise. First, if *kāraka* in this definition stands only for an animate *kartṛ*, then an inanimate *kartṛ* will not be included and the activities of an inanimate *kartṛ* will not be called *kriyā*. But in the sentence {*khaṭvā kampate* 'a bed is shaking'}, the activity of the bed, which is an inanimate *kartṛ*, should also be called *kriyā*.[33] Second, in the sentence {*pāṇinā māṃsaudanaṃ bhuṅkte* 'he is eating rice mixed with meat with his hand'}, a hand, which is *karaṇa* and not *kartṛ*, can act impetuously or slowly towards rice with meat.[34] How can you say that the *Bhāṣyakāra* intends only *kartṛ*?

It is somewhat difficult to understand the answer to this question. This view says that *pravṛttiviśeṣa* is accidentally distinguished (*upalakṣita*) by *saṃrambha* and *mandatā* in the passage of the *Mahābhāṣya*, and general activities other than those distinguished by *saṃrambha* and *mandatā* of *kartṛ* are not excluded by *saṃrambha* and *mandatā*. And we have to probably interpret the word *kartṛ* in the answer as that which is in the form of *kartṛ* in actual expression without reference to whether it is animate or not and whether it is the agent of the main act (*pradhānakartṛ*) or that of a subordinate act (*guṇakartṛ*). This fourth view analyses the compound *pravṛtti-viśeṣa* as *pravṛttir eva viśeṣaḥ* 'speciality in the form of activity'.[35] In this view, the argument concerning *karman* is rather obscure. This view says that the fact that Patañjali states *kārakāṇām* and not *kartṝṇām*, shows that the word *kāraka* in this definition intimates (*sūcita*) *karman* also.[36] The most likely explanation is that the activities of *kartṛ* are predominant over those of *karman*.

Now the following question arises. The *Mahābhāṣya* says "*atha kaḥ paceḥ pradhāno 'rthaḥ/ yā 'sau taṇḍulānāṃ viklittiḥ*".[37] In short, this statement means that the main meaning of the root *pac* is softening (*viklitti*)

33 Ambākartrī (VPŚ, page 404, lines 18-19): *atra kecid vadanti – cetanasyaiva sasaṃrambhā mandā vā pravṛttiḥ saṃbhavati ity acetanaḥ kartā na gṛhītaḥ syāt iti tatpravṛttiḥ kriyeti noktaṃ syād khaṭvā kampate ityādau/*

34 Ambākartrī (VPŚ, page 405, lines 1-2): *kiñ ca pāṇinā māṃsaudanaṃ bhuṅkte ityādisthale māṃsaudanau pāṇyādirūpāṇāṃ karaṇādīnāṃ api saṃrambhavattvāt tat katham kartaivātra nirdiṣṭa iti /*

35 VPŚ (page 405, line 8) reads *pravṛtter eva viśeṣaḥ* for *pravṛttir eva viśeṣaḥ* in VPI. This reading intends to exclude activities of *kārakas* other than *kartṛ*.

36 VPI, page 3, line 10.

37 VPI, page 3, line 12. But original text reads "*iha paceḥ kaḥ pradhānārthaḥ*"/ See MBh on P.3.1.26. (MBh I., vol. 2, page 32, lines 24-25).

of rice grains. And this softening of rice grains is an activity of *karman* and not that of *kartṛ*. And the activity of *kartṛ* is *vikledana* 'making [rice grain] soft'. Does this *Bhāṣya* passage conflict with the fourth view?

This view answers as follows. In this passage Patañjali investigates the problem from an objective (*vastvartha*) point of view and not from a *śābda* point of view. From an objective point of view, the main meaning of the root *pac* is *viklitti*. But from the *śābda* point of view, *vikledana* is the main meaning of the root *pac*.

As regards the case that *Lakāra* is introduced in the sense of *karman* after the root, some think that only *viklitti*, which is the activity of *karman*, is the meaning of the root *pac*, and others think *viklitti* to which *vikledana* is subordinated is the meaning of *pac*.

2.5 The Fifth View[38]

The fifth view is based on the first alternative {*sarveṣāṃ kārakāṇāṃ ekaḥ pravṛttiviśeṣaḥ*}, and rests on the authority of the *Mahābhāṣya*.[39] There are some variant readings, and I adopt the reading "*pravṛttimātram agṛhīta-viśeṣaṃ sakalakārakānuyāyi*".[40]

This view establishes a single *pravṛttiviśeṣa* as a characteristic common to all the *kārakas*. They all produce a single result. It is true that all the *kārakas* have their own activities.[41] But these activities produce one result. Therefore, so far as the result is concerned, there is no difference between them.

In this view, the compound "*pravṛttiviśeṣa*" is a *karmadhāraya*, as is shown by the paraphrase {*pravṛttiś cāyam viśeṣaś ca*}.[42] And the meaning of the whole expression is "[*kriyā* is] a special function [which is called *jananā* 'producing',] common to all the *kārakas*".

38 I may divide this view and the next view at VPI, page 4, line 4, *pravṛttir ity.../* for convenience' sake. See the next view.

39 MBh on P.1.4.23. (MBh I, vol. 1, page 326, line 15): *...sāmānyabhūtā kriyā vartate.../*. For a discussion of this passage, see Joshi, S.D. & Roodbergen, J.A.F. 1975, page 44.

40 VPŚ, page 403, lines 5-6: *pravṛttimātram agṛhītaviśesam* sakalakārakānuyāyi** kriyeti manyante/* *VPŚ reads *pravṛttimātragṛhītaviśeṣam* for VPI *pravṛttimātram agṛhītaviśeṣam*. **VPI reads *sakalakārakānuyāyinī* for VPŚ *sakalakārakānuyāyi*.

41 Namely, *avāntaravyāpāra* of each *kāraka*.

42 Helārāja on KSk.1 (VPI, page 3, line 2).

2.6 The Sixth View

There is a difference of viewpoint between the preceding five views and this sixth view. The former five are concerned with the relation between *kāraka* and *kriyā* with respect to one *kriyā*. On the other hand, the sixth view is concerned with the difference between two *kriyās*.

This sixth view, which seems to be adopted by Kaiyaṭa and Nāgeśa,[43] is also based on the first alternative, that is {*sarvesām kārakānām ekaḥ pravṛttiviśesaḥ*}. In this view, the compound *pravṛttiviśesa* means 'difference from another activity'. And this difference is of two kinds. The one is *sajātīya* 'of same kind' and the other is *vijātīya* 'of a different kind'. In order to illustrate the former (*sajātīya*), this view quotes the passage of the *Mahābhāṣya* which is also quoted by the fourth view above, namely, "*anyathā kārakāṇi śuṣkaudane pravartante anyathā māṃsaudane.*"[44] This quotation means that act-participants act impetuously towards rice with meat, and do so indifferently towards dried rice. The purpose of this is to show that, for example, the act of eating (*bhujikriyā*) rice with meat is different from the act of eating dried rice.[45] This is the difference from an activity 'of the same kind'.

Next, we will take up the difference from a different kind of activity. It is clear that the act of cooking is different from the act of reciting (*paṭhikriyā*). There is no need for further explanation.

Here, it may be worth pointing out that Helārāja does not draw a sharp line between the fifth view and the sixth view, although he does so elsewhere. And this sixth view is not contradictory to the fifth view above. In this connection, we may say that this view provides additional information to or constitutes a more elaborate interpretation of, the fifth view.[46]

43 Pradīpa on P.1.3.1. (MBh II., vol. 2, page 123, col. 2, lines 10-11, 25-26): *pravṛttiviśeṣa iti/ sarvā pravṛttiḥ pravṛttyantarād bhidyate ity asty eva sarvasyāh kriyātvam/.../ yady evam iti/ atrāpi pravṛttyantarāpekṣayāsty eva pravṛttiviśesarūpatvam ity arthah/*
Uddyota on P.1.3.1. (MBh II, vol. 2, page 123, col. 2, lines 17-19): *nanu pravṛttiviśesasya kriyātve pravartata ity atra kriyātvānāpattir ata āha – sarveti/ pacyādyapekṣayā sāpi viśeṣa eveti bhāvaḥ/*

44 VPI, page 4, line 8.

45 *bhujikriyā* means *kriyā* which is expressed by the verbal root *bhuj* 'to eat'.

46 It seems that the meaning of *as, bhū* or *vid* is called *kriyā* on the basis of this sixth view. See Helārāja on KSk.1 (VPI, page 6, line 1-page 7, line 10). But these arguments are not clear for me at present.

3. Conclusion

It is not easy to decide which view is adopted by Helārāja himself. And from Bhartṛhari's and Helārāja's standpoint of *sarvapārṣada* we need not decide which one is their own. But when we remember Bhartṛhari's definition which we referred to in the first half of this paper, it seems that the fifth view that '*kriyā*' is defined as a special function (*pravṛttiviśeṣa*) found in all the act-participants, is adoptable. The sixth view, in which '*kriyā*' is defined as that which is differentiated from other activities, and which is not clearly separated from the fifth view by Helārāja, cannot be excluded.

It is to be regretted that Helārāja's work *Kriyāviveka*, in which he dealt with *kriyā* in detail, is not available.[47]

Bibliography

A. Primary Sources and Abbreviations.

Ambākartrī: Raghunātha Śarma's commentary. See VP.

KS: Bhartṛhari's *Kriyāsamuddeśa*. See VP.

VSM: *Vaiyākaraṇa-siddhānta-mañjūṣā by Nāgeśa Bhaṭṭa*. Edited by K.P. Sukla, Varanasi, 1977: Sampurnanand Sanskrit Vishvavidyalaya.

MBh I.: *The Vyākaraṇa=Mahābhāṣya*. Edited by F. Kielhorn, Third edition revised and furnished with additional readings, references, and select critical notes by K.V. Abhyankar. 3 volumes, Poona, 1962-1972: Bhandarkar Oriental Research Institute.

II.: *Vyākaraṇamahābhāṣya*. Edited with Kaiyaṭa's *Pradīpa* and Nāgeśa's *Uddyota* by Bhargavasastri Joshi, Sivadatta D. Kudala, and Raghunathasastri. 6 parts, Nirnaya Sagar Press. Reprinted, 1982-91, Delhi: Chaukhamba Sanskrit Pratishthan.

Nirukta: *The Nirukta of Yāska*. Edited with Durga's commentary by H.M. Bhadkamkar, vol. 1, 1918. Reprinted, 1985, Poona: Bhandarkar Oriental Research Institute.

NK: *Nyāyakośa or Dictionary of Technical Terms of Indian Philosophy by Mahāmahopādhyāya Bhīmācārya Jhalakīkar*, Poona, 1978: Bhandarkar Oriental Research Institute.

NS: *Nyāyadarśana*. Edited by Taranatha Nyaya-Tarkatirtha and Amarendramohan Tarkatirtha. Calcutta, 1936-44. Reprinted, 1985, New Delhi: Munshiram.

Pradīpa: Kaiyaṭa's *Pradīpa*. See MBh II.

Uddyota: Nāgeśa's *Uddyota*. See MBh II.

47 See Helārāja on KSk. 1 (VPI, page 7, line 20).

VP: Bhartṛhari's *Vākyapadīya*.

VPI: Edited with Helārāja's commentary by K.A. Subramania Iyer, Kāṇḍa III, part ii. Poona, 1973: Deccan College.

VPŚ: Edited with Helārāja's commentary and Raghunātha Śarma's Ambākartrī by Raghunātha Śarma. Part III, vol. II (Sarasvatī Bhavana Granthamalā 91) Varanasi, 1979: Sampurnanand Sanskrit Vishvavidyalaya.

VPR: Edited by Wilhelm Rau. *Bhartṛharis Vākyapadīya: Die Mūlakārikās nach den Handschriften herausgegeben and mit einem Pāda-Index versehen.* (Abhandlungen für die Kunde des Morgenlandes XLII. 4.) Wiesbaden, 1977: Steiner.

B. Others

Bandini, Giovanni.: 1980, *Die Erörterung der Wirksamkeit. Bhartṛharis Kriyāsamuddeśa und Helārājas Prakāśa zum ersten Male aus dem Sanskrit übersetzt, mit einer Einführung und einem Glossar*, Wiesbaden (Beiträge zur Südasienforschung. Südasien-Institut Universität Heidelberg, Band 61).

Cardona, George.: 1974, 'Pāṇini's kārakas: Agency, Animation and Identity', *JIP* 2:231-306.

-do-: 1991, 'A Path Still Taken: Some Early Indian Arguments Concerning Time', *JAOS* 111.3: 445-464.

Joshi, S.D. & Roodbergen, J.A.F.: 1975, *Patañjali's Vyākaraṇa-Mahābhāṣya Kārakāhnika (P.1.4.23.-1.4.55), Introduction, Translation and Notes*, Poona. (Publications of the Centre of Advanced Study in Sanskrit, Class, C No. 10).

Rocher, Rosane.: 1969, 'The Concept of Verbal Root in Indian Grammar (A Propos of Pāṇini 1.3.1.)', *FL* 5.1: 73-82.

-do-: 1983, 'Review of Bandini 1980', *JAOS* 103.4.: 778-9.

Subrahmania Iyer, K.A.: 1951, 'The Conception of Action Among the Vaiyākaraṇas', *JGJRI* 8.2.: 165-188.

-do-: 1969, *Bhartṛhari. A Study of the Vākyapadīya in the light of the Ancient Commentaries*, Poona. (Deccan College Building Centenary and Silver Jubilee Series 71).

-do-: 1974, *The Vākyapadīya of Bhartṛhari, Chapter III, pt. II. English Translation with Exegetical Notes*, Delhi (Motilal Banarsidass).

WHO ARE BHARTṚHARI'S *PADADARŚINS*? ON THE DEVELOPMENT OF BHARTṚHARI'S PHILOSOPHY OF LANGUAGE*

Jan E.M. Houben, Utrecht

One of the major problems discussed in the second book of the Vākyapadīya (VP) concerns the primary unit of language: Is it the sentence *(vākya)* or the word *(pada)?* In the context of the discussion of this problem, two groups of thinkers are opposed in kārikā 2.57: the *vākyavādins* or upholders of the sentence and the *padadarśins* or upholders of the word.[1]

Kārikā 2.57 is the only place in the VP where these two groups are explicitly juxtaposed.[2] But the opposition between the views which present the sentence as the primary unit and those which present the word as the primary unit pervades the entire second book of the VP, and also plays a role in the first and third book.[3] According to Puṇyarāja, the upholder of the sentence is the grammarian, and the intention of Bhartṛhari would have been to refute the views of the upholders of the word.[4]

* The author is happy to acknowledge the financial assistance he received from the Netherlands Organization for Scientific Research (NWO) and from the State University Utrecht, which enabled him to present this paper at the Bhartṛhari Conference at the University of Poona (January 6-8, 1992). His thanks are also due to Professor dr. J. Bronkhorst, Professor dr. H.W. Bodewitz and Professor dr. A.N. Aklujkar for their critical comments on earlier drafts of this paper.

1 VP 2.57: *abhedapūrvakā bhedāḥ kalpitā vākyavādibhiḥ /*
bhedapūrvān abhedāṁs tu manyante padadarśinaḥ //
In the context of the whole discussion this may be translated as follows: "Those who speak of the sentence (as being the primary linguistic unit) postulate the divisions (i.e. words) as preceded by the undivided (sentence). Those who perceive the word (as the primary linguistic unit) think that the undivided (sentences) are preceded by the divisions (i.e. the words)."

2 In VP 2.217, the word *padārthadarśanam* evokes the opposition without mentioning the other group.

3 See for instance VP 1.72-74, 91-95; 3.1.1-2; 3.4.1-2.

4 The opposition between the upholder of the sentence and the upholder of the word is very much emphasized in the commentary ascribed to Puṇyarāja, the oldest commentary available for the second book. Puṇyarāja summarizes the purpose of the discussion in the second book as follows (VP II:4.26-28):

tatra vaiyākaraṇasyākhaṇḍa evaiko 'navayavaḥ śabdaḥ sphoṭa-lakṣaṇo vākyam, pratibhaiva vākyārthaḥ, adhyāsaś ca saṁbandha iti padavādi-pakṣa-dūṣaṇa-paraḥ paraṁ ṭīkā-kāro vyavasthāpayatīty asya kāṇḍasya saṁkṣepaḥ.

"For the grammarian the indivisible *śabda*, 'linguistic unit', without parts, defined as the *sphoṭa*, is the sentence; *pratibhā* 'intuition' is the sentence meaning; and *adhyāsa*

Who are these upholders of the word, these *padadarśins* as they are called by Bhartṛhari himself in kārikā 2.57? Commentators and interpreters have identified them, mainly and with increasing emphasis, as Mīmāṁsā-thinkers.[5] It is true that many of the arguments used in the VP

'superimposition' the relation: it is this that is here being established as the highest by the author of the (Mahābhāṣya-) Ṭīkā (i.e. Bhartṛhari), being intent upon refuting the view of the upholder of the word."

(The word *paraṁ* after *-dūṣaṇaparaḥ* is a bit odd and would not be missed if deleted. It may be due to an erroneous repetion by a scribe.)

5 Bhartṛhari enumerates several definitions of the sentence in the first two kārikās of the second book. From of old, Bhartṛhari's enumeration has been read and interpreted in different ways (K. Kunjunni Rāja, ALB vol. 26 (1962): 206-210). The oldest grammarian commentary available for these kārikās (the one attributed to Puṇyarāja) recognizes references to eight different views in Bhartṛhari's enumeration, and categorizes them as either 'indivisible sentence' view or 'divisible sentence' view. It is the upholder of the sentence who accepts the sentence as primary and in principle indivisible. According to Puṇyarāja, Bhartṛhari mentions five 'divisible sentence' views; three of them accept *anvitābhidhāna* and two *abhihitānvaya* (VP II:1.10-14). These terms, *anvitābhidhāna* and *abhihitānvaya*, characteristic for the opposition between the later Mīmāṁsā schools of Prabhākara and Kumārila, are not used by Bhartṛhari himself. By using them Puṇyarāja may create the impression that the criticism of the upholder of the word is mainly a criticism of Mīmāṁsā-ideas. Elsewhere, the Mīmāṁsakas are explicitly referred to (VP II:10.10, 32.12). Yet Puṇyarāja recognizes that thinkers of other schools too had their own ideas about the primary unit of language. Their views, however, are in one way or the other implied in the views discussed by Bhartṛhari (VP II:3.284.18). Puṇyarāja is also aware of a sentence definition in the tradition of grammar which accepts individual words. But this definition is only *pāribhāṣika* 'technical', and it is, moreover, implicit in one of the eight main views enumerated by Bhartṛhari (VP II:2.17-19). Thus, while showing awareness of other upholders of the word, Puṇyarāja suggested that the Mīmāṁsakas occupied at least an important place among them.

Perhaps partly on the basis of Puṇyarāja's commentary, modern scholars have strongly emphasized the importance of the Mīmāṁsakas as Bhartṛhari's opponents and upholders of the primacy of the word. According to Iyer, "the doctrine of the reality and indivisibility of the sentence and the sentence-meaning was put forward in opposition to the Mīmāmsakas who believe in the reality of the individual word and its meaning" (Iyer, 1969:188). Gaurinath Sastri identifies the Mīmāṁsaka with the *padavādin*: "In seeking to develop the thesis that a sentence is an indivisible unit he [i.e. Bhartṛhari, JH] has to unfold and examine the view of the Mīmāṁsist (or, *padavādin*) who regards terms as ultimate elements and vehemently repudiates the view that they are unreal abstractions" (Gaurinath Sastri, 1959:83). Biardeau makes the following remark with regard to Bhartṛhari's ideas about the sentence: "Cependant, Bhartṛhari connaît les idées de Śabara et des Mīmāṁsaka sur ce point (...), et ce sont elles principalement que son exposé vise à réfuter, tantôt en paraissant suivre Patañjali ou tel autre grammairien, tantôt en retournant simplement contre la Mīmāṁsā les arguments qu'elle avance" (Biardeau, 1964:402). According to Coward (*Bhartṛhari*, 1976:129, note 21), Bhartṛhari establishes in the second chapter "the *vākya* or sentence *sphoṭa* over against the view of the Mīmāṁsakas." And in a very recent book, B.K. Matilal (1990:106) says that "In *Vākyapadīya*, ch. 2, Bhartṛhari (1965 edn.) notes that there are two principal philosophical theses regarding the notion of the sentence and sentence-meaning: one is called the to support the reality of the individual word presuppose Mīmāṁsā-principles;[6] but there also seem to have been upholders of the individual word among other groups including the grammarians themselves. The view that the sentence is divisible and that words are individual units may be subdivided into five views, in accordance with (Puṇyarāja's interpretation of) Bhartṛhari's enumeration of views on the sentence at the beginning of the second Kāṇḍa. Among these 'divisible sentence' views, one in particular has very close connections with the grammarians themselves rather than with the Mīmāṁsakas.

The view I have in mind is identified as *saṁghātapakṣa* by Puṇyarāja, with reference to the word *saṁghāta* 'collection' or 'coalescence' in Bhartṛhari's enumeration in kārikās 2.1-2.[7] Bhartṛhari discusses the view more elaborately in kārikās 41-48. The first two kārikās of this group are as follows[8]:

41. Whatever is expressed by a single word as the meaning, that much it expresses if it is in the sentence.

'indivisibility' thesis (*a-khanda-paksa*) and the other is the 'divisibility' thesis (*khanda-paksa*). [note that these two terms are used in Punyarāja's commentary but not in the kārikās, JH.] The first thesis is what Bhartṛhari himself maintains while the second is held by his opponents, the Mīmāṁsakas."

Here I will not investigate to what extent there is a basis in the available Mīmāṁsā sources from about Bhartṛhari's time, to consider the Mīmāṁsakas as upholders of the word. I only want to point out that we know of ancient Mīmāṁsā-thinkers who defended the individual phonemes (*varnas*) as eternal, but that the theoretical step from these eternal phonemes to eternally meaningful larger units remains rather vague in the earliest sources. See the discussion of this problem by Frauwallner, "Mīmāṁsāsūtram I, 1, 6-23" (WZKSO 5,1961), and D'sa, *Śabdaprāmāṇyam in Śabara and Kumārila*, Vienna 1980 (Publications of the De Nobili Research Library), esp. pp. 34, 93f, 113f.

6 Especially the passage VP 2.64-87 contains numerous references to the principles and technicalities of Mīmāṁsā.

7 Whereas Punyarāja is aware of a merely 'technical' (*pāribhāṣika*) definition of the grammarians in which individual words are accepted and which is included in one of the main views (VP II:2.17-19), he presents the *saṁghāta*-view as one of the main 'divisible sentence' views. This view receives full attention in those parts of the second Kāṇḍa in which the 'divisible sentence' views and 'indivisible sentence' views are explained and contrasted or opposed (this happens roughly speaking in the whole second Kāṇḍa up to and including 2.413-446, the last passage in which the two groups of views are confronted). From this one may infer that Bhartṛhari too considered the *saṁghāta*-view as one of the main 'divisible sentence' views.

8 41. *kevalena padenārtho yāvān evābhidhīyate /*
vākyasthaṁ tāvato 'rthasya tad āhur abhidhāyakam //
42. *saṁbandhe sati yat tv anyad ādhikyam upajāyate /*
vākyārtham eva taṁ prāhur anekapadasaṁśrayam //

42. But what arises as different and additional when there is a relation *(sambandha)* [between several words], that's what they call the sentence meaning, residing in several words.

These kārikās are reminiscent of some passages in the MBh. It is 42 in particular which is evocative of a sentence occurring a few times in the discussion of P 2.3.46 and 50 (MBh 2.3.46, 1:462.4; 2.3.50, 1:464.1012): *yad atrādhikyaṁ vākyārthah sah* 'what is additional here (namely, in the sentence in comparison with the separate words), that is the sentence meaning'. Because wording and context are so similar, there can be little doubt that 42 is a direct reference to this sentence.[9] The sentence is also cited by Puṇyarāja and in the Vṛtti on this kārikā. Kārikā 42 and the immediately preceding 41 should therefore be considered a reference to this statement in the grammarians' tradition rather than to a Mīmāṁsā view.

The close connection with the grammarians becomes especially clear from the Vṛtti. It is in the Vṛtti on kārikā 42 that we find the expression *tatrabhavat* 'His Honour' for the first time[10]: Time being limited it is not possible to enter here into a detailed discussion of the remarks by *tatrabhavat* 'His Honour', but I think there can be little doubt that the character of his remarks point to a grammarian rather than to a Mīmāṁsaka. Attention should be paid to the fact that the passage attributed to him constitutes a major citation in the text of one of the main 'divisible sentence' views. There is no indication that this grammarian *tatrabhavat* thought that the sentence would, in fact, be indivisible. Words and smaller divisions like the nominal stem and the ending are accepted in the passage attributed to him without apparent reservations. Is it possible that this

9 Another relevant passage which is not so close to these VP-kārikās in its wording is found in a discussion of Vārttika 4 on MBh 1.2.45, according to which from a sentence not only the word meanings are understood but also the relation between them (MBh 1.2.45, 1:217.25-218.10).

10 "And this difference between what is additional in the sentence and what is additional in the word has been explained in the (Mahā)bhāṣya. Hence *tatrabhavat* 'His Honour' says: While the meaning belonging to a single word becomes the cause of correct formation (*saṁskāra*) of a word [read: *padasaṁskārahetur*] with regard to an utterance [read: *vacanaṁ prati*] within the nominal stem (*prātipadika*), [the meaning] belonging to a single word – the very cause of correct formation of the word – is not the cause with regard to the joining/employment of endings: [as for instance in] *grāmo, grāmo ramaṇīyah*. But the meaning of the sentence, residing in several words, is said to be a cause for establishing 'loss of accent' and all these things (*pratinighātādi*)" (VP II:210.24-211.3).

For the use of *tatrabhavat* outside the context of drama as a very general honorific (at least from the time of the MBh), cf. Aklujkar, 1972:186-187. In the MBhD *atrabhavat* is sometimes used to refer to a grammarian or thinker on grammatical subjects.

tatrabhavat 'His Honour' was actually a grammarian who upheld the reality of the individual word?

Tatrabhavat is referred to at one or two other places in the Vṛtti. First, *tatrabhavat* is cited in the Vṛtti on 2.447 in the context of a discussion of a sūtra in Pāṇini's grammar that presupposes a certain view on the sentence. Again there is no indication that the sentence is considered as the primary linguistic unit that would, in fact, be indivisible.[11]

The other relevant place is the Vṛtti on 2.453. Although the text contains a gap, there seems to be another reference here to *tatrabhavat* 'His Honour'. The context is a discussion of general and more particular actions implied in the meaning of a verb. It can be shown that there is again a close connection between an idea attributed to *tatrabhavat*, and a view which accepts individual word meanings. As in the case of the reference in the Vṛtti on 42, the idea attributed here to *tatrabhavat* is closely related to the view called *saṁghātapakṣa* by Puṇyarāja, one of the main 'divisible sentence' views.[12]

11 The viewpoint attributed to *tatrabhavat* makes use of the notion of *ākāṅkṣā* (syntactic or semantic expectancy), which shows that the sentence is considered to be a composite whole. (The notion of *ākāṅkṣā* is used not only in Mīmāṁsā, but also in the MBh, together with *apekṣā*).

tatrabhavanto manyante – bahuṣv api tiṅanteṣu yeṣv arthalakṣaṇā kācid ākāṅkṣā vidyate teṣām ekavākyatvaṁ na vyāvartyate / tathā ca sūtre 'rthavān tiṅparyudāso bhavati (VP II:315.9-11).

12 The idea attributed here to 'His Honour' is as follows:
sāmānyamātram eva tatra vivakṣitaṁ viśeṣās tv anumeyāḥ, na teṣāṁ śabdena saṁsparśo 'stīti. "There (*tatra*) only the general is intended, the particulars are to be inferred; language (*śabda*) does not touch these [particulars]." (VP II:317.8-10).
The problem of whether a word expresses a general or a specific meaning has been discussed in the context of views which accept individual words. According to one view, the word in a sentence expresses in fact a particular meaning. Yet, the word considered in isolation seems to express a general meaning. This is expressed in VP 2.17, and according to Puṇyarāja the idea presupposes *anvitābhidhāna*. There is another view in this context, which is closer to the idea attributed to *tatrabhavat*. It is expressed in one of the kārikās of the passage 41-48 (*saṁghātapakṣa* according to Puṇyarāja), namely 44:

sarvabhedānuguṇyaṁ tu sāmānyam apare viduḥ /
tad arthāntarasaṁsargād bhajate bhedarūpatām //

Others consider the general (meaning) to be in accordance with all particulars; on account of combination (*saṁsarga*) with other meanings, it partakes of the state of being a particular.

Here the meaning of the word is first of all something general, next this general meaning acquires the status of a particular meaning on account of the combination with other words in the sentence. All this is in perfect accord both with the view attributed to *tatrabhavat* and with *abhihitānvaya*. Again, there is a close connection between an idea attributed to *tatrabhavat*, and a view which accepts individual word meanings.

It should be pointed out that even according to the view that the sentence is the primary unit, it is acceptable to divide the sentence secondarily into words and these into smaller parts. It is therefore not impossible that even *tatrabhavat* considered the sentence as actually one and indivisible. However, the fact is that he is cited three times in the context of views accepting individual words, but not in the context of the views which Bhartṛhari ultimately seems to prefer and for which he has become famous, namely those that emphasize that the sentence is the primary, indivisible unit of language.[13]

What is clear is that one of the main views accepting individual words is closely connected with grammarians. As for the identity of *tatrabhavat* referred to at two or three places in the Vṛtti, it is difficult to arrive at definite conclusions, other than that he was a grammarian cited in the context of 'divisible sentence' views.

Let us now turn to the Mahābhāṣya-dīpikā (MBhD), often held to be a work by the same Bhartṛhari who wrote the VP. The MBhD is in several respects similar to the VP. Similar grammatical problems are discussed in a comparable way, and it seems to have originated in an almost identical cultural-intellectual *milieu*.[14] While all these similarities are there, there is also an important difference. Whereas the upholders of the sentence and the upholders of the word appear as two well-established groups in the VP, the upholders of the sentence are by no means prominent in the MBhD. It should be remembered that a student of the MBhD is severely

13 The identification of *tatrabhavat* with Bhartṛhari, the author of the kārikās himself, has played a role as a possible argument in the discussion about the authorship of the Vṛtti. But this identification has now become somewhat problematic. Cf. Iyer, 1965:xxxif, xxxvi; 1969:31f, 35f and Aklujkar, 1972:186-188, who have not accepted this identification as a strong argument. Bronkhorst, 1988:109-110, however, used it again as an argument for different authorship. For my own standpoint in this discussion, see "Bhartṛhari and the ancient Vṛtti" (in preparation). The tentative conclusions at which I will arrive below, make the identification with Bhartṛhari *in an earlier stage of his development* again possible, though by no means necessary.

14 About the similar Vedic background of the two works see Rau, 1980 and Bronkhorst, 1981 and 1987. Aklujkar, 1972:188 speaks of "the overwhelming similarities of diction, thought, and sources that are noticed in the V, kārikās, and Tripādī [= the VP Vṛtti, VP kārikās and Mahābhāṣya-dīpikā, JH]". Cf. Svaminathan (1963:59-70), Yudhisthir (*saṁvat* 2020:347), and Iyer (1965:xxvi-xxix). In my view, the evidence that can be adduced shows (1) that the MBhD and the VP were *considered* to be the works of one and the same Bhartṛhari for many centuries; (2) that the author of the MBhD and the author of the VP, if they were not identical, had at least a very similar background and were familiar with the same grammatical tradition. That it is for the moment very difficult to go beyond this conclusion is clear from the parallel case of the authorship of the VP-kārikās and Vṛtti, for which cf. the preceding note.

handicapped by the inferior quality of the single and incomplete manuscript available, on which all present editions are based. For this reason, all conclusions with regard to the MBhD necessarily have a merely tentative character. In numerous instances a few emendations are necessary to make a passage understandable. And perhaps future research and detailed comparisons with related texts like Kaiyaṭa's Pradīpa will suggest new emendations which will alter the meaning of some of the passages. On the basis of the imperfect and problematic material, I would still like to present a few examples from this work that illustrate its distinctive perspective on the primary unit of language.

First of all, the author of the MBhD distinguishes between the language of Vedic literature and everyday language. In Vedic language words are not used in isolation, they occur in fixed sequence in a sentence; but in everyday language there is no fixed word order (MBhD 1:1.16-19). The difference between sentences in Vedic texts and sentences in everyday language is that in the former there is permanence in use (*prayoga-nityatvam*), whereas in the latter there is impermanence (MBhD 1:17.18-21). In the kārikās of the VP such distinction is not made.[15] In two places there is a reference to tradition in support of the idea that sentences are permanent. The first place is VP 2.58-59, which contains a reference to a passage in the MBh applying strictly speaking only to the transmitted texts of Vedic literature. Yet the immediate context of this passage suggests that the conclusion should be applied to all sentences. The second reference to tradition, VP 2.344-345, concerns a minority view referred to in the Nirukta, a text outside the grammarians' tradition.[16] The view applies to sentences in everyday life. This illustrates how the domain in which sentences are permanent in the 'indivisible sentence' views in the VP is not restricted to Vedic sentences as in the MBhD.

Second, the MBhD enumerates different views on the permanence of *śabda* (MBhD 1:16.26-17.26). At the corresponding place the MBh only asks the question: Is the word permanent or impermanent? It does not

15 As far as I know, no such distinction is made in the Vṛtti either, nor is it made in any of the views in Puṇyarāja's commentary, either in his 'divisible sentence' views or his 'indivisible sentence' views.

16 Grammar (Vyākaraṇa) and Nirukta are two of the six traditionally accepted 'ancillary disciplines of the Veda' (Vedāṅgas). The MBh considers grammar the most important one among the six ancillaries (MBh 1:1.19). As for the Nirukta, it draws a distinction between views accepted in this discipline itself and those accepted by grammarians (Nirukta, 1.12, 9.5, 13.9). The interpretation of the phrase *padaprakṛtiḥ saṁhitā* favoured in the VP (2.58-59) is exactly opposite to the one accepted in the Nirukta (1.17).

mention different views at all, so the author of the MBhD must have felt free to expound on the issue according to his own insights. The views he mentions are quite divergent; it seems that he even refers to the view of the Jainas, according to which only *prākṛta* words are permanent (MBhD 1:16.9). As we have seen, permanence in the case of Vedic sentences has indeed been defended in this context (MBhD 1:17.18-21). However, there is no trace of a view that the *śabda* which is permanent would ultimately be the sentence in all cases. If the author of the MBhD accepted the sentence as primary in the way explained in the VP, i.e. in a general sense and not only in Vedic sentences, one would expect that this view would have been, if not discussed in some detail, at least referred to at this place.

Third, in a few places the author of the MBhD says explicitly that both words and sentences are meaningful units. And here the meaningfulness of the word is not made dependent upon the meaningfulness of the sentence, whereas according to the 'indivisible sentence' views in the VP, the sentence would be the primary meaningful unit and the word would be secondary. In MBhD 2:8.27-28 it is said that *śabda*, interpreted as either the word or the sentence, is meaningful and permanent, and that it is a collection of phonemes.[17] Another passage in the MBhD comments upon the MBh-expression *atha kim idam akṣaram iti* 'Now, what is this *akṣara*?' (MBh 1:36.5), which occurs at the end of the critical study of the alphabet or list of phonemes. Therefore, *akṣara* must have been intended as 'phoneme' by Patañjali. However, for the author of the MBhD this immediate context is not decisive. He mentions that according to some thinkers *akṣara* is *varṇa* 'phoneme', but that according to others it is *pada* 'word' or *vākya* 'sentence'. It is clear that the MBhD-author prefers the latter two options.[18] In the MBh-passage which concludes the study of the

17 *śāstre hy arthavataḥ śabdasya nityatvaṁ pratijñātam, padasya vākyasya vā / sa ca samudāyo'bhyupagataḥ śāstre / samudāyaś ca varṇātmaka eva.*

18 He mentions an earlier MBh-passage in which *akṣara* was used, apparently as an illustration of its meaning of *pada* 'word' or *vākya* 'sentence' (although the meaning 'phoneme' would do very well too). Thus he diverts the attention from the preceding discussion about the phonemes. In the discussion of the following Ślokavārttikas about *akṣara* he also finds occasion to bring forward the interpretation as 'word' and 'sentence'. One of the explanations of *akṣara* in the first Ślokavārttika is that it is derived from *aś* with the suffix *sara*. This is further explained in the MBhD as follows: "because it pervades (*aśnute* = *vyāpnoti*) meaning, (and) because it is pervaded by meaning, therefore *akṣara* (is so called)" (2:39.8-9). Next he mentions as examples of meaningful units only *pada* 'word' and *vākya* 'sentence'. Thus he forgets that in the preceding discussion Patañjali accepted that in some cases phonemes may be meaningful, namely if they happen to be roots, affixes or certain particles. At any rate, the preceding passage dealt with phonemes

list of phonemes it is also said that *akṣara* is the place where *brahman* resides (MBh 1:36.14). Commenting on this statement, the author of the MBhD mentions the *pada*[19] as the place where *brahman* explained as the Veda resides, and not the *varṇa* (which is what one would expect on the basis of the context in the MBh) nor the *vākya* (which one would expect on the basis of the second Kāṇḍa of the VP, especially as it is interpreted by Puṇyarāja). In other words, the word and the sentence are presented here as linguistic units which are on the same footing as far as their meaningfulness is concerned, perhaps with a certain preference for the word. In spite of the immediate context, the importance of the phoneme is neglected. And unlike the preferred views in the VP, the MBhD at this place does not make the meaningfulness of the word dependent on the meaningfulness of the sentence.

Finally, it is certainly not the case that there is no reference at all to the sentence in the MBhD. Such references, however, are usually compatible with Puṇyarāja's 'divisible sentence' views (*anvitābhidhāna* or *abhihitānvaya*). Still, I have found a reference to a view which seems very close to an 'indivisible sentence' view as found in the VP. It is the following (MBhD 6b:27.18-19)[20]:

> "Or, it is possible (to say) that just as phonemes (are) meaningless, words (in a sentence) are also meaningless. Thus the meaning is understood from the sentence."

It is clear that this is very reminiscent of a VP kārikā such as 2.413.[21] In the VP, kārikā 2.413 is connected with an important, and even preferred view on the sentence. In contrast, the reference in the MBhD represents just one out of many approaches to the problems posed by P 1.1.44: *na veti vibhāṣā*. Further, it is also introduced by the MBhD-author as just a possible viewpoint. It is not presented either as an important viewpoint of a well-established group of thinkers, or as the only view ultimately accepted by the author.

(and the question whether they are meaningful or not), not with words and certainly not with sentences.

19 MBhD 2:39.16-17. Palsule's *pade* in MBhD 2:39.17 on the basis of the parallel in Kaiyaṭa's Pradīpa and instead of *yade* (MS, AL, Sw) is an improvement.

20 *atha vā śakyam evānarthavadvarṇavat padāny anarthakāny eva / evam eva ca vākyāt evārthapratipattiḥ* / The view is adopted here as one of the possible ways to avoid the conclusion that in some circumstances an individual word loses its (external) meaning and has only its own form as meaning.

21 *yathaivānarthakair varṇair viśiṣṭo 'rtho 'bhidhīyate / padair anarthakair evam viśiṣṭo 'rtho 'bhidhīyate //*

The main points made above may be summarized as follows: First, in the MBhD, as in the VP, it is recognised that sentences may be considered permanent. In the MBhD, however, this applies in full only to Vedic sentences. In the places in the VP where the permanence of sentences is defended, no such restriction is made. Secondly, the view of the sentence being the primary, indivisible unit of language is not mentioned in places in the MBhD where one would expect this if the view was really important to its author. Thirdly, the author of the MBhD explicitly presents the word and the sentence as linguistic units which are on the same footing as far as their meaningfulness is concerned. He does not make the meaningfulness of the word dependent upon that of the sentence. However, more than an indirect, dependent meaningfulness of the word cannot be accepted if the 'indivisible sentence' views of the VP are adhered to. And finally, in a rare instance in which the MBhD does refer to an 'indivisible sentence' view similar to an 'indivisible sentence' view in the VP, it is not presented as an important view of a well-established group.

The author of the MBhD is therefore by no means as committed to the indivisible sentence as the author of the VP seems to be.[22] Does this mean that the VP and the MBhD did not have the same author? Perhaps it does. But another explanation is possible, one that will do justice to the overwhelming number of similarities between the two works in terms of ideas and approaches to problems. It is not possible to demonstrate in this paper in detail how significant these similarities are. It may suffice to point out that the approach to the problem of the relation between word and phoneme is very similar in the two works.[23] The only difference is that in the VP it is applied not just to the relation between word and phoneme, but also to the relation between sentence and word.[24]

22 That the two are identical and have the same convictions with regard to the indivisible sentence seems to have been presupposed by V.B. Bhagavat and Saroja Bhate, in their edition with translation and notes of the 6th Āhnika of the MBhD. They mention the *vākyasphota*-view twice in reference to certain passages (MBhD 6a:4.11-12 and MBhD 6a:4.13-17) in the MBhD. Whereas the translation of these passages brings out correctly that they are about words and their constituents, not about the relation between words and sentences, the notes on p. 100 introduce without proper basis in the MBhD itself 'the theory of *vākyasphota*' and the idea that 'the word itself does not have an existence'. See also note 24 below.

23 Cf. references in note 14 above for some similarities between the MBhD and the VP kārikās. Similarities that can be traced back directly to the MBh are of course much less significant than those that cannot.

24 To give only one example, all that can be learned from the MBhD passages mentioned in note 22 (MBhD 6a:4.11-12 and MBhD 6a:4.13-17) is that the approach to the problem

Moreover, a problem which occupied the author of the MBhD was: How is it possible for one word to refer to a whole sentence or its meaning? Much attention is paid to this problem even where this would not seem necessary from the point of view of the MBh.[25] In the VP the fact that a single word, even a single phoneme, can refer to the meaning of a whole sentence is used as an argument for the sentence meaning being one and indivisible (VP 2.40, 444).

Is it possible to do justice both to the similarities and this one important difference between the VP and the MBhD? At this point we have to estimate what is historically probable and what not. Different scholars will have different ideas about this. Here, one hypothetical explanation of the facts just described will be put forward. It seems quite possible that the two works were written by the same author, but at different stages of his life. Apart from the great number of passages in the MBhD which express ideas very close to ideas expressed in the VP-kārikās, there is even one VP-kārikā that occurs in exactly the same form in the MBhD. On the basis of this fact, Joshi and Roodbergen have suggested that the VP must have been the earlier work, and that the MBhD cites from the VP (Joshi-Roodbergen, 1986:212-213, notes 904 and 908).[26] However, it is possible that this kārikā is cited in both cases from a third source. Or, if we want to maintain that one and the same Bhartṛhari is the author of both the VP and the MBhD, and also of the kārikā in question, we might propose that while writing the MBhD, he also

of the status of different units of language (MBhD 6a:4.12 *paramārtha-darśane ca sarvatraivāyaṁ pravibhāgo nāsti*) is similar to an approach well-known from the VP (e.g. VP 1.74: *pade na varṇā vidyante varṇesv avayavā na ca / vākyāt padānām atyantaṁ pravibhāgo na kaś ca na //*). The important difference is that in the MBhD this approach is not applied to the sentence.

25 The most striking case is in the second Āhnika, when the author of the MBhD starts to discuss the problem how the word *idam* in a phrase in the MBh can possibly refer to a whole sentence-meaning. From the point of view of the MBh the whole discussion is rather far-fetched (MBhD 2:16.23-17.2). In the discussion of the MBh-passage on the *saṁprasārana-sūtra* (P 1.1.45, MBhD AL:269) the consideration of this problem is more at its place. Commenting on the MBh on P 1.1.44, the author of the MBhD investigates in great detail how *vibhāsā* can be the name of the expression *na vā* (MBhD 6b:23.18-25.2). While following the broad outlines of the discussion in the MBh, he treats of the issues raised there in an elaborate and rather independent way, and even adds numerous related issues on his own.

26 In the introduction of Joshi-Roodbergen, 1986, the authors mention the Mahābhāsya-dīpikā as "a work written after the composition of the VP" (Joshi-Roodbergen, 1986, introduction:ii).

started to put some of his thoughts in the form of kārikās, at least one of which found its place in the later VP.

Indeed, because of the difference explained earlier, it seems to be more likely that the MBhD was written or finalised earlier than the VP, than the other way round.[27] To explain: There is no denying that both the MBhD and the VP have a strong tendency to enumerate different views on topics related to language and grammar. If the 'indivisible sentence' views were as important in grammatical circles as suggested by the discussions in the VP, why were they so much neglected in the MBhD, even there where its author felt free to discuss the views of quite divergent schools of thought? It is difficult to account for this if the MBhD was written later.[28] But if the MBhD was written earlier, it is not difficult to see why very little attention is paid by its author to 'indivisible sentence' views. Maybe there were a few thinkers who adhered to such views, but they were not prominent and the views were possibly not fully developed. The MBhD is still close to the MBh which, while taking the sentence into account in numerous instances, places no emphasis on its importance, let alone on the idea that it would constitute the primary and indivisible unit of language. In between the writing of the MBhD and the VP someone among the grammarians, perhaps the author of the MBhD himself, became increasingly interested in some of the existing 'indivisible sentence'

27 K. Kunjunni Rāja, in the Encyclopedia of Indian Philosophies volume 5, suggests that the MBhD was written earlier than the VP without discussing arguments pro or con: "Bhartrhari's philosophical ideas are found in their fully developed form in the *Vākyapadīya*, which is his magnum opus; but the germs of his theories may be found in his commentary on the *Mahābhāsya* ... Some of the ideas that were *developed later* into a cogent system are found scattered here and there in the commentary on the *Mahābhāsya*" (Encyclopedia of Indian Philosophies, volume 5: The Philosophy of the Grammarians, ed. H.G. Coward and K. Kunjunni Rāja, pp. 172-173, my emphasis).

28 Because of their similar cultural background, it seems not very likely that either one was written and finalised and the author of the other one remained completely unaware of its existence. It should also be kept in mind that the purpose and scope of the MBhD and VP overlap to a considerable extent (for which cf. Aklujkar, 1980/81, p. 599 and notes 21 and 22). Both are commentaries on the MBh, both - not only the MBhD but also the VP - follow the MBh very closely. There is no topic in the VP which is not also somewhere a topic of the MBh. The difference is that the MBhD follows mainly the sequence of the exposition in the MBh and the VP not. Most importantly, both the author of the MBhD and the author of the VP are anxious to take numerous alternative views on a certain topic into account, adding even views beyond the different views directly referred to in the MBh. This gives both works the character of a 'compendium', and it is precisely the 'compendium' character of the MBhD which makes one expect references to the 'indivisible sentence' views at several places if they were as important as suggested in the VP.

views and developed them. By the time the VP was written, these views had become prominent enough to figure as major views in grammatical discussions. If it was the author of the VP himself who had developed these views, then it is also clear why these views figure suddenly so prominently in the VP: In his eyes these views were simply very important and probably even superior to views which accept the independent meaningfulness of words. Whereas the permanence of sentences was restricted to Vedic sentences in the MBhD, such a restriction was no longer necessary in the fully developed 'indivisible sentence' view in the VP.

This is, of course, nothing more than a hypothetical explanation on the basis of the facts pointed out above, and it is as a hypothetical explanation that it is being presented to the scholars assembled here today. Much more research will be needed to determine whether such an explanation can really do justice to both texts and to their treatment of a wide range of divergent views. We may now return to the question asked at the beginning of this paper: Who are the so-called upholders of the word, the *padadarśins* referred to in kārikā 2.57 of the VP? The emphatic identification by later commentators and interpreters of these upholders of the word with Mīmāṁsakas, has obscured the fact that there were important upholders of the word among the grammarians themselves, including probably the one referred to in the Vṛtti as *tatrabhavat* 'His Honour'. In the MBhD, the word is usually presented as being individually meaningful, not as an abstraction from an indivisible sentence. In the VP, in contrast, there are indications that its author ultimately preferred the view that it is the indivisible sentence which is primary. Yet, the author of the VP also discusses in a positive way views in which individual words are accepted as meaningful and the sentence as divisible. In so doing, he discusses views which were accepted among grammarians, and perhaps - if he is the same person who wrote the MBhD - even by himself at an earlier stage of his development.

Abbreviations

AL = Abhyankar and Limaye's edition of the Mahābhāṣya-dīpikā (Poona: Bhandarkar Oriental Research Institute, 1970).

MBh = Patañjali's Vyākarana-Mahābhāṣya (Kielhorn's edition).

MBhD = 1. Mahābhāṣya-dīpikā
2. The recent Mahābhāṣya-dīpikā edition (with translation and notes) by a team of scholars (Poona, 1985-1991). Numbers following MBhD refer to this edition as follows: MBhD (number of Āhnika):(page).(line). 6a and 6b as number of the Āhnika refer to MBhD Āhnika VI, Part I (Poona, 1986) and Āhnika VI, Part II (Poona, 1990) respectively.

MS = manuscript of the Mahābhāṣya-dīpikā, as referred to in the editions.

P = Pāṇini's Aṣṭādhyāyī.

Sw = Swaminathan's (partial) edition of the Mahābhāṣya-dīpikā (under the title Mahābhāṣya Ṭīkā, Varanasi: Banaras Hindu University, 1965).

VP = Bhartṛhari's Vākyapadīya; references to the kārikās (with two or three arabic numerals separated by periods) follow W. Rau's critical edition of the kārikās (Rau, 1977).

VP II = Iyer's edition: *The Vākyapadīya of Bhartṛhari, Kāṇḍa II, With the Commentary of Puṇyarāja and the ancient Vṛtti*, Delhi etc.: Motilal Banarsidass, 1983. For Puṇyarāja's commentary reference is made to this edition as follows: VP II:(page).(line).

Bibliography

Aklujkar (1972): Ashok Aklujkar, "The Authorship of the Vākyapadīya-Vṛtti", *WZKSOA* 16:181-198.

Aklujkar (1980/81): Ashok Aklujkar, "Interpreting Vākyapadīya 2.486 historically (part 1)", *ALB*, 581-601.

Biardeau (1964): Madeleine Biardeau, *Théorie de la connaissance et philosophie de la parole dans le brahmanisme classique*. Paris - La Haye. (École Pratique des Hautes Études - Sorbonne. Sixième Section: Sciences Économiques et Sociales. Le Monde d'Outre-Mer. Passé et Présent. Première Série: études XXIII.)

Bronkhorst (1981): Johannes Bronkhorst, "On some Vedic quotations in Bhartṛhari's works", *Studien zur Indologie und Iranistik* (Reinbek) no. 7: 73-175.

Bronkhorst (1987): Johannes Bronkhorst, "Further remarks on Bhartṛhari's Vedic affiliation", in: *Studies in Indian Culture, Professor S. Ramachandra Rao Felicitation Volume*, Bangalore: 216-223.

Coward (1976): Harold Coward, *Bhartṛhari*, Boston.

Iyer (1965): K.A. Subramania Iyer (tr.), *The Vākyapadīya of Bhartṛhari with the Vṛtti*, Chapter I, English Translation. Poona. (Deccan College Building Centenary and Silver Jubilee Series, 26.)

Iyer (1969): K.A. Subramania Iyer, *Bhartṛhari, A Study of the Vākyapadīya in the light of the Ancient Commentaries*. Poona. (Deccan College Building Centenary and Silver Jubilee Series, 68.)

Joshi-Roodbergen (1986): S.D. Joshi and J.A.F. Roodbergen (ed., tr.), *Patañjali's Vyākaraṇa-Mahābhāṣya, Paspaśāhnikā*. Poona. (Publications of the Centre of Advanced Study in Sanskrit, Class C, No. 15.)

Matilal (1990): Bimal K. Matilal, *The Word and the World, India's contribution to the study of language*. Delhi: Oxford University Press.

Rau (1977): Wilhelm Rau (ed.), *Die* mūlakārikās *nach den Handschriften herausgegeben und mit einem* pāda-*Index versehen von Wilhelm Rau*. Wiesbaden. (Abhandlungen fur die Kunde des Morgenlandes XLII, 4).

Rau (1980): Wilhelm Rau, "Bhartṛhari und der Veda", *Studien zur Indologie und Iranistik* (Reinbek), no. 5/6:167-180.

Subramania Iyer, K.A., see Iyer, K.A.S.

Svaminathan (1963): V. Svaminathan, "Bhartṛhari's authorship of the commentary on the Mahābhāṣya", *Adyar Library Bulletin* no. 27:59-70.

Yudhisthir (*saṁvat* 2020): Yudhisṭhir Mīmāṁsaka, *Saṁskṛta Vyākaraṇa-Śāstra kā Itihāsa*, Sonipat: Rāma Lāl Kapūr Trust, vol. 1.

MEANING AND THE LIMITS OF ANALYSIS: BHARTṚHARI AND THE BUDDHISTS, AND POST-STRUCTURALISM*

John D. Kelly, Princeton

I would like to begin with some questions, questions that I offer as my primary contribution to these deliberations. I am still very much a student of Sanskrit grammar and the history of *vyākaraṇa*, my research and study still in progress. So I will focus here on questions, explain my reasons for asking them, and then will outline the directions my efforts to answer them are taking.

Questions

In short, I want to pose two main questions about Bhartṛhari and the Vākyapadīya/Trikāṇḍī text. The first is whether the text is making a general argument that all formal analytic systems are limited in their potential to explain or even describe linguistic phenomena: whether the text is an argument for limits to formal analysis of meaning. The second question is whether this argument, or any of the text's arguments, are directed specifically as a response to Buddhist arguments about language and meaning, especially those of Nāgārjuna or the Vijñānavādins.

* My research for this project was conducted in Pune in 1990 under the auspices of AIIS. Thanks are owed to S.D. Joshi, who was my research guide, and to both Deccan College and the University of Poona for hospitality. I also want to specially thank Dr. (Mrs.) Saroja Bhate, and Pandit Vamanśāstri Bhagavat, for their patience and insights as they led my reading of the vākya kāṇḍa, and the jātisamuddeśa, of the Vākyapadīya. Edwin Gerow began my Sanskrit education, my education in Indian philosophy and my reading of the Vākyapadīya; my debts to him are enormous. This paper has been improved by valuable criticisms and suggestions from colleagues at Princeton and by participants in the International Conference on Bhartṛhari; thanks especially to Jim Boon, Jan Houben and Johannes Bronkhorst. In this case more than in the usual sense, all errors and infelicities of interpretation are obviously my own.

Let me develop the first question first. To begin, what are we to make of the perplexing argumentative style of the Vākyapadīya? On the one hand, from the beginning it clearly presents itself as a text delivering wisdom, wisdom relevant to liberation. But on the other hand it is clearly, in large sections at least, a *saṃgraha*, a collection of views. While more critical of some views than others, the text abjures final judgments of preference on specific analytic questions, especially in the most technical passages of the third kāṇḍa. How do these two aspects of the text cohere? Pandit Vamanśāstri Bhagavat, who showed me the wisdom of reading the text as a *saṃgraha*, directed me to 2.489 as the explanation:

prajñā vivekaṃ labhate bhinnair āgamadarśanaiḥ /
kiyad vā śakyam unnetuṃ svatarkam anudhāvatā // 2.489

"The intellect gains discernment by means of the different perceptions (*darśanas*) of tradition. / How much can be ascertained by someone following their own reason?"

tat tad utprekṣamāṇānām purāṇair āgamair vinā /
anupāsitavṛddhānāṃ vidyā nātiprasīdati // 2.490[1]

"The knowledge of those who have not sat at the feet of seniors, who conjecture this and that without the established traditions, will not become clear."

As well as a warning to young scholars, these kārikās might also be the cornerstone for the bridge between the text's own argument and its *saṃgraha* form: the intellect gains discernment by means of *different* darśanas. Thus the text is, as it describes itself in 2.487, an **āgama-saṃgraha**, a collection of traditions.

Is the argument above connected to the argument about *prakriyā*, *avidyā* and *śāstra* in 2.233? Let us first consider 2.233 and a bit of its neighborhood[2]:

1 In my numeration and citation I am following the Rau 1977 text. Aklujkar (1978, 1991) doubts that the controversial set of kārikās at the end of the second kāṇḍa, including the two cited here, are written by Bhartṛhari himself. He prefers to read them as the work of one of Bhartṛhari's students. As he argues for the more controversial kārikās in this much disputed set, they still have great value as comments on the text and its position in the history of vyākaraṇa. However, if he is right it clearly puts more burden on the rest of my evidence for my conjecture concerning Bhartṛhari's attitude towards difference of traditions and limits to analysis.

2 Another kārikā almost identical to 2.233 is included in the Abhyankar and Limaye Vākyapadīya text as 3.14.78, but is not included by Rau. It will be left aside here.

vyavahārāya manyante śāstrārthaprakriyā yataḥ // 2.232/cd

"Thus the constructions (*prakriyā*) of meaning in *śāstra* are thought of for worldly use."

śāstreṣu prakriyābhedair avidyaivopavarṇyate /
anāgamavikalpā tu svayaṃ vidyopavartate // 2.233

"Only *avidyā* is described by the differences of construction in the *śāstras*. / Truth (*vidyā*) arises by itself, not as an alternative of tradition."

anibaddhaṃ nimitteṣu nirupākhyaṃ phalaṃ yathā /
tathā vidyāpy anākhyeyā śāstropāyeva lakṣyate // 2.234

"Just as an effect is indescribable and unconnected to causes, / just so, truth (*vidyā*) also, though not fit to be interpreted, is characterized as if it had *śāstra* as a means."

Bhartṛhari's stance on tradition is quite as complex as the organization of his text. *Śāstra* is indispensable, but is not itself the cause of truth. *Śāstra* is characterized as if it were the means to truth, and it is the best hope the intellect has for becoming clear and achieving understanding, but the truth arises by itself, not dependent on causes nor existing for worldly use. On the one hand, then, Bhartṛhari seems skeptical of the adequacy of any analytic formalism. In kārikās 2.226-227 Bhartṛhari makes it clear that **doṣās tu prakriyāgatāḥ**, "Errors are produced by *prakriyā*," when grammatical *śāstra* devises means for explaining complex formations (*vṛtti*) to the ignorant (*abudha*). The various analyses of negative compounds figure predominance among the imputed elements differently, when the object of analysis is undivided in fact. *Prakriyā* here, and in 2.232-33, seems clearly to refer to analytical constructions, grammatical explanations, and neither these nor *śāstra* are themselves actual means to truth. But on the other hand, Bhartṛhari is clearly a defender of tradition, clearly committed to Vedic ritual, an Upaniṣadic Brahman, and also to Patañjali and Pāṇini in particular.

Why is tradition so useful? Why is Bhartṛhari not a Buddhist? And why is *prakriyā* used, also, in Vākyapadīya 1.1? Is this use of *prakriyā* separate in sense from that in 2.233, as for example the glossary to the Abhyankar and Limaye Vākyapadīya text suggests? Perhaps the various *prakriyā* of grammarians and others are false, the *prakriyā* of Brahman real, the first errors, the second the world. Or perhaps the *prakriyā* of the grammarians are a minor part of the ongoing *prakriyā* of Brahman. Or perhaps both. The same question could also be posed about *artha* as used in 1.1, in relation to *artha* discussed in the rest of the text. Resolving such matters is beyond me, but clearly the theological commitment should not be bracketed from the position being taken on the *avidyā* of *śāstra*. Let us compare *prakriyābheda*, difference in construction, as discussed in 1.22 and 2.13:

> yad ekaṃ prakriyābhedair bahudhā pravibhajyate /
> tad vyākaraṇam āgamya paraṃ brahmādhigamyate // 1.22
>
> "... that which is one, divided variously by differences in construction, / That highest Brahman is apprehended when the science of grammar is attained."
>
> śabdasya na vibhāgo 'sti kuto 'rthasya bhaviṣyati /
> vibhāgaiḥ prakriyābhedam avidvān pratipadyate // 2.13
>
> "There are no divisions of the uttered word (*śabda*). How will there be divisions of the meaning (*artha*)? The ignorant conceives difference in constructions by divisions."

Kārikā 1.22 caps the discussion explaining why and how a science of grammar is the royal road to Brahman, for those who can learn to see through the manifested forms to the unitary cause of all. Kārikā 2.13 caps the first presentation in the vākya kāṇḍa of the view of word and sentence that comes to be called the *sphoṭavādin* view.[3] Analytical processes based on observation of similarities and differences can, for practical purposes, lead to the separation (*apoddhāra*) of words in a sentence, just as they can lead to division of base and suffix in a word. But these formal techniques are to aid the ignorant: indeed, the kārikās ending the first kāṇḍa seem to suggest that the learned (*śiṣṭa*) create the *smṛti* literature in general, and grammatical treatises in particular, "in deference to the differing capacities of individuals and by taking into consideration the changed capacities of expressions as far as merit and demerit are concerned" (as Aklujkar summarizes, Aklujkar 1990: 137).

Many have traced the connection between Bhartṛhari's theology and the *sphoṭavādin* semiotics, through various paths and into controversial theological matters.[4] I am asking not about where to position Bhartṛhari in relation to other theologies, but about how to read him as a theorist of

3 Joshi (1967) argues persuasively that the author of the kārikās did not use the term *sphoṭa* as freely and widely as has the later tradition in using it to refer to the wholeness of sentence and utterance meaning. However there is surely little doubt that the author of the kārikās intended to present powerful arguments in favor of taking sentence/utterance meanings as undividable unities. The literature on the *sphoṭa* concept is vast – see also Brough, Dasgupta, Gaurinath Sastri, Raja, Coward, and Matilal.

4 For example, Iyer and Gaurinath Sastri disagree on how to place Bhartṛhari in relation to later Vedāntic arguments; see also Coward 1980: 79ff. Coward himself, and Dasgupta before him, locate Bhartṛhari in close relation to Yoga.

language structure and functions. Let us reformulate the original question, about the *saṃgraha* form of the text, and the emphasis in 2.489 on studying many *different āgamadarśana*. I wonder whether it is part of Bhartṛhari's point that all formalizations are limited, and that reasonable analytical traditions will be plural, because of the way language (and God) really work in the world: that the student gains wisdom from the formal study of language not by deciding on a best formal system but by realizing the virtues, and limits, of each, as each grapples with language phenomena that make, remake, and transcend their own means.

My other question then follows. It can be posed independently of the thoughts above, and simply: Is Bhartṛhari arguing against specific Buddhist arguments about language and meaning? If so, which Buddhists and which arguments?

If I am on the right track in my reconstruction of Bhartṛhari's project, then these questions can be reformulated more precisely: is Bhartṛhari's argument about the unity of sentence/utterance meaning, and the utility of contemplating the powers and limits of formal approaches to linguistic analysis, meant as a response to the deconstructive Madhyamaka dialectics, or to the vijñānavāda psychological formalization of Madhyamaka, or both? Is Bhartṛhari encompassing both into a vision of language and the world that better respects the reality of meaning and the powers of traditions, while still accepting and even privileging the lessons of deconstruction as well?

It is this last question that is most important to me, not simply as a student of Bhartṛhari's thought, but also as a student of anthropological linguistics in particular and contemporary social theory in general. Perhaps there is a post-structuralism in Bhartṛhari's arguments that gets significantly beyond the post-structuralisms now discussed in literary criticism, history, and anthropology.

Bhartṛhari and Post-Structuralism

While I am intent on reading Bhartṛhari in his own terms and in relation to the discourse of his own time, these are not my only interests. I am also interested in trying to relate his ideas to those of my own discipline at present. In this, I don't think I am unusual. B.K. Matilal and many others have done painstaking work reconstructing Indian philosophical systems, while also comparing them with Western philosophy. Harold Coward and many others have worked to raise comparative theological as well as philosophical questions while reading Bhartṛhari. Linguists working on vyākaraṇa in relation to Western linguistics have abounded. We have works and work in progress juxtaposing Bhartṛhari and Wittgenstein, Nāgārjuna and Nietzsche, Pāṇini and Chomsky, Diṅnāga and Saussure. If I am unusual it is simply that from the perspective of American anthropology, I want to ask questions about meaning in practice, and this leads me to juxtapose Bhartṛhari with Whorf and Bakhtin.

Juxtapositions of this sort have always run against the grain of philological technique and intention, and they have challenged the tendency to separate radically "the Orient" as a thought-world and mentality from "the West" and "the Modern." Along such lines I want to make a few points about my own comparisons. First, I do apologize for my trespasses against philological structures of feeling. George Steiner puts it well: "philology insists on the holiness of the particular" (1989: 106). When philologists criticize comparative juxtapositions of culturally and historically separated thinkers, their concern to protect ancient and obscure texts from misreading is admirable. As Steiner argues, in reading our understandings are always provisional, and there should be "cardinal discretions" in any encounter with a text (1989: 176). If my questions seem to be the sort that "diminish both the object of our questioning and ourselves" (ibid), my defense for posing them is a hope that might be naive, the hope (with Vološinov 1983, but without his rancor) that we might find in the works of Bhartṛhari the kind of meaning that elicits response as well as respect. Second, my comparison will not be of East versus West. We have the privilege of living in interesting times; we inherit many and contradictory disciplines and methods for the study of language and culture. In our present intellectual world it has become risky to assert, or deny, relationships of sameness, or difference, between phenomena across cultures. I am persuaded by Edward Said's critique of the past premises of Orientalist discourse (see Said 1978) that it is dangerous, especially, for the goal of comparative scholarship to be to locate essential differences between Eastern and Western intellectual history. But third, I do not conclude from this that it should be our goal to find and assert essential similarities. Instead, my sense is that judgments of similarity or difference work well as conceits for launching a comparative investigation, but are peculiar as conclusions to them.

It is easy, and arbitrary, to prove that Nāgārjuna's arguments are different from those of Jacques Derrida, for example, or to find that they are fundamentally similar. My right hand is clearly different from my left, and clearly similar to it. Such comparisons need to have a larger purpose.

Otherwise, as Gerald Larson recently argued, they run the risk of being "mechanical, one-dimensional, forced, anachronistic, and worst of all, tedious" (Larson 1989: 15). Heretofore, that purpose has often been the delineation of Oriental difference, even when that difference is positively valued, as for example in Frits Staal's article on "Euclid and Pāṇini" (1965). The cost is then homogenization: in Staal's case, Euclid's method is presented as the classical foundation of all Western science, Pāṇini's as the classical foundation for all Indian sciences. I would rather use comparison to launch in a different direction, into the dialogues and debates within each intellectual history, including debates now raging in my own field. The clearest evidence of a limit to the difference between India's intellectual history and the West's is that the history of linguistics connects them. The Western comparative philologists learned a great deal from Pāṇini, no matter how quickly the debt was suppressed. Despite denigrating gatekeepers such as Whitney, later generations of Western linguists still learned things from vyākaraṇa, including arch-rivals Bloomfield and Whorf and more recent scholars. Recently, French semiotic luminaries Julia Kristeva and Tzvetan Todorov have each tried their hands at interpreting, respectively, Bhartṛhari and Abhinavagupta. But my own premise is that much more can be said: that Bhartṛhari might still have work to do.

I would like to begin, therefore, by asserting the similarity of Derrida and the Buddhists, especially Derrida and Nāgārjuna.[5] Derrida insists on the centrality of language to science and history, on the primacy of signifiers over signifieds, and on the dangers of signification. No one can actually establish the things signified, especially in a written discourse. But

5 Harold Coward has recently called into question "current suggestions that Derrida can be understood as a Mādhyamikan Buddhist" (1991: 157; see also 1990a, 1990b), suggesting instead that the arguments of Bhartṛhari are more similar to those of Derrida. While I agree that one finds the lessons of deconstruction well assimilated in Bhartṛhari's argument, I disagree with Coward mainly in his reading of Derrida. Coward goes so far as to suggest a hidden Christian theology in Derrida's arguments (1991: 155-56); in this and other aspects of his reading I think Coward takes Derrida "beyond" the critique of the metaphysics of presence, and thereby evicts him from his residence. Thus with many others, notably the translator of *Of Grammatology*, Gayatri Chakravorti Spivak (personal communication), I see more of a family resemblance between the arguments of Derrida and Nāgārjuna: in both, the primary commitment and tactic is deconstruction. However, my intention in this essay is not to overturn Coward's reading – I became aware of it after this paper was written – but simply to continue, as he suggests, to think about the issues raised by these comparisons. For other interesting efforts to calibrate Indian and Western language theories discussed here see Matilal 1990: 120-32 on Derrida and Bhartṛhari, and Chatterjee 1985 on Whorf and Wittgenstein, with reference also to Derrida and Mādhyamika Buddhism.

the signifiers convey the presence of the objects anyway, by appearing to be dependent on the things they merely stand for. Derrida seeks to "deconstruct" this sense of presence by revealing the entrapping power of the signifiers, to change philosophy and science by "deconstructing" the metaphysics of presence on which they have been founded up to now. Similarly, Nāgārjuna is clearly skeptical about the adequacy of any full signification. If anything, Nāgārjuna's four-fold negation (*catuṣkoṭi*) is more thoroughgoing than anything Derrida offers as a rejection of the possibility of finding truth or reality through use of signs. The way Nāgārjuna reports it, no predications are adequate, and no *dharma* of anything or anyone was asserted by the Buddha. Derrida is more neurotic: he announces that he is "destroying the concept of "sign" and its entire logic" (1974: 7), but many other places insists that the sign concept is "necessary," (e.g., 1974: 13), and that he is simply out to reverse the dependence of semiotics on logic (1974: 48).

Deconstructing *āstika dharma*, among other things, Nāgārjuna's Buddhism identifies predicative cognitions, attachments of signs to each other and agents to signs, as the locus of worst trouble. Derrida's deconstruction leads not to a four-fold negation but to strange sentences - such as "the sign ~~is~~ that ill-named ~~thing~~, the only one, that escapes the instituting question of philosophy, 'what is...?'" (1974: 19) - precisely because his deconstruction of the sign is *less* thoroughgoing. Derrida is conventionally thought of as a "post-structuralist." It is a good label, in a sense, because it connects his thought intrinsically to structuralism, and after all his linguistics still depends deeply on Saussure's.[6] On the Buddhist side, a formal description comparable to Saussure's of signs as arbitrary, gaining their identity by a system of negations, seems not to have arisen until after Nāgārjuna's time: the Indian philosopher whose views most closely resemble Saussure's is probably Diṅnāga, as Raja 1963 was perhaps the first to point out. As Diṅnāga saw it, the things meant by words came into being through exclusion of others, and thus their identities are entirely relational - Saussure would say, their identities are entirely their values in a structure. But for Diṅnāga, as for the other Buddhists, the point was not the utility of such a value system. In Buddhism the deconstructive implications of a structuralist definition of meaning units was obvious from

6 On this point, to stick with *Of Grammatology*, consider his admission: "I should like to approach, as a privileged example, the project and texts of Ferdinand de Saussure. That the particularity of the example does not interfere with the generality of my argument is a point which I shall occasionally try not merely to take for granted" (p. 29).

the beginning of analysis of cognition in terms of systems of concepts (*vikalpa*), and what was deconstructed was *dharmas*.

In the recent past many anthropologists, along with scholars in several other disciplines, committed themselves to privileging formal models of sign systems as the vehicle for interpretation and explanation of everything. To the "structuralists," the sign systems were themselves the core social and cultural realities. My discipline now seeks to find its way back from the interiors of abstracted semiotic realms, and its current favored definition of the real and target for analysis is "practice." It seems to me that it needs to do more thinking about meaning, meaning units, and the general prospects for formal analysis of meaning, and that leads me to Bhartṛhari because he, also, addressed such topics in the wake of, and perhaps in response to, a powerful deconstructive formalization of meaning.

Bhartṛhari and the Buddhists

So what is Bhartṛhari's relationship to the Buddhist semiotic claims? I can only lay out here what I am looking at to try to answer this question. In a preliminary way, let us move backwards. We know Diṅnāga read Bhartṛhari carefully, quoted him respectfully, but sought in the end an approach to meaning focussed on word-level units and **apoha**, meaning-determining exclusion. Hattori (1979) and Herzberger (1986) show that this response to Bhartṛhari was crucial to Diṅnāga's philosophy. However, the way Warder (1980) tells Diṅnāga's story is also interesting: that Diṅnāga was following the critique of the Sarvāstivādin Abhidharma of his teacher Vasubandhu, and developing it into a general theory of knowledge (Here see also Hattori 1977). Hattori's and Herzberger's works are important, though they have more to say about Diṅnāga than Bhartṛhari, because they move against the grain of Buddhist scholarship and *āstika* scholarship, against the tendency to trace the main lines of dialogue and influence simply within purely Buddhist or purely *āstika* genealogies. Indeed, when scholars note a Buddhist influence on an *āstika* thinker, or an *āstika* influence on a Buddhist, it is frequently with subtle or not-so-subtle regret.[7] The Sarvāstivāda/Sautrāntika controversy surely cannot be

7 Consider for example Lindtner on influences on Nāgārjuna: "it must be conceded that he could not escape the impact which orthodox Brahmin dialectics (*vāda*), natural philosophy, arts, crafts and sciences indirectly exerted upon the Buddhist milieu. ... From his birth to his death Nāgārjuna must as a member of the community have received an

separated from themes and questions of *āstika* philosophy, however. Look at the dilemma: The Sarvāstivādins, populating new intellectual centers and writing in Sanskrit under royal patronage, codify and interpret Abhidharma, and even infer lost sūtras, "following probably the Mīmāṃsaka system of inferring the existence of lost Vedic texts" (Warder p. 346). The Buddhists contesting Sarvāstivādin technique have their critiques rejected, and perforce become a new and separate school, the Sautrāntikas. Shortly thereafter Nāgārjuna emerges, also writing in Sanskrit, and argues against definitions and predications altogether. He deconstructs the Abhidharma project, and contests as well with *āstika* schools, especially the emerging Nyāya (see Bronkhorst 1985, Lindtner 1982). Centuries later the Sautrāntika Vasubandhu is still in the business of abhidharma critique but, Warder tells us (p. 449), provokes his student Diṅnāga to shift focus from abhidharma definition dilemmas to the more general problem of pramāṇas.

So we have Diṅnāga influenced by his teacher Vasubandhu and/or his worthy adversary Bhartṛhari. In constructing his story Warder notes the existence of Paramārtha's life of Vasubandhu (and follows Frauwaller in dividing it into the mixed lives of two Vasubandhus), but makes no reference to another interesting character in Vasubandhu's life as described by Paramārtha: grammarian Vasurāta, Bhartṛhari's teacher. Quoting from Takakusu's (1905: 45) account of Paramārtha's text[8]:

> Vasurāta was, according to Paramārtha, a Brahmin, husband of a sister, i.e. a brother-in-law, of King Bālāditya. He was well-versed in the vyākaraṇa treatise. When Vasubandhu composed the Abhidharmakośa, this Brahmin attacked his composition on the authority of the Vyākaraṇa, thinking that the Buddhist disputer would certainly [not?] defend his own work when the grammatical faults were thus pointed out. Vasubandhu answered: – "If I do not understand the Vyākaraṇa, how can I ever understand the admirable truth of Buddhism?" Thereupon he composed a treatise utterly refuting the thirty-two chapters of the Vyākaraṇa. Thus the Vyākaraṇa was lost, while the Abhidharmakośa survived. The King and the Queen-mother gave him some lacs of gold. Vasurāta further tried to defeat him through the intervention of another scholar. The vyākaraṇa mentioned here will in all probability be the "Candra-vyākaraṇa" when we see that what Bhartṛhari (died 650) obtained through Vasurāta (though not necessarily directly) was Candragomin's grammar.

Takakusu's Bhartṛhari date is wrong, obviously. We have a cast of five characters – Vasubandhu and his worthy opponent Vasurāta, their con-

incessant flow of impressions and convictions, prejudices and superstitions from the Hindu society surrounding him" (1982: 250-51).

8 I have not read Paramārtha's text. At this point I am simply working from accounts of its content.

temporary Candragomin, and their students Bhartṛhari and Diṅnāga. I know of no reason not to accept that these five were closely connected in time, perhaps literally connected in face to face dialogues, and definitely connected by these contests for reputation and influence. What a peculiar question: "If I do not understand the Vyākaraṇa, how can I ever understand the admirable truth of Buddhism?" But what text is it that is refuted and "lost"? The thirty-two chapters makes it sound like Pāṇini's Aṣṭādhyāyi. Was Pāṇini's text replaced by another in some sort of official curriculum, replaced, for example, by Candragomin's twentyfour chapter grammar? We also have other candidates for lost texts, of course: Patañjali's Mahābhāṣya, Vyāḍi's Saṃgraha, the latter an interesting candidate especially since it clearly *was* lost at some point. Does this problem remind anyone of another passage about lost and waning texts and struggles over vyākaraṇa? I refer of course to the problematic final kārikās of Bhartṛhari's vākya kāṇḍa.

For certain, I have no new overall interpretation of these problematic kārikās.[9] Perhaps with Bronkhorst (1983) we should see the Saṃgraha lost, the Mahābhāṣya not properly studied, and the Aṣṭādhyāyī suffering.

9 I do have one tiny contribution to offer, in regard to the problematic term **pratikañcuka** in kārikā 2.484. Aklujkar, Bronkhorst and others have debated whether to read this term as "protective armor." In the same kārikā is another puzzling term: **śuṣkatarkānusārin**, "pursuers of dry reason." Why this metaphor? I stumbled across the following aphorism in one of Apte's dictionaries (1988: 326): *nindati kañcukakāraṃ prāyaḥ śuṣkastanī nārī*. "A dry-breasted woman usually reviles her blouse-maker." Apte glosses it by comparing it to "A bad workman quarrels with his tools"; perhaps his reticence is similar to that which drives later scholars away from milk and towards war metaphors. In any case, we have here a connection between *śuṣka* and *kañcuka*:

baijisaubhavaharyakṣaih śuṣkatarkānusāribhiḥ //
ārṣe viplāvite granthe saṃgrahapratikañcuke // 2.484
(alternate reading: *saṃgrahe pratikañcuke*)
"When the Ṛṣi's (or Ṛṣis') book, that was like a blouse for the Saṃgraha (or, for which the Saṃgraha was blouse-like), was mutilated by the dry-reason pursuing Baiji, Saubhava and Haryakṣa..."
(with alternate text:) "When the book of the Ṛṣis, the Saṃgraha, was mutilated like a blouse by the dry-reason pursuing...

Abhyankar and Limaye report this text variant, but Rau does not. Either version makes sense. In the first the wrecked text is either the Mahābhāṣya, blouse for Vyāḍi's Saṃgraha, or in the more grisly version, the Aṣṭādhyāyī, for which the Saṃgraha was blouse-like. The text variant makes the Saṃgraha itself both the blouse and the mutilated text, and is perhaps the best fit with the aphorism. In any case, this way of interpreting the kārikā accords with the second kāṇḍa's humor, confidence, and tendency to cryptic intertextuality. The image of reason (*tarka*) as a dry breast, and implicitly, *śāstra* and *śabda-pramāṇa* as the means to milk, is also in accord with kārikās 489-490, quoted at the outset of this essay.

Going back to Paramārtha's text, the debate between Vasubandhu and Vasurāta is situated in turn in a history of competition for royal bequests between Buddhists and Sāṃkhya philosophers; Vasubandhu avenged defeat of his own teacher, and won royal favor and money, only to be challenged by the grammarian Vasurāta, who was said also to have invited Saṃghabhadra to launch a new Sāṃkhya challenge to Vasubandhu (Takakusu 1905: 46). Should we then expect that the vyākaraṇa of Vasurāta was specifically Sāṃkhya? We may not want to go so far with this account, but unless we disregard it wholly, I think we can conclude that vyākaraṇa's mode of knowing, and *śabda* as a *pramāṇa*, were under debate in Vasurāta's time, and with this in mind I think we should look more closely at Candragomin. What kind of Buddhist was Candragomin? And what was Bhartṛhari's attitude toward his grammar?

In the Candra-vyākaraṇa, "the influence of the Mahābhāṣya is evident," Scharfe tells us, "at every step" (1977: 164). But Candra discarded the rules relating to Vedic forms and accents, and sought to discard, also, all defined terms, calling his vyākaraṇa **asaṃjñaka**, "termless" (II.2.68, quoted in Scharfe 1977: 165). According to Scharfe, "To an astonishing degree he has succeeded in using only enumerations, contractions or descriptive expressions and in avoiding defined terms" (ibid). The most significant casualty of this move is the kārakas; Candra reduces Pāṇini's three levels in syntax logic to two (on this change see also Radicchi's contribution to this volume). "Shall we assume," Scharfe asks, "that Candragomin dropped the objective relations under the influence of Buddhist mentalistic philosophy?" (1977: 166). I think we can move the question closer to those of Vasubandhu and Vasurāta's day. First, returning to the all-Buddhist perspective, where does Candragomin's project fit in? Whose side is he on among the Buddhists? Surely the anxiety to jettison all definition-commitments sounds like an effort to meet Sautrāntika strictures against Sarvāstivādin reifications. Shall we suppose, then, that vyākaraṇa was also attacked for dependence upon reifications? Was Candragomin's grammar an effort to save vyākaraṇa from attachment to definitions, indeed an answer to criticisms of vyākaraṇa made by Vasubandhu, teacher of Diṅnāga?

Second, whose side was Candragomin on, between Vasurāta and Vasubandhu? Jettisoning all the Vedic references and explanations certainly sounds like a Buddhist thing to do, so we need not doubt that he was a Buddhist. But (at least as reported by Takakusu) Paramārtha presents him as an ally of Vasurāta, a defender of vyākaraṇa. The boundary between two sides begins to blur. Perhaps, with friends like this the Pāṇinians did not need enemies. But recall that Candra was cited, apparently favorably, in one of the closing kārikās (2.486) of the vākya kāṇḍa. By most suggested readings of the disputed kārikās, Candra was favored as a defender of vyākaraṇa technique in general and Patañjali's interpretations in particular. Was it, any port in a storm? How complete was Bhartṛhari's endorsement of Candra?

The key kārikā 2.486 is another obscure one (see Aklujkar 1991, etc.), and I won't attempt a whole translation:

> parvatād āgamaṃ labdhvā bhāṣyabījānusāribhiḥ /
> sa nīto bahuśākhatvaṃ candrācāryādibhiḥ punaḥ // 2.486

Is there any way we can construe the *āgama* from "the mountain" as a reference to Candra and others following, also, a different *āgama*? Whatever the resolution of *parvatād*, here Candra and company are lucky not to be *śuṣkatarkānusārin* but instead *bhāṣyabījānusārin*, following not dry reason (see 2.484, and note 9 above) but the seeds of the Bhāṣya (see also 2.482); in consequence their action carries vyākaraṇa to many-branchedness. In short they get somewhere. The metaphor has switched from milk to seeds and trees, but the contrast is clearly between strategies that do and do not produce growth.

More generally, did Bhartṛhari accept Candra's innovations? Surely Bhartṛhari was a committed and loyal follower of the Pāṇinian tradition. In his texts, discussion abounds of problems in Vedic interpretation. But what about the kāraka theory? Can we say that Bhartṛhari accepted Candra's abandonment of kārakas and other technical definitions? Clearly not. The bulk of the Sādhanasamuddeśa, and much discussion elsewhere, presents and discusses kāraka theory for reader edification, and includes Bhartṛhari's new formulations discussed by Radicchi. But can we say that Bhartṛhari therefore rejected Candra's formulation of vyākaraṇa? No special judgment need be made if all *śāstra* is *avidyā*. And clearly, Candra's vyākaraṇa was presented within the fold of a many-branched vyākaraṇa, itself part of a diversity of edifying, albeit indirectly edifying, darśanas.

If Bhartṛhari was making a general response to Buddhist attacks, in defense of *śabda pramāṇa*, *śruti* and *smṛti*, and Vedic *āgama*, his principal opponent was not Candragomin. How to sort out other candidates? In the absence of direct references, suppose we try to connect works that respond to each other's concepts, metaphors and examples. Which Buddhist discussions did Bhartṛhari play with? Here I will mainly consider Nāgārjuna as a candidate.

In the Paspaśāhnika, the first day-session of Patañjali's Mahābhāṣya, the meaning of **siddha** is discussed, in relationship to Patañjali's argument that Pāṇini's grammar concerns rules for a language in which word (*śabda*) meaning (*artha*) and their relation (*saṃbandha*) are already established (*siddha*)(Bhāṣya I.1.61; here I follow the numbering in Joshi and Roodbergen). If established meant permanent, then how could the relationship be permanent if the meaning was a particular thing (*dravya*) that could be destroyed, etc.? Patañjali's answer was that the relationship was permanent when the particular things with the meanings, even if themselves impermanent, had a permanent relationship with the meanings (see I.1.74-75). (Something like, the cow is a cow for as long as it exists.) Looking into Bhartṛhari's commentary, the Mahābhāṣyadīpikā, on these Bhāṣyas, we find him going farther into the question of the nature of these permanent relationships. He proposed, and did not reject, the possibility that the relationship is *samavāya*, inherence. Then he suggested that the relationship is **aśūnyatā**, non-emptiness. Rather than insist that the particular cow is inherently a cow, and this connects word and meaning, this version of the established nature of a *dravya* meaning simply asserts that the *śabda* is never empty: the *śabda* can only be if it is in relation to some meaning.

The deconstructionist argument is that such relations are never actually established. Nāgārjuna advanced no arguments out of awareness that all predications are actually **śūnya**. In his first samuddeśa on *dravya* in the Vākyapadīya/Trikāṇḍī, was Bhartṛhari playing with Nāgārjuna's fourfold negation? Discussing *tattva*, the ultimate *dravya*, Bhartṛhari reported that by *āgama atattva* is not different from it, but is simply *tattva* ill considered, given different form. Kārikās 3.2.12 and 3.2.13 sound like versions of the third and fourth planks of a fourfold negation: *na tad asti na tan nāsti*, etc., then, *tan nāsti vidyate tac ca*, etc. But Bhartṛhari *affirmed* the propositions, offering them rather than rejecting them. The next kārikā begins,

> tasya śabdārthasaṃbandharūpam ekasya dṛśyate /
>
> "Of the one, a form as word, meaning and relation is seen."

As he did in his commentary on Mahābhāṣya I.1.75, Bhartṛhari argued here that *dravya* meanings unfold into a unity, oneness, an ultimate substance behind all forms. The words cannot help but refer to the real by means of unreal limiting factors. In the dravya samuddeśa, the example of the gold and the bracelet followed (3.2.15-16). The gold takes on the form of the bracelet, without compromising its purity as gold. (Implicitly, then, the gold is and is not the bracelet, etc.) What is really expressed by all words is the ultimate *prakṛti* that is real beyond all transformations. The words seem plural in nature but are not really separate from this basis, and express it in all their forms. This would seem a Sāṃkhya style rebuttal (perhaps Vasurāta's?) to the fourfold negation; the next kārikā invokes a key Advaitin metaphor, comparing word plurality to dream images. Can either be said to be Bhartṛhari's *own* solution? Despite the fact that the text, especially the third kāṇḍa, is a *saṃgraha*, I suspect one answer is closer to his heart than the others, but that it is none of these!

Before going on with Bhartṛhari's analysis of the problem of establishment of *dravyas*, let us note that the gold and the bracelet are discussed as well in the Mahābhāṣya itself, in I.1.76, the Bhāṣya immediately after those discussed above. As Joshi and Roodbergen note (p. 113), the Mahābhāṣya shifts remarkably in its discussion of *dravya* from Bhāṣya 75 to Bhāṣya 76, from considering *dravya* as impermanent individuals of permanent types, to considering, with the gold and the bracelet, the *dravya* as the substance, the gold, to be more permanent than the bracelet form. The first clearly is the Mīmāṃsā view of *dravya*. The second, Joshi and Roodbergen speculate, might be a doctrine from Sāṃkhya or Buddhist *vijñānavāda*. I haven't found any Buddhist discussions of the example from Bhartṛhari's time or before, let alone from Patañjali's time or before (which was surely before the rise of the *vijñānavādins* proper); any references would be welcome. But can we speculate that Buddhist/Sāṃkhya contests, or other Buddhist contentions, had changed and raised the philosophical stakes for discussions of meaning, even by Patañjali's time?

As Madhav Deshpande has pointed out, problems in the analysis and practice of encoding, moving into word form, are quite different from problems in the analysis and practice of decoding, moving from word form to meaning.[10] Pāṇini was clearly concerned primarily with the first set of problems, problems still addressed in a vast continuing science of formal linguistics, now including the work of Joshi, Cardona, Kiparsky, and Staal. But by Patañjali's time, questions from the other problem set were also

10 I heard Deshpande make this argument in lectures at the University of Poona in May 1990. This distinction between encoding and decoding sciences could also be applied fruitfully to restate one of Frits Staal's strangest arguments (see Staal 1982, 1988a, 1988b), the argument that only ancient India developed a science of ritual. As an anthropologist, I am still put off by Staal's clearly intentional dismissal of the history of ritual study in cultural anthropology, but the point is well taken if it is simply that the ritual literature from Veda to Mīmāṃsā concerns increasingly complex problems in the analysis and practice of the encoding of rituals, while the Western sciences of ritual have overwhelmingly concerned interpreting rituals already performed and observed.

being posed.[11] Controversy over combining the two types of grammatical inquiry continues; Joshi, for example, calls for separating out the linguistic elements of arguments, even Bhartṛhari's arguments, from the questions of "metaphysical and semantic philosophy of language," thus banishing semantics from linguistics proper (1967: 54). Patañjali would seem to be his ally. As Joshi and Roodbergen note (1986: 106), Patañjali's discussion of the gold and the bracelet has "a different point' than Bhartṛhari's. Patañjali concluded that it is futile to try to specify what about *artha* is *siddha* or *nitya*, except the fact that it is the word meaning (I.1.79). Bhartṛhari agreed that the *dravya* is established (*siddha*) by its relation to the *śabda* - but he sees nothing futile about the point.

Let us return, then, to Bhartṛhari's discussion of options for delineating *dravya*. For the ultimate *tattva* to be a *dravya* would after all place a limiting factor on *tattva*. After discussing *saṃbandha* Bhartṛhari offered his shortest samuddeśa, a further samuddeśa on *dravya*, with a very different point. After announcing that the rest of the samuddeśas will discuss things abstractly separated from sentence meanings by *śāstra*, Bhartṛhari argued in 3.4.3, final kārikā of this samuddeśa, that *dravya* emerge as a power of grammar. *Dravya* are whatever is intended to be separated as things, existing in the grammatical positions where pronouns, thing designators, are used. The point is reaffirmed in the next samuddeśa, on *guṇas*, where he showed that any dependent quality can be grammatically recast into the position of primary substantive under discussion. In one sense, *dravya* is thereby deconstructed: no essential *dravyas* are left. But the signs are saturated with grammatical *śakti*, and cannot be emptied of it.

Similarly, in the jātisammudeśa Bhartṛhari privileged grammatical *śakti* in *artha*, as in the example of the *khadira* post referred to in a Vedic injunction to sacrifice. The *khadira* is clearly a type of tree, but we understand that a *khadira* twig will not do, and what kind of other posts would be suitable alternatives, because we are understanding "*khadira*" within the whole injunction.

11 They are said to have already been under discussion by Vyāḍi and others as well, especially in the missing Saṃgraha. Very hard to say, when we have neither the text nor a complete and reliable account of it. Was the Saṃgraha Bhartṛhari's model even for his own *saṃgraha* strategy? No doubt, in a simple sense. Quite possibly a Vyāḍi did launch discussion of sentence as the unit of meaning. But I would be very surprised if the earlier text connected the theological, epistemological, grammatical-formal, and genre issues in as complex, elegant, and coherent a fashion as Bhartṛhari's text does, and in particular if it responded as coherently to deconstructive arguments.

ato jātyabhidhāne 'pi śaktihīnaṃ na gṛhyate //3.1.4cd

"Thus, even though the denotation is of *jāti*, nothing devoid of *śakti* is grasped."

Types of things, and particular things in question, are shaped by the whole sentences. The fact the *khadira* of the injunction is and is not the *khadira* species reveals gaps between signifiers, signifieds, and referents only if we seek a unit of meaning at the level of the sign. The ability of reanalysis to reconfigure the relationships between signs, things and classes is indeed deconstruction of the sign as unit, but only further evidence of the power of grammar to communicate meanings through whole sentences and utterances.

To get back to the search for markers of dialogical relationship, from Nāgārjuna to Bhartṛhari: Another possible connection point is a metaphor, lamps and light. One target of Nāgārjuna's deconstruction was *pramāṇa* theory. As Bronkhorst has recently shown, the Nyāya sūtras and the possibility of a Nyāya darśana distinct from Vaiśeṣika emerged in Nāgārjuna's day, and Nāgārjuna challenged the Nyāya sūtras even while the final form of the Nyāya sūtra text was still being compiled. The Nyāya sūtras, rules for debate, raised the problem of how to establish *pramāṇa* as means of knowledge without an infinite regress, since thinking about them transformed them from means to object of knowledge (*prameya*). The Nyāya solution was that the *pramāṇas* were means of knowledge of themselves as well as other objects, just as the light of a lamp (*pradīpaprakāśa*) illuminated itself and other things. Two of Nāgārjuna's texts, the Vigrahavyāvartanī and the Vaidalyaprakaraṇa, criticized this theory at great length (See Bronkhorst 1985, Lindtner 1982, Bhattacarya 1986, Santina 1986). The subject cannot be the object of its own act; if fire illuminated itself it would also burn itself (see Bhattacharya 1986: 117n[12]). Nāgārjuna may go so far as to argue that the lamp cannot illuminate anything, itself or another object, whether in contact or not (see Lindtner 1982: 88).

Bhartṛhari, on the other hand, gets heavy use out of *prakāśa* metaphors. Does he privilege things known by seeing over those known by hearing, as when *śruti* and *smṛti* are elaborated by all-*seeing* Ṛsis for those who do not already see and understand? (See Vākyapadīya 1.36ff) In any case, in *śabda* he connects seeing to hearing, because *śabda* involves both;

12 Bhattacarya et al point out that Śaṃkara borrows and repeats this argument of Nāgārjuna, when disputing with Vijñānavādins. Thus Śaṃkara moves against the grain of Bhartṛhari's return to self-illuminating means of knowing – in criticism of a Buddhist school!

the words heard, like light, illuminate at least their own form if received, and if received and grasped properly, their meaning as well (Vākyapadīya 1.56ff). This is the crucial general capacity (*śakti*) of *śabda*. How does Bhartṛhari's formulation evade the logical difficulties demonstrated by Nāgārjuna? Perhaps by new deployment of the deconstructionist's main conclusion, that semiotics do not follow logic, but rather the reverse. Relations such as that of subject, means and object are constituted by grammatical powers themselves, as Bhartṛhari discusses at length in the Sādhanasamuddeśa. In such a sentence as "He kills himself with his own hands," a physical unity is established separately and simultaneously as subject, object, and means, with no contradiction.

I am not at all sure that Nāgārjuna himself is the Buddhist theorist most important to Bhartṛhari. (Vasubandhu would be an obvious alternative, still to be investigated; and if Warder is right that there are two Vasubandhus, then both of them, the Vijñānavādin and the Sautrāntika.) But some scholars have emphasized the Nāgārjuna connection. Lindtner, a formidable Nāgārjuna specialist, has declared that Nāgārjuna's distinction of worldly from ultimate truths had "a decisive impact" on Bhartṛhari, "though this fact and its far-reaching implications seem to have escaped the notice of the modern interpreters of the Vākyapadīya" (1982: 280). Has it escaped Lindtner's notice, in turn, how much of Nāgārjuna's theory and method Bhartṛhari encompasses and overturns?

Bhartṛhari, Whorf, Bakhtin and Meaning

The reception and revision of Bhartṛhari's arguments has been widely studied, especially their reception and revision by Diṅnāga, Śaṃkara, the Mīmāṃsakas and the Rhetoriticians (see, e.g., Coward 1980, Matilal 1990). As we know vyākaraṇa itself was eclipsed by other disciplines, later to be revived. If I am right about Bhartṛhari's argument, surely it was greatly revised within vyākaraṇa as well, by his more formalistic successors after the great gap. The process might be poignantly indicated by Nāgeśa's clean, tidy, clear and economical reading of a line of Kaiyaṭa. Kaiyaṭa's introductory verses to the Mahābhāṣya appear, from Joshi and Roodbergen's translation, remarkably close in style and substance to Vākyapadīya formulations. He begins his text, like the Brahman kāṇḍa, with a salute to the ultimate. The highest ātman has no form but takes on all form, has passed beyond a nature of being and nonbeing. How to construe this last phrase? Joshi and Roodbergen (1986: 4) report and endorse Nāgeśa's explanation, "That is to say, he can be described as *sat* 'being' only."

My own research into Bhartṛhari and his times is clearly impelled by my interest in decoding as well as encoding problems. I am trying to seize the flash - I do not pretend, even to myself, to have accomplished it well - in both Bhartṛhari's sense and also in Walter Benjamin's sense (1968: 255): seizing the flash when a fragment of the past is recalled at a present moment of danger. As I have already said, the present moment that concerns me is the search for a post-structuralist semiotics, a search which sometimes seems to have become a contest between fatuous nihilism based on deconstructive wisdom, and reductive power-functionalisms working from materialist and political-economic premises. My sense is that we need a much more powerful reconsideration of meaning itself to resolve the impasse, and that Bhartṛhari might help.

The two other theorists I find useful here are Benjamin Lee Whorf, an American anthropological linguist of the mid-twentieth century, and Mikhail Bakhtin (and his student V.N. Vološinov), recently rediscovered literary critic whose work was suppressed for its heterodoxy in Stalinist Russia. Both have many points of affinity, and difference, with Bhartṛhari and with each other. What all three have in common is great skepticism about meaning as something built up from real, individual sign units.[13]

Whorf, like Bhartṛhari, suggests that even in our imagination, imputed "word" meanings are the meanings of sentences; to think "chair" is to think "a chair exists" (See Vākyapadīya 2.270, Whorf 1956: 67). The sentence, for Whorf as for Bhartrhari, is the real meaning-bearing unit. Like Bhartṛhari Whorf focusses upon grammatical powers, what he calls among other things "configurative rapport," that give form to formless

13 Others have suggested comparing Bhartṛhari with George Steiner, especially with respect to Steiner's critique of deconstruction in *Real Presences* (1989). Steiner like Bhartṛhari seeks meaning in sentence and larger units, values formal analytic systems while also insisting on their limits, and unlike Whorf and even Bakhtin, puts explicit weight on divinity, divine presence, as the foundation for creative acts. Ironically, it is in his account of the relation of human and divine creativity that Steiner seems to me to be most different from Bhartrhari. Steiner finds human creativity in "the impulse to rivalry with a 'jealous God'" (1989: 207); both divinity and humanity seem specifically Judeo-Christian here. But of course the more consequent divergence is no doubt the one between Steiner's "wager on transcendence" (1989: 214) and my own disciplinary commitment to meaning that is, indeed, humanly made and immanent in our world. The disciplinary commitment of anthropology to ethnographic study of real human communities is itself a clear wager that Steiner is wrong to dismiss the mundane, daily, commonsensical, and empirical as a source for real presences (cf. Steiner 1989: 133-34, 199), a wager with Vico on human eloquence and self-fashioning (cf. Said 1985).

whole thoughts and intentions, and allow thoughts and intentions to be determined in the reverse process upon reception of the sentences of others. And the two theorists' linguistic traditions are not wholly separate. Whorf's sources for information on vyākaraṇa and the rest of Indian philosophy were apparently quite pedestrian. But he was impressed both by the linguistic accomplishments,[14] and by what he described, using Sanskrit terms, as the Indian philosophical interest in discussing meaning that was *arūpa* as well as meaning in *nāma* and *rūpa* (1956: 253). Perhaps the most important difference between Whorf and Bhartṛhari is that Whorf insisted on difference, and equality, between the grammars of different languages. He spent his intellectual life comparing different language grammars, especially European languages with Hopi, a Native American language without verb tenses. While the Indo-European languages make "thing" a term of cosmic scope of reference, dividable into formless substances plus forms (alas, no mention of gold and bracelet), in Hopi grammar, temporality is thought intrinsic to substantives. Rather than events being a kind of thing, our "things" are depicted as enduring sorts of events. Like Bhartṛhari, Whorf saw linguistic skills as something to be developed, not mistrusted, not because the formal operations were themselves the vehicle of truth but because insight into their powers led to clearer understanding. His prescription was not devotion to traditional proprieties, however, but study of multiple languages.

In contrast to both, Bakhtin prescribes study of a "translinguistics" above simple encoding linguistics, study of dialogue, genres, and the movement of style into grammar. Bakhtin focusses not on basic syntax, or on sentences, but on the use of "captured speech" in new speech, and on utterances as units of meaning. People may write or say more or less than a grammatically complete sentence, but whatever their utterance's style and length (a word or a book) it is intended to convey something and this is the proper unit of meaning. Further, its method is to use items not out of a dictionary or a Saussurean langue, but to reply to already extant speech and writing, to "capture" fragments of existing discourse and com-

14 Whorf wrote, "the science of linguistics was founded, or put on its present basis, by one Panini ... It was the Greeks who debased the science. They showed how infinitely inferior they were to the Hindus as scientific thinkers, and the effect of their muddling lasted two thousand years. Modern scientific linguistics dates from the rediscovery of Panini by the Western world in the early nineteenth century" (1956: 232). Compare, for example, Kristeva (1989: 104): "By positing the bases of modern reasoning, Greek philosophy also provided the fundamental principles that have enabled language to be thought about up to our day."

ment on them. Unlike Whorf, and like Derrida, Bakhtin and Vološinov directly criticized Saussure, and in this sense are literally "post-structuralists." But their critique took them in this different and productive direction. Like Bhartṛhari, they insist that mere reception of a word and reception of its meaning should be distinguished, and that the latter involves reception and evaluative response to actual claims about truth and falsehood, existence and non-existence, right and wrong, good and evil, etc. (See for example Vākyapadīya 1.56-61 and 2.427-429, Vološinov 1983: 40-41.) From Bhartṛhari they would no doubt wish to hear more about practice (*abhyāsa*), the foundation of the expertise that goes beyond inference (Vāk. 1.35), the practice that might explain the arising of the capacity for *pratibhā*, intuition of meaning (Vāk. 2.116-118, 143-152, 402-403). Like Whorf, Bakhtin and Vološinov are aware of the origins of linguistics in India, but they are less flattering, arguing that the connection of linguistics to priests, sacred texts, and authoritative interpretation of tradition is precisely the problem with all of philology, even to the present. Philologists, they argue, treat all language as dead, and never deal with the kind of meaning that elicits active response (Vološinov 1983: 44-45). On this point they would no doubt criticize Whorf as well as Bhartṛhari.

The theorists would also disagree over whether the genealogy of language leads back to divinity or primates, and over the types of liberation available through understanding of grammatical processes. Not small questions. But all three contribute, as I see it, to getting us past the type of "post-structuralism" that is represented by Derrida in contemporary Western thought: past the discovery of instability in signs, and the irreducibility of acts of power in their use. All three make important contributions to continuing efforts to understand how real meaning arises, abides and changes. I agree with Whorf about the plurality of grammars, and with Bakhtin about the significance of dialogue, captured speech and the utterance as the real meaning-bearing unit. But Bhartṛhari is especially important because, of the three, he is the only one providing a sustained critique of a sign-unit approach to meaning, the only one responding to and encompassing the lessons of a deconstructivist sign theory. We left Derrida stuck on his sentence so difficult to think, "the sign is that ill-named thing, the only one, that escapes the instituting question of philosophy: 'what is ...'?" Must we let it escape? Why not find it a better name, or better yet, a clearer way to think about it? Following Whorf (and Bhartṛhari on *dravya*) this "thingness" of the sign is a projection of a grammar in which thingness is a default characteristic of nouns; with Whorf consider the sign an event. Or turn to Bhartṛhari's metaphors: the sign like light, illuminating an object-meaning received in an event of understanding. Derrida insists that the signifier is a trace, Bhartṛhari that it disappears when the meaning becomes clear (see Vāk. 2.298-299, 2.420). I want to finish, though, with another of Bhartṛhari's metaphors: the sign as a tool. Plows, swords, and pestles have form (*rūpa*) and powers (*śakti*) suiting them as means (*sādhana*) especially for certain activities, but also in other ways for others; they are applied within their limits to the necessary tasks. So it is with *śabda* (Vāk. 2.275-277). Signs don't have their own meanings, they are used to make meanings. Why should we imagine that signs have meaning? Do tools have gardening, fighting, or cooking?

Works Cited

Abhyankar, Kashinath Vasudeva, and Vishnu Prabhakar Limaye, eds. 1965 *Vākyapadīya of Bhartṛhari*. Poona: University of Poona Sanskrit and Prakrit Series.

Aklujkar, Ashok (with Karl Potter) 1990 Summary of Trikāṇḍī or Vākyapadīya, in Harold G. Coward and K. Kunjunni Raja, eds., *Encyclopedia of Indian Philosophies. vol. 5: The Philosophy of the Grammarians*. Delhi: Motilal Banarsidass.

Aklujkar, Ashok 1978 "The Concluding Verses of Bhartṛhari's Vākya-kāṇḍa" *Annals of the Bhandarkar Oriental Research Institute* 48-49: 9-26.

Aklujkar, Ashok 1991 "Interpreting Vākyapadīya 2.486 Historically (Part 3)" In Madhav M. Deshpande and Saroja Bhate (eds.) *Pāṇinian Studies: Professor S.D. Joshi Felicitation Volume*. Ann Arbor: Center for South and Southeast Asian Studies, University of Michigan.

Apte, Vaman Shivram 1988 *The Practical Sanskrit-English Dictionary*. Delhi: Motilal Banarsidass.

Benjamin, Walter 1968 *Illuminations*. New York: Schocken Books.

Bhattacharya, Kamaleswar, E.H. Johnston and Arnold Kunst 1986 *The Dialectical Method of Nāgārjuna: the Vigrahavyāvartanī*. Second edition. Delhi: Motilal Banarsidass.

Bronkhorst, Johannes 1983 "On the History of Pāṇinian Grammar in the Early Centuries Following Patañjali" *Journal of Indian Philosophy* 11: 357-412.

Bronkhorst, Johannes 1985 "Nāgārjuna and the Naiyāyikas" *Journal of Indian Philosophy* 13: 107-132.

Bronkhorst, Johannes, trans. 1987 *Mahābhāṣyadīpikā of Bhartṛhari* Fasc IV: Āhnika I. Poona: Bhandarkar Oriental Research Institute.

Chatterjee, Ranjit 1985 "Reading Whorf Through Wittgenstein: A Solution to the Linguistic Relativity Problem" *Lingua* 67: 37-63.

Coward, Harold G. 1980 *The Sphoṭa Theory of Language: A Philosophical Analysis*. Delhi: Motilal Banarsidass.

Coward, Harold G. 1990a "Derrida and Bhartṛhari's Vākyapadīya on the Origin of Language" *Philosophy East and West* 40: 3-16.

Coward, Harold G. 1990b *Derrida and Indian Philosophy*. Albany: State University of New York Press.

Coward, Harold G. 1991 "Speech Versus Writing' in Derrida and Bhartrhari," *Philosophy East and West* 41: 141-62.

Coward, Harold G., and K. Kunjunni Raja 1990 *The Philosophy of the Grammarians*, vol. 5 of *Encyclopedia of Indian Philosophies*. Delhi: Motilal Banarsidass.

Dasgupta, Surendranath 1920 "Sphoṭavāda: Semantic Theory," in S. Dasgupta, *A Study of Patanjali*. Delhi: Motilal Banarsidass.

Derrida, Jacques 1976 *Of Grammatology*. Baltimore: The Johns Hopkins University Press.

Gaurinath Sastri 1980 *A Study in the Dialectics of Sphoṭa*. Delhi: Motilal Banarsidass.

Hattori, Masaaki 1977 "The Sautrāntika Background of the **Apoha** Theory" *In* Leslie S. Kawamura and Keith Scott (eds.) *Buddhist Thought and Asian Civilization: Essays in Honor of Herbert V. Guenther on His Sixtieth Birthday*. Emeryville, Ca: Dharma Publishing.

Hattori, Masaaki 1979 "**Apoha** and **Pratibhā**" *In* M. Nagatomi, B.K. Matilal, J.M. Masson and E. Dimock (eds.) *Sanskrit and Indian Studies*. Reidel.

Herzberger, Radhika 1986 *Bhartṛhari and the Buddhists*. Dordrecht (Studies of Classical India, vol. 8).

Iyer, K.A. Subramania 1969 *Bhartṛhari: A Study of the Vākyapadīya in the Light of the Ancient Commentaries*. Poona: Deccan College Postgraduate and Research Institute.

Joshi, S.D. 1967 "Introduction: The Sphoṭa Theory," in *The Sphoṭanirṇaya of Kauṇḍa Bhaṭṭa*, S.D. Joshi trans. Poona: University of Pooṇa.

Joshi, S.D. and J.A.F. Roodbergen, trans. 1986 *Patañjali's Vyākaraṇa-Mahābhāṣya: Paspaśāhnika*. Pune: University of Poona.

Kristeva, Julia 1989 *Language - The Unknown: An Initiation into Linguistics*. New York: Columbia University Press.

Larson, Gerald James 1988 "Introduction: The 'Age-Old Distinction Between the Same and the Other'" in G.S. Larson and Eliot Deutsch, eds., *Interpreting Across Boundaries: New Essays in Comparative Philosophy*. Delhi: Motilal Banarsidass.

Lindtner, Chr. 1982 *Nagarjuniana: Studies in the Writings and Philosophy of Nāgārjuna*. Delhi: Motilal Banarsidass.

Matilal, Bimal Krishna 1990 *The Word and the World: India's Contribution to the Study of Language*. Delhi: Oxford University Press.

Raja, K. Kunjunni 1963 *Indian Theories of Meaning*. Madras: The Adyar Library and Research Centre.

Rau, Wilhelm (ed.) 1977 *Bhartṛharis Vākyapadīya*. Wiesbaden: Deutsche Morgenländische Gesellschaft.

Said, Edward 1978 *Orientalism*. New York: Vintage Books.

Said, Edward 1985 *Beginnings: Intention and Method*. New York: Columbia University Press.

Santina, Peter Della 1986 *Madhyamaka Schools in India*. Delhi: Motilal Banarsidass.

Scharfe, Hartmut 1977 *Grammatical Literature*. vol 5, fasc 2 of Jan Gonda, ed., *A History of Indian Literature*. Wiesbaden: Otto Harrassowitz.

Sprung, Mervyn 1977 "Nietzsche and Nāgārjuna: The Origins and Issue of Scepticism" in Harold Coward and Krishna Sivaraman, eds., *Revelation in Indian Thought*. Emeryville, California: Dharma Publishing.

Staal, Frits 1965 "Euclid and Pāṇini" *Philosophy East and West* 15: 156-66. reprinted in Frits Staal, *Universals: Studies in Indian Logic and Linguistics*. Chicago: University of Chicago Press, 1988.

Staal, Frits 1982 *The Science of Ritual*. Poona: Bhandarkar Oriental Research Institute.

Staal, Frits 1988a "Is There Philosophy in Asia?" in Gerald James Larson and Eliot Deutsch, eds., *Interpreting Across Boundaries: New Essays in Comparative Philosophy*. Delhi: Motilal Banarsidass.

Staal, Frits 1988b *Universals: Studies in Indian Logic and Linguistics*. Chicago: University of Chicago Press.

Steiner, George 1989 *Real Presences*. Chicago: University of Chicago Press.

Takakusu, J. 1905 "A Study of Paramārtha's Life of Vasubandhu and the Date of Vasubandhu" *Journal of the Royal Asiatic Society* 57: 33-53.

Vološinov, V.N. 1983 "The Latest Trends in Linguistic Thought in the West" in Ann Shukman, ed., *Bakhtin School Papers*.

Warder, A.K. 1980 *Indian Buddhism*. Delhi: Motilal Banarsidass.

Whorf, Benjamin Lee 1956 *Language, Thought, and Reality: Selected Writings of Benjamin Lee Whorf*. Cambridge, Mass: The M.I.T. Press.

LINKING UP BHARTṚHARI AND THE BAUDDHAS

Chr. Lindtner, Copenhagen

1. There is, as will be recalled, a good tradition (Puṇyarāja and Siṃhasūri) to the effect that Vasurāta was at one time the *guru* of Bhartṛhari. According to another source (Paramārtha), the Bauddha teacher Vasubandhu was attacked by Vasurāta, the grammarian, i.e. Bhartṛhari's teacher.[1]

On the basis of these pieces of independent external evidence only, it would be natural to conclude that Bhartṛhari cannot have been absolutely ignorant about at least some of the writings of "the master of 1000 *śāstra*-s", as the Chinese sources occasionally speak of Vasubandhu (thus, probably, not implying more than that Vasubandhu was an extremely prolific author). When I here speak of Vasubandhu, I am, to be sure, speaking of the author of *Abhidharmakośa, Karmasiddhi, Pañcaskandhaka, Viṃśatikā, Triṃśikā, Vyākhyāyukti*, etc. - to mention only the most important of his authentic works.

Naturally, the question then arises, whether we can detect any palpable pieces of influence from Vasubandhu in Bhartṛhari's *magnum opus*, the *Vākyapadīya* (VP).[2] We might then find ourselves in a position to understand what I-ching had in mind when he reported that Bhartṛhari was "intimately acquainted with the doctrine of *vijñaptimātratā* (Chinese: *wei-shih*)".[3]

1 For the references, see E. Frauwallner, *Kleine Schriften*, Wiesbaden 1982, p. 857 (= "Landmarks in the History of Indian Logic", in *WZKSO* 5 (1961), pp. 125-148).

2 I am here mostly using Rau's critical edition, *Bhartrharis Vākyapadīya*, Wiesbaden 1977, and his most useful *Bhartrharis Vākyapadīya. Vollständiger Wortindex zu den mūlakārikās*, Wiesbaden/Stuttgart 1988. In addition to these, K.A. Subramania Iyer's standard edition with the extant commentaries: VP I, Poona 1966; VP II, Delhi 1983; VP III, Poona 1963 (i) and 1973 (ii). - For Bhartrhari and the Buddhists, see also (somewhat outdated) D. Seyfort Ruegg, *Contributions à l'histoire de la philosophie linguistique indienne*, Paris 1959, pp. 57-93.

3 This is the translation of John Brough in "I-ching on the Sanskrit grammarians" in *BSOAS* 36 (1973), pp. 248-260. The old translation of Takakusu was "sole knowledge (Vidyāmātra)", which is impossible. But *wei-shih* could also, and more likely, be rendered *vijñānamātra*, or even *cittamātra*, any of which is preferable to Brough's *vijñaptimātratā* (*ibid*., p. 260). Brough (*ibid*., p. 259) gives further ref. to the question of Bhartrhari and the Buddhists, which he, absurdly, regards as a "dead issue". - See also H. Nakamura's "Buddhist influence upon the *Vākyapadīya*", in *Journal of the Ganganatha Jha Research Institute* 29 (1973), pp. 367-388.

I think there is sufficient evidence to show that I-ching was right. Perhaps it is superfluous of me to quote the first verse of Vasubandhu's *Triṃśikā* (T).[4] Anyhow, here it is:

> *ātmadharmopacāro hi vividho yaḥ pravartate /*
> *vijñānapariṇāme 'sau pariṇāmaḥ sa ca tridhā //*

Also, T 17 and 18ab should be kept in mind:

> *vijñānapariṇāmo 'yaṃ vikalpo yad vikalpyate /*
> *tena tan nāsti tenedaṃ sarvaṃ vijñaptimātrakam //*
> *sarvabījaṃ hi vijñānaṃ (pariṇāmas tathā tathā /)*

Of these verses I cannot help hearing an echo in VP I.124:

> *śabdasya pariṇāmo 'yam ity āmnāyavido viduḥ /*
> *chandobhya eva prathamam etad viśvaṃ pravartate //*[5]

If required to describe the philosophy of Vasubandhu and Bhartṛhari in a single word, it could well be *vijñānapariṇāma-* and *śabdapariṇāmavāda*, respectively. No doubt Bhartṛhari deliberately alludes to Vasubandhu. This would have been recognized immediately by the contemporary learned reader.

For Bhartṛhari the absolute, Brahman, is *eka* (I.29), but as a result of various powers (*śakti*, I.2c) and forces (*kratu*, I.52b, a Vedic term never used by the Bauddhas) it develops (*vivartate*, I.1c = *vartate*, I.2d = *pravartate*, I.124b) so as to *appear* manifold. The ultimate reason for this, as in Buddhism, is *avidyā*. As a grammarian Bhartṛhari likes to call the absolute *śabdatattva*, and he speaks of its manifestation, also in grammatical terminology, as *prakriyā*, formation. When VP I.4 furthermore says of Brahman that it is *sarvabīja*, and that it appears as *bhoktṛ*, *bhoktavya* and *bhoga*, we again hear Buddhist echoes. Vasubandhu makes a distinction between *grāhya* and *grāhaka*. So does Bhartṛhari. Bhartṛhari speaks of the three (or four?) forms of *vāk*, viz. *vaikharī*, *madhyamā* and *paśyantī* (VP I. 159-

4 There are, as known, many editions and translations of Vasubandhu's *Triṃśikā*. See, most recently, S. Anacker, *Seven Works of Vasubandhu*, Delhi 1984. Here the Sanskrit text is given on pp. 422-423. See also the facsimile edition given in K. Mimaki *et al.* (eds.), *Three Works of Vasubandhu in Sanskrit Manuscript*, Tokyo 1989. (There are *no* significant variants.)

5 In the *Viṣṇupurāṇa* (as quoted in PW, s.v. *pariṇāma*) there is an interesting variant, probably of VP:
haviṣāṃ pariṇāmo 'yaṃ yad etad akhilaṃ jagat /

170).[6] Likewise Vasubandhu speaks of three kinds of *pariṇāma (vipāka, mananā* and *viṣayavijñapti)*, and of three characters *(parikalpita-, paratantra-* and *parinispannasvabhāva*). Both are concerned about three forms of the absolute. The terminology and the details certainly differ, but the structural similarity is too striking to be purely coincidental. Moreover, technical terms such as *saṃghāta* and *upalabdhi*, so common in Vasubandhu, may also have been borrowed by Bhartṛhari in whose VP they are quite common, too.[7]

It is true that Bhartṛhari never uses the term *vijñapti(-mātratā)*. Even *vijñāna* rarely occurs. One could perhaps go as far as to say that he carefully avoids it! In any case, internal evidence certainly supports I-ching's remark about Bhartṛhari being intimately acquainted with the doctrine of *vijñaptimātratā* (or *vijñāna-mātra)*, i.e. with the philosophical works of Vasubandhu.

2. Paul Hacker, in particular, has stressed that there is an important distinction to be drawn between *vivarta-* and *pariṇāmavāda* in Indian philosophy.[8] In case of *pariṇāmavāda*, the material cause and its product is held to be essentially the same. In case of *vivartavāda* (...ist vom monistisch-illusionistischen Vedānta ausgebildet worden), we are here dealing with the concept of "Scheinentfaltung". As Hacker points out, Bhartṛhari uses the term *vivarta* in the sense of "Scheinentwicklung", and one can characterize his point of view "als *illusionistischen Bhedābhedavāda*". To Bhartṛhari *vivarta* (also *vikāra*) and *pariṇāma* are more or less synonyms. Finally, Hacker suggests that Bhartṛhari's usage of *vivarta* has a Buddhist background.[9]

Unfortunately, Hacker only gives a few vague references to the use of *vivartate/vivarta* in Buddhist sources. Hacker is quite right, though, that *vivartate* (Pāli: *vivaṭṭati*) belongs to a cosmological context. Though it cannot be said to be very common in the Buddhist *sūtra*-s the idea is known from several early *sūtra*-s of Mahāyāna. We have a nice example

6 On all this, see K.A. Subramania Iyer's classical work, *Bhartṛhari. A study of the Vākyapadīya in the light of the Ancient Commentaries*, Poona 1969. – For a discussion of *śabdādvaita*, etc., see also the same author's *The Vākyapadīya – Some Problems*, Poona 1982.

7 For the references, see Rau's *Wortindex*, s.s.v.

8 See his *Vivarta. Studien zur Geschichte der illusionistischen Kosmologie und Erkenntnistheorie der Inder*, Wiesbaden 1953.

9 *Op. cit.*, p. 16.

from a most important chapter of the *Samādhirājasūtra*, recently edited by C. Cüppers (IX.1-2):

yada lokadhātūna vivartu bhotī
ākāśu bhotī ayu sarvaloke /
yathaiva taṃ pūrvi tathaiva paścāt
tathopamāṃ jānatha sarvadharmān // (IX.1)
idam jagad yāvata kiñci vartate (v.l.: *kiṃ vivartate!*)
adhastam etī ayam āpaskandhaḥ /
yathaiva taṃ heṣṭi tathaiva ūrd(h)vaṃ
tathopamāṃ jānatha sarvadharmān // (IX.2)[10]

Here then, in an early and influential Mahāyāna text, we are clearly confronted with a *vivartavāda* according to which the entire world (*lokadhātu, idaṃ jagat*) evolves from one single principle, *ākāśa*, into which it also, in the course of time, reverts again. This sort of "monistic illusionism" is most characteristic of Mahāyāna. In Vasubandhu, however, *ākāśa* is replaced by *vijñāna*, in Bhartṛhari by *śabda(-tattva)*. The concepts of *vivarta* and *pariṇāma* were certainly not invented by Bhartṛhari.

Since we are here dealing with the Buddhist sources that may have influenced Bhartṛhari, it is reasonable to ask whether there is any evidence that would allow us to say anything about his knowledge of Buddhist *sūtra*-s. There is no definite answer to this question, at least on the basis of the VP. There is a nice case, though, which shows Bhartṛhari using specific Buddhist terminology. This is, in Rau's critical edition, VP II.238ab:

upāyāḥ śikṣamāṇānāṃ bālānām upalāpanāḥ /

The reading *upalāpanāḥ* is significant. It is given in the *Mūlakārikā*-s and in the Commentary of Puṇyarāja (ed. K.A.S. Iyer, Delhi 1983, p. 98). In the *Vṛtti*, however the reading has been changed to *apalāpanāḥ*.[11] This is definitely a wrong reading. If the author of the *Vṛtti* actually did write (or read) *apalāpanāḥ* (which is not certain, for it could be a scribal error), we can be quite sure that its author was *not* Bhartṛhari. How so?

First of all, it may be noted that Iyer has misunderstood the meaning of the verse in his translation: "These *śāstras* which are a means (of attaining knowledge) are really misleading to ignorant people."[12] The version

10 C. Cüppers, *The IXth Chapter of the Samādhirājasūtra*, Stuttgart 1990, p. 17.
11 Thus also, e.g. K. Raghavan Pillai, *The Vākyapadīya*, Delhi 1971, p. 91.
12 K.A. Subramania Iyer, *The Vākyapadīya of Bhartṛhari, Chapter II,* Delhi 1977, p. 103.

of K. Raghavan Pillai is also on the wrong track: "Means are intended as a concealment of the truth for the sake of the unwise who are learning".[13]

In Buddhist texts we occasionally find expressions such as *bālalāpana, bālollāpana, bālapralāpa, bālopalāpana* and *bālālāpana*.[14] The expression is used about a teaching which is not really true, but nevertheless useful and good for beginners. In other words something that is true *vyavahārataḥ*, but not *paramārthataḥ*.[15] In Mahāyāna texts it belongs to the context of *satyadvaya*, as indeed it also does in the VP. Hence *upāyāḥ ...upalāpanāḥ*, in VP, should be translated with a positive connotation, e.g.: "When dealing with young students still learning ("freshmen") (their teacher may use) pedagogical means".

There can hardly be any doubt that Bhartṛhari derived the expression *bālānām upalāpanāḥ* from some Buddhist text, and therefore, of course, the reading *apalāpanāḥ* must be erroneous.

We cannot be sure precisely from *which* Bauddha text Bhartṛhari borrowed this expression, but it may be worthy of note that *bālalāpana* occurs in Nāgārjuna's *Acintyastava* 7, especially so since it is not impossible that VP III. 2.1.:

> *ātmā vastu svabhāvaś ca śarīram tattvam ity api /*
> *dravyam ity asya paryāyās tac ca nityam iti smṛtam //*

is moulded upon *Acintyastava* 45ab:

> *svabhāvaḥ prakṛtis tattvaṃ dravyaṃ vastu sad ity api /*[16]

Whether this be so or not, the fact remains that there are numerous echoes of typical Madhyamaka arguments and doctrines to be found scattered around in Bhartṛhari's VP.

It may, incidentally, be pointed out that Nāgārjuna's *Acintyastava* shows a considerable influence from *Samādhirajasūtra* IX, not just with regard to *vivartavāda* (see above), but also, among other things, with

13 See n. 11.

14 See my *Nagarjuniana. Studies in the Writings and Philosophy of Nāgārjuna*, Copenhagen 1982, p. 143, n. 7. For the idea cf. also *Yuktisaṣṭikā* 30, *ibid.*, p. 110.

15 This *satyadvayavibhāga* is about as common in the VP as in Mahāyāna texts in general – not to speak of other Vedānta texts.

16 This seems first to have been pointed out by O. Qvarnström, *Hindu Philosophy in Buddhist Perspective,* Lund 1989, p. 130.

regard to the question of *pramāṇa*-s, a topic to which we shall revert soon. For now I shall just point out that *Acintyastava* 20:

jaḍatvam apramāṇatvam athāvyākṛtatām api /
viparītaparijñānam indriyāṇāṃ tvam ūcivān //[17]

without any doubt is based on *Samādhirājasūtra* IX.24:

yasmād ime indriya apramāṇā
jaḍāḥ svabhāvena avyākṛtāś ca /
tasmād ya nirvāṇapathena arthikaḥ
sa āryamārgeṇa karotu kāryam //[18]

We here have an early canonical source to the effect that *indriya-pratyakṣa* cannot be considered a *pramāṇa*.[19]

3. We are on safer ground when we turn to Buddhist authors *after* Bhartṛhari. The first to come into consideration would be Dignāga.

As already pointed out long ago, Dignāga, towards the end of his *Pramāṇasamuccaya* (PS) V, quotes at least two verses from VP, viz. II. 158 and 155.[20] There are numerous other references to VP in the PS, and there can, therefore, be no doubt that Dignāga knew Bhartṛhari, and that he should also be placed *after* that author in time.[21]

17 Quoted from my *Nagarjuniana*, p. 146, where I failed to identify the original source.

18 Cüppers, *op. cit.*, p. 39.

19 Nāgārjuna accepts four *pramāṇa*-s (as does e.g. Candrakīrti, his celebrated commentator), but, naturally, only *vyavahārataḥ*. This is clear from his *Vigrahavyāvartanī* and *Vaidalyaprakaraṇa*. Probably also from his **Upāyahṛdaya* (?), provided Y. Kajiyama is justified in accepting its authenticity, see his recent paper "On the Authorship of the *Upāyahṛdaya*" in E. Steinkellner (ed.), *Studies in the Buddhist Epistemological Tradition*, Wien 1991, pp. 107-117. I still regard my hesitations as valid, see *Nagarjuniana*, p. 17, n. 44.

20 Frauwallner, *op. cit.*, p. 856, with ref. - See also M. Hattori (ed.), *The Pramāṇasamuccayavṛtti of Dignāga. Chapter Five,* Kyoto 1982, pp. 147 & 149, for the Sanskrit and Tibetan.

21 Many examples in R. Herzberger, *Bhartṛhari and the Buddhists - An Essay in the Development of Fifth and Sixth Century Indian Thought*, Dordrecht 1986, *passim*. Apart from this very problematic book, one may refer to M. Hattori's "*Apoha* and Pratibhā", in M. Nagatomi *et al.* (eds.), *Sanskrit and Indian Studies. Essays in Honour of Daniel H.H. Ingalls*, Dordrecht 1980, pp. 61-73. In the opinion of Hattori, Dignāga "adopted" his concept of *pratibhā* from VP. - See also, F. Tola and C. Dragonetti, "Some Remarks on Bhartṛhari's Concept of Pratibhā", in *JIP* 18 (1990), pp. 95-112. - There is no single word to cover all the meanings of this important term in VP. It covers notions such as:

Quite interesting in this connection is Dignāga's *Traikālyaparīkṣā*, a text in 33 verses available in an old Tibetan translation. Or rather, since (apart from its initial and final verses) it is but an extract from the *Saṃbandhasamuddeśa* (VP III.3.53-85, with some omissions), it is also still available as such in Sanskrit.[22]

The final verses occur in the *Vṛtti* to VP I.1. They are often quoted, and Frauwallner may be right in suggesting that their original source was Bhartṛhari's now lost *Śabdadhātusamīkṣā*:

yathā viśuddham ākāśam timiropapluto janaḥ /
saṃkīrṇam iva mātrābhis citrābhir abhimanyate //
tathedam amṛtam brahma nirvikāram avidyayā /
kaluṣatvam ivāpannam bhedarūpaṃ vivartate //

There is, as already pointed out by Frauwallner, a small and significant change introduced here by Dignāga, who replaces Bhartṛhari's subject *(amṛtaṃ) brahma* with *rnam śes*, i.e. *vijñānam* (and *hi*?). It is hard to say exactly what Dignāga wished to achieve by adapting Bhartṛhari's verses, but by replacing *brahma* with *vijñāna* he at least affirms that Bhartṛhari's monism is acceptable to the Bauddhas, i.e. to Yogācāra, provided *vijñāna*, not *brahma*, is read. By making this replacement Dignāga brings the verses closer to the idea expressed e.g. in *Madhyāntavibhāga* (I. 16, 21-22, especially), which may indeed have been one of Bhartṛhari's original sources for the distinction between *brahma/vijñāna/citta* as originally pure, but under normal circumstances rendered impure by *kleśa*-s, above all *avidyā*. In a word, Dignāga brings the verses back into their original Buddhist form. Dignāga was, like I-ching, very much aware of Bhartṛhari's Buddhist leanings.

Later on we find Bauddhas such as Bhavya and Śāntarakṣita accusing Gauḍapāda and others of having "stolen" their ideas from the Buddhist texts.[23] Dignāga is saying the same thing in a more diplomatic language.

The fact that Dignāga's *Traikālyaparīkṣā* is thus based on Bhartṛhari's *Prakīrṇa(ka)* (VP III), tallies very nicely with the tradition that the celebrated Dharmapāla wrote a commentary (*vṛtti*) on that very chapter

intelligence, instinct, intuition, bright idea, and the like. Thanks to experience and intelligence, some people are more "bright" than others. Even animals and children possess *pratibhā* telling them what to do in a given situation.

22 Sanskrit and Tibetan texts in Frauwallner, *op. cit.*, pp. 821-828.

23 The charge of having stolen from the Buddhists is almost a *locus communis*, cf. Qvarnström, *op. cit.*, pp. 101-104.

of the VP. Its title was, according to Durvekamiśra, *Prakīrṇavṛtti.*[24] Apart from fragments, and as opposed to Dharmapāla's incomplete commentary on Dignāga's *Ālambanaparīkṣā*, it now, as known, seems to have been irreparably lost. But all this is nevertheless sufficient to show that by the time of Dignāga the works of Bhartṛhari were carefully studied by the Bauddhas, especially by those belonging to Yogācāra.

4. Kambala and Dharmakīrti are among those Bauddhas in whose extant works we can detect traces of their having read Bhartṛhari. A few obvious instances must be sufficient to establish this point.
First Kambala (ca. 450-525 A.D.). In his *Navaśloka* 9ab:

> *yoginām api yaj jñānaṃ tad apy ākāśalakṣaṇam /*

has a nice parallel in his *Ālokamālā* 110ab:

> *yoginām api yaj jñānaṃ tad apy ajñānam eva hi /*

This is based on VP I.30cd:

> *ṛṣīṇām api yaj jñānaṃ tad apy āgamapūrvakam /*

Likewise, there can hardly be any doubt that *Ālokamālā* 111:

> *sarvam saṃvṛtimaj jñānam paṇḍitasyetarasya ca /*
> *grahaṇe vyapadeśe ca samam eva pravartate //*[25]

is based on VP III.3.55:

> *rūpaṇavyapadeśābhyāṃ laukike vartmani sthitau /*
> *jñānaṃ praty abhilāpaṃ ca sadṛśau bālapaṇḍitau //*

Whether Kambala got it directly from VP, or from Dignāga's *Traikālyaparīkṣā* (where it comes as verse 4) is difficult to decide.
Ālokamālā 19 and 20 run:

> *abhinnam api bhedena bahiś cāpy abahirgatam /*
> *viṣayākārakaluṣaṃ khyāti cittam anekadhā //*

24 Frauwallner, *op. cit.*, p. 857, n. 27.

25 Kambala's *Ālokamālā* was edited by me in *Miscellanea Buddhica*, Copenhagen 1985, pp. 109-221.

sūryacandramasau vyoma tārācakraṃ vasuṃdharā /
saritsāgaradikśailāś cittasyaitā vibhūtayaḥ //

We are here, when it comes to *kāluṣya, kaluṣatva*, not just reminded of VP III.3.57 (= *Traikālyaparīkṣā* 6, cf. 4), but especially VP III.7.41:

dyauḥ kṣamā vāyur ādityaḥ sāgarāḥ sarito diśaḥ /
antaḥkaraṇatattvasya bhāgā bahir avasthitāḥ //

See also *Ālokamālā* 85, 146, 157, 162, 177 and 193 for further references etc. to Bhartṛhari by Kambala.

Dharmakīrti, too, knew his Bhartṛhari. Not only does the style and the very title of his *Saṃbandhaparīkṣā*[26] recall Bhartṛhari's *Saṃbandhasamuddeśa*, but especially in Dharmakīrti's own commentary to the first chapter of the *Pramāṇavārttika* there are numerous places reminiscent of VP.[27] The learned readers in those days would, of course, immediately recognize such allusions and they would appreciate them, just as one cannot fail to appreciate what in poetics is called *dhvani*. Indeed, as I have now tried to point out, such *sat sapienti* allusions must have been a characteristic and much cherished feature of sophisticated Sanskrit literature in the period we are here dealing with. A failure to recognize this device can easily lead to wrong judgements about the proper historical context.

I would not here want to go into the problem of the authenticity of the collection of poems ascribed to Bhartṛhari, i.e. the *Śatakatraya* (or *Subhāṣitatriśatī*, etc.).[28] Personally, I have no hesitation at all in accepting its authenticity whatever its *original* form may have been. Dharmakīrti, too, composed poems, including some very nice ones in the *śṛṅgāra* style.[29] He may, indeed, have been inspired by the example of Bhartṛhari to do so. In any case, by the time of Dharmakīrti, Bhartṛhari was almost a part of the Buddhist heritage.

When Dharmakīrti in the *Pramāṇasiddhi* chapter of his PV discusses *pramāṇa*, reliable knowledge, he also deals with language, which, for him,

26 Edited and translated by Frauwallner, *op. cit.*, pp. 490-529. The original Sanskrit text (including the *Ṭīkā* of Vinītadeva) was recently discovered in Tibet, but still awaits publication.

27 R. Gnoli (ed.), *The Pramāṇavārttikam of Dharmakīrti. The First Chapter with the Autocommentary*, Roma 1960, *passim*.

28 For a discussion (with further ref.) see e.g. Harold G. Coward, *Bhartṛhari*, Boston 1976, pp. 95-104.

29 The references are listed in L. Sternbach, *Poésie sanskrite conservée dans les anthologies et les inscriptions, Tome II*, Paris 1982, pp. 130-132.

can be reduced to *anumāna*. (Or rather: which for him *must* be reduced to *anumāna*, since his system does not, for various reasons, permit more than two *pramāṇa*-s.) Language, speech and communication can be reliable for practical purposes to the extent that it tells us what other people have in mind. But how things actually are is not something we can be sure of merely on the basis of what other people tell us. Reliable knowledge is knowledge we can actually use for some meaningful practical purpose. We always have to try out whether it works. Dharmakīrti defines reliability, *avisaṃvādana*, as *arthakriyāsthiti*, the ability of being of any practical use. When he says, PV II.2cd:

> *(prāmāṇyaṃ tatra śabdasya) nārthatattvanibandhanam* /

we are not wrong in taking this as an allusion to VP I.13ab:

> *arthapravṛttitattvānāṃ śabdā eva nibandhanam* /.

Of course, it is not quite fair of Dharmakīrti to refute Bhartṛhari in this way, because *śabda* means much more than just words and language in the VP. So Dharmakīrti's criticism is here a bit onesided.[30]

When Dharmakīrti defines reliable knowledge in terms of *arthakriyā* he certainly has Bhartṛhari in mind, even though the term can be traced back as far as Nāgārjuna.[31] The idea that real things are *arthakriyāsamartha*, or *kāryakriyāsamartha*, is an old one in Indian thought.

In his PVin II.5-6, Dharmakīrti quite clearly has VP I. 33-35 in mind. The "hints" are given by the example of the *maṇi*-, and by VP 33b: *tāṃ tāṃ arthakriyāṃ prati*, which in PVin II.5d becomes: *viśeṣo 'rthakriyāṃ prati*.

Bhartṛhari's argument is that real things (*dravya*) may have the ability to do this or that (*arthakriyā*), but under various circumstances other things may prevent them from doing so. This, however, is *not* something we can be sure of by means of *anumāna*. It requires a sort of expertise,

30 Cf. my paper "The Initial Verses of the *Pramāṇasiddhi* Chapter of the *Pramāṇavārttika*", in the volume of proceedings edited by E. Steinkellner (see n. 19), pp. 155-159. Dharmakīrti, to be sure, was not the first to employ *avisaṃvādana* as a criterion of valid knowledge. The term *avisaṃvāda* is found in *Pramāṇasamuccaya* II. 5ab, *Ślokavārttika, Śūnyavāda, Codanā* 80, *Tarkajvālā* ad MHK IV.38 (*...bslu ba med pa ni bden pa yin par rigs kyi...*), and even as early as *Ratnāvalī* II.35 (ed. M. Hahn, Bonn 1982, p. 52).

31 In the author's own commentary to VV 2 we thus read: *atha śūnyāḥ sarvabhāvā na ca kāryakriyāsamarthā bhavanti mā bhūd...* This implies that something real must be *kāryakriyāsamartha*, which is much the same as *arthakriyāsamartha*.

such as the one that a jeweller has based on long experience (*abhyāsa*). Such an expertise is inherited from a long cultural tradition, it depends on *āgama*. For Bhartṛhari *āgama* has things in common with perception, but is clearly a third *pramāṇa* in its own right apart from *pratyakṣa* and *anumāna*.[32] For Dharmakīrti, on the other hand, the validity of cognition is not a question of *abhyāsa* (at least in this context!) but rather one of seeing whether our ideas actually work:

> *arthakriyānurodhena pramāṇatvaṃ vyavasthitam* /[33]

In Dharmakīrti there is no room for *āgama* as a third sort of *pramāṇa*. He therefore has to adapt, or interpret, this passage in the VP (with which, as we shall see, Buddhist philosophers were very much concerned) so as to suit the demands of his own system of two *pramāṇa*-s.

I have no doubt that future research will show that Dignāga and Dharmakīrti are heavily indebted to Bhartṛhari for much of their technical terminology. Here I just want to point out one such case. Speaking of an ignoramus with a "limited horizon", Dharmakīrti at least twice uses the expression *tshu rol mthoṅ ba*. This corresponds in Sanskrit to *arvāgdarśana*, a term which can be traced back to the *Vṛtti* to VP I.134, which may well, directly or indirectly, be Dharmakīrti's source.[34]

5. The term *arvāgdarśana* also occurs in another Buddhist author before Dharmakīrti, namely Bhavya, to whom I shall now turn my attention.

That Bhavya knew Bhartṛhari has already been established long ago. Let us briefly review some of the evidence before we try to determine the

32 Cf. A. Aklujkar "The Number of Pramānas according to Bhartṛhari" in WZKS 33 (1989), pp. 151-159. – See also Aklujkar and Potter's summary of the VP in H.G. Coward and K. Kunjunni Raja (eds.), *Encyclopedia of Indian Philosophies. Volume V: The Philosophy of the Grammarians*, Delhi 1990, pp. 121-172.

33 PVin II.6cd, quoted from E. Steinkellner (ed.), *Dharmakīrti's Pramāṇaviniścayaḥ. Zweites Kapitel: Svārthānumānam. Teil I*, Wien 1973, p. 27.

34 *Ibid.*, p. 66: *de la tshu rol mthoṅ ba bdag ñid kyi mṅon sum log pa tshad mar byed pa ni des gzuṅ bar 'os pa ñid dgag pa pa rigs kyi thams cad ni de lta ma yin pa'i phyir thams cad 'gog pa ni ma yin no*. – In PVin III (Peking ed., Ce 319b6) we read: *tshu rol mthoṅ ba 'dis*... In the *Vṛtti* to VP I. 134. (ed. Iyer, p. 221) we have what is probably the source of Dharmakīrti (and, as we shall see, Bhavya): *arvāgdarśanānām tu puruṣānām prāyena sātiśayāḥ pratighātinyaḥ sāparādhāḥ śaktayaḥ*. The term also occurs in the *Vṛtti* to VP I. 151 (ed. Rau), see Iyer, *op. cit.*, p. 205 (ad VP I. 127). Cf. also E. Steinkellner (trans.), *Dharmakīrti's Pramāṇaviniścayaḥ. Zweites Kapitel: Svārthānumānam.* Teil II, Wien 1979, p. 79, n. 258 for some *later* references. No source earlier than VP seems to be known.

extent to which Bhartṛhari exerted a positive influence upon Bhavya's way of thinking. As we shall see, it was very considerable.

In his *Madhyamakahṛdayakārikā* (MHK) IX.13-14 Bhavya has these two verses presenting the view of Mīmāṃsā:

dūṣayitvā trayīmārgam hetubhir hetuvādinaḥ /
anumānapradhānatvāt svanayaṃ dyotayanti ye //
pādasparśād ivāndhānāṃ viṣame pathi dhāvatām /
anumānapradhānānāṃ pātaḥ teṣāṃ na durlabhaḥ //[35]

This includes an almost literal quotation from VP I.42:

hastasparśād ivāndhena viṣame pathi dhāvatā /
anumānapradhānena vinipāto na durlabhaḥ //

The same verse, to be sure, is also cited by Bhavya in his *Prajñāpradīpa* IX, which, incidentally, confirms the variant readings:

/loṅ ba rkaṅ pa'i tshod dpag kyi(s)//nam ṅa'i lam du rgyug pa ltar/
/rjes su dpag pa gtsor 'dzin pa//rnam par lhuṅ ba mi dka' 'o/[36]

On the basis of this there can be no doubt that Bhavya knew the VP. Before proceeding further it may be useful briefly to recall the ideas expressed in VP I.30-42. Bhartṛhari's fundamental position is that *dharma* can only be stablished by means of *āgama*. Even the cognition of saints is based on *āgama*. It is impossible to figure out what *dharma* is merely by *tarka* or *anumāna* (VP I.30):

na cāgamād ṛte dharmas tarkeṇa vyavatiṣṭhate /
ṛṣīṇām api yaj jñānaṃ tad apy āgamapūrvakam //[37]

What Bhartṛhari disavows is not *tarka* or *anumāna* as such, but merely its limitations, and therefore also those philosophers who put too much emphasis on "reason", those who are *anumānapradhāna*. As long as *tarka* is ancillary to *āgama* it is fully acceptable to Bhartṛhari (VP I. 151ab):

vedaśāstrāvirodhī ca tarkaś cakṣur apaśyatām /

35 Quoted from S. Kawasaki (ed.), *The Mīmāṃsā Chapter of Bhavya's Madhyamaka-hṛdaya-kārikā: Sanskrit and Tibetan Texts*, Tsukuba 1976, 1987, 1988, p. 12 (with a few changes).

36 Cf. Kawasaki, *op. cit.*, p. 13, n. 7, for the source of the Tibetan.

37 As will be recalled, Kambala also referred to this verse, in *Navaśloka* 9ab and *Ālokamālā* 110ab, both quoted above (p. 202).

Bhartṛhari's view can certainly be considered "orthodox". In the verse just quoted he seems to have had in mind *Manu* XII.106 (or some such passage):

> *ārṣaṃ dharmopadeśaṃ ca vedaśāstrāvirodhinā /*
> *yas tarkeṇānusaṃdhatte sa dharmaṃ veda netaraḥ //*

He has nothing against *tarka* or *anumāna* as such, but only against those who are *śuṣkatarkānusārin* (VP II. 484b, cf. *Mahābhārata* III. 13463, quoted in PW, s.v.),[38] or *anumānapradhāna*. Logic and reason are all right as long as they are not in conflict with the holy tradition.

The hostile attitude towards "dry logicians" (*tārkika*) is by no means specific to Manu and the VP. According to Nāgārjuna, for instance, even the Buddha took exception to *tārkika*-s.[39] And let us not forget that in early Buddhist texts *nirvāṇa* is said to be inaccessible to reason (*atarkāvacara*).[40]

To sum up Bhartṛhari's position: He accepts three *pramāṇa*-s, true, but they are by no means on a par. When one has to make the right decision (*dharma, itikartavyatā*) in matters of religion, ethics and grammar (!) one must resort to *āgama*. As we would say, *āgama* has to do with *values*, with good and bad, rather than with "facts". *Āgama* can be supported by *anumāna* and *tarka*, but never challenged or questioned by reason and logic. *Āgama* works as a sort of perception, but it covers much more than normal perception. This sort of *āgama* is the most fundamental of the three *pramāṇa*-s accepted by Bhartṛhari.

When it comes to Bhavya the situation is much the same, at least in principle. His attitude towards *āgama* is partly inherited from Bhartṛhari though it certainly also has a Buddhist background, and, of course, his conception of what *dharma* is has nothing in common with Bhartṛhari. Moreover, it should not be forgotten that the antithesis *āgama-tarka* expressed by Manu and VP has an old parallel in the Buddhist distinction between *āgama* and *yukti*.[41]

38 The expression is also known to Śaṃkara, see *Adyar Library Bulletin* 54 (1990), p. 147. See also Manu II. 12.

39 See *Lokātītastava* 21, in my *Nagarjuniana*, p. 134.

40 Cf. *A Critical Pāli Dictionary* for ref.

41 This distinction is already known to Nāgārjuna, cf. his *Ratnāvalī* III.14a: *rigs pa daṅ ni luṅ bstan pa...yukti* and *āgama*...

Let us now look at some of the most significant passages in question. To Bhartṛhari, *āgama* is, roughly speaking, the Veda with all its *upāṅga*-s, etc., and those civilized people (*śiṣṭa*) who follow it. With Bhavya it is otherwise. The correct teaching is to be found in the Buddhist scriptures, the Buddha being the most competent authority. How can we be sure? Because it is the least unreasonable of all teachings, according to Bhavya. (This again implies that one has to check all other teachings, to see that they are unreasonable. This again explains the doxographical nature of Bhavya's main works.) See MHK V.8-9:

> *(atrocyate) pramāṇam naḥ sarvam tāthāgatam vacaḥ /*
> *āptopadeśaprāmāṇyād bhadro hi pratipadyate //*
>
> *nāgamāntarasaṃdigdhaviparyastamatiḥ paraḥ /*
> *tasmāt tatpratipattyartham tanmṛgyo yuktimannayaḥ //*[42]

The Buddhist scriptures tell us what *tattva* is, and what *dharma* is. "Reason", on the other hand, shows us that all other opinions entertained by our opponents, are, in the final analysis, wrong. Still, the ultimate *tattva* of the Bauddhas (*śūnyatā, anutpāda, dharmakāya*, etc.) is beyond the range of reason (but not, as we shall see, beyond the range of "personal experience"). This is clear from MHK V. 104-105:

> *tattvasyātarkagocarāt tadbodho nānumānataḥ /*
> *nātas tarkeṇa dharmāṇāṃ gṛhyeta dharmateti cet //*
> *ihānumānān nirdoṣād āgamānuvidhāyinaḥ /*
> *kalpitāśeṣavividhavikalpāpāṃ nirākṛteḥ //*

When Bhavya here speaks of *anumāna* as having to be *nirdoṣa* and *āgamānuvidhāyin*, it is in principle similar to Manu's *tarka* which must be *vedaśāstrāvirodhi(n)*, a term taken over, as we have seen, by VP I.151. Bhavya can therefore say, MHK V.107:

> *ato 'numānaviṣayaṃ na tattvaṃ pratipadyate /*
> *tattvajñānavipakṣo yaḥ tasya tena nirākriyā //*

One can, on this basis, speak of Bhavya's "negative dialectics", and in this sense Bhavya's *tattva* is, as he says in MHK V. 113, *yuktāgamopeta*, i.e. based on *āgama*, supported by logic.

42 Quoted from the critical edition of the text (in prep. by myself and M.D. Eckel). It is based on the only available Sanskrit Ms., for which see Qvarnström, *op. cit.*, p. 23. (The following verses come from the same source.)

In the commentary to MHK IX.7 the Bauddhas are accused of reducing *āgama* to *anumāna*.[43] This would, at least in a sense, apply to Dignāga and, later on, Dharmakīrti, but not to Bhavya. The issue is taken up by Bhavya later on in his *Prajñāpradīpa*. Here, he agrees that *āgama* and *anumāna* have the same *viṣaya*. They deal with the same thing. There is nothing wrong with *anumāna* as such, but one must not place too much emphasis on *anumāna*. This is exactly the position of Bhartṛhari, as we have already seen.[44]

What, then, is the relationship between *āgama* and *tattva*, for, surely, *āgama* is not identical with *tattva*? Bhavya attempts to solve this problem by saying that the words of the Buddha are *ji lta ba bźin*, or *yathāvat*, they are adequate in the sense that they "correspond" to reality. This idea comes very close to VP I.5 which describes the Veda (i.e. *āgama*) as a *prāptyupāya* and an *anukāra* ("image, imitation") of *(śabda-)tattva*. The scriptures are valid because they somehow reflect true reality. The rest is logic, and it is yoga, in Bhartṛhari as well as in Bhavya.

We would have liked to know what exactly Bhartṛhari has in mind when he refers to *śabdapūrvayoga* (VP I.20c) and to *adhyātmaśāstra* (VP I.174c). Is it the sort of "OM-mysticism" mentioned e.g. in Patañjali's YS I. 25-27, or in the first chapter of the *āgamaśāstra* of Gauḍapāda?

43 TJ IX ad MHK IX.7 (Peking ed. Dsa 311b5): *gaṅ yaṅ saṅs rgyas pas luṅ gis rjes su dpag pa'i khoṅs su gtogs so źes btags pa de ni bden pa ma yin te/ gaṅ gi phyir/*

pratyakṣam anumānaṃ ca śābdaṃ copamayā saha /
arthāpattir abhāvaś ca hetavaḥ sādhyasādhakāḥ //

Cf. Kawasaki, *op. cit.*, p. 9, n.5. See also TJ ad IX.18 for *āgama*.

44 *Prajñāpradīpa* IX (Peking ed. Tsha 154a 4), just after the citation of VP I. 42...*luṅ ni rjes su dpag pa las don tha dad pa ma yin par gzuṅ bar bya ste/ mṅon sum ma yin pa'i don rtogs pa'i rgyu yin pa'i phyir/ dper na/ rjes su dpag pa'i raṅ gi bdag ñid bźin no// kha cig na re/ luṅ ni rjes su dpag pa las don tha dad pa kho na yin te/ de las yul tha dad pa'i phyir dper na mṅon sum bźin no// de ltar yaṅ rjes su dpag pa ni dbaṅ pos gzuṅ ba'i don gyi yul can yin la/ sgra'i mtshan ñid kyi tshad ma ni dbaṅ po las 'das pa mtho ris daṅ byaṅ grol gyi yul can yin pas/ de'i phyir luṅ ni rjes su dpag pa las don tha dad pa kho na yin no/ źe na/ luṅ ni rjes su dpag pa las yul tha dad pa ñid ma yin te/...yaṅ na mtho ris daṅ thar pa yod do// źes bya ba/ de bźin gśegs pa'i luṅ gaṅ yin pa de ni ji lta ba bźin te...*
Bhavya, in MHK IX. 19-20, goes as far as to say that everything that is handed down *and* makes sense, is *āgama*:

yat parīkṣākṣamaṃ yuktyā vacanaṃ cet tad āgamaḥ /

With this in mind, it is understandable why Candrakīrti would accuse Bhavya of *priyānumānatā* (*Prasannapadā*, p. 16), a predilection for logic. Cf. also the very title Bhavya chose for his work: *Tarkajvālā*. Still, the accusation is not quite fair, as we see once we also keep MHK V. 104-107 in mind (quoted above). Bhavya is also very much aware of the limitations of logic.

We cannot be sure. In any case, Bhavya's position is clear enough. The ideal is to obtain *vajropamasamādhi*, or *tattvajñāna*, i.e. to experience *śūnyatā* and *anutpāda* personally. First one learns the doctrine of *anutpāda* etc. from Buddhist *āgama* (esp. *Prajñāpāramitā*). Then one refutes all other *āgama*-s with the help of *yukti, tarka* and *anumāna*.[45] This brings one to the truth. Finally one realizes the reality behind truth through "auto-suggestion", or *bhāvanā*. This reflects the old Buddhist distinction between three degrees of *prajñā*, partly modified by Bhavya himself.

Of course Bhavya accepts a *tattvajñāna*, as all Mādhyamikas always do. This *jñāna*, however, is neither *savikalpa* nor *avikalpa*, see e.g. MHK III. 285cd (speaking of the *dharmakāya*):

savikalpāvikalpena jñānenāpy eṣa durdṛśaḥ //[46]

or MHK III.265:

nirvikalpārthaviṣayā nirvikalpāpi dhīr mṛṣā /
anātmādisvabhāvatvāt tadyathā savikalpadhīḥ //[47]

or MHK VIII.104:

savikalpāvikalpā ca yadā buddhir nivartate /
dhiyām aviṣaye tasmin prapañcopaśamaḥ śivaḥ //[48]

This is a bit surprising, and this terminology - neither *savikalpa* nor *nirvikalpa (avikalpa)* - ought to strike us as odd. One would have expected Bhavya to say that *tattva* was the object of some sort of *nirvikalpajñāna*, as Mahāyāna texts otherwise invariably do. Bhavya seems to be the only Bauddha to express himself in this curious way, if I am not mistaken.

There is a very specific historical background for this oddity. The clue is to be found in the commentary to MHK III.285. Here we are told that *anumāna* is *savikalpa* and determined by *vikalpa* and *anusmṛti*, whereas *pratyakṣa* is *nirvikalpa* and grasps *vastumātra* as its object.[49] The *dharma-*

45 See e.g. MHK IX. 18 with TS.

46 Quoted from the edition of Y. Ejima, *Chūgan-Shisō no Tenkai-Bhāvaviveka Kenkyū*, Tokyo 1980, p. 340.

47 *Ibid*., p. 334.

48 Quoted from Qvarnström, *op. cit.*, p. 48 (cf. p. 153 for Tib.). Cf. *ibid*., p. 95, n. 118 for further references.

49 TJ ad MHK III.285: *rtog pa daṅ bcas pa ni rjes su dpag pa ste/ rtog pa daṅ rjes su dran pa'i rnam par rtog pa yod pa'i phyir ro// rnam par rtog pa med pa ni mṅon sum gyi śes*

kāya, according to MHK III.286, is *tārkikānām agocaraḥ*. Bhavya obviously has certain *tārkika*-s in mind when he says that *tattva* cannot be known by *anumāna* or *pratyakṣa*. Logicians who accept only two *pramāṇa*-s. That Bhavya here has Dignāga (to whom he explicitly refers in MHK V) in mind is quite clear. His terminology is a reaction against the epistemology of Yogācāra *sākāravāda*.[50] In other words, Bhavya does not accept merely two *pramāṇa*-s, as does Dignāga etc. To him, as to Bhartṛhari, *āgama* is the most fundamental *pramāṇa*, provided, naturally, that one does not forget to practise yoga.

When Dignāga speaks of a *yogipratyakṣa(-jñāna)*, Bhavya speaks of *jñānakṣaṇa* (MHK III.291), *ekakṣaṇajñāna* (ad MHK I.6, and MHK 268), *svayaṃbhūjñāna*, or the like. The difference, of course, is hardly more than one of terminology in the final analysis.

Finally, in the first chapter of the *Madhyamakaratnapradīpa*, there are some unmistakable echoes of VP when Bhavya opines that *tārkika*-s who are *anumānapramāṇapradhāna* are unable to understand *tattva*, etc., because their cognition is too limited, being that of *arvāgdarśana*.[51]

6. Also in later Buddhist literature we find references to Bhartṛhari's opinion about the limitations of *anumāna*. In his *Tattvasaṃgraha* (TS) 1460-1462, for instance, Śāntarakṣita quotes VP I.32-34. But a little later (TS 1476-1477) Śāntarakṣita, by adding *na*, indicates that he does not agree:

pa ste/ dṅos po tsam la dmigs pa'i phyir ro//. This is based on Dignāga. The idea that *pratyakṣa* has *vastumātra* as its "object" comes up again in Dharmakīrti. The scriptural origin of the term *vastumātra* (or *paratantrasvabhāva*, as the "object" of *pratyakṣa*) seems to be the *Tattvārthapaṭala* of the *Bodhisattvabhūmi*. The terms *svalakṣaṇa* and *vastumātra* thus become almost interchangeable, depending on the context. - See also TJ ad MHK IV.67.

50 See my "Bhavya's Critique of Yogācāra in the Madhyamakaratnapradīpa, Chapter IV", in B.K. Matilal and R.D. Evans (eds.), *Buddhist Logic and Epistemology*, Dordrecht 1986, pp. 239-263.

51 MRP I: *'di ltar* ***rjes su dpag pa'i tshad ma gtso bor byed pa'i rtog ge pas*** *ni de kho na ñid daṅ/ saṅs rgyas kyi sku daṅ ye śes śin tu lkog tu gyur pa dag brtags śiṅ dpyad pas śes par mi 'gyur te/* ***tshu rol mthoṅ ba'i śes par yin pa'i*** phyir ro//
ñi ma dmus loṅ yul min bźin//mtho ris sdig can yul ma yin/
/de ñid daṅ ni bsgrub bya de//rtog ge pa yi yul ma yin/
/nor bu rin chen brtag pa la//loṅ ba tshad ma yin nam ci/
These verses contain echoes of MHK III. 286 (Ejima, *op. cit.*, p. 340) and (as later on also *Pramāṇaviniścaya*, as we have seen, II.5-6) VP I.35cd: *maṇirūpyādivijñānaṃ tadvidāṃ nānumānikam*. Cf. also the *Vṛtti* to VP I.127 (ed. Iyer, p. 205).

avasthādeśakālānāṃ bhedād bhinnāsu śaktiṣu /
bhāvānāṃ anumānena nātaḥ siddhiḥ sudurlabhā //
yatnenānumito 'py arthaḥ kuśalair anumātṛbhiḥ /
nānyathā sādhyate so 'nyair abhiyuktatarair api //[52]

Another late Buddhist author who often quotes the VP, is Jñānaśrībhadra, who composed a *Vṛtti* to the *Laṅkāvatārasūtra*. He was active in the 11th century A.D., and is quoted by Jñānavajra, the author of the only other Indian commentary on the *Laṅkāvatārasūtra* that has come down to us. Both seem now to have been lost in the original Sanskrit. All in all Jñānaśrībhadra quotes about fourty verses from Bhartṛhari ("Bha ta hari") and other grammarians. Among these it will here be sufficient to cite a sample which, when compared with the corresponding Sanskrit original, shows a few interesting variants, but otherwise serves to corroborate the *textus receptus*.[53]

This list of extracts can be seen as a supplement to the useful preliminary set of testimonia in K.V. Abhyankar and V.P. Limaye's edition of the *Vākyapadīya*, Poona 1965.

1. *anādinidhanaṃ brahma śabdatattvaṃ yad akṣaram /*
vivartate 'rthabhāvena prakriyā jagato yataḥ //
/ thog ma med pa'i tshaṅs pa rtag//yaṅ dag sgra ni yig 'bru gaṅ/
/ gaṅ las don dṅos 'byuṅ ba daṅ//'gro ba'i rab tu byed pa yaṅ /
2. *yaḥ sarvaparikalpānāṃ ābhāse 'py anavasthitaḥ /*
tarkāgamānumānena bahudhā parikalpitaḥ //
/ gaṅ yoṅs rtogs pa thams cad la//snaṅ bar yaṅ ni mi gnas te/
/ rtog pa luṅ daṅ rjes dpag pas//rnam pa du mar kun brtags pa'o/
3. *vyatīto bhedasaṃsargau bhāvābhāvau kramākramau /*
satyānṛte ca viśvātmā pravivekāt prakāśate //

52 Quoted from A. Kunst, *Probleme der buddhistischen Logik in der Darstellung des Tattvasaṅgraha*, Kraków 1939, p. 100. (To Śāntarakṣita *tattva* is also beyond *anumāna*, as in case of Bhavya. But *vyavahārataḥ* both accept an *anumāna* that is *nirdoṣa*, which, in case of Śāntarakṣita, means that it follows the rules of Dharmakīrti.)

53 For Jñānaśrībhadra, who also wrote a commentary on *Pramāṇaviniścaya*, see E. Steinkellner, *op. cit.*, 1973, p. 15. His commentary on the *Laṅkāvatāra* is also mentioned in the splendid (but often rather uncritical) work of H. Nakamura, *A History of Early Vedānta Philosophy*, Delhi 1983, pp. 257-258. – In the verses here quoted from VP (*Vṛtti* – or *Śabdadhātusamīkṣā*?) I & III, there seem to be some variant readings, e.g., in 1, *anādi hi nityam ... 'rthabhāvaś ca*, etc. – In the Tibetan I have corrected in 4b *'gram daṅ riṅ* (for *'gran daṅ rim*) and 8a *rig* (for *rigs*). Read, perhaps, also *nam yaṅ* for *rnam dag* in 8d. – Other quotations from various grammarians are found 74a2 (2 v. from VP), 74a4 (11 v. from VP), 74b1 (1 v. from gžon nu can gyi mur byed pa), 133a (2 v. from VP), 140a2 (3 v. from VP), 140a8 (1 v. from VP), 242b5 (2 v. from VP), and 276a6 (6 v. from VP).

/ 'das kyaṅ 'du 'dzi byed pa daṅ//dṅos daṅ dṅos med rim mi rim/
/ bden daṅ brdzun par sna tshogs bdag//dben pa las ni rab tu snaṅ/

4. *antaryāmī sa bhūtānām ārād dūre ca dṛśyate /*
so 'tyantamukto mokṣāya mumukṣubhir upāsyate //

/ 'byuṅ po rnams kyi naṅ rgyu ba// 'gram daṅ riṅ du'aṅ snaṅ ba ste/
/ thar pa rab tu grol ba de//grol 'dod rnams kyis bstan par byed/

5. *prakṛtitvam api prāptān vikārān ākaroti saḥ /*
ṛtudhām eva grīṣmānte mahato meghasaṃplavān //

/ de yi tshor ba gcig po yaṅ//rnam pa maṅ por rab tu 'byed/
/ 'jig pa 'byuṅ ba'i me mdag daṅ//chu yi phuṅ por chu bźin du/

6. *tasmād ākṛtigotrasthād vyaktigrāmā vikāriṇaḥ /*
mārutād iva jāyante vṛṣṭimanto balāhakāḥ //

/ de phyir da rod rigs gnas pa// gsal ba'i groṅ rnams 'gyur ba ni/
/ sprin rnams char daṅ ldan pa rnams//rluṅ las 'byuṅ ba bźin du 'o/

7. *trayīrūpeṇa tajjyotiḥ paramaṃ parivartate /*
pṛthaktīrthapravādeṣu dṛṣṭibhedanibandhanam //

/ gsum gyi gzugs su de snaṅ ba//mur smra tha dad rnams la ni/
/ mchog gi yoṅs su 'gyur ba ste// lta ba tha dad kyis ni bciṅs/

8. *śāntavidyātmako yo 'ṃśaḥ tad uhaitad avidyayā /*
tayā grastam ivājasraṃ yā nirvaktuṃ na śakyate //

/ źi źiṅ rig bdag tshaṅs pa ste// de las byuṅ ba'i ma rig pa/
/ des ni srin po bźin du med//gaṅ smra mi nus rnam dag go/

9. *yathā viśuddham ākāśam timiropapluto janaḥ /*
saṃkīrṇam iva mātrābhiś citrābhir abhimanyate //

/ ji ltar nam mkha' rnam dag par//rab rib 'khrul pa'i skyes bu yis/
/ ri mo rnam pa sna tshogs kyis//kun tu gaṅ bar sems pa pa/

10. *tathedam amṛtaṃ brahma nirvikāram avidyayā /*
kaluṣatvam ivāpannaṃ bhedarūpaṃ vivartate //

/ de ltar tshaṅs pa bdud rtsi 'di//'gyur ba med pa ma rig pas/
/ rñog pa lta bur byas pas na//tha dad gzugs su snaṅ ba ste/

11. *dyauḥ kṣamā vāyur ādityaḥ sāgarāḥ sarito diśaḥ /*
antaḥkaraṇatattvasya bhāgā bahir avasthitāḥ //

/ lha sa rluṅ daṅ nam mkha' daṅ//ri daṅ chu daṅ phyogs rnams kyaṅ/
/ naṅ du byed pa'i yaṅ dag gi// cha rnams phyi rol bźin du gnas/

12. *ekam eva yad āmnātaṃ bhinnaśaktivyapāśrayāt /*
apṛthaktve 'pi śaktibhyaḥ pṛthaktveneva vartate //

/ tshul ni gcig ñid gaṅ yin las// tha dad mthu ni rnam gnas pas/
/ mthu las tha dad ma yin yaṅ// tha dad bźin du 'byuṅ ba'o/

13. *brahmedaṃ śabdanirmāṇaṃ śabdaśaktinibandhanam /*
vivṛttaṃ śabdamātrābhyas tāsv eva pravilīyate //

/ tshans sgra'i 'di ni sprul pa ste//sgra yi mthu las gnas pas ni/
/ sgra tsam las ni byuṅ ba yaṅ//de dag ñid du źa bar 'gyur/

14. *yad ekaṃ prakriyābhedair bahudhā pravibhajyate /*
tad vyākaraṇam āgamya paraṃ brahmādhigamyate //

/ rab tu byed pa gcig 'byed la//maṅ por rab tu phye ba pa/
/ de ni luṅ ston rtogs pa las//tshaṅs pa mchog ni chud par 'gyur/

POINTS OF AGREEMENT AND DIFFERENCE BETWEEN THE VĀKYAPADĪYA AND THE MAHĀBHĀṢYA-DĪPIKĀ IN THE MATTER OF SPOṬA

G.B. Palsule, Pune

Now that the publication of the Critical Edition of the *Mahābhāṣya-Dīpikā* (henceforth *Dīp.*) undertaken by the Bhandarkar Oriental Research Institute, Pune, has been complete (i.e. as far as the text is available in the unique Berlin Ms), it is possible to study this oldest commentary on the *Mbh.* in a variety of ways. One of the lines of study could be a sort of comparative study of the *Vākyapadīya* (henceforth *Vākyap.*) and the *Dīp.*, both assigned to Bhartṛhari since Vardhamāna, the author of the *Gaṇaratnamahodadhi*, who says: *bhartṛharir vākyapadīyaprakīrṇakayoḥ kartā mahābhāṣyatripādyā vyākhyātā ca.*

I am interested in the Sphoṭa theory propounded by Bhartṛhari since a long time. I have much tried to understand this theory, but I am not still sure that I have correctly understood it. Therefore, with the appearance of this new edition of the *Dīp*. I renewed my interest in this topic and tried to ascertain what Bhartṛhari has to say about the Sphoṭa in the *Dīp*. In the present paper I have collected his occasional statements on Sphoṭa in the *Dīp*. (in all three, in the Āhnikas I and II), and have compared them with his statements on the same in the *Vākyap*. Frankly, this is not an exhaustive or thorough study: I have only jotted down points of agreement and difference regarding Sphoṭa in the two works and have offered a few passing observations.

I. The fundamental thesis:
   (1) The sounds, the revealers of the Sphota, and
   (2) The Sphoṭa, the conveyor of meaning.

In the view of both, the *Vākyap*. and the *Dīp*., the physical sounds uttered by the speaker do not convey any meaning directly. Their only purpose is to manifest the Sphoṭa which, the latter, conveys the meaning.[1]

1 Direct statements for the meaninglessness of phonemes are very rare in these two texts, such as *ke cin manyante yo vā 'yam uccāryate kramavān avaraḥ / kaś cid anyaḥ akramaḥ śabdātmā buddhistho vigāhate / tasmād arthapratipattiḥ / kutaḥ? yathaivārthāntaranibandhano nārthāntaram pratyāyayati evam svarūpanibandhano notsahate pratyāyayitum* (Dīp. I.3.13-15) / Elsewhere there is no dearth of such express statements. Kaiy. for

II. Some points of difference between the sounds and the Sphoṭa: According to both the Vākyap. and the Dīp. -

(1) The sounds are sequential (*kramajanman*), while the Sphoṭa is without any sequence (*akrama*).[2]

(2) The sounds are transitory (*anitya*), while the Sphoṭa is permanent (*nitya*).

(3) The sounds are transitory because they are produced (*karanebhyo vivrttena dhvaninā* - Vākyap. I. 47), while the Sphoṭa is permanent (*nitya*) because it is only to be manifested, and not to be produced (*vyajyamāne tathā vākye... Vākyap.* I.90).[3]

(4) Therefore the sounds are called *vyañjaka* 'manifestor' while the Sphoṭa is called *vyaṅgya* 'manifested' (*pratyekaṃ vyañjakā bhinnā varnavākyapadeṣu ye* I.88).[4]

instance says: *varṇānāṃ pratyekaṃ vācakatve dvitīyādivarṇoccāraṇānarthakyaprasaṅgāt, ānarthakye tu pratyekam utpattipakṣe yaugapadyenotpattyabhāvāt, abhivyaktipakṣe tu kramenaivābhivyaktyā samudāyābhāvāt, ekasmṛtyupārūḍhānām vācakatve sarah rasah ityādāv arthapratipattyaviśesaprasaṅgāt tadvyatiriktah sphoṭo nādābhivyaṅgyo vācako vistareṇa vākyapadīye vyavasthāpitah* [on the Mbh. 1.1.10.11: *yenoccāritena sāsnālāṅgūlaviṣāṇinām sampratyayo bhavati/*].

Although Kaiy. expressly mentions here the *Vākyap*. in connection with the meaninglessness of phonemes, I have not come across such an explicit statement in that text. Still there is no doubt whatsoever that such a statement is implied there, since otherwise it will take the bottom clean out of the argument in favour of the Sphoṭa theory. For the meaningfulness of the Sphoṭa, see *aparo'rthe prayujyate* Vākyap. I.44. *jāter arthasya pratipattiḥ / etac ca arthasvarūpam /sphoṭo 'yam eva śabdātmā nityaḥ /* Dīp. I.3.17,18 [*ke cin manyante*] *yo vāyam uccāryate, [sa] kramavān avaraḥ / kaś cid anyaḥ akramaḥ śabdātmā buddhistho vigāhate / tasmād arthapratipattiḥ /* (quoted above). *Tatra yadāyam pakṣaḥ vṛkṣādayaḥ śabdāḥ kramajanmānaḥ ayugapatkālāḥ vṛkṣaśabdatvākṛter akramāyā abhivyaktihetavo bhavanti - tadā vṛkṣaśabdatvād arthapratipattiḥ / sā ca nityā / - tatra caitad uktam "ubhayataḥ sphoṭamātraṃ pratinirdiśyate, raśruter laśrutiḥ" iti*. Dīp. I.17.4ff.

2 *nādasya kramajanmatvāt* Vākyap. I.48; Dīp. I.17.4ff. *na pūrvo na paraś ca saḥ / akramaḥ* - Vākyap. I.48.

3 Also: *anekavyaktyabhivyaṅgyā jātiḥ sphoṭa iti smṛtā* Vākyap. I.93 *yasyāpi śabdavyaktiḥ tasyāpi nityaḥ śabdaḥ / sa tu nādābhivyaṅgyaḥ* Dīp. I.17.9 *kramajanmānaḥ - vṛkṣaśabdatvākṛter akramāyā abhivyaktihetavaḥ* (Dīp. I.17.4, 5)

4 Also: *vyañjakadhvanibhedānupātena* Vṛtti on Vākyap. I.46; *nādaḥ sphoṭam avadyotayati* Vṛtti on Vākyap. I.48; *dhvaniprakāśite śabde* Vākyap. I.83.

III. Both the *Vākyap.* and the *Dīp.* mention different views regarding where exactly the *saṁskāra* (perfection) is effected by the sounds which helps the grasping of the word (*indriyasya, śabdasya, ubhayoḥ*).[5]

IV. Both the *Vākyap.* and the *Dīp.* also state that the manifested word (Sphoṭa) only apparently seems to partake of the properties of the sounds which manifest it; the Sphoṭa, in reality, is above the distinctions made by the properties of the sounds.[6]

5 *indriyasyaiva saṃskāraḥ śabdasyaivobhayasya vā /*
kriyate dhvanibhir vādās trayo 'bhivyaktivādinām // Vākyap. I.78
indriyasyaiva saṃskāraḥ samādhānāñjanādibhiḥ /
viṣayasya tu saṃskāras tadgandhapratipattaye// I.79
cakṣuṣaḥ prāpyakāritve tejasā tu dvayor api
viṣayendriyayor iṣṭaḥ saṃskāraḥ sa kramo dhvaneḥ // I.80
sa ca nādaḥ śrotrasyānugrahe vartate / tadanugṛhītam śrotram śabdopalabdhau samartham bhavati / yathākṣnor añjanam ity eke / apare śabdasyaiva / yathā prokṣaṇam pṛthivyā eva na ghrāṇasya / ubhayor ity apare / Dīp. I.17.15-17.

6 *nādasya kramajanmatvān na pūrvo na paraś ca saḥ /*
akramaḥ kramarūpeṇa bhedavān iva jāyate // Vākyap. I.48
The Vṛtti on this: *asau [sphoṭaḥ] ekatvam anatikrāman saṃsargiṇo nādasya bhedarūpam upasaṃgṛhṇāti /* (sequentialness)
pratibimbaṃ yathānyatra sthitaṃ toyakriyāvaśāt /
tatpravṛttim ivānveti sa dharmaḥ sphoṭanādayoḥ // 49 (number)
sphoṭasyābhinnakālasya dhvanikālānupātinaḥ /
grahaṇopādhibhedena vṛttibhedaṃ pracakṣate // 75 (speed of utterance)
svabhāvabhedān nityatve hrasvadīrghaplutādiṣu /
prākṛtasya dhvaneḥ kālaḥ śabdasyety upacaryate // 76 (length of vowels)
On this, Vṛṣabha: *dhvanisphoṭayor vibhāgāparicchedād dhvanikṛtam bhedaṃ sphoṭe paśyanti.*
śabdasyordhvam abhivyakter vṛttibhedaṃ tu vaikṛtāḥ /
dhvanayaḥ samupohante sphoṭātmā tair na bhidyate // 77
prakāśakānāṃ bhedāṃś ca prakāśyo 'rtho 'nuvartate
tailodakādibhede tat pratyakṣaṃ pratibimbake // 99
The Vṛtti: *dṛṣṭam abhivyaṅgyānām abhivyañjakabhedānuvidhānam / tad yathā / nimneṣv ādarśatalādiṣu mukhapratibimbam unnatam dṛśyate, unnateṣu nimnam, khaḍge dīrgham, priyaṅgutaile śyāmam cīnaśastrayavanakācādiṣv ādarśapramāṇabhedānupātī parimāṇo bhedavikalpaḥ / saṃkhyābhedo' pi ādarśabhede jalataraṅgabhede ca dṛśyate sūryādipratibimbānām /*
Dīp.: *yathādarśamaṇḍalādiṣu pratibimbāni dīrghāṇi parimaṇḍalāni mahānti anyāni ca dṛśyante, evaṃ śabdā api nādabhedena bhidyante / yathā salile taraṅgabhedena ekaś candro 'neka upalabhyate / pradīpabhedāc ca chāyā bhidyate / ādarśabhedāc ca pratibimbabhedaḥ / tasmān niyatanādābhivyaṅgyā nādavṛddhihrāsānuvidhāyino vyaktiśabdā api nityāḥ* (I.17.11-14)

V. Both the *Vākyap*. and the *Dīp*. mention the different views held by different linguists as regards what exactly constitutes the Sphoṭa. They are:

(1) The inner or mental word, the inner Word-principle which constitutes the reality of every being (*buddhisthaḥ śabdaḥ*,[7] *antaḥśabdatattvam*)[8]

(2) The universal or the class notion (*jātiḥ, ākṛtiḥ*)[9]

(3) A single word entity (*vyakti*)[10]

(4) The sound (i.e. the first sound) produced by the activity of the speech organs (*yaḥ saṃyogavibhāgābhyāṃ karaṇair upajanyate / sa sphoṭaḥ* Vākyap. I. 102)[11]

The first three make the sphoṭa *nitya* while according to the last view it is *anitya*, since it is produced (and not just revealed) (*anityapakṣe sthānakaraṇaprāptivibhāgahetukaḥ prathamābhinirvṛtto yaḥ śabdaḥ sa sphoṭaḥ ity ucyate*, the Vṛtti on Vākyap. I.102).[12]

7 *araṇisthaṃ yathā jyotiḥ prakāśāntarakāraṇam/*
tadvac chabdo 'pi buddhisthaḥ śrutīnāṃ kāraṇaṃ pṛthak // Vākyap. I.46
kaś cid anyaḥ akramaḥ śabdātmā buddhistho vigāhate / tasmād arthapratipattiḥ / (Dīp. I.3.13-14)

8 *Yad antaḥśabdatattvaṃ tu nādair ekaṃ prakāśitam /*
tad āhur apare śabdaṃ ...// Vākyap. II.30
See also 12 below.

9 *anekavyaktyabhivyaṅgyā jātiḥ sphoṭa iti smṛtā /*
kaiś cid vyaktaya evāsya dhvanitvena prakalpitāḥ // Vākyap. I.93
On this the Vṛtti: *ākṛtinityatvāc chabdanityatvam ācakṣāṇāḥ ... sphoṭaśabdavācyaṃ ... śabdākṛtim ācakṣate /*
For the Dīp. (I.3.13-14 and 17-18) see Note 1 above.

10 *avikārasya śabdasya nimittair vikṛto dhvaniḥ /*
upalabdhau nimittatvam upayāti prakāśavat // Vākyap. I.94
On this the Vṛtti: *anye tv ākṛtivyaktivyavahāraprakriyāvaidharmyād ekam eva śabdatattvaṃ nityaṃ ... abhivyajyata ity āhuḥ /*
Dīp. (I.17.9ff.): *yasyāpi śabdavyaktiḥ tasyāpi nityaḥ śabdaḥ / sa tu nādābhivyaṅgyaḥ / ... niyatanādābhivyaṅgyā nādavṛddhihrāsānuvidhāyino* vyaktiśabdā *api nityāḥ /*

11 *atha vā kāryavad buddhiṃ kṛtvā idam ucyate* [viz. "*ubhayataḥ ... bhavati*" Mbh.] / *tatra kāryapakṣe sphoṭa eva saṃyogāt, vibhāgāt, saṃyogavibhāgābhyāṃ vā niṣpadyate / yat tv anuraṇanaṃ tac chabdata eva / tena ya evāsau sphoṭasya niṣpādakaḥ karaṇasya vyāpāras tāvata evāśrayaṇam* / Dīp. II.25.19-21.

11a *ya ete śabdāḥ kiṃ te śabdākṛtayaḥ āhosvid śabdavyaktayaḥ iti ... niyatanādābhivyaṅgyāḥ vyaktiśabdā api nityāḥ* / Dīp. I.17.3-14

12 Cf. also *athāyam āntaro jñātā sūkṣmavāgātmanā sthitaḥ /*
vyaktaye svasya rūpasya śabdatvena vivartate // [I.113]
Similarly,
api prayoktur ātmānaṃ śabdam antar vyavasthitam /
prāhur mahāntaṃ vṛṣabhaṃ yena sāyujyam iṣyate // I.122

VI. Observations:

(1) It must have been seen that there is agreement on most of the points concerning the Sphoṭa in both the texts.

(2) Still there are some differences on a few minor points and in the matter of preferences. Thus, (i) the *Dīp.* speaks (foot note (11a)) of the *śabdavyaktayaḥ* (in plural). The *Vākyap.* (I.94) is not very clear on this point. The *Vṛtti* on it speaks of *ekam eva śabdatattvam* (a single Word-principle) manifested by sounds while on *Vākyap.* I.23 it speaks of *nityāṁ sabda-vyaktim.* Vṛṣabha commenting on the stanza I. 94 introduces it thus: *apare tv ākāśagata ekaḥ sphoṭavarṇa ity āhuḥ - avikārasya iti.*[13] Though the author of the Vṛtti and Vṛṣabha speak differently about this *Vyaktisphoṭa* as being either the (inner) *śabdatattva* or external Sphoṭa-phoneme, both of them take it as a single entity which appears in the forms of myriads of individual utterances. The *Dīp.* however seems to hold that for every word there is a different *vyakti-sphoṭa* (*ya ete śabdāḥ kiṃ te śabdākṛtaya āhosvit śabdavyaktaya iti* I. 17.3)

(ii) There is a difference of preferences as regards the *buddhistha śabda* vs. *ākṛti/vyakti*. The way the topic of Sphoṭa is introduced in the *Vākyap.* beginning with the *buddhistha śabda* (I.46) makes it almost certain that that is the author's own view. The *ākṛti* and the *vyakti* views, on the other hand, are mentioned (I.93,94) casually at the end and dismissed summarily. Exactly opposite is the treatment in the *Dīp.* where the *buddhistha śabda* is casually mentioned only once (I.3.14) and, there too, this view is indifferently ascribed to *kecit*! - while the *ākṛti* and the *vyakti* views are explained in detail (I.3.15 ff; I.17.2 ff; II. 25.21 ff).

(3) How is this difference in the preference to be explained? One explanation could be that in the *Dīp.* Bhartṛhari was commenting on the *Mbh.* Now, the *Mbh.* has in all probability used the word Sphoṭa only in a phonetic context. Further, only two views, *ākṛti* and *vyakti*, are mentioned in this context in the *Mbh.* (Pratyāhārāhnika, *Mbh.* on Vārttikas

13 Nāgeśa - *sarvadhvanibhir ekasya sphoṭasyaiva tattadrūpeṇa abhivyañjanāt* / (the Pradīpa: *ekaivākāravyaktiḥ* on the Vār. *ekatvād akārasya siddham* / [pratyāhārāhnika])

5 - 15. Vol. I. p. 16-18). That may be the reason why Bhartṛhari gives prominence to these views in the *Dīp*. In the *Vākyap*. on the other hand he is free to give full scope to his own views. That is why he gives prominence to the *buddhistha śabda* there. It is also probable that, if he wrote *Dīp*. first and the *Vākyap*. afterwards, his own views may have been crystalised in course of time and so he stated the *buddhistha śabda* view prominently in the *Vākyap*. He may have mentioned the *ākṛti* and the *vyakti* views briefly, because he did not want to do any injustice to them by dropping them altogether.

Friends, as I said in the beginning, I do not claim to have made any substantial contribution to the subject under study. Still I may say this much:

(1) The statements in the two works regarding different aspects of Sphoṭa are near-identical (and may indicate a common authorship, if, indeed, a proof of the identity of the authors of the two works was needed), and

(2) the difference between the preferences as regards the exact nature of Sphota (*ākṛti* / *vyakti* vs. *buddhistha śabda*) may indicate that initially Bhartṛhari was under the influence of Patañjali but in the *Vākyap*., free from that influence, he has given his own view prominently.

VIVAKṢĀ IN THE VĀKYAPADĪYA

Anna Radicchi, Cagliari

Vivakṣā's terminology occurs frequently in the *kārikās* of Bhartṛhari's Vākyapadīya[1]; *vivakṣā* changes meaning and implications according to context.

The first context in which the term *vivakṣā* appears, in the I Kāṇḍa, is clearly a phonetic one.

It is found in a *kārikā* quoted from the Pāṇinīya Śikṣā,[2] the last in a series following VP.I.110 (the series, numbered I.111-119 in W. Rau's edition, is missing in the southern branch of the *kārikās'* manuscript tradition), which reviews opinions of the *śikṣākāras* regarding the production of articulated sound, the *śabda*. This review is certainly not complete but is important nevertheless.

Whether the basic element of the *śabda* lies in the air, *vāyu*, the atom, *aṇu*, or knowledge, *jñāna*, the setting in motion of the prime matter, *prāna vāyu aṇu*, and then the arrival of the flow at the points of articulation, *sthāna*, remains a constant in the various representations. The mind, *manas*, takes on the impulse and guides the movement. Above and beyond the *manas*, the *buddhi* or a *jñātṛ*, an internal knower, is mentioned. There are also terms indicating heat: these are less technically associated with sound production than is *prayatna*, which basically means the articulatory effort or the predisposition of the organs, *karana*, to the articulatory effort.

It is in this context that the term *vivakṣā* appears in the Pāṇinīya Śikṣā's *kārikā* (I,6), included in the review. It is said that after the *buddhi* has formed its vision of things, the desire of the individual to express

1 All occurrences of *vivakṣā* terminology in the *kārikās* of the Vākyapadīya have been considered, verifying them in W. Rau's edition, "Bhartṛharis Vākyapadīya. Die *mūlakārikās* nach den Handschriften hrsg. und mit einem *pāda*-Index versehen", Abhandlungen für die Kunde des Morgenlandes XLII 4, Wiesbaden 1977 & "Bhartṛharis Vākyapadīya. Vollständiger Wortindex zu den *mūlakārikās*", Akademie der Wissenschaften und Literatur, Mainz, Abhandlungen der Geistes- und Sozialwissenschaftlichen Klasse Jg. 1988, Nr. 11. In Rau's Index the occurrences are listed under *vivakṣā*, *°vivakṣā* (also separately under *anyaśabdavivakṣā*, *saṃkhyāvivakṣā*, etc.), *vivakṣāniyamāśraya*, *vivakṣita*, *vivakṣitanibandhana*, *vac* (for *vivakṣyate* and *vivakṣyante*), *avivakṣā*, *°avivakṣā* (also separately under *upamānāvivakṣā*), *avivakṣātas*, *avivakṣita*, *prativivakṣita*.

2 VP.I.119 in the numbering of the above-cited edition by W. Rau. This numbering is followed unless otherwise specified.

himself resorts to the *manas*, which stimulates the energy needed for articulation; thus *marut* is produced.

The *vivakṣā* in this *kārikā* seems to be the equivalent of the *vaktur icchā*, the 'desire to speak', the expression used in another *kārikā*, VP.I.111, of the same series, which simply explains that, moved by the effort resulting from the desire to speak, air, *vāyu*, beats against the points of articulation, producing articulated sound.

The specificity of the opinions reviewed in this series of *kārikās* is clarified by the *vṛtti*, which repeats that they are viewpoints of the *śikṣākāras*, the phoneticians. On the other hand, the *vṛtti* itself extends the investigation beyond the immediate, contingent speech organs; following a course opposite to that of exhaled air, it attempts to reach what appears to be the beginning of the motion of the air itself. Important stages which were part of traditional physiology are mentioned: first *nābhi*, the navel, and also *koṣṭha*, the abdomen, then *kaṇṭha*, the throat.

Under VP.I.121 the *vṛtti* speaks of the *prāṇa* which, penetrated by the *buddhi*, rises like a flame in the direction of the organs of articulation.

This motion of the *prāṇa* does not seem to be distinguishable from what the first tāntric texts call the motion of the *kuṇḍalinī*. The *kuṇḍalīśakti* according to Ahirbudhnya-Saṃhitā (XVI,55 foll.)[3] moves up from the *mūlādhāra*, first reaches the navel, then proceeds to the heart; from there, 'desiring to express the *vācya*', *vācyavivakṣayā* (XVI,63), turns towards the throat where phonemes are produced.

The motion of the *prāṇa-kuṇḍalinī* is spontaneous, just as man's speech is a spontaneous phenomenon coming before its acoustic, grammatical or philosophical interpretation.

In the phonetic context, the *vivakṣā* is simply a datum of experience. Without the natural function of speech, which man naturally wants to exercise, there would be no production of articulated sound.

However, correct speech is the subject-matter of grammar.

Proceeding with the *kārikās* of the I Kāṇḍa, in I.152 we encounter that *sato'vivakṣā* - if that is the correct reading - which immediately refers to the Mahābhāṣya.

3 Ed. M.D. Ramanujacharya, under the supervision of F.O. Shrader, rev. V. Krishnamacharya, Vol. I, second ed., first rep., Adyar, Madras 1986, pp. 147-149.

The Mahābhāṣya is the first of the two known fundamental stages through which grammatical tradition reached Bhartṛhari; the other is the Cāndravyākaraṇa.[4]

It is with the Mahābhāṣya that the *vivakṣā* appears in the history of grammar; it certainly existed before Patañjali because it occurs in the formulation of *vārttikas* he commented on.

B.A. Van Nooten presented a paper on *vivakṣā* especially in the Mahābhāṣya some time ago.[5] The investigation, on Pathak and Chitrao's Index, is far from definitive; on the contrary, it does not hit the mark in important points.

It is first necessary to distinguish *vivakṣā* in Kātyāyana's *vārttikas* from *vivakṣā* in Patañjali's dialectics.

For the few occurrences in the *vārttikas*, one could simplistically say that *vivakṣā*, or rather *(a)vivakṣitatva*, is resorted to only in the attempt to resolve difficulties in the interpretation and application of Pāṇini's *sūtras*. For example, *sūtra* 1.4.24 which gives the *saṃjñā* of *apādāna*, contemplating a fixed point, *dhruvam*, from which the movement of departure begins, would seem to have no validity for moving objects, in which there is no fixed point. *Vārtt*. 3 under the *sūtra* eliminates the difficulty: the speaker may not wish to present the object in motion but only the separation from that object. Pā. 1.4.24 remains valid also in these cases.

On the other hand, in Patañjali's dialectic *vivakṣā* enters at times with a vitality demanding revision of F. Kielhorn's old opinion,[6] never denied, i.e., *vivakṣā*, like *anabhidhāna*, is an artifice "of no value whatever".

Patañjali is still far from the medieval scholasticism of the Bhāṣāvṛtti and the Durghaṭavṛtti, which will reduce *vivakṣā* to a pure expedient, even if often ingenious, used to justify difficult forms which would otherwise be aberrant with respect to the rules.

From Patañjali comes the formula, quasi *paribhāṣā: itikaraṇaḥ kriyate tataśced vivakṣā*, "*iti* is there, from it *vivakṣā* is deduced". That is, only in Pāṇini's *sūtras*, in whose formulation *iti* appears, the *vivakṣā* can

4 See also the recent Th. Oberlies, "Studie zum Cāndravyākaraṇa. Eine kritische Bearbeitung von Candra IV.4.52-148 und V.2", Alt- und Neu-Indische Studien hrsg. Institut für Kultur und Geschichte Indiens und Tibets an der Universität Hamburg, Stuttgart 1989, pp. 11-14, "Die Datierung Candragomins und Dharmadāsas".

5 "*Vivakṣā-*, or intention to speak, as a linguistic principle", Proceedings of the International Seminar on Studies in the *Aṣṭādhyāyī* of Pāṇini, Publications of the Centre of Advanced Study in Sanskrit, Class E 9, University of Poona, 1983, pp. 43-52.

6 F. Kielhorn, "Notes on the Mahabhashya, 7. Some devices of Indian grammarians", Ind. Ant. 16 (1887), pp. 244-252.

legitimately be invoked; there the *vivakṣā* dispenses with additions or modifications.

Omitting arguments regarding rules and grammatical technique, two points about *vivakṣā* seem particularly interesting in Patañjali's remarks.

The first has been misunderstood in Van Nooten's paper. It is what Patañjali explains under 5.1.16 (Vol. II, pp. 342-43); he says there are two types of *vivakṣā: prāyoktrī* and *laukikī*.

The *prāyoktrī* is present when one uses 'tender, affected, slippery' words, yielding to an individual taste for speech. The series of adjectives Patañjali uses, *mṛdūn snigdhān ślakṣṇān*, seems to reach with a crescendo that 'corrupt', *apabhraṃśān*, with which Kaiyaṭa's comment below the passage[7] frankly annotates the series. They are clearly individual affectations which others must not and cannot imitate; there is no limit, Kaiyaṭa says, to personal freedom.

The *laukikī vivakṣā* is of a different type: there we have majority consent, *prāyasya sampratyayaḥ*; that is, it expresses a generally perceived tendency and so its established use regards the general run of language users. Grammatical tradition, Kaiyaṭa further states, has its roots in usage: *prayogamūlatvād vyākaraṇasmṛteh*. Here the *vivakṣā* goes well beyond that spontaneity accorded it by phoneticians. A strictly linguistic factor has been added: the recognition of tendencies that assert themselves in language.

The other interesting point about *vivakṣā* in Patañjali's discourse is found under 1.4.24, after the above-cited *vārtt*. 3 and then passim, under 2.3.50, etc. Patañjali says that one may not wish to communicate things that objectively exist, just as one may wish to express things that do not exist: *sato'py avivakṣā bhavati.....asataś ca vivakṣā*.

Bhartṛhari's *kārikā* I.152 follows Patañjali's wording.

The ocean may seem a basin and the Vindhya a large pile of rice: that is to say that fantasy is free and the language following it must not be questioned. The stylistic and rhetorical implications deriving from this are remarkable.

There have been contrasts and errors in evaluation on the part of scholars concerning the use the Cāndravyākaraṇa makes of *vivakṣā*.[8]

7 Ed. Vedavrata, Haryāṇā Sāhitya Saṃsthāna, Gurukula Jhajjar (Rohatak), Vol. IV, 1963, p. 21.

8 See M. Deshpande, "Candragomin's syntactic rules, some misconceptions", Indian Linguistics, Vol. 40 (1979), pp. 133-145, which criticizes S.D. Joshi and J.A.F. Roodbergen,

An index of all occurrences of the term and connected terminology in the *sūtras* and the *vṛtti* must still be compiled.[9]

The theory of the *kārakas* in the Cāndravyākaraṇa is interesting. Candra reunified in Ca. 2.1.43-98 Pāṇini's two sections 1.4.23-55 and 2.3.1-70, in addition to including the treatment of the *upapada*.

Pā. 1.4.23-55 had roughly sketched out sectors of activity, which make themselves known in language through verbs and syntactic operators, *kārakas,* while Pā. 2.3.1-70 had given the related detailed use of case endings, *vibhaktis*. Reunifying Pāṇini's two sections, Candra directly connected cases of the declension with actions that are carried out and require an accusative in language to indicate the object, an instrumental to indicate the agent or the instrument, and so on.

The speaker may wish to express the object - this is the *vyāpyavivakṣā* - or an instrument - this is the *karaṇavivakṣā* - and thus uses a particular ending. The *vivakṣā* does not violate the rules. These are useful for learning the correct usage, only by using the correct cases can we express what we mean. But the use of cases serves the speaker, who wants to express events in his own way. This is the meaning of the well-known *paribhāṣā*, in the form presented under Ca. 2.1.49: *vivakṣāto hi kārakāṇi bhavanti.*[10]

We would rather emphasize the freedom the *vivakṣā* allowed, according to Cāndravyākaraṇa, freedom in using the rules, and stylistic freedom.

That dichotomy between reality, *kārakas*, and language, *vibhaktis*, not resolved in Pāṇini's two sections and overcome in Candra by simple superimposition, is philosophically systematized in Bhartṛhari.

In the Sādhanasamuddeśa in the III Kāṇḍa of the Vākyapadīya, as well as elsewhere in this great work, the *sādhana-kārakas* are clearly seen to

"Patañjali's Vyākaraṇa-Mahābhāṣya: Kārakāhnika (P.1.4.23-1.4.55)", Publications of the Centre of Advanced Study in Sanskrit, Class C 10, University of Poona 1975, "Introduction".

9 I plan to read a paper on this subject at the 9th World Sanskrit Conference in Melbourne.

10 "*Vivakṣātaḥ kārakāṇi bhavanti*" is the title of a chapter Cārudevaśāstrī dedicated to *vivakṣā* in "Prastāvataraṅginī". Haridāsa-Saṃskṛta-Granthamālā 201, Benares 1950, pp. 188-196. There a valid philological discussion on *vivakṣā* had already been set out, meant to constitute orthodox teaching rather than supply elements of historical criticism on the evolution of the concept among grammarians. As far as I know, there are no other later monographic studies on *vivakṣā* untill the above-cited article by Van Nooten. The scholar who seems to have shed more light on the subject is L. Renou, with his edition of "La Durghaṭavṛtti de Śaraṇadeva. Traité grammatical en sanskrit du XIIe siècle", Collection Émile Senart, I 1-3, II 1-3, Paris 1940-1956.

act on the level of mental activity. There is an interior vision of things which is individualistic and free; in it action is represented in various ways and the elements of reality assume the roles of the various *kārakas*.

When the desire to translate the interior vision into words comes with the *vivakṣā*, at that point grammar acts as a guide and the *vibhaktis* are used. The *vibhaktis* are on the level of the *śabda*, the translation of mental representation into words.

Thus the *vivakṣā* acts as a link between the mental plane of the *kalpanā*, *buddhikalpanā*, where the *kārakas* operate and the plane of expressed words, which use the *vibhaktis*.

There is another *paribhāṣā* in the Cāndravyākaraṇa which we briefly wish to call attention to: *vivakṣāvyāpter iṣṭāvasāyaḥ*. It is what one wants to express that commands the desiderata of grammar, that indicates what forms we want to see regularized by grammar.

Here the field is that of word formations, *śabdasaṃskāra*, in which the *vivakṣā* will have a long way to go before arriving at medieval scholasticism and beyond.

The way the Cāndravyākaraṇa presents the process is clearly seen from the *vṛtti* under 5.2.44; see also the Kāśikā under 6.3.45. How can we justify the form *śreyastarā* which the rule accepting *śreyasitarā* and *śreyasītarā* does not sanction? It is justified because one does not want to express the feminine form with it, and this choice occurs before the suffix denoting the degree of comparison is added. In terms of the *vṛtti*: *prakarṣayogāt prāk strītvasyāvivakṣitatvāt siddham.*

In Bhartṛhari as well, in the Vṛttisamuddeśa in the III Kāṇḍa, the *kārikās* repeatedly point out that forms - see the use of the suffix *vat*, compounds, the expression of *upamāna*, etc. - are explained as grammatically correct only by considering the *vivakṣā*. Why *mṛgadugdhā*, for example?: because the first member does not mean to express the feminine form (419). Surely here *vivakṣā* appears channeled into normative grammar to correctly and efficiently unfold itself according to rules valid for everyone.

It is also conditioned by the cultural milieu. Children inherit a linguistic patrimony at birth (VP.I. 129, foll.). Their organs are already predisposed for articulating words.

It is Bhartṛhari the philosopher, not a linguist, who is speaking. From time to time his discourse is tinged with psycholinguistics, sociolinguistics and linguistic speculation; it is never purely linguistic.

The idea emerging in Patañjali's dialectics on the *laukikī vivakṣā*, of the language as an autonomous organism in which tendencies develop, disappears in the philosopher Bhartṛhari.

In the II Kāṇḍa of the Vākyapadīya, which presents and debates the two fundamental themes of grammar, *vākya* and *pada*, we find sections containing interesting cues regarding textual and stylistic analysis.

Verses 64-87 contain a sequence of objections that *padavādins* raised against the *akhaṇḍavādins*, based on specific observations: a word, for example *vrīhi*, which must be substituted in the prescription of a rite, when that material is not available; an unfamiliar word like *pika*, which is taken out of context for explanation; the difference between direct statement and syntactical connection; attention paid to secondary clauses; finally, a number of elements in a clause from which are understood the sequence, the primary action, etc., elements depending on the reading of the text, important because their correct interpretation involves the fruit, *phala* (named in 83), of the sacrificial act itself. The *padavādins* argued that it was impossible to deny the *pada* a meaning independent of that of the *vākya*.

In these twenty-four verses the terminology of *vivakṣā*, or here rather of non-*vivakṣā* (69: *avivakṣitāḥ, avivakṣā*; 80: *na vivakṣitaḥ*; 83: *avivakṣitaḥ*), appears quite conspicuously, considering the total number of appearences in the II Kāṇḍa. Other terminology used is also interesting. An important part is played by the *śruti*, direct statement; in contrast there is *sāmarthyam*, what is gathered from context, which is indicated, *lakṣita*, or contained in an indication, *lakṣaṇā*, derived from context, *sāmarthya-lakṣaṇa*. The *abhidhā*, or more precisely the *śabdo'bhidhāyakaḥ*, the *śabda* having denotative power, also appears.

Understanding the *vivakṣā*, which is what the text wants to convey, means interpreting it correctly and acting accordingly.

Other instances of *vivakṣā* terminology in the II Kāṇḍa (301: *vivakṣite, avivakṣitam*; 304: *avivakṣitam*) are found in the final part of a long section, II.250-324, presenting theories and opinions on the meaning of the word and above all on the difference between the primary meaning, *mukhya*, and secondary meaning, *gauṇa*.[11]

It is stated (298) that, just as a lamp reveals not only the objects it is meant to illuminate but also others nearby, in the same way a word used in one meaning involves others along with the desired one. *Vivakṣita* is the desired meaning; other meanings automatically involved are *avivakṣita* (301).

11 There is an article by K.A. Subramania Iyer, dealing in detail with passages contained in this section of the II Kāṇḍa, which never mentions *vivakṣā* at all: "Bhartṛhari on the primary & secondary meanings of words", Indian Linguistics, Vol. 29 (1968), S.M. Katre Felicitation Volume Part I, pp. 97-112.

Further on (314 and 315) are two lists of determining elements for assigning meaning to a word: the clause in which it is found, *vākya*, the context, *prakaraṇa*, the meaning of the other words, *artha*, the propriety, *aucitya*, place, *deśa*, and time, *kāla*. The second list which follows is broader, repeating two elements, *artha* and *prakaraṇa*, already considered in the first one. The subject had evidently been debated.

The accepted conclusion, in simple terms, is that the word has many meanings which are used according to context. Here *vivakṣā* is the intention of conveying one meaning rather than another.

There is also an indirect way of making oneself understood, and this seems the most interesting stylistic suggestion. This occurs when one does not simply wish to use the primary or one of the secondary meanings. For instance, the "crows" from which the boy is asked to protect the *sarpis* also means "dogs" or similar animals (312). The *dhātu bhuj*, used in the sense of "to feed", also implies washing the dishes in which the food was eaten and the pots in which the food was cooked (313). It is said that the sacred texts expressing praise or blame, this being the only way to incite or dissuade from action, should not be taken literally, *ayathārthām* (319).

The discourse presented in these passages of the II Kāṇda of the Vākyapadīya is one of textual criticism, using specific terminology and examining Vedic texts.

Before Bhartṛhari, the meaning of the *mantra* had long been an object of criticism, at times hostile. Kautsa's judgement stated in Nirukta I.15 was categorical: *anarthakā hi mantrāḥ*, "*mantras* have no meaning at all". Kautsa's objections and their refutations will have broad repercussions long after Bhartṛhari.

The meaning Kautsa could not find in the *mantras* was in effect the common meaning, difficult to extract from an archaic, at times obscure language which often expressed itself in contradictory terms.

The meaning of the *mantras*, or more precisely the *mantravākyārtha* (Nirukta VII.3), was considered in another context: that of hymns of praise to the divinity. These varying visions of the *mantras, ṛṣīṇām mantradṛṣṭayaḥ*, were broadened and consolidated in a list of thirty-six different *vākya, vividhāni vākyāni*, that the Bṛhaddevatā exemplifies in I.46-60. They are modes of expression, whose purpose is to praise the divinity but which sometimes directly express *nindā*, blame, or *saṃśaya*, doubt, praise to the divinity remaining a matter of inference.

Here the analysis of the meaning of the *vākya* had already become a stylistic-rhetorical investigation linked, in the type of texts under examination, to the expression of praise to the divinity.

Nirukta and Bṛhaddevatā are far from Bhartṛhari, but they are the first well-known texts in which the meaning of the *mantra* undergoes an investigation oriented toward the textual and stylistic criticism we will later on find in Bhartṛhari. Moreover, the texts investigated are at least in part the ones Bhartṛhari himself will consider.

The *vivakṣā* which is read in the Vākyapadīya in these contexts of the II Kāṇḍa returns in what are properly regarded the first texts on rhetoric.

The *vivakṣita artha*, "the understood meaning", already appears in the analysis of the *doṣa bhinnārtha* in that schematic compendium of the essentials of poetic art given by the Nāṭyaśāstra and concluding with their use in the presentation of the *rasas*.[12] It is the first sign of that familiarity with the *vivakṣā* constantly found in the first *alaṃkārikas*, in Bhāmaha, Daṇḍin, Udbhaṭa, where the *vivakṣā* is resorted to in order to enter into the intricacies of the figures. In Vāmana as well (4.3.27), the *vivakṣā* is used to define an *alaṃkāra*, the *alaṃkāra ākṣepa*; then in the last adhyāya of the Kāvyālaṃkārasūtrāni, in a strictly grammatical context, that of *śabdaśuddhi*.

Ānandavardhana emphasized the presence of the *vivakṣā* as a stylistic and poetic element. The two broad categories of true poetry, *dhvani kāvya*, already contain *vivakṣā* in their own definitions of *avivakṣita-vācya* and *vivakṣitānyapara-vācya*. Ānandavardhana is certainly a long way from Bhartṛhari; he reconciled the contrasts of the various schools: of the systems of the *rasa, alaṃkāra, rīti*. In any case the indebtedness of Ānandavardhana to Bhartṛhari has been pointed out several times.

Even without definitively ascertaining Bhartṛhari's date, we can say that Bhartṛhari lived more or less between Bharata and Bhāmaha, in a period relatively lacking in documentation on rhetorical studies. His historical position is extremely interesting as his field is still the Vedic. From this point of view, the dramatic texts Bharata deals with and above all the *kāvya* texts from which Bhāmaha and the other rhetoricians take their examples are traditionally considered more modern. But Bhartṛhari is certainly near to them, in the use he makes of the term *vivakṣā*.

12 Adhyāya 16, v. 91 in "Nāṭyaśāstra with the commentary of Abhinavagupta", ed. M. Ramakrishna Kavi, Vol. II, Gaekwad's Oriental Series LXIII, Baroda 1934, p. 332. The line was overcorrected by V. Raghavan, "Bhoja's Śṛṅgāra Prakāśa", p. 222 in the first edition, Madras 1963. However *vivakṣita-* can be read unequivocally.

Two conclusions can clearly be drawn from the observations on the above-examined occurrences of *vivakṣā* terminology in the II Kāṇḍa of the Vākyapadīya.

The first is that the sections considered should by right be included among Indian works on rhetoric. Seeing the scarcity of such documents for the period preceding Bhāmaha, it would be reasonable to treasure them.

The second conclusion regards the term *vivakṣā* and is a corollary of the first. The occurrences of *vivakṣā* terminology in these sections assume their full meaning only in light of the Indian rhetorical theories of the period.

Phonetics, grammar, stylistics: they represent three different currents which carry the idea of *vivakṣā* and a terminology for *vivakṣā*.

However, Bhartṛhari's discourse is principally philosophical; phonetics, stylistics and normative grammar are only secondarily involved. The grand design running from the first to the third Kāṇḍa of the Vākyapadīya moves from the *Śabdabrahman* of the first Kāṇḍa, through the two great themes, *vākya* and *pada*, in the second Kāṇḍa, to the detailed review of linguistic aspects and principles to which the third Kāṇḍa is dedicated. It almost follows the *Vāc* - the observation has been made several times - which descends from the level of *paśyantī*, through the *madhyamā*, to the world level with the *vaikharī*.

The *vivakṣā* enters into this grand design even if it is not the object of particular attention. There is a turning point in the *madhyamā vāc*, this *Vāc* being of an ambivalent nature precisely because it is intermediate. It is the moment when the *vāc madhyamā*, even with the sequence suppressed or contracted, according to how one interprets "*saṃhāra*" in the expression *kramasaṃhārabhāve* in the *vṛtti* under I.159, despite resorting to a motion of subtle *prāṇa*, *sūkṣmaprāṇavṛttyanugatā*, is yet according to some *vyaktaprāṇaparigrahā*, that is, as Iyer nicely translates, "it has distinct functioning of breath in it". Vṛṣabha explains that this is made clear when one recites something silenty to oneself: *svayam apy asyopāṃśutaraṃ paṭhataḥ tat spaṣṭam*. This *vāc madhyamā* is interior and in a certain sense contains sequence, and the *buddhi* is its sole foundation: *madhyamā tv antaḥsaṃniveśinī parigṛhītakrameva buddhimātropādānā* (*vṛtti*). Vṛṣabha says that the *madhyamā* is interior because it is the form of the word in the *buddhi* before it is pronounced: *na karaṇasthā kiṃ tv enaṃ śabdaṃ samuccārayāmīti buddhau yaḥ śabdākāraḥ*, "it is not in the articulatory organs, but it is the form of the *śabda* which is in the *buddhi*, when the intention is to pronounce those particular words".[13]

This is the turning point: the moment in which the *madhyamā vāc* prepares itself to be translated into the *vāc vaikharī* which will be articulated by the speech organs. This translation, substantially unbiased in literary production, is also the common source of action. Because one desires to intervene or decides to intervene depending on "how he views reality", *saṃdarśana* (VP.III.7.16). Then one action develops from another and determines activity. Regardless of whether the articulated word is accompanied by an action or whether there is only the word, it is this desire to express oneself that constitutes the *vivakṣā*. It is due to this desire that the constructions of the *buddhi* are translated one after another into language.

VP.III.7.17 states that it is *caitanya*, "sentience", that is the means to the "vision" of things and as such comes before all activity and "vision" itself. With the *caitanya* one finally arrives at that life principle of which is to be recognized "the ultimate identity with *brahman*, the postulated starting point of the world of our experience".[14]

It is true that Bhartṛhari has not reserved particular treatment for that epistemology whose elements he accepts and uses in his discourse. However, it seems certain that for him it is the *buddhi* that constructs images of the reality; these images the listener comprehends. This clearly means, in another context, VP.III.3.32: "the word is understood (by the listener) with the meaning present in the *buddhi* (of the speaker)".

Somānanda was not mistaken, proposing his precious testimony at the beginning of the II āhnika of the Śivadṛṣṭi. Summing up before proceeding to the confutation, the position of the *vaiyākaraṇas*, i.e., substantially that of Bhartṛhari, regarding levels of reality, gives *paśyantī*, which is for them the *parā sthitiḥ*, corresponding to the level of *Sadāśiva*, then *madhyamā* which is *śabda* on the mental plane of *vijñāna*, ready to express things, finally *vaikharī*. Somānanda uses the term *vivaksā* in this context: *āste vijñānarūpatve sa śabdo'rthavivakṣayā / madhyamā kathyate saiva*. And

13 See "Vākyapadīya of Bhartṛhari with the Vṛtti and the Paddhati of Vṛṣabhadeva. Kāṇḍa I", ed. K.A. Subramania Iyer, Deccan College Monograph Series 32, Poona 1966, p. 214 & K.A. Subramania Iyer, "The Vākyapadīya of Bhartṛhari with the Vṛtti. Chapter I. English translation", Deccan College Building Centenary & Silver Jubilee Series 26, Poona 1965, p. 125.

14 Quoted from A. Aklujkar: "Bhartṛ-hari's concept of the Veda", p. 7, Panels of the VIIth World Sanskrit Conference, Vol. V, *Pāṇini and the Veda*, Leiden 1991, pp. 1-18.

again, about the grammarians' *madhyamā*: "It is the *madhyamā* that is united with the *buddhi*, whose nature is that of constructing images".[15]

Bhartṛhari will have great influence on Indian thought in the following centuries.

The paragraph in the *vṛtti* under VP.I.159 relative to *paśyantī* will be entirely quoted by Abhinavagupta in the Īśvarapratyabhijñāvivṛttivimarśinī and attributed to Bhartṛhari himself.[16]

Of all Abhinavagupta's speculations regarding *Vāc*, here it is interesting to recall and compare what is contained in ten verses at the end of the III āhnika of the Tantrāloka.[17]

After having developed the theme of the emanation of phonemes, which is also the unfolding of creation, Abhinavagupta presents multiplicity as a triple body, *vapus*, named *paśyantī, madhyamā* and *vaikharī*. Each of these three *Vāc* has a triple nature: *sthūla, sūkṣma* and *para*.

Sthūlā paśyantī is the *nādarūpiṇī* of music consisting only of notes, without the harshness of distinct phonemes. *Sthūlā madhyamā* is *dhvani* in the music made, for example, by drums, which also knows how to be sweet when imitating singing. *Sthūlā vaikharī* is that of spoken language, with its phonemes and clauses.

The stage preceding the *sthūla* for each, *paśyantī, madhyamā* and *vaikharī*, is the *sūkṣma*. This consists of an *anusandhāna*, planning, let us say an intention. It can be formulated with the words of common experience: now I am going to make music, now I am going to play an instrument, now I am going to talk.

Beyond this level, for the three *Vāc*, is the supreme, *para*, which reaches Śiva.

It is the *sūkṣma* stage that interests us here.

Jayaratha's comment on the meaning of *anusandhāna* expresses no doubts. It has the nature of desire; in its three varieties, corresponding to *paśyantī, madhyamā* and *vaikharī*, it is respectively the desire to sing, *jigāsā*, to play an instrument, *vivādayiṣā*, and finally to speak: *vivakṣā*.

In Abhinavagupta's conception, the three stages, *sthūla, sūkṣma* and *para*, constitute a stairway within each of the three *Vāc*, which descends

15 Cf. ed. Madhusūdan Kaul Shāstrī, KSTS LIV, Srinagar 1934, pp. 36-42 and p. 59.

16 Cf. ed. Madhusūdan Kaul Shāstrī, KSTS LXII, Bombay 1941, Vol. II, p. 226.

17 See "The Tantrāloka of Abhinavagupta with the Commentary of Jayaratha", ed. R.C. Dwivedi and Navajivan Rastogi, enlarged edition, Delhi 1987, Vol. II Chapters 1-3, pp. 577-584.

from heaven to earth and then reascends. The *paśyantī* does not remain outside the world but descends there and is incorporated into sublime music, and the *vaikharī* is not only in the world but goes beyond it, as far as Śiva.

If we look for the *vivakṣā* in this grandiose conception, in which all conflicts and polemics about *Vāc* levels are overcome, we find it at the point in which the *Vāc* is about to present itself in the world, just before the *sthūla* stage of the *vaikharī*.

BIBLIOGRAPHY ON BHARTṚHARI

Yves Ramseier, Lausanne

This bibliography is divided into three parts:

– PART 1: the editions of the *Vākyapadīya*. The numbering follows the bibliography of Wilhelm RAU (1977 and 1988), and the presentation of these editions is also inspired by his.

– PART 2: the editions of the *Mahābhāṣyadīpikā*.

– PART 3: the rest, i.e. studies, translations and book reviews. Some works editing the text and translating it into any language appear twice.

The content of RAU's bibliography is of course completely integrated here, and the initials W.R. refer to his remarks (kārikās to his edition: nº 16a). Important were also CARDONA 1976 and COWARD and RAJA 1990. Many persons helped me in my task, and I thank them all, among them specially Johannes BRONKHORST, Mr GOSVAMI, librarian at the *Centre of Advanced Studies in Sanskrit* (Poona University), Jan HOUBEN, S.D. LADDU, Mr. MANJUL, librarian at the *Bhandarkar Oriental Research Institute*, and TANIZAWA Junzō. I also implore the compassion of the reader for some important items I may have omitted in this bibliography.

Editions of Vākyapadīya

(For a complete word-index, see nº 16b and 25.)

1. Vākyapadīya. A treatise on the philosophy of Sanskrit grammar by Bhartṛhari with a commentary by Puṇyarāja on the 1st and 2nd kāṇḍas and Helārāja's commentary on the 3rd kāṇḍa. Edited by RĀMAKṚṢṆA ŚĀSTRĪ alias TĀTYĀ ŚĀSTRĪ PAṬAVARDHANA, GAṄGĀDHĀRA ŚĀSTRĪ MĀNAVALLĪ, RĀMACANDRA ŚĀSTRĪ KOṬIBHĀSKARA and GOSVAMI DĀMODARA ŚĀSTRI, Benares (Benares Sanskrit Series, Work nº 6: [fascicle] nº 11, 1884, pp. (1)-(2), 1-96 [I.1 - II.73]; nº 19, 1886, pp. 97-192 [II.74 - 266]; nº 24, 1887, pp. 193-292 [II.267 to end] = Volume I. — Nº 95, 1905, pp. 1-96 [III.1.1 - III.2]; nº 102, 1905, pp. 97-192 [III.3 - III.7.24]; nº 130, 1907, pp. 193-288 [III.7.25 - 162]; nº 160, 1928, pp. 289-384 [III.7.162 - III.9.101]; nº 161, 1930, pp. 385-480 [III.9.102 - III.14.60]; nº 162, 1933, pp. 481-576 [III.14.61 - 260]; nº 163/4, 1937, pp. 577-744 [III.14.261 to end] = Volume II).

2. Śrībharttṛhariviracitavākyapadīyabrahmakāṇḍaḥ. So [']yam... śrīDRAVYEŚA-JHĀpraṇītapratyekārthaprakāśikāsamākhyayā vyākhyayopetaḥ. Śrīvṛndāvane paṃ° RĀMANIVĀSAŚARMAdvārā śrī 'brajendra'mudraṇālaye sammudrya prākāśyaṃ nītaḥ. Saṃvat 1983 [= 1926/7].

3a. Bhagavadbhartṛhariviracitaṃ vākyapadīyam. Tatra haryyupajñavṛttisanāthaṃ vṛṣabhadevaṭīkāsaṃkṣepasaṃyutaṃ prathamaṃ kāṇḍam. Pariṣkartā CĀRUDEVAḤ ŚĀSTRĪ pāṇinīyaḥ. Lavapura [=Lahore], vikramavatsarāḥ 1991 [= 1934].

3b. Vākyapadīyam. Bhartṛharyupajñavṛttisanāthaṃ puṇyarājaṭīkāsaṃyutaṃ dvitīyaṃ kāṇḍam (dvitīyabhāge prathamakhaṇḍaḥ). Śrīmatyā Rāmalālakapūranyāsasamityā prakāśitam. Pariṣkarttā CĀRUDEVAḤ ŚĀSTRĪ pāṇinīyaḥ. [Lahore], vikramābdaḥ 1996 [= 1939/40].

4a. The Vākyapadīya (3rd Kāṇḍa) with the commentary Prakīrṇakaprakāśa of Helārāja son of Bhūṭirāja. Part. I. Edited by K. SĀMBAŚIVA ŚĀSTRĪ, Trivandrum 1935 (Trivandrum Sanskrit Series. No. CXVI. Śrī Citrodayamañjarī. nº V) [III.7.156 - III.13].

4b. Part II. Edited by L. A. RAVI VARMĀ. Trivandrum 1942, (University of Travancore Sanskrit Series No. CXLVIII) [III, 14 complete].

5. The Vākyapadīya – Brahmakāṇḍam of Bhartri-Hari. With The Prakash Commentary of Pt. NARAIN DATT TRIPATHI. ... Edited by Pt. AVADH BIHARI MISHRA. Benares 1937.

6. The Vākyapadīya. A treatise on the philosophy of Sanskrit grammar by Bhartrī Hari [sic]. (Brahma Kāṇḍa). Edited with the Bhāvapradīpa commentary and notes by SŪRYANĀRĀYAṆA ŚŪKLA [sic]. Benares 1937 (Kashi Sanskrit Series 124).

7a. The Vākyapadīya. A treatise on the philosophy of Sanskrit grammar by Bhartṛhari. (Brahma Kāṇḍa). With the Bhāvapradīpa Sanskrit commentary and notes by SŪRYANĀRĀYAṆA ŚUKLA. Edited with Hindi commentary etc. by RĀMAGOVINDA ŚUKLA. Varanasi 1961 (Kashi Sanskrit Series 124).

7b. Vākyapadīyam: Brahmakāṇḍam. Mahāvaiyākaraṇaśrībhartṛhariviracitam. SŪRYANĀRĀYAṆA ŚUKLENA svapraṇītena Bhāvapradīpākhyavyākhyānena ṭippaṇena ca samalaṅkṛtam. RĀMAGOVINDAŚUKLENA hindīvyākhyayā viśiṣṭayā bhūmikayā ca samalaṅkṛtya sampāditam. Pariśiṣṭalekhakaḥ Rudraprasādo vasthī. 5. saṃskaraṇam. Vārāṇasī: Caukhambā Samskṛta Saṃsthāna 1984 (Kāśīsaṃskṛtagranthamālā 124).

8a. Vākyapadīya with the commentary Ambākartrī by RAGHUNĀTHA SHARMA. Part I (Brahma-Kāṇḍa). Varanasi 1963 (Sarasvatī Bhavana Granthamālā vol. 91).

8b. Vākyapadīyam Part II (Vākyakāṇḍam) with the Commentary Ambākartrī by RAGHUNĀTHA SHARMA. Varanasi 1968 (Sarasvatī Bhavan Granthamāla vol. 91).

8c. Vākyapadīyam Part III (Pada Kāṇḍa) (Jāti, Dravya and Sambandha Samuddeśa) with the Commentary Prakāśa by Helārāja and Ambākartrī by Pt. RAGHUNĀTHA SHARMA. Varanasi 1974 (Sarasvatībhavana-Granthamālā Vol. 91).

8d. Vākyapadīyam [Part III, Vol. II] [Bhūyodravya- Guṇa- Dik- Sādhana- Kriyā- Kāla- Puruṣa- Saṃkhyā- Upagraha- and Liṅga- Samuddeśa) with the commentary Prakāśa by Helārāja and Ambākartrī by Pt. RAGHUNĀTHA ŚARMA. Varanasi 1979 (Sarasvatī Bhavana Granthamālā [vol. 91]).

8e. Vākyapadīyam [Part III] (Padakāṇḍa) (Vṛttisamuddeśa) with the commentary Prakāśa by Helārāja and Ambākartrī by Pt. RAGHUNĀTHA SARMA. Varanasi 1977 (Sarasvatī Bhavana Granthamālā Vol. 91).

9a. Vākyapadīya of Bhartṛhari with the commentary of Helārāja. Kāṇḍa III, Part I. Edited by K.A. SUBRAMANIA IYER. Poona 1963 (Deccan College Monograph Series 21). [III.1.1 - III.7 end].

9b. Vākyapadīya of Bhartṛhari with the commentaries Vṛtti and the Paddhati of Vṛṣabhadeva, kāṇḍa I. Critically edited by K.A. SUBRAMANIA IYER. Poona 1966 (Deccan College Monograph Series 32).

9c. Vākyapadīya of Bhartṛhari with the Prakīrṇaprakāśa of Helārāja. Kāṇḍa III, Part II. Critically Edited by K.A. SUBRAMANIA IYER. Poona 1973. [III.8.1 - III.14 end].

10. Bhartṛhari. Vākyapadīya Brahmakāṇḍa. Avec la Vṛtti de Harivṛṣabha. Texte reproduit de l'édition de Lahore. Traduction, introduction et notes par Madeleine BIARDEAU. Paris: de Boccard 1964 (Publications de l'Institut de Civilisation Indienne, Serie in-8°, fascicule 24).

11. Vākyapadīya of Bhartṛhari. Edited by K. V. ABHYANKAR and V. P. LIMAYE. Poona 1965 (University of Poona Sanskrit and Prakrit Series, Volume II).

12. Śrīmadbhartṛhariviracitaṃ svopajñaṭīkāsamanvitaṃ vākyapadīyam (brahmakāṇḍam). Ed. Pandit VĀMANA BĀLAKRISHNA BHAGAVATA. Tilak Maharashtra Vidyapeeth, Poona 1965 (Grantha-Saṃśodhana-Prakāśana-Maṇḍala, Publication nº 2). [Text and Marathi translation].

13. Vākyapadīyam (Brahmakāṇḍa) of Shrī Bhartṛhari, The great linguist & grammarian, with trilingual commentary by Dr. SATYAKAM VARMA. New Delhi: Munshi Ram Manohar Lal 1970. [Sanskrit - English - Hindi].

14. The Vākyapadīya. Critical Text of Cantos I and II [with English Translation, Summary of Ideas and Notes]. By K. RAGHAVAN PILLAI. Delhi: Motilal Banarsidass 1971 (Studies in the Vākyapadīya, vol. I).

15. Vaakyapadiiyamu (VAKYAPADIYAMU): Sanskrit Original: Bhartṛhari; Telugu translation: Sri PERI SURYANARAYANA Sastri, Sriman SRIBHASHYAM APPALACHARYULU, Dr. Pullela SRIRAMACHANDRUDU and Sri Appalla SOMESWARA SARMA; Scrutiniser: Professor G. J. SOMAYAJI. Telugu Akademi, Hyderabad 1974. [lst and 2nd kāṇḍa].

16a. Bhartṛharis Vākyapadīya. Die *mūlakārikās* nach den Handschriften herausgegeben und mit einem Pāda-Index versehen von Wilhelm RAU. Wiesbaden: Franz Steiner 1977 (Abhandlungen für die Kunde des Morgenlandes XLII, 4).

16b. INDEX: Bhartṛharis Vākyapadīya Vollständiger Wortindex zu den *mūlakārikās*, von Wilhelm RAU, Stuttgart: Franz Steiner Verlag 1988 (Akademie der Wissenschaften und der Literatur, Abhandlungen der Geistes- und Sozialwissenschaftlichen Klasse, Jahrgang 1988, nº 11).

17. Yogirājamahāvaiyākaraṇaśrīmadbhatṛhariviracito Vākyapadīyabrahmakāṇḍaḥ parīkṣopayoginyā ṭīkayā saṃvalitaḥ. Ṭīkākāra – YogiŚAṄKARANĀTHAḤ PHALEGRAHIḤ. Avedyanāthena Yatīndravartmanā ''tmanā mudā Vākyapadīyapustakam. Svakīyarikthena vikāśitaṃ mude vicakṣaṇānāṃ padavartmavartinām. Kalpasaṃ° 1972949053, vi° saṃ° 2009 [= 1952]. Sarvādhikārasaṃrakṣikā yogapracāriṇī Gorakṣaṭillā Kāśī, saṃrakṣaka yo° pra° upapradhāna, śrī Avedyanātha Vedāntavāgīśa Tarkacūḍāmaṇi Gorakṣapura.

18. Vākyapadīya of Bhartṛhari (An ancient Treatise on the Philosophy of Sanskrit Grammar). Containing the Ṭīkā of Puṇyarāja and the Ancient Vṛtti. Edited by K. A. SUBRAMANIA IYER. With a Foreword by Ashok AKLUJKAR. Kāṇḍa II. Delhi: Motilal Banarsidass 1983.

19. Vākyapadīyam śrīmanmahāvaiyākaraṇabhartṛhariviracitam. Nṛsiṃhāparanāmadheyena paṇḍitaśrīNĀRĀYAṆADATTATRIPĀṬHINĀ kṛtayā prakāśavyākhyayā sanātham. Saṃpādakaḥ PaṇḍitaśrīRĀMEŚACANDRAPĀṆḌEYAḤ. Dvitīyam saṃskaraṇam. Vārāṇasī: Sudhi Prakāśanam 2041 [=1984]. vol. I: Brahmakāṇḍam. [To be complete in three volumes].

20. Bhartṛhari's Vākyapadīya with Gujarati Translation and Notes by Jayadev Mohanlal SHUKLA. Ahmedabad 1984 (Lalbhai Dalpatbhai Series 98).

21. Vākyapadīyam (Brahmakāṇḍam) of Bhartri Hari with 'Pratibhā' Sanskrit – Hindi commentaries by VAMDEV Acharya. Edited by Satyanarayan KHANDURI Shastri. Varanasi 1987 (Krishnadass Sanskrit Series 97).

22. Vākyapadīya of Śrī Bhartṛhari, along with his own Vṛtti (First: Brahmakāṇḍa). Edited with Hindi Commentary by Dr. Shiv Shankar AVASTHI Shastri, M.A. etc. Varanasi: Chowkhamba Vidyabhawan 1990 (Vidyabhavan Sanskrit Granthamala 168).

23. Bhartṛharis Vākyapadīya II: Text der Palmblatt-Handschrift Trivandrum S. N. 532 (=A), von Wilhelm RAU. Stuttgart: Franz Steiner Verlag 1991 (Akademie der Wissenschaft und der Literatur, Abhandlungen der Geistes- und Sozialwissenschaftlichen Klasse, Jahrgang 1991, nº 7).

24. Vakyapadīyam-Brahmakāṇḍa: Text and English translation, by Korada SUBRAHMANIAM, Delhi: Sri Satguru Publications 1992 (Sri Garib Dass Oriental Series nº 146).

25. Word Index to the Vākyapadīya of Bhartṛhari (together with the complete text of the Vākyapadīya), by Saroja BHATE and Yashodhara KAR. Delhi: Eastern Book Linkers 1992.

Editions of Mahābhāṣyadīpikā

1. Partly edited by Brahmadatta JIJÑĀSU, *Suprabhātam* saṃvat 1991 [=1933]. [Covers only the first Āhnika up to p.11, l.19 in the 'critical edition', ed. Bronkhorst].

2. Partly edited by V. SVAMINATHAN under the title Mahābhāṣya Ṭīkā (Āhnikas 1-4). Varanasi: Banaras Hindu University, 1965 (Hindu Vishvavidyalaya Nepal Rajya Sanskrit Series, vol. 11).

3. Edited by K. V. ABHYANKAR and V. P. LIMAYE. Poona: Bhandarkar Oriental Research Institute, 1970 (Post-Graduate and Research Department Series nº 8).

4. Manuscript reproduced. Poona: Bhandarkar Oriental Institute, 1980.

5. 'Critical edition', with English translation, Bhandarkar Oriental Research Institute, Poona:

   Āhnika I (Fascicule IV), critically edited by Johannes BRONKHORST, Post-Graduate and Research Department Series nº 28, 1987.

   Āhnika II (Fascicule V), critically edited by G. B. PALSULE, Post-Graduate and Research Department Series nº 31, 1988.

   Āhnika III (Fascicule I), critically edited by G. B. PALSULE, Post-Graduate and Research Department Series nº 22, 1985.

Āhnika IV (Fascicule VI), critically edited by G. V. DEVASTHALI and G. B. PALSULE, Post-Graduate and Research Department Series nº 32, 1989.

Āhnika V (Fascicule II), critically edited by V. P. LIMAYE, G. B. PALSULE, and V. B. BHAGAVAT, Post-Graduate and Research Department Series nº 23, 1985.

Āhnika VI, Part I (Fascicule III), critically edited by V. B. BHAGAVAT and Saroja BHATE, Post-Graduate and Research Department Series nº 25, 1986.

Āhnika VI, Part II (Fascicule VII), critically edited by V. B. BHAGAVAT and Saroja BHATE, Post-Graduate and Research Department Series nº 34, 1990.

Āhnika VII (Fascicule VIII), critically edited by G. B. PALSULE and V. B. BHAGAVAT, Post-Graduate and Research Department Series nº 37, 1991.

Studies and translations

AKAMATSU, Akihiko

1992 "The evolution of linguistic theory in classical India", *Jinbun Gakuhō* (Kyōto University) nº 60: 203-227. [In Japanese].

1993 "*Pratibhā* and the meaning of the sentence in Bhartṛhari's Vākyapadīya", *Asiatische Studien / Études Asiatiques* nº 47, Proceedings of the First International Conference on Bhartṛhari, Pune, January 6-8 1992 [= the present volume]: 37-43.

AKLUJKAR, Ashok Narhar

1969 "Two textual studies of Bhartṛhari", *Journal of the American Oriental Society* (New Haven) nº 89: 547-563.

1970a *The philosophy of Bhartṛhari's Trikāṇḍī*, doctoral dissertation, Harvard University, Cambridge Mass. [Unpublished].

1970b "Ancient Indian Semantics", *Annals of the Bhandarkar Oriental Research Institute* (Poona) nº 51: 11-29.

1971a "Nakamura on Bhartṛhari", *Indo-Iranian Journal* (The Hague) nº 13: 161-175.

1971b "Mahābhāṣya-dīpikā or Tripādī?", *Adyar Library Bulletin* (Madras) nº 35: 159-171.

1971c "The number of kārikās in Trikāṇḍī, book I", *Journal of the American Oriental Society* (New Haven) nº 91: 510-513.

1972 "The authorship of the Vākyapadīya-vṛtti", *Wiener Zeitschrift für die Kunde Südasiens* (Wien) nº 16: 181-198.

1974 "The authorship of the Vākya-kāṇḍa-ṭīkā", in *Charudeva Shastri Felicitation Volume*, Delhi, pp. 165-188.

1976 Review of RAU 1971, *Orientalistische Literaturzeitung* (Berlin) nº 71, Jahrgang nº 3: 285-292.

1978a "The concluding verses of Bhartṛhari's Vākya-kāṇḍa", *Annals of the Bhandarkar Oriental Research Institute* (Poona) nº 58/59 (Diamond Jubilee Volume): 9-26.

1978b "The number of kārikā-s in Trikāṇḍī book II", *Adyar Library Bulletin* (Madras) nº 42: 142-163.

1979 "Emendation of some verses in Bhartṛhari's Trikāṇḍī", *Wiener Zeitschrift für die Kunde Südasiens* (Wien) nº 23: 63-74.

1980/81 "Interpreting Vākyapadīya 2.486 historically (part 1)", *Adyar Library Bulletin* (Madras) nº 44/45 (Dr. K. Kunjunni Raja Felicitation Volume): 581-601.

1982 "Interpreting Vākyapadīya 2.486 historically (part 2)", in *Indological and Buddhist Studies* (Volume in Honour of Professor J. W. de Jong on his Sixtieth Birthday), edited by L. A. Herscus et al. Canberra: Faculty of Asian Studies, pp. 1-10.

1983 Foreword to the edition of the Vākyapadīya, kāṇḍa II, by K. A. Subramania Iyer. [See edition nº 18 above].

1989a "Saṃbandha and abhisaṃbandha", *Journal of Indian Philosophy* (Dordrecht) nº 17: 299-309.

1989b "The number of pramāṇas according to Bhartṛhari", *Wiener Zeitschrift für die Kunde Südasiens* (Wien) nº 33: 151-158.

1989c "Prāmāṇya in the philosophy of the grammarians", in *Studies in Indology* (Professor Rasik Vihari Joshi Felicitation Volume), edited by Avanindra Kumar et al., New Delhi: Shree Publishing House, pp. 15-28.

1990 Chapter on Bhartṛhari's Trikāṇḍī or Vākyapadīya, with Vṛtti on books 1 and 2, in COWARD AND RAJA 1990: 122-172; on Harivṛṣabha or Vṛṣabhadeva: 179.

1991a "Bhartṛhari's concept of the Veda", in *Pāṇini and the Veda*, edited by Madhav M. Deshpande (Panels of the VIIth World Sanskrit Conference, vol. V). Leiden: E.J. Brill, pp. 1-18.

1991b "Interpreting Vākyapadīya 2.486 historically (part 3)", *S. D. Joshi Felicitation Volume*, edited by M. Deshpande & S. Bhate, Ann Arbor, pp. 1-47.

1991c "Syntactic gleanings from Bhartṛhari's Trikāṇḍī", in *Studies in Sanskrit Syntax* – A volume in honor of the centennial of Speijer's Sanskrit Syntax (1886-1986), edited by Hans Henrich Hock. Delhi: Motilal Banarsidass, pp. 1-11.

1993a "An introduction to the study of Bhartṛhari", *Asiatische Studien / Études Asiatiques* nº 47, Proceedings of the First International Conference on Bhartṛhari, Pune, January 6-8 1992 [= the present volume]: 7-36.

1993b "Once again on the authorship of the Trikāṇḍī-Vṛtti", *Asiatische Studien / Études Asiatiques* nº 47, Proceedings of the First International Conference on Bhartṛhari, Pune, January 6-8 1992 [= the present volume]: 45-57.

BALADEVA UPĀDHYĀYA

1968 "Vākyapadīyadvitīyakāṇḍagatāmbākartryupodghātaḥ", *Sarasvatībhāvanagranthamālā* 91, dvitīyaḥ bhāgaḥ: ka-ña. [See edition nº 8b above].

BANDINI, Giovanni

1980 *Die Erörterung der Wirksamkeit. Bhartṛharis Kriyāsamuddeśa und Helārājas Prakāśa* zum ersten Male aus dem Sanskrit übersetzt, mit einer Einführung und einem Glossar. Wiesbaden: Franz Steiner (Beiträge zur Südasienforschung. Südasien-Institut Universität Heidelberg, Band 61).

1982 "Die Erörterung der Person. Bhartṛharis *Puruṣasamuddeśa* und Helārājas *Prakāśa* zum ersten Male übersetzt und mit einem Kommentar versehen", *Zeitschrift der Deutschen Morgenländischen Gesellschaft* (Wiesbaden) nº 132: 150-173.

1986 "Bhartṛharis Begriff der Wirksamkeit: Einige Gedanken zum Thema, ausgehend von Vākyapadīya III.8.21", *Sanskrit and World Culture*, Proceedings of the Fourth World Sanskrit Conference, edited by W. Morgenroth. Berlin: Akademie-Verlag, pp. 405-414.

BANDYOPADHYAY, Nandita

1988 *Being, meaning and proposition: a comparative and critical study of Bhartṛhari, Russell, Frege and Strawson*. Calcutta: Sanskrit Pustak Bhandar.

BERGDAHL, Roland R.

1988 *The sādhanasamuddeśa (Ka. 1-44) of Bhartṛhari's Vākyapadīya with the commentary Prakāśa of Helārāja*, doctoral dissertation, University of Pennsylvania, 1987. Ann Arbor: UMI 8804883.

BHĀGAVATA, Śaraṇa Śukla

1989 "Vyākaraṇaśāstre jātisvarūpavimarśaḥ", *Journal of the Gaṅgānātha Jhā Kendrīya Sanskrit Vidyāpeeth* (Allahabad) nº 42: 241-251.

BHĀGAVATA, Pt. Vāman Bālkrishna Śāstrī

1965 *Śrīmadbhartṛhariviracitaṃ svopajñaṭīkāsamanvitaṃ vākyapadīyam (brahmakāṇḍam)*. Tilak Maharashtra Vidyapeeth, Poona (Grantha-Saṃśodhana-Prakāśana-Maṇḍala, Publication nº 2). [Text and Marathi translation].

1980 "Śabdaḥ, śabdārthaḥ, tayoḥ saṃbandhaḥ", *Proceedings of the Winter Institute on Ancient Indian Theories on Sentence-meaning* (Held in March 1979). Edited by S. D. Joshi, Pune: University of Poona, pp. 235-237. [In Sanskrit].

1985 *Pāṇinīya Vyākaraṇ āṇi Bhāṣā-Tattvajñān*, Maharashtra Rajya Sahitya Saṃskriti Mandal, Mantralay. Bombay. [In Marathi].

1993 "Śrīmadbhartṛhariḥ Nāgeśaś ca", *Asiatische Studien / Études Asiatiques* nº 47, Proceedings of the First International Conference on Bhartṛhari, Pune, January 6-8 1992 [= the present volume]: 59-65. [In Sanskrit].

BHAT, M. S.

1973 "Two passages from the Vākyapadīya", *Journal of the University of Bombay* 42, nº 78: 54-58.

BHATE, Saroja

1992 *Word Index to the Vākyapadīya of Bhartṛhari* (together with the complete text of the Vākyapadīya). Delhi: Eastern Book Linkers. [In collaboration with Yashodhara KAR].

1993 "Bhartṛhari on language and reality", *Asiatische Studien / Études Asiatiques* nº 47, Proceedings of the First International Conference on Bhartṛhari, Pune, January 6-8 1992 [= the present volume]: 67-73.

BHAṬṬACHARYA, Bishnupada

1962 *A Study in Language and Meaning*, Calcutta: Progressive Publishers.

1985a *Vākyapadīya (Brahmakāṇḍa)*, Calcutta. [Bengali translation].

1985b *Bhartṛhari's Vākyapadīya and Linguistic Monism*. Professor K. V. Abhyankar Memorial Lectures (Third Series), Poona (BORI Post-Graduate and Research Department Series nº 25).

BHATTACHARYA, Ram Shankar

1954 "A new verse of the Saṃgraha", *The Poona Orientalist* (Poona) nº 19: 4-5. [= Vākyapadīya 2.266 – W.R.].

1958 "Some broad aspects of indian grammar and the theory of sphoṭa", *Journal of the Gangānātha Jhā Research Institute* (Allahabad) nº 15: 83-92.

1966 "Vākyapadīya kā eka sāṃśayika śloka", in *Pāṇinīya vyākaraṇa kā anuśīlana*, Varanasi, pp. 410-412. [In Hindi].

BIARDEAU, Madeleine

1960 Review of RUEGG 1959, *Indo-Iranian Journal* (The Hague) nº 4: 170-172.

1964a *Théorie de la connaissance et philosophie de la parole dans le brahmanisme classique*. Paris - La Haye: Mouton & Co (École Pratique des Hautes Études - Sorbonne. Sixième Section: Sciences Économiques et Sociales. Le Monde d'Outre-Mer. Passé et Présent. Première Série: études XXIII).

1964b *Bhartṛhari Vākyapadīya Brahmakāṇḍa. Avec la Vṛtti de Harivṛṣabha*. Paris: de Boccard (Publications de l'Institut de Civilisation Indienne, fascicule 24).

1964c Review of RAJA 1963, *Indo-Iranian Journal* (The Hague) nº 8: 228-232.

1975 Review of IYER's editions of Vākyapadīya, above nº 9a, 9b, 9c, translations and studies 1965a, 1969, 1971 and 1974a, *Journal Asiatique* (Paris) nº 263: 470-472.

BRONKHORST Johannes

1981 "On some Vedic quotations in Bhartṛhari's works", *Studien zur Indologie und Iranistik* (Reinbeck) nº 7: 173-175.

1982 Review of RAU 1981b, *Kratylos* (Wiesbaden) nº 27: 78-81.

1983 "On the history of Pāṇinian grammar in the early centuries following Patañjali", *Journal of Indian Philosophy* (Dordrecht) nº 11: 357-412.

1985 "The origin of an Indian dietary rule: evidence for a lost Mānava work on Dharma", *Aligarh Journal of Oriental Studies* nº 2 (1-2) (Ram Suresh Tripathi Commemoration Volume): 123-132.

1986 "Tantra and prasaṅga", *Aligarh Journal of Oriental Studies* nº 3: 77-80.

1987a "Further remarks on Bhartṛhari's Vedic affiliation", in *Studies in Indian Culture* (Professor S. Ramachandra Rao Felicitation Volume), Bangalore, pp. 216-223.

1987b "The text history of the Mahābhāṣya", in *Three Problems pertaining to the Mahābhāṣya*, Pandit Shripad Shastri Deodhar Memorial Lectures (Third Series), Poona (BORI Post-Graduate and Research Department Series nº 30).

1988 "Études sur Bhartṛhari, 1: L'auteur et la date de la Vṛtti", *Bulletin d'Études Indiennes* (Paris) nº 6: 105-143.

1989 "Studies on Bhartṛhari, 2: Bhartṛhari and Mīmāṃsā", *Studien zur Indologie und Iranistik* (Reinbeck) nº 15: 101-117.

1990 "Vārttika", *Wiener Zeitschrift für die Kunde Südasiens* (Wien) nº 34, 123-146.

1991a "Studies on Bhartṛhari, 3: Bhartṛhari on spoṭa and universals", *Asiatische Studien / Études Asiatiques* nº 45.1: 5-18.

1991b "Two literary conventions and their consequences", *Asiatische Studien / Études Asiatiques* nº 45.2: 210-227.

1992 "Études sur Bhartṛhari, 4: L'absolu dans le Vākyapadīya et son lien avec le Madhyamaka", *Asiatische Studien / Études Asiatiques* nº 46.1 (Études bouddhiques offertes en hommage à Jacques May): 56-80.

1993 "Studies on Bhartṛhari, 5: Bhartṛhari and Vaiśeṣika", *Asiatische Studien / Études Asiatiques* nº 47, Proceedings of the First International Conference on Bhartṛhari, Pune, January 6-8 1992 [= the present volume]: 75-94.

BROUGH, John

1951 "Theories of general linguistics in the Sanskrit grammarians", *Transactions of the Philological Society* 1951 (Oxford): 27-46. [Reprinted in *A Reader on the Sanskrit Grammarians*, edited by J. F. Staal, Massachussets Institute of Technology 1972. Indian edition: Delhi: Motilal Banarsidass 1985, pp. 402-414].

1952 "Audumbarāyaṇa's theory of language", *Bulletin of the School of Oriental and African Studies* (London) nº 14: 73-77.

1953 "Some Indian Theories of Meaning", *Transactions of the Philological Society* 1953 (Oxford): 164-167. [Reprinted in *A Reader on the Sanskrit Grammarians*, edited by J. F. Staal, Massachussets Institute of Technology 1972. Indian edition: Delhi: Motilal Banarsidass 1985, pp. 414-423].

1973 "I-ching on the Sanskrit grammarians", *Bulletin of the School of Oriental and African Studies* (London) nº 36: 248-260.

BÜHLER, Georg

1882 "Über die Erklärung des Wortes *āgama* im Vākyapadīya II, 1-6 [=2.485-490 – W.R.]", *Zeitschrift der Deutschen Morgenländischen Gesellschaft* (Leipzig) nº 36: 653-654.

CARDONA, George

1968 Review of JOSHI 1967, *Journal of the Oriental Institute* (Baroda) nº 17: 445-450.

1976 *Pāṇini. A survey of research*, The Hague: Mouton & Co. [Indian reprint: Delhi: Motilal Banarsidass 1980].

1978 "Still again on the History of the Mahābhāṣya", *Annals of the Bhandarkar Oriental Research Institute* nº 58-59 (Diamond Jubilee Volume): 79-99.

1980 Review of RAU 1977, *Indo-Iranian Journal* (The Hague) nº 22.1: 53-56.

1991 "A path still taken: some early Indian arguments concerning time", *Journal of the American Oriental Society* (New Haven) nº 111: 445-464.

CARPENTER, David Wesley

1985 "Revelation and experience in Bhartṛhari's Vākyapadīya", *Wiener Zeitschrift für die Kunde Südasiens* (Wien) nº 29, 185-206.

1987 *The Light of the Word. A comparative study of the phenomenon of revelation* (Volume One), doctoral dissertation, University of Chicago. [Unpublished].

CHAKRABARTI, Prabhat Chandra

1931 *The Philosophy of Sanskrit Grammar*, Calcutta.

1933 *Linguistic Speculations of the Hindus*, Calcutta.

CHARUDEVA Shastri

1930 "Bhartṛhari: a critical study with special references to the Vākyapadīya and its commentaries", *Proceedings of the fifth Indian Oriental Conference* (Lahore 1928), Lahore. Vol. 1, pp. 630-655.

1967 Review of *Mahābhāṣya Ṭīkā* [=*Mahābhāṣyadīpikā* edition nº 2 above], *Vishveshwaranand Indological Journal* (Hoshiarpur) nº 5.

CHATURVEDI, Mithilesh

1973 "Notes on a kārika ascribed to Bhartṛhari", *Journal of the Gaṅgānātha Jhā Kendrīya Sanskrit Vidyāpeeth* (Allahabad) nº 29: 203-209.

1974a "Bhartṛhari on the number of words to be compounded simultaneously", *Indological Studies* nº 3, Journal of the Department of Sanskrit, University of Delhi (A. D. Pusalker Commemoration Volume): 31-38.

1974b "Kakaṭaliya – a Grammatical Analysis by Bhartṛhari", *Sri Venkateswara University Oriental Journal* (Tirupati) nº 17: 93-99.

1975 "On Some Formations Involving luk-elision", *Vishveshwaranand Indological Journal* (Hoshiarpur) 13: 42-49. Also *Journal of the Gaṅgānātha Jhā Kendrīya Sanskrit Vidyāpeeth* (Allahabad) nº 33/4: 19-30.

1976a "Yugapadadhikaraṇavacanatā in Dvandva – a critical appraisal by Bhartṛhari", *Vishveshwaranand Indological Journal* (Hoshiarpur) nº 14: 82-92.

1976b "The Negative Compound in Sanskrit – a Semantic Analysis by Bhartṛhari", *Adyar Library Bulletin* (Madras) nº 40: 1-40.

1980-81 "Upamāsamuddeśa – a Part of Vṛttisamuddeśa of Vākyapadīya", *Journal of the Oriental Institute* (Baroda) nº 30: 195-197.

COWARD, Harold (G.)

1976a *Bhartṛhari*, Boston: Twayne Publishers.

1976b "Language as Revelation", *Indian Philosophical Quarterly* (Poona) nº 3: 447-472.

1977 "Bhartṛhari versus Śankara on the overcoming of error", in *Buddhist Thought and Asian Civilisation* (Essays in Honor of Herbert V. Guenther on his Sixtieth Birthday), edited by Leslie S. Kawamura and Keith Scott, Emeryville (California): Dharma Publishing, pp. 1-15.

1980 *Sphoṭa theory of language*, Delhi: Motilal Banarsidass.

1982a "The meaning and power of mantras in Bhartṛhari's Vākyapadīya", SR (*Studies in Religion / Sciences Religieuses*) nº 11: 365-375. [Also published in *Understanding Mantras*, edited by Harvey P. Alper. Albany: State University of New York Press 1989, pp. 165-176].

1982b "Time (Kāla) in Bhartṛhari's Vākyapadīya", *Journal of Indian Philosophy* (Dordrecht) nº 10: 277-288.

1985 "The Yoga of the word (*śabdapūrvayoga*)", *Adyar Library Bulletin* (Madras) nº 49: 1-13.

1990 "Derrida and Bhartṛhari's Vākyapadīya on the origin of language", *Philosophy East and West* (Hawai) nº 40: 3-16. [Reprinted in *Derrida and Indian Philosophy*, New York 1990. Indian edition: Delhi 1991, pp. 27-48].

1991 "'Speech versus writing' in Derrida and Bhartṛhari", *Philosophy East & West* (Hawai) nº 41 (2): 141-162. [Reprinted as "Derrida and Bhartṛhari on speech and writing", *Derrida and Indian Philosophy*, New York 1990. Indian edition: Delhi 1991, pp. 49-79].

COWARD, Harold G., and RAJA, K. Kunjunni (ed.)

1990 Encyclopedia of Indian Philosophies, Vol. V: *The Philosophy of the Grammarians*. Delhi: Motilal Banarsidass. See AKLUJKAR 1990 and RAJA 1990.

DANGE, Sadashiv A.

1980 "Sphoṭa - a reappraisal", *Proceedings of the Winter Institute on Ancient Indian Theories on Sentence-meaning* (Held in March 1979). Edited by S. D. Joshi. Pune: University of Poona, pp. 69-78.

DASH, Narendra Kumar

1988 "Sphoṭatattvasamīkṣā", *Viśva-saṃskṛtam* (Hoshiarpur) nº 25. [In Sanskrit].

DAVIS, Lawrence Ward

1979 *Studies in Bhartṛhari's Vākyapadīya*, doctoral dissertation, Graduate School of the University of Massachusetts. Ann Arbor: UMI 7901990.

DESHPANDE, Madhav M.

1980 *Evolution of syntactic theory in Sanskrit Grammar*: syntax of the Sanskrit infinitive -tumUN, Ann Arbor: Karoma Publishers (Linguistica Extranea Studia 10).

1981 "Sanskrit gerund constructions: syntactic disputations", *Indo-Iranian Journal* (The Hague) nº 23: 167-185.

1986 "Sanskrit grammarians on diglossia", in *South Asian Languages*: Structure, Convergence and Diglossia (MBLD Series in Linguistics, vol. III). Edited by Bh. Krishnamurti. Delhi: Motilal Banarsidass, pp. 312-321.

1991 "Ditransitive passive in Pāṇini", *Indo-Iranian Journal* (The Hague) nº 34: 19-35. [P. 27 on the *Sādhanasamuddeśa*].

1992 "Bhartṛhari", in *Philosophy of Language*, An International Handbook of Contemporary Research, edited by M. Dascal, D. Gerhardus, K. Lorenz & G. Meggle. Berlin - New York: Walter de Gruyter. Vol.1: 269-278.

1993 "The changing notion of *śiṣṭa* from Patañjali to Bhartṛhari", *Asiatische Studien / Études Asiatiques* nº 47, Proceedings of the First International Conference on Bhartṛhari, Pune, January 6-8 1992 [= the present volume]: 95-115.

DRAGONETTI, Carmen

1990 "Some remarks on Bhartṛhari's concept of pratibhā", *Journal of Indian Philosophy* (Dordrecht) nº 18: 95-112. [In collaboration with Fernando TOLA].

DRAVID, Raja Ram

1972 *The problem of universals in Indian Philosophy*, Delhi: Motilal Banarsidass. [Ch. IX: The Grammarian's view of word and meaning: 209-263].

DVIVEDI, Kapila Deva

1956 *Arth-vijñān aur vyākaraṇ-darśan*, Allahbad: Hindusthani Academy. [In Hindi].

DWIVEDI, S. S.

1974 *Bhartṛhari-kṛta Mahābhāṣya-dīpikā*: *eka adhyayana* [A study of Bhartṛhari's Mahābhāṣya-dīpikā], doctoral dissertation, Gujarat University. [In Gujarati, unpublished].

FILLIOZAT, Jean

1954 "À propos de la religion de Bhartṛhari", *Silver Jubilee Volume of the Zinbun-Kagaku-Kenkyusyo*, Kyōto University: 116-120. [English version published in *Religion Philosophy Yoga*, a selection of articles by Jean Filliozat, Maurice Shukla tr. Delhi: Motilal Banarsidass 1991. Chapter 3: "About the religion of Bhartṛhari", pp. 41-46].

FRAUWALLNER, Erich

1959 "Dignāga, sein Werk und seine Entwicklung", *Wiener Zeitschrift für die Kunde Süd- und Ostasiens* (Wien) nº 3: 83-164.

1961 "Landmarks in the history of Indian Logic", *Wiener Zeitschrift für die Kunde Süd- und Ostasiens* (Wien) nº 5: 125-148.

GANGULI, Hemanta Kumar

1963 *Philosophy of logical construction; an examination of logical atomism and logical positivism in the light of the philosophies of Bhartṛhari, Dharmakīrti and Prajñākaragupta*, Calcutta.

1967-69 "Metaphysics of Meaning", *Anviksa* nº 2.1, 1967: 38-48; nº 2.2., 1967: 13-24; nº 3.1, 1968: 61-72; nº 3.2, 1969: 71-84.

GAURINĀTHA Śāstrī

1937 "A Study in the Dialectics of Sphoṭa", *Journal of the Department of Letters* nº 29, University of Calcutta. [See 1980 for the remodelled version].

1939 "The doctrine of Śabdabrahman – a criticism by Jayanta Bhaṭṭa", *Indian Historical Quarterly* (Calcutta) nº 15: 441-453.

1956 "Philosophy of Bhartṛhari", *Journal of the Asiatic Society* (Calcutta) nº 22: 71.

1959a *The Philosophy of Word and Meaning*. Some Indian approaches with special reference to the philosophy of Bhartṛhari. Calcutta (Calcutta Sanskrit College Research Series nº 5, studies nº 2). [Reprint: 1981].

1959b "Absolute consciousness as Bhartṛhari views it", *Summaries of Papers, All India Oriental Conference* 19 (Delhi 1957), Delhi, pp. 144-145.

1968 "Monism of Bhartṛhari", *Wiener Zeitschrift für die Kunde Süd- und Ostasiens* (Wien) nº 12-13 (Festschrift Frauwallner): 319-322.

1980 *A Study in the Dialectics of Sphoṭa*, Delhi: Motilal Banarsidass.

1991 *The philosophy of Bhartṛhari*, Delhi – Varanasi: Bharatiya Vidya Prakashan.

GILLON, Brendan

1993 "Bhartṛhari's solution to the problem of *asamartha* compounds", *Asiatische Studien / Études Asiatiques* nº 47, Proceedings of the First International Conference on Bhartṛhari, Pune, January 6-8 1992 [= the present volume]: 117-133.

GOGOI-CHUTIA, Laksahira

1988 "A note on the concept of Lakṣanā in the Vyākaraṇa Literature", *Gauhati University Journal of Arts* 34: 203-210.

GONDA, Jan

1963 *The Vision of the Vedic Poets*, The Hague: Mouton & Co. [Chapter XV: "Pratibhā", pp. 318-348].

1966 Review of BIARDEAU 1964a, *Linguistics* (The Hague) nº 27: 112-120.

GRAY, J. E. B.

1968 Review of BIARDEAU 1964a and IYER 1965a, *Foundations of Language* (Dordrecht), vol. 4: 70-75.

HALBFASS, Wilhelm

1991 *Tradition and Reflection*. Exploration in Indian Thought. Albany: State University of New York Press 1989.

1992 *On Being and what there is*. Classical Vaiśeṣika and the History of Indian Ontology. Albany: State University of New York Press 1989.

HARADA, Wasō

1987 "Intuition and self cognition as the denotation of a word (I): Dignāga vs. Bhartṛhari (1)", *Bukkyō Gakkaihō* (Kōyasan) nº 13: 22-39. [In Japanese].

1988 "The theories of *abhidhāna*, *ākṣepa*, and *ākāṅkṣā* (I) - Dignāga vs Bhartṛhari (2)", *The Mikkyō Bunka* (Kōyasan) nº 165: 84-57. [In Japanese].

1989a "Intuition and self cognition as the denotation of a word (II): Dignāga vs. Bhartṛhari (1)", *Bukkyō Gakkaihō* (Kōyasan) nº 14: 69-83. [In Japanese].

1989b "The development of *arthakriyā* from Bhartṛhari to Dignāga", *Journal of Indian and Buddhist Studies* (*Indogaku Bukkyōgaku Kenkyū*) (Tōkyō) nº 39-1. 423-420. [In Japanese].

1989c "The theories of *abhidhāna*, *ākṣepa*, and *ākāṅkṣā* (II) - Dignāga vs Bhartṛhari (2)", *The Mikkyō Bunka* (Kōyasan) nº 167: 88-73. [In Japanese].

1989d "The theories of *abhidhāna*, *ākṣepa*, and *ākāṅkṣā* (III) - Dignāga vs Bhartṛhari (2)", *The Mikkyō Bunka* (Kōyasan) nº 168: 78-43. [In Japanese].

1990 "Intuition and self cognition as the denotation of a word (III): Dignāga vs. Bhartṛhari (1)", *Bukkyō Gakkaihō* (Kōyasan) nº 15: 27-53. [In Japanese].

1991 "Intuition and self cognition as the denotation of a word (IV): Dignāga vs. Bhartṛhari (1)", *Bukkyō Gakkaihō* (Kōyasan) nº 16: 29-53. [In Japanese].

HATTORI Masaaki

1977 "The Sautrāntika Background of the *Apoha* theory", in *Buddhist Thought and Asian civilization*, (Essays in Honor of Herbert V. Guenther on his Sixtieth Birthday), edited by Leslie S. Kawamura and Keith Scott, Emeryville (California): Dharma Publishing, pp. 47-58.

1980 "Apoha and pratibhā", *Sanskrit and Indian Studies* (Essays in Honour of Daniel H. H. Ingalls), edited by M. Nagatomi et al. (Studies of Classical India vol.2), Dordrecht: D. Reidel, pp. 61-73.

1987 "Indo Gengotetsugaku ni okeru Ningenkan" ("The concept of Man in the linguistic Philosophy of Classical India"), *Tōyō ni okeru Ningenkan*, edited by S. Mayeda. Tōkyō: The University of Tōkyō Press, pp. 181-200.

1993 "Kamalaśīla's interpretation of some verses in the Vākyakāṇḍa of Bhartṛhari's Vākyapadīya", *Asiatische Studien / Études Asiatiques* nº 47, Proceedings of the First International Conference on Bhartṛhari, Pune, January 6-8 1992 [= the present volume]: 135-140.

HERZBERGER, Hans G.

1981 "Bhartṛhari's paradox", in *Studies in Indian Philosophy* (A memorial volume in Honour of Pandit Sukhlalji Sanghvi), edited by N. J. Shah and D. Malvania (L.D. Series 84), Ahmedabad, pp. 279-299. [In collaboration with Radhika HERZBERGER. Also published in *Journal of Indian Philosophy* (Dordrecht) nº 9: 1-17].

HERZBERGER, Radhika

1981 See HERZBERGER, Hans G. 1981.

1986 *Bhartṛhari and the Buddhists.* An essay in the development of 5th and 6th century Indian thought (Toronto Univ. Diss.). Dordrecht: Reidel (Studies of Classical India, vol. 8).

HONDA, Yoshichika

1993 "Bhartṛhari's definition of *kriyā*", *Asiatische Studien / Études Asiatiques* nº 47, Proceedings of the First International Conference on Bhartṛhari, Pune, January 6-8 1992 [= the present volume]: 141-154.

HOUBEN, Jan E. M.

1990 "The sequencelessness of the signifier in Bhartṛhari's theory of language", *Indologica Taurinensia* nº 15-16: 119-129.

1992a "Bhartṛhari's *samaya* / Helārāja's *saṃketa*: a contribution to the reconstruction of the grammarians' discussion with the Vaiśeṣikas on the relation between 'śabda' and 'artha'", *Journal of Indian Philosophy* (Dordrecht) nº 20.

1992b *The saṃbandha-samuddeśa and Bhartṛhari's philosophy of language*. A study of Bhartṛhari's Saṃbandha-samuddeśa in the context of the Vākyapadīya, with a translation of Helārāja's Commentary Prakīrṇaprakāśa on the Saṃbandha-samuddeśa. Doctoral dissertation, University of Utrecht (3 volumes). [Unpublished].

1993 "Who are Bhartṛhari's *padadarśins*? On the development of Bhartṛhari's philosophy of language", *Asiatische Studien / Études Asiatiques* nº 47, Proceedings of the First International Conference on Bhartṛhari, Pune, January 6-8 1992 [= the present volume]: 155-169.

forthc. "Bhartṛhari en de structuur van het Sanskrit: 'God's truth' of 'hocus-pocus'?", *Handelingen van het 41e Filologencongres* (15 december 1990). [In Dutch].

IHARA, Shōren

1975 "Bhartṛhari and Pāṇini 3.2.123", *Tetsugaku Nempō* (Fukuoka): 358-344. [In Japanese].

1976 "A controversy over the theory of the present tense according to the Vākyapadīya", in *Okuda Jiō sensei kinen Bukkyō shisō ronshū*. Kyōto: Heirakuji shōten. [In Japanese].

1988 "The idea of time according to Bhartṛhari - a study of Kālasamuddeśa of Vākyapadīya", *Journal of Naritasan Institute for Buddhist Studies* nº 12: 1-12. [In Japanese].

IWASAKI, Yoshiyuki

1992 "*Sādhya* and *sādhana* in the Vākyapadīya", *Journal of Indian and Buddhist Studies* (*Indogaku Bukkyōgaku Kenkyū*) (Tōkyō) nº 40-2: 992-990. [In Japanese].

IYENGAR Rangaswami, H. R.

1951 "Bhartṛhari and Diṅnāga", *Journal of the Bombay Branch of the Royal Asiatic Society* nº 26: 147-149.

IYER, K. A. Subramania

1937 "Who are the anityasphoṭavādins?", *Proceedings of the All-India Oriental Conference* 8 (Mysore 1935), Bangalore, pp. 258-263.

1941 "Pratibhā as the meaning of a sentence", *Proceedings of the All-India Oriental Conference* 10 (Tirupati 1940), Madras, pp. 326-332.

1947 "The doctrine of Sphoṭa", *Journal of the Gangānātha Jhā Research Institute* nº 5 : 121-147.

1948 "The point of view of the vaiyākaraṇas", *Journal of Oriental Research* (Madras) nº 18: 84-96. [Reprinted in *A Reader on the Sanskrit Grammarians*, edited by J. F. Staal, Massachussets Institute of Technology 1972. Indian edition: Delhi: Motilal Banarsidass 1985, pp. 393-400].

1954 "The concept of Upagraha among the Vaiyākaraṇas", *Journal of Oriental Research* (Madras) nº 23: 79-88. [Summary in *Summary of Papers, All-India Oriental Conference* 17 (Ahmedabad 1953), p.240].

1963 "Vākyapadīyaprathamakāṇḍagatāmbākartryupodghātaḥ", *Sarasvatībhāvana-granthamālā* 91, prathamaḥ bhāgaḥ: a-ṭa (3rd ed.1988: 2.1-11). [See editions of Vākyapadīya above, nº 8a]. [In Sanskrit].

1964a "Bhartṛhari on *vyākaraṇa* as a means of attaining mokṣa", *Adyar Library Bulletin* (Madras) nº 28: 112-31. [Reprinted in: *Proceedings of the twenty-sixth International Congress of Orientalists*, New Delhi, January 4-10, 1964. Vol. III, part I, Poona 1969, pp. 238-245. Summary in *Summaries of papers, 26th International Congress of Orientalists*, New Delhi, p. 129].

1964b "Bhartṛhari on *apabhraṃśa*", *Vishveshwaranand Indological Journal* (Hoshiarpur) nº 2: 242-246.

1964c "Citranibandhanāvalyupodghātaḥ", [see RAGHUNĀTHA ŚARMA 1964].

1965a *The Vākyapadīya of Bhartṛhari with the Vṛtti.* Chapter I, English translation, Poona (Deccan College Building Centenary & Silver Jubilee Series 26).

1965b "Bhartṛhari on *dhvani*", *Annals of the Bhandarkar Oriental Research Institute* (Poona) nº 46: 49-65.

1967 "Bhartṛharer abhipretaḥ śabdārthasaṃbandhaḥ", *Viśva-saṃskṛtam* (Hoshiarpur) nº 4: 207-219. [In Sanskrit].

1968 "Bhartṛhari on the primary and secondary meanings of words", *Indian Linguistics* (Poona) nº 29: 97-112.

1969 *Bhartṛhari. A study of the Vākyapadīya in the light of the Ancient Commentaries*, Poona (Deccan College Building Centenary and Silver Jubilee Series: 68).

1970a "Bhartṛhari and Bhoja", *Bhoja Seminar*, Vikram University, Ujjain.

1970b "Tatrabhavadbhartṛharyabhipretaṃ sādhanarūpam", *Ṛtam* (Akhila Bhāratīya Saṃskṛta Pariṣad, Lucknow), vol. I-II: 1-8. [In Sanskrit].

1971 *The Vākyapadīya of Bhartṛhari,* Chapter III, pt. I. English translation, Poona (Deccan College Building Centenary and Silver Jubilee Series 71).

1974a *The Vākyapadīya of Bhartṛhari*, Chapter III, pt. II. English Translation with Exegetical Notes, Delhi: Motilal Banarsidass.

1974b "Bhartṛhari on *taddhita* formations involving comparison", *Charudeva Shastri Felicitation Volume*, Delhi, pp. 241-257.

1974c "Vākyapadīyatṛtīyakāṇḍagatāmbākartryupodghātaḥ", *Sarasvatībhāvanagranthamālā* 91, tṛtīyo bhāgaḥ, ka-ca [see editions of Vākyapadīya above, nº 8c]. [In Sanskrit].

1975 "Some lost works on Vyākaraṇa", *Sanskrit and Indological Studies* (Dr. V. Raghavan Felicitation Volume), Delhi, pp. 137-144.

1977 *The Vākyapadīya of Bhartṛhari. Kāṇḍa II.* English translation with exegetical notes, Delhi: Motilal Banarsidass.

1980 "Bhartṛhari on grammatical analysis (*apoddhāra*)", *Vishveshwaranand Indological Journal* (Hoshiarpur) nº 18 = *Bhāratī-Bhānam* (Light of Indology) being Dr. K. V. Sarma Felicitation Volume = *Panjab University Indological Series* nº 26: 69-79.

1980/1 "Bhartṛhari on the sentence", *Adyar Library Bulletin* (Madras) nº 44/45: 15-49.

1982 *The Vākyapadīya: some problems*, Professor K. V. Abhyankar Memorial Lectures (First Series), Poona (BORI Post-Graduate and Research Department Series nº 14).

JAMBUVIJAYA Muni

1949 "On the date of Bhartṛhari, the author of the Vākyapadīya", *Summaries of Papers, All India Oriental Conference* 14 (Darbhanga 1948), Allahabad, pp. 50-51.

1951a "Ācārya bhagavān Mallavādikṣamāśramaṇa ane Bhartṛharino samaya", *Śrī Jaina Satya Prakāśa* (Ahmadabad), varṣa 17, nº 2: 26-30. [In Gujarati].

1951b "Jainācārya Śrīmallavādī ane Bhartṛharino samaya". *Buddhiprakāśa* (Ahmadabad), *Pustaka* 98, nº 11: 332-335. [In Gujarati].

1952 "Bhartṛhari ane Diṅnāga", *Jaina Ātmānanda Prakāśa* (Bhavnagar) nº 50, nº 2: 22-27. [In Gujarati].

1954 "Bhartṛhari aur Diṅnāga kā samaya", *Nāgarī Pracāriṇī Patrikā*, Nāgarī Pracāriṇī Sabhā (Varanasi) nº 60 3/4: 227-233. [In Hindi].

JOSHI, S. D.

1965 Review of *Mahābhāṣya Ṭīkā* [=*Mahābhāṣyadīpikā* edition nº 2 above], *Annals of the Bhandarkar Oriental Research Institute* nº 46: 178-180.

1967 *The Sphoṭanirṇaya of Kauṇḍa Bhaṭṭa*, Centre of advanced Study in Sanskrit, University of Poona, Class C nº 2. [Introduction: 1-91].

1976 "Sanskrit Grammar", in *Ramakrishna Gopal Bhandarkar as an Indologist*, edited by R. N. Dandekar, Poona, pp. 113-142.

1977 "Bhartṛhari's Concept of *pratibhā*: A Theory on the Nature of Language Acquisition", in *Some aspects of Indo-Iranian Cultural Traditions* (Commemoration Volume of Dr. V. G. Paranjpe), Delhi, pp. 71-76.

KAHRS, Eivind G.

1992a "What is a *tadbhava* word?" *Indo-Iranian Journal* (The Hague) nº 35: 225-249.

1992b "Exploring the *Saddanīti*", *Journal of the Pali Text Society* nº 17: 1-212. [Ch.2-2.5 refer to the *Sādhanasamuddeśa*].

KAPILA DEVA Śāstrī

1964a "Bhartṛhari kī dṛṣṭi meṃ aṣṭādhyāyī kā prakāra śabda", *Nāgarī Pracāriṇī Patrikā*, Nāgarī Pracāriṇī Sabhā (Varanasi) nº 69: 302-315. [In Hindi].

1964b "Bhartṛhari's discussion on *sāmānādhikaraṇya*", *Adyar Library Bulletin* (Madras) nº 28: 41-54.

1964c "Bhartṛhari's discussion on the relation between *upamāna* and *upameya* in his Vākyapadīya", *Indian Linguistics* (Poona) nº 25 (Baburam Saksena Felicitation Volume): 229-233.

1964d "Bhartṛhari on the relation between *upamāna* and *upameya*", *Vishveshwaranand Indological Journal* (Hoshiarpur) nº 2, pt. i: 87-92.

1965 "*Upamāna, upameya* and *sāmānyavacana* according to the Vākyapadīya of Bhartṛhari", *Vishveshwaranand Indological Journal* (Hoshiarpur) nº 3: 19-28.

1966a "Catvāri vāk parimitā padāni ity atra Bhartṛhariḥ", *Viśva-saṃskṛtam* (Hoshiarpur) nº 3: 144-153. [In Sanskrit].

1966b "Bhartṛhari on *samānādhikaraṇa taddhitavṛtti*", *Summaries of Papers, All India Oriental Conference* 23 (Aligarh 1966), pp. 62-65.

1968 "Vaiyākaraṇānāṃ sphoṭavādaḥ", *Viśva-saṃskṛtam* (Hoshiarpur) nº 4: 40-51. [In Sanskrit].

KAR, Yashodhara

1992 *Word Index to the Vākyapadīya of Bhartṛhari* (together with the complete text of the Vākyapadīya). Delhi: Eastern Book Linkers. [In collaboration with Saroja BHATE].

KAVIRAJ, Gopinath

1924 "The doctrine of *pratibhā* in Indian Philosophy", *Annals of the Bhandarkar Oriental Research Institute* nº 5: 1-18 & 113-132. [§3: "Vyākaraṇa", pp. 11-18].

KELLY, John

1993 "Meaning and the limits of analysis: Bhartṛhari and the Buddhists, and post-structuralism", *Asiatische Studien / Études Asiatiques* nº 47, Proceedings of the First International Conference on Bhartṛhari, Pune, January 6-8 1992 [= the present volume]: 171-194.

KENGHE, C. T.

1961 "Bhartṛhari's commentary on the Vākyapadīya-kārikās: its nature and extent", *Summaries of Papers, All India Oriental Conference* 21 (Srinagar 1961), Srinagar, pp. 47-48.

KHARWANDIKAR, D. K.

1973 "Mnemonic verses in the Padamañjarī of Haradatta Miśra", *Journal of the Gangānātha Jhā Kendrīya Sanskrit Vidyāpeeth* (Allahabad) nº 29: 285-294. [Eighty-one from the Vākyapadīya – W.R.].

KIELHORN, Lorenz Franz

1874 "The concluding verses of the second or Vākya-Kāṇḍa of Bhartṛhari's Vākyapadīya", *Indian Antiquary* (Bombay) nº 3: 285-287. [Also in: Franz KIELHORN, *Kleine Schriften*. Mit einer Auswahl der epigraphischen Aufsätze herausgegeben von Wilhelm RAU, Wiesbaden 1969: 154-156].

1875 "Note on Rājataraṅgiṇī I.176", *Indian Antiquary* (Bombay) nº 4: 107-108. [Also in *Kleine Schriften*: 156-157].

1883a "On the grammarian Bhartṛhari", *Indian Antiquary* (Bombay) nº 12: 226-227. [Also in *Kleine Schriften*: 185-186].

1883b Preface to the first edition, vol. II, of *The Vyākaraṇa-Mahābhāṣya of Patañjali*, published in the 3rd edition, vol. III, by K. V. Abhyankar, Bhandarkar Oriental Research Institute, Poona 1972, pp. 11-29.

KIYOSHIMA, Hideki

1984 *Indian Philosophy of Language, with reference to the Vākyapadīya* (chapter II), doctoral dissertation, University of Delhi.

KRISHNAMOORTHY, K.

1983 "Bhartṛhari's idea of grammar", *Journal of the Oriental Institute* (Baroda) nº 33: 11-16.

KUANPOONPOL, Priyawat

1991 *Pratibhā: the concept of intuition in the philosophy of Abhinavagupta*, doctoral dissertation, Harvard University. [Available on microfilm].

KUNHAN RAJA, C.

1936 "I-tsing and Bhartṛhari's Vākyapadīya", in *S. Krishnaswami Aiyangar Commemoration Volume*, Madras, pp. 285-298.

KUNJUNNI RAJA K. *see* RAJA, K. Kunjunni

LADDU, S. D.

1981 "A reconsideration of the history of the Mahābhāṣya", *C.A.S.S. Studies* nº 6, Poona, pp. 187-198.

1982 "Ancient Sanskrit grammarians and the literary records", *Vishveshwaranand Indological Journal* (Hoshiarpur) nº 9: 315-322.

LA TERZA, Ermenegildo

1899 "Su Bhartṛhari", *Proceedings of the International Congress of Orientalists* 12, Rome, Vol. 1, Section Inde et Iran, pp. 201-206. [In Italian].

LIMAYE, V. P.

1966 "Dhyānagraha-kāra or Dhyāna-kāra: A pre-Bhartṛhari grammarian", *Vishveshwaranand Indological Journal* (Hoshiarpur) nº 4: 228-229.

1984 "Nāgayajñopavītin", in *Amṛtadhārā* (R. N. Dandekar Felicitation Volume), Delhi: Ajanta Publications, pp. 509-511.

LINDTNER, Christian

1993 "Linking up Bhartṛhari and the Bauddhas", *Asiatische Studien / Études Asiatiques* nº 47, Proceedings of the First International Conference on Bhartṛhari, Pune, January 6-8 1992 [= the present volume]: 195-213.

MADHAVA KRISHNA SARMA, K., *see* SARMA, K. Madhava Krishna

MATILAL, Bimal Krishna

1985 *Logic, Language and Reality*, an introduction to Indian Philosophical Studies. Delhi: Motilal Banarsidass.

1990a *The Word and the World*, India's contribution to the study of language. Delhi: Oxford University Press.

1990b "On Bhartṛhari's Linguistic Insight", in *Sanskrit and Related Studies, Contemporary Researches and Reflections*, Delhi: Sri Satguru Publications, pp. 3-13 (Sri Garib Dass Oriental Series nº 84).

1992 "The Sphoṭa doctrine of the Indian Grammarians", in *Philosophy of Language*, An International Handbook of Contemporary Research, edited by M. Dascal, D. Gerhardus, K. Lorenz & G. Meggle. Berlin - New York: Walter de Gruyter. Vol.1: 609-620.

MAZUMDAR, Pradip Kumar

1977 *The philosophy of language*, Calcutta: Sanskrit Pustak Bhandar.

MĪMĀṂSAKA, Yudhiṣṭhira

1973 *Saṃskṛta Vyākaraṇa-śāstra kā itihāsa* (*tīn bhāgoṃ meṃ pūrṇa*), [History of Sanskrit Grammar] Sonipat: Rāma Lāl Kapūr Trust [vol. 1: 3rd edition, vol. 2: 2nd edition, vol. 3: 1st edition. Previous editions: Ajmer: Bhāratīya-Prācyavidyā-Pratiṣṭhāna, i.e. Vol. 1. 1st ed.: 1950, 2nd ed. 1963. Vol.2. 1st ed. 1966]. [In Hindi].

MISHRA, K. K.

1986 "Bhartṛhari's theory of sphoṭa", *Indologica Taurinensia* nº 13 (1985-86): 115-121.

MIŚRA, Ājāda

1986 "Vaiyākaraṇānāṃ sattādvaitavādaḥ", *Journal of the Gangānātha Jhā Kendrīya Sanskrit Vidyāpeeth* (Allahabad) nº 42: 269-276. [In Sanskrit].

MURTI, M. S. Narayana

1972 "Bhartṛhari on '*viśeṣaṇānāṃ cājāteḥ*' of Pāṇini", *Sri Venkateswara University Oriental Journal* (Tirupati) nº 15: 49-62.

1973 "Philosophy of grammar", *Sri Venkateswara University Oriental Journal* (Tirupati) nº 16: 37-54.

1980/1 "Bhartṛhari on *svaṃ rūpaṃ śabdasyāśabdasaṃjñā*", *Adyar Library Bulletin* (Madras) nº 44/45: 602-613.

1981 "Time According to Bhartṛhari", *Vishveshwaranand Indological Journal* (Hoshiarpur) nº 19: 140-146.

1983 "The import of the negative sentence according to Bhartṛhari", *Journal of the Gangānātha Jhā Kendrīya Sanskrit Vidyāpeeth* (Allahabad) nº 37 [1981] (Baladeva Upādhyāya Felicitation Volume): 217-226.

MURTI, P. Srirama

1992 "Pratibhā, sphoṭa and dhvani", in *Language and Text* (Studies in Honour of Ashok R. Kelkar), Delhi: Kalinga Publications, pp. 51-56.

MURTI, T. R. V.

1963 "The philosophy of language in the Indian context", *Proceedings of the 37th Session, Indian Philosophical Congress* [Reprinted in *Studies in Indian Thought*: The Collected Papers of Professor T. R. V. Murti, Delhi 1983, pp. 357-376].

1974 "Some comments on the philosophy of language in the Indian context", *Journal of Indian Philosophy* (Dordrecht) nº 2: 321-331.

NAGAR, R. S.

1974 "Indebtedness of Ānandavardhana to Bhartṛhari", *Indological Studies* (Delhi) nº 2: 78-85.

NAKADA, Jikidō

1976 "Mahābhāṣyadīpikā wayaku" (A japanese translation of the Mahābhāṣyadīpikā, Abhyankar & Limaye p.2, l.1 - p.4, l.25) in *Okuda Jiō sensei kinen Bukkyō shisō ronshū*. Kyōto: Heirakuji shōten, 1195-1203.

NAKAMURA, Hajime

1955 "Tibetan citations of Bhartṛhari's verses and the problem of his date", in *Studies in Indology and Buddhology* presented in Honour of Professor Susumu Yamaguchi on the Occasion of his Sixtieth Birthday, Kyōto, pp. 122-136.

1956 *Kotoba no keijijōgaku* ("*Metaphysics of language*"), Tōkyō: Iwanami Shōten [Reprint: 1981]. [In Japanese].

1960 "Bhartṛhari the scholar", *Indo-Iranian Journal* (The Hague) nº 4: 282-305.

1972 "Bhartṛhari and Buddhism", *Journal of the Gaṅgānātha Jhā Kendrīya Sanskrit Vidyāpeeth* nº 27/28: 395-405.

1973 "Buddhist influence upon the Vākyapadīya", *Journal of the Gaṅgānātha Jhā Kendrīya Sanskrit Vidyāpeeth* nº 29: 367-387.

1981 "The concept of brahman in Bhartṛhari's philosophy", *Journal of Oriental Research* (Madras) nº 40/41 [1970/72] (Kuppuswami Sastri Research Institute Silver Jubilee Volume): 135-150.

1983 *A History of Early Vedānta Philosophy*, Delhi: Motilal Banarsidass.

NARAYANA MURTI, M. S., *see* MURTI, M. S. Narayana

OETKE, Claus

1986 Review of BANDINI 1980, *Zeitschrift der Deutschen Morgenländischen Gesellschaft* (Wiesbaden) nº 136: 150-165.

PALSULE, G. B.

1980 "Bhartṛhari's concept of *vākya* and *vākyārtha*", *Proceedings of the Winter Institute on Ancient Indian Theories on Sentence-meaning* (Held in March 1979). Edited by S. D. Joshi, Pune: University of Poona, pp. 1-8.

1993 "Points of agreement and difference between the Vākyapadīya and the Mahābhāṣya-Dīpikā in the matter of sphoṭa", *Asiatische Studien / Études Asiatiques* nº 47, Proceedings of the First International Conference on Bhartṛhari, Pune, January 6-8 1992 [= the present volume]: 215-220.

PANDA, Ramesh Chandra

1983 *The Mahābhāṣya-dīpikā: a critical study*, doctoral dissertation, University of Poona. [Unpublished].

PĀṆḌEYA Narendranātha

1992 *Vākyapadīyapāṭhabhedanirṇaya*, Part II. Sarasvatī Bhavana Granthamālā (Sampurnananda Sanskrit University) nº 116, Varanasi. [In collaboration with RAGHUNĀTHA ŚARMA].

PANDEYA, Ramajna

1954 *An Introduction to the Philosophy of Sanskrit Grammar*. Allahabad - Government Sanskrit Library Banaras (The Princess of Wales Sarasvati Bhavana Studies, vol. XI). [In Sanskrit].

PANDEYA, Rama Chandra

1963 *The Problem of Meaning in Indian Philosophy*. Delhi: Motilal Banarsidass.

PATHAK, Kashinath Bapuji

1890-4a "Bhartṛhari and Kumārila", *Journal of the Bombay Branch of the Royal Asiatic Society* nº 18: 213-238.

1890-4b "Was Bhartṛhari a Buddhist?", *Journal of the Bombay Branch of the Royal Asiatic Society* nº 18: 341-349.

PATNAIK, Tandra

1988 "Language, thought and communication: an appraisal of Bhartṛhari's theory of language", *Indian Philosophical Quarterly* (Poona) nº 15 (3): 349-368.

1989 "Some reflections on Bhartṛhari's notion of sentence meaning", *Visva Bharati Journal of Philosophy* nº 24.2 (Feb.1988) & 25.1 (August 1988): 118-129.

1991 "A note on Bhartṛhari's theory of Sphoṭa", *Prajñā* (Research Bulletin of the Department of Philosophy, Uktal University) (Bhubaneswar) nº 11: 59-65.

PERI, Sarveswara Sharma

1972 *The Kālasamuddeśa of Bhartṛhari's Vākyapadīya*, together with Helārāja's commentary translated from the Sanskrit for the first time, Delhi: Motilal Banarsidass.

1974 "What is the *atyadbhutā vṛtti* (miraculous course of action) in the Vākyapadīya?", *Vishveshwaranand Indological Journal* (Hoshiarpur) nº 12: 351-360.

1977 "Vyākaraṇasya darśanatvam", *Veda Pariṣad* (Guntur, Andhra Pradesh): 11-14 [In Sanskrit; 6 pages – pagination unusual].

1979 "Kâiyaṭa and his work", *Bhāratīya Vidyā* 39: 5-13.

1981a "The idea of power (*śakti*) in the Vākyapadīya", *Bhāratīya Vidyā* nº 41: 75-79.

1981b *see* RAU 1981b.

1983 "Puṇyarāja's ṭīkā on the Vākya-kāṇḍa of the Vākyapadīya of Bhartṛhari", *Bhāratīya Vidyā* nº 42: 1-21.

1985/7 "Some problems raised with regard to the concluding verses of the Vākya-kāṇḍa of Bhartṛhari's Vākyapadīya", *Bhāratīya Vidyā* nº 45/47: 1-12.

1987a "What is *apoddhāra* in Bhartṛhari's Vākyapadīya?", *Aligarh Journal of Oriental Studies* nº 4: 105-118.

1987b "Eight topics which form the subject-matter of the Vākyapadīya", *Studien zur Indologie und Iranistik* (Reinbeck) nº 13/14: 219-233.

PERI, Sūryanārāyaṇa Śāstrī *et al.*

1974 Telugu translation of the Vākyapadīya (lst and 2nd kāṇḍa). [See edition nº 15 above].

PILLAI, K. Raghavan

1971 *The Vākyapadīya*. Critical Text of Cantos I and II [with English Translation, Summary of Ideas and Notes], Delhi: Motilal Banarsidass (Studies in the Vākyapadīya, vol. I).

PILLAI, N. Gopala

1942 "The conception of time according to Bhartṛhari", *Shri Citra – The Sanskrit College Magazine* (Trivandrum) nº 2/2: 1-6.

RADICCHI, Anna

1993 "*Vivakṣā* in the Vakyapadīya", *Asiatische Studien / Études Asiatiques* nº 47, Proceedings of the First International Conference on Bhartṛhari, Pune, January 6-8 1992 [= the present volume]: 221-233.

RAGHAVAN, V.

1975 "The dates of Helārāja and Kaiyaṭa", *Ṛtam* (Akhila Bharatiya Parishad, Lucknow), vol. II-VI: 105-109.

RAGHUNĀTHA ŚARMA

1964 *Citranibandhâvaliḥ* (*Vividhāśāstrīyanibandhanānāṃ saṃgrahaḥ*), Delhi: Motilal Banarsidass. [In Sanskrit. For the original journal issues, see CARDONA 1976: 97-98].

1980 *Vākyapadīyapāṭhabhedanirṇaya*, Part I. Sarasvatī Bhavana Granthamālā (Sampurnananda Sanskrit University) nº 116, Varanasi. [lst and 2nd kāṇḍa].

1992 *Vākyapadīyapāṭhabhedanirṇaya*, Part II. Sarasvatī Bhavana Granthamālā (Sampurnananda Sanskrit University) nº 116, Varanasi. [In collaboration with PĀṆḌEYA Narendranātha].

RAJA, K. Kunjunni

1957 "Yāska's definition of the 'verb' and the 'noun' in the light of Bhartṛhari's explanation", *Annals of Oriental Research* (Madras) nº 13: 86-88.

1961 "Bhartṛhari's list of sentence-definitions: the textual problem", *Summaries of Papers, All India Oriental Conference* 21 (Srinagar 1961), Srinagar, pp. 197-198.

1962 "Bhartṛhari's list of sentence-definitions", *Adyar Library Bulletin* (Madras) nº 26: 206-210.

1963 *Indian theories of meaning*, ^{2}Madras 1969 (The Adyar Library Series, vol. 91). [First edition: Madras 1963].

1983 "Bhartṛharir Diṅnāgaś ca", *Surabhi* (Sreekrishna Sarma Felicitation Volume), Tirupati. Sanskrit Section: 35-40. [In Sanskrit].

1990 Chapter on Bhartṛhari's Ṭīkā on Patañjali's Mahābhāṣya, in COWARD AND RAJA, 1990: 172-174.

RAMAKRISHNA KAVI, M.

1930 "The discovery of the author's vṛtti on the Vākyapadīya", *Journal of the Andhra Historical Research Society* (Rajamundry) nº 4: 235-241.

RAMASWAMI Śāstrī, V. A.

1936/7 "Bhartṛhari a Bauddha?", *Annamalai University Journal* nº 6: 65-69. [A shorter version has been published in the *Proceedings of the All-India Oriental Conference* 8 (Mysore 1935), Bangalore 1937, pp. 254-257].

1938 "Bhartṛhari a pre-Śaṅkara Advaitin", *Annamalai University Journal* nº 8: 42-53. [Also in the *Proceedings of the All-India Oriental Conference* 9 (Trivandrum 1937), Trivandrum 1940, pp. 548-562].

1952 "Bhartṛhari as a Mīmāṃsaka", *Bulletin of the Deccan College Research Institute* (Poona) nº 14: 1-15. [A short summary is available in the *Summaries of Papers, All India Oriental Conference* 17 (Ahmedabad 1953), pp. 133-134].

1955/6 "Bhartṛhari's interpretation of '*grahaṃ saṃmārṣṭi*' and '*paśunā yajeta*'", *Journal of Oriental Research* (Madras) nº 25: 74-78. [Also published – though without diacritics – in the *Proceedings of the All-India Oriental Conference* 18 (Annamalainagar 1955), pp. 185-188].

RANGASWAMI IYENGAR, H. R., *see* IYENGAR Rangaswami, H. R.

RANGASWAMI, O. P.

1937 "Bhartṛhari and the Bhāgavṛtti", *Journal of Oriental Research* (Madras) nº 11: 45-50.

RAO, P. S.

1957 "Bhartṛhari", *Prabuddha Bhārata* (Calcutta) nº 62: 347-352.

RASTER, Peter

1983 "Die verborgenen drei Viertel", in *Allgemeine Sprachwissenschaft, Sprachtypologie und Text linguistik*. (Festschrift für Peter Hartmann), Tübingen: Gunter Narr, pp. 211-220.

RAU, Wilhelm

1962 "Über sechs Handschriften des Vākyapadīya", *Oriens* (Leiden) nº 15, 374-398.

1964 "Handschriften des Vākyapadīya. Zweiter Teil. MSS 7-10 (GK)", *Oriens* (Leiden) nº 17: 182-198.

1971 *Die handschriftliche Überlieferung des Vākyapadīya und seiner Kommentare*. München: Wilhelm Fink Verlag (Abhandlungen der Marburger Gelehrten Gesellschaft, Jahrgang 1971, nº 1).

1977 "Zwei neue Vākyapadīya-Handschriften", *Studien zur Indologie und Iranistik* (Reinbeck) nº 3: 114-123.

1978 "Metrical peculiarities in Bhartṛhari's Vākyapadīya", *Annals of the Bhandarkar Oriental Research Institute* (Poona) nº 58/59: 263-269.

1980 "Bhartṛhari und der Veda", *Studien zur Indologie und Iranistik* (Reinbeck) nº 5/6 (Festschrift Paul Thieme): 167-80.

1981a "Erwiderung", *Studien zur Indologie und Iranistik* (Reinbeck) nº 7: 175 [on BRONKHORST 1981].

1981b *Vākyapadīyaprameyasaṃgraha*. Ein anonymes Scholion zum Zweiten Kāṇḍa des Vākyapadīya. München: Wilhelm Fink Verlag (Abhandlungen der Marburger Gelehrten Gesellschaft, Jahrgang 1978, nº 2). [In collaboration with PERI Sarveswara Sharma].

1984 "Three further kārikā-manuscripts of the Vākyapadīya" in *Amṛtadhārā*, (R. N. Dandekar Felicitation Volume), Delhi: Ajanta Publications, pp. 343-349.

1985 "Ein bisher unzugängliches Trivandrum-MS des Vākyapadīya", *Studien zur Indologie und Iranistik* (Reinbeck) nº 10: 3-7.

1988 *Bhartṛharis Vākyapadīya Vollständiger Wortindex zu den* mūlakārikās, Stuttgart: Franz Steiner Verlag (Akademie der Wissenschaften und der Literatur, Abhandlungen der Geistes- und Sozialwissenschaftlichen Klasse, Jahrgang 1988, nº 11).

1991 *Bhartṛharis Vākyapadīya II*: Text der Palmblatt-Handschrift Trivandrum S.N.532 (= A), Stuttgart: Franz Steiner Verlag (Akademie der Wissenschaften und der Literatur, Abhandlungen der Geistes- und Sozialwissenschaftlichen Klasse, Jahrgang 1991, nº 7).

RENOU, Louis

1953 *L'Inde Classique*, vol.II, Paris-Hanoi, §1532: 93-94. [Reprint: Paris: Adrien Maisonneuve 1985].

ROCHER, Rosane

1983 Review of BANDINI 1980, *Journal of the American Oriental Society* (New Haven) nº 103-4: 778-779.

RUDOJ, V.

1979 "Some premises of the ancient Indian philosophy of grammar", *Sanskrit and Ancient Indian Culture* (Articles and papers presented by the Soviet scholars to the IVth World Sanskrit Congress, Weimar GDR, 23-30 May, 1979), Moscow, pp. 108-15. [In Russian].

RUEGG, David Seyfort

1959 *Contributions à l'histoire de la philosophie linguistique indienne*. Paris: de Boccard (Publications de l'Institut de Civilisation Indienne, Fascicule 7).

1960 Review of GAURINĀTHA ŚĀSTRĪ 1959a, *Indo-Iranian Journal* (The Hague) nº 4: 173-179.

1971 Review of JOSHI 1967, *Indo-Iranian Journal* (The Hague) nº 13: 292-295.

RUKMANI, T.S.

1987 "Patañjali's prajñā and Bhartṛhari's pratibhā: a comparative study", *Indian Philosophical Quarterly* (Poona) nº 14 (1): 81-90.

SADHU RAM

1953 "Bhartṛhari's date", *Journal of the Gangānātha Jhā Research Institute* (Allahabad) nº 9 (1952): 135-151.

1956 "Authorship of some kārikās & fragments ascribed to Bhartṛhari", *Journal of the Gangānātha Jhā Research Institute* (Allahabad) nº 13: 51-79.

SAKSENA, B. R.

1975 Review of IYER 1969, *Ṛtam* (Akhila Bharatiya Parishad, Lucknow), vol. II-VI: 353-356.

ŚĀNTI BHIKṢU Śāstrī

1963 "Āgamasamuccaya alias Vākyapadīya-Brahmakāṇḍa of Bhartṛhari", *Wissenschaftliche Zeitschrift der Karl-Marx-Universität*, 12. Jahrgang, Leipzig (Gesellschafts- und Sprachwissenschaftliche Reihe, Heft 1): 191-228.

SARMA, E. R. Sreekrishna

1962 "Some aspects of Bhartṛhari's philosophy", *Sri Venkateswara University Oriental Journal* (Tirupati) nº 5: 37-42.

1983 Review of DESHPANDE 1980, *Adyar Library Bulletin* (Madras) nº 49: 243-244.

1986 "Bhartṛhari as an Advaitin", *Adyar Library Bulletin* nº 50 (Golden Jubilee Volume): 579-585.

SARMA, K. Madhava Krishna

1940a "Bhartṛhari not a Buddhist: evidence from nearer home", *The Poona Orientalist* (Poona) nº 5: 1-5.

1940b "Śabdadhātusamīkṣā: a lost work of Bhartṛhari", *Annals of the Sri Venkateswara Oriental Institute* (Tirupati) nº 1.3: 670.

1940c "Bhartṛhari: a great post-Upanishadic intuitionist", *The Aryan Path* (Bombay) nº 11: 538-539.

1942 "Gleanings from the commentaries on the Vākyapadīya", *Annals of the Bhandarkar Oriental Research Institute* (Poona) nº 23 (Silver Jubilee Volume): 405-412.

1943a "Helārāja, not a disciple of Bhartṛhari", *Indian Historical Quarterly* (Calcutta) nº 19: 79-82.

1943b "Vāk before Bhartṛhari", *The Poona Orientalist* (Poona) nº 8: 21-36.

SARMA, V. Anjaneya

1965 "The *śabdabrahman* and the *prasthānatraya*", *Sri Venkateswara University Oriental Journal* (Tirupati) nº 8: 31-36.

SATYAVRAT Śāstrī

1953 "Bhartṛhari's conception of time", *Summaries of Papers, All India Oriental Conference* 17 (Ahmedabad 1953), Ahmedabad, p. 244.

1957 "Conception of space (*dik*) in the Vākyapadīya", *Journal of the Asiatic Society of Bengal* (Calcutta) nº 23: 21-26. [Revised version in *Essays in Indology* (1963): 205-215].

1958 "The conception of time according to Bhartṛhari" *Annals of the Bhandarkar Oriental Research Institute* (Poona) nº 39: 68-78. [Revised version in *Essays in Indology* (1963): 165-90].

1963 "The text of the Dik and the Kāla samuddeśa of the Vākyapadīya and its commentary", in *Essays in Indology*, Delhi: 42-45.

SEREBRYAKOV, Igor D.

1986 "Bhartṛhari problem in contemporary Indology" *Sanskrit and World Culture, Proceedings Fourth World Sanskrit Conference*, Berlin, pp. 663-666.

SHAH, K. J.

1991 "Perspectives on the philosophy of Meaning: Bhartṛhari and Wittgenstein", *Tradition, modernity and svaraj*, vol. 1.1, Delhi, pp. 80-95.

SCHARFE, Hartmut

1977 *Grammatical literature*, vol. 5.2 of *A History of Indian Literature*, Wiesbaden: Otto Harrassowitz. [Chapter XI: "The later Pāṇini school", pp. 170-175].

SHIMIZU, Shin'ichi

1985 "Bhartṛhari on a model of the dhvani theory", *Journal of Indian and Buddhist Studies* (*Indogaku Bukkyōgaku Kenkyū*) (Tōkyō) nº 34/1: 415-412. [In Japanese].

SHRIRAMAMURTI, P.

1980a "Grammarians and Literary Critics on pratibhā in Sanskrit", *Proceedings of the All-India Oriental Conference* 29 (Poona 1978), Poona, pp. 301-305.

1980b "The meaning of the sentence is pratibhā", *Proceedings of the Winter Institute on Ancient Indian Theories on Sentence-meaning* (Held in March 1979). Edited by S. D. Joshi, Pune: University of Poona, pp. 9-16.

SHUKLA, Jayadev Mohanlal

1954 *Bhartṛhari's contribution to the philosophy of Sanskrit Grammar*, doctoral dissertation, University of Bombay. [Unpublished].

1956 "The Concept of time according to Bhartṛhari", *Proceedings of the All-India Oriental Conference* 17 (Ahmadabad 1953), Ahmadabad, pp. 379-384.

1966 "Vākyapadīya-kāra Bhartṛhari", *Svādhyāya* (Baroda) nº 3: 185-212, 277-300. [In Gujarati].

1982 Review of VĪRENDRA ŚARMA 1975a, *Journal of the Oriental Institute* (Baroda) nº 31: 316-318.

1984 *Bhartṛhari's Vākyapadīya* with Gujarati Translation and Notes, Ahmedabad (Lalbhai Dalpatbhai Series 98).

SHUKLA, Bhagavat Śaraṇa, *see* BHAGAVAT, Śaraṇa Śukla

SREEKRISHNA, E. R. SARMA *see* SARMA, E. R. Sreekrishna

STAAL, J. F.

1969 "Sanskrit philosophy of language", in *Current Trends in Linguistics* 5, edited by Thomas A. Sebeok. The Hague, Paris: Mouton & Co, pp. 499-531.

1976 "Sanskrit philosophy of language", *History of Linguistic Thought and Contemporary Linguistics*, edited by Herman Parret. Berlin, New York: Walter de Gruyter: 102-136.

SUBRAHMANIAM, Korada

1992 *Vakyapadīyam-Brahmakāṇḍa*: Text and English translation, Delhi: Sri Satguru Publications (Sri Garib Dass Oriental Series nº 146).

SUBRAHMANYAM, K. G.

1927 "A note on the manuscript entitled Vākya Padīya Ṭīkā, deposited in the Government Oriental Manuscripts Library Madras (nº I-33-29)", *Journal of Oriental Research* (Madras) nº 1: 185-187.

SUBRAMANIA IYER, K. A., *see* IYER, K. A. Subramania

SVAMINATHAN, V.

1961 "Bhartṛhari and Mīmāṃsā", *Proceedings of the All-India Oriental Conference* 20 (Bhubaneshwar 1959), Poona (BORI), vol. II, pp. 309-317.

1963 "Bhartṛhari's authorship of the commentary on the Mahābhāṣya", *Adyar Library Bulletin* (Madras) nº 27: 59-70.

1967 "On the date of Helārāja", *Sri Venkateswara University Oriental Journal* (Tirupati) nº 10: 23-35.

TAKAKUSU, Junjirō.

1896 *The Buddhist Religion as practised in India and in the Malay archipelago, by I-Tsing* (A.D. 671-695), Oxford: Clarendon Press, pp. 178-180. [Reprint: Delhi 1966].

TANIZAWA, Junzō

1984 "Bhartṛhari on pratyakṣa", *Journal of Indian and Buddhist Studies* (*Indogaku Bukkyōgaku Kenkyū*) (Tōkyō) nº 33-1. 368-366. [In Japanese].

1987a "Bhartṛhari on pravṛttinimitta", *Journal of Indian and Buddhist Studies* (*Indogaku Bukkyōgaku Kenkyū*) (Tōkyō) nº 35-2: 980-978. [In Japanese].

1987b "A solution of the liar paradox in Indian philosophy (with special reference to Bhartṛhari)", in *Takasaki Jikidō hakushi kanreki kinen ronshū*, Tōkyō: Shunjūsha, pp. 155-164. [In Japanese].

1987c "Indian grammarians' theory of meaning with regard to negation", *Bukkyō Bunka* (Tōkyō) nº 17: 69-91. [In Japanese].

1989a "The problem of 'meaning' for Indian grammarians", *Tōhōgaku* (*Eastern Studies*; edited by the Institute of Eastern Culture, Tōkyō) nº 77: 128-118. [In Japanese].

1989b "*Yadṛcchabda* and *saṃjñā*: from the point of view of proper names", *Journal of Indian and Buddhist Studies* (*Indogaku Bukkyōgaku Kenkyū*) (Tōkyō) nº 37-2: 1008-1003. [In Japanese].

1991a "Two elements of meaning: Bhartṛhari and Frege", *Studies in Comparative Philosophy* (*Hikaku Shisō Kenkyū*) (Tōkyō) nº 17: 39-45. [In Japanese].

1991b "Pāṇinian Theory of *guṇasamudāya*", *Journal of Indian and Buddhist Studies* (*Indogaku Bukkyōgaku Kenkyū*) (Tōkyō) nº 39: 1049-1045.

1991c *Bhartṛhari's Vākyapadīya* 3-14, *Vṛttisamuddeśa*, Japanese Translation and Notes (1), Tōkyō: the Sankibo Press. [In Japanese].

TOLA, Fernando

1990 "Some remarks on Bhartṛhari's concept of pratibhā", *Journal of Indian Philosophy* (Dordrecht) nº 18: 95-112. [In collaboration with Carmen DRAGONETTI].

TORELLA, Raffaele

1987 "Examples of the Influence of Sanskrit Grammar on Indian Philosophy", *East and West*, (Rome) nº 37: 151-164.

TRIPATHI, Dipti S.

1986 "Apabhraṃśa in Sanskrit grammar. An appraisal of Bhartṛhari's view", *Aligarh Journal of Oriental Studies* nº 3: 81-92.

TRIPATHI Rama Sureśa

1972 *Saṃskṛt vyākaraṇ-darśan*. Delhi – Patna: Rajkamal. [In Hindi].

VARMA, Satya Kam

1964a *Bhāṣātattva aur Vākyapadīya* [Linguistics and the Vākyapadīya], with a summary in English. New Delhi: Bhāratīya Prakāshan. [In Hindi].

1964b "Bhartṛhari as a Linguist and a Grammarian", *Summaries of Paper, 26th International congress of Orientalists*, Delhi, p. 262.

1970 *Vākyapadīyam (Brahmakāṇḍa) of Shri Bhartṛhari, the great linguist & grammarian*, with trilingual commentary, New Delhi: Munshi Ram Manohar Lal. [Sanskrit - English - Hindi].

1971 *Vyākaraṇa kī dārśanika bhūmikā (Bhartṛhari par mukhyataḥ ādhārita)*; The Philosophy of Grammar according to Bhartṛhari. New Delhi: Munshi Ram Manohar Lal. [In Hindi].

1973 "Śabdapūrvako yogaḥ", in *Śrīcārudevaśāstryabhinandanagranthaḥ* [Charudeva Shastri felicitation volume], Head of the editorial committee: Satyavrat Sastri, Delhi, pp. 124-129. [In Sanskrit].

1976a "Tradition and Bhartṛhari", in *Studies in Indology*, New Delhi, pp. 185-200.

1976b "Bhartṛhari: Works and Achievements", in *Studies in Indology*, New Delhi, pp. 201-223.

1976c "Linguistic Contents in Vākyapadīya", in *Studies in Indology*, New Delhi, pp. 224-237.

1976d "Śabdapūrvayoga", in *Studies in Indology*, New Delhi, pp. 238-247.

1980 "Sentence-meaning according to Bhartṛhari", *Proceedings of the Winter Institute on Ancient Indian Theories on Sentence-meaning* (Held in March 1979). Edited by S. D. Joshi, Pune: University of Poona, pp. 17-37.

1984 "Definition of sentence: Bhartṛhari's view", *International Journal of Dravidian Linguistics* nº 13.1:171-176.

VĪRENDRA ŚARMA

1975a *Critical Study of Sambandha Samuddeśa of Vākyapadīya in the Light of Helārāja's Commentary*, doctoral dissertation, Kurukshetra University.

1975b "Is the eternal verbum of Bhartṛhari a dynamic principle?", *Vishveshwaranand Indological Journal* (Hoshiarpur) nº 13: 337-350.

1977 *Vākyapadīya. Sambandha-Samuddeśa. A critical study with special reference to the commentary of Helārāja*. Hoshiarpur (Panjab University Indological Series 9). [In Hindi].

WAYMAN, Alex

1981 "The citations of Bhartṛhari's Vākyapadīya in the Tattvasaṃgraha of Śāntarakṣita and Kamalaśīla" (summary), *Summary of the World Sanskrit Conference* 5, Delhi, pp. 185-186.

WEZLER, Albrecht

1974 "Ein bisher mißverstandener Vers in der Vākyapadīyavṛtti", *Münchener Studien zur Sprachwissenschaft* nº 32: 159-164.

ZIMMERMANN, Francis

1987 Review of HERZBERGER 1986. *Bulletin d'études Indiennes* (Paris) nº 5: 19*-23*.

INDEX OF REFERENCES TO WORKS ASCRIBED TO BHARTṚHARI

References in this index are to RAU's edition of the Vākyapadīya, to IYER's edition of the Vṛtti (books I and II), and to the 'critical edition' of the Mahābhāṣyadīpikā (the roman numeral refers to the Āhnika concerned, VIa and VIb to the two volumes covering Āhnika VI). Since the contributors to this volume have not all referred to the editions here specified, adjustments have been made in the index where necessary.

Vākyapadīya

Brahmakāṇḍa

Prakīrṇakāṇḍa

Vṛtti

Mahābhāṣyadīpikā

CONTRIBUTORS

AKAMATSU, Prof. Dr. Akihiko, c/o Indian Philosophy, Faculty of Letters, Kyushu University, 6-19-1 Hakozaki, Higashi-ku, 812 Fukuoka, Japon

AKLUJKAR, Prof. Dr. Ashok, University of British Columbia, Department of Asian Studies, 2075 Wesbrook Mall, Vancouver B.C., Canada V6T 1W5

BHAGAVAT, Pt. V.B., Bhandarkar Oriental Research Institute, Law College Road, Pune 411 004, Inde

BHATE, Prof. Dr. Saroja, Dept. of Sanskrit & Prakrit, University of Poona, Pune - 411 007, Inde

BRONKHORST, Prof. Dr. Johannes, Section de langues et civilisations orientales, Université de Lausanne, BFSH 2, CH-1015 Lausanne

DESHPANDE, Prof. Dr. Madhav M., Department of Asian Languages and Cultures, University of Michigan, 3070 Frieze Bldg., Ann Arbor, Michigan 48109, USA

GILLON, Dr. Brendan, Département de linguistique, Université McGill, 1001, rue Sherbrook Ouest, Montréal, Québec, Canada H3A 1G5

HATTORI, Prof. Dr. Masaaki, 40-6 Sakuradani-cho, Shishigatani, Sakyo-ku, Kyoto 606, Japon

HONDA, Mr. Yoshichika, Dept. of Sanskrit, Fac. of Letters, Kyoto University, Yoshida-honmachi, Sakyo-ku, Kyoto, Japan 606-01

HOUBEN, Dr. J.E.M., Postbus 85281, 3508 AG Utrecht, Pays-Bas

KELLY, Prof. John D., Department of Anthropology, Princeton University, Princeton NJ, USA 08544-1011

LINDTNER, Prof. Dr. Christian, Tovesvej 6, DK-2850 Naerum, Denmark

PALSULE, Prof. Dr. G.B., Bhandarkar Oriental Research Institute, Pune - 411 004, Inde

RADICCHI, Prof. Anna, Viale Avignone, 19, 53100 Siena, Italie

RAMSEIER, Monsieur Yves, Éterpeys 22, CH-1010 Lausanne